Posts and Pasts

SUNY series

EXPLORATIONS

in

POSTCOLONIAL STUDIES

Emmanuel C. Eze, editor

Patrick Colm Hogan, *Colonialism and Cultural Identity: Crises of Tradition in the Angophone Literatures of India, Africa, and the Caribbean*

Alfred J. Lopez, *Posts and Pasts: A Theory of Postcolonialism*

S. Shankar, *Textual Traffic: Colonialism, Modernity, and the Economy of the Text*

John C. Hawley, editor, *Postcolonialism, Queer: Theoretical Intersections*

Posts

and

Pasts

A Theory of Postcolonialism

ALFRED J. LÓPEZ

State University of New York Press

Published by
STATE UNIVERSITY OF NEW YORK PRESS, ALBANY

Printed in the United States of America

For information, address State University of New York Press,
90 State Street, Suite 700, Albany, NY 12207

Production by Marilyn P. Semerad
Marketing by Dana E. Yanulavich

Library of Congress Cataloging-in-Publication Data

López, Alfred J., 1962-
Posts and pasts : a theory of postcolonialism /Alfred J. López.
p. cm.—(SUNY series, explorations in postcolonial studies)
Includes index.
ISBN 0-7914-4993-9 (alk. paper)—ISBN 0-7914-4994-7 (pbk. : alk. paper)
1. Criticism—History—20th century. 2. Developing countries—Literatures—History and criticism—Theory, etc. 3. Postcolonialism. I. Title. II. Series.

PN98.P62 L67 2001
801′.95′0904—dc21

00-046357

10 9 8 7 6 5 4 3 2 1

For Susan, Olga, and Sofia, the newest "Post-"

Contents

Acknowledgments		ix
Introduction	Posts and Pasts	1
Chapter One	"The Other! The Other!": Conrad, Wilson Harris, and the Postcolonial "Threshold of Capacity"	43
Chapter Two	Specters of the Nation: Resistance, *Criollismo,* and the Ambivalence of the "Neo-"	65
Chapter Three	Whiteness and the Colonial Unconscious	85
Chapter Four	"Toward a New Humanism. . . .": Fanon, Hegel, and the Crisis of Mastery	121
Chapter Five	Reason, "the Native," and Desire: A Theory of "Magical Realism"	143
Conclusion	Magic, "Realism," and the "Post-"	205
Notes		211
Biblography		257
Index		265

Acknowledgments

It is beyond cliché in both academic and commercial publishing for authors to open their acknowledgments with the rather sheepish confession that theirs has not been a solitary endeavor; that, on the contrary, they have depended upon the support, financial, moral, editorial, and so forth, of any number of institutions and colleagues. While this book is no exception, neither has it been blessed by the outpouring of resources in the form of research grants, and lavish release time, which a more pointedly utilitarian project, or one hailing from a more elite institution, might have received. I managed to make significant progress toward this book while working as a "part-time" adjunct instructor at a technical college in the southern United States, teaching five courses of English composition and/or freshman literature per semester. Upon securing the relative comforts of a tenure-track position at Florida International University, I have completed the process of writing and revising the book, as well as that of seeking a publisher, thanks largely through two teaching-load reductions that I have received through the good graces of Professor and Chair Donald Watson, to whom I am eternally grateful.

I mention all of this not to draw attention to my particular situation, nor to elicit sympathy to my relative plight ("relative" because, of course, there are those colleagues who remain at that technical college, and who labor as adjunct instructors at my present institution). Rather, I present my own example as a way of questioning whether administrators, not only at my institution but elsewhere, adequately balance the research demands they place upon junior faculty (i.e., a book, at many other institutions, two) with the amount of support, in terms of research grants, sabbaticals, and so on, which they are willing to dedicate to that end. I suspect that the answer at many colleges and universities across our great nation, paradoxically at a moment in America of unprecedented prosperity, is no. Before moving on to those to whom I certainly owe a great deal in the preparation of this book, I cannot help but pose the perhaps naíve question of why, during the very moment of America's ascendancy as *the* global economic and political power, institutional support for the humanities should be thus neglected. There is undoubtedly a need to theorize and think through this obscure relation between America's millennial position of global wealth and power on the one hand and its converse disregard, even disdain, for the humanities on the other. This is, admittedly, not the time nor the place to further pursue this or related questions.

Aside from Professor Watson, then, I wish to thank my colleagues at Florida International who have been helpful in reading and helpfully commenting on parts of *Posts and Pasts: A Theory of Postcolonialism:* to Harry Antrim, Rick Schwartz, Chuck Elkins, and Maneck Daruwala. I also owe a debt of gratitude to the members of the postcolonial-studies course "Whiteness After Empire," which I taught at FIU during the summer of 1998, not only for helping me formulate the thesis and supporting ideas for chapter 3, "Whiteness and the Colonial Unconscious," but for allowing me to use excerpts from their in-class writings (anonymously, I should add) as an integral part of my own critique of postcolonial whiteness.

This book began life, as do so many first scholarly monographs, as a dissertation. I thus owe a great debt to many at the University of Iowa (and to some who have moved on) for their guidance and mentorship during this critical incubation period: Peter Nazareth, Cheryl Herr, Adriana Méndez, Linda Bolton, Herman Rapaport, and Fred Moten. I thank you all for your support and, when necessary, the occasional kick in the rear. Thanks also to the University of Iowa for their Opportunity Fellowship, without which there would be one less Latino Ph.D. in the world, and the English Department at Iowa for the Sherman Paul/Prairie Lights Dissertation Scholarship that allowed me to complete the document that serves, however unrecognizably, as the basis for this book. A special thank-you is in order to Faber and Faber, not only for their permission to use an excerpt from Wilson Harris's magisterial novel *Jonestown* as an epigraph for the book, but also and especially for the unbelievable speed with which they responded to my request for permission. Finally, to my wife and partner Susan M. López, who has stuck it out with me through both the dissertation and manuscript-preparing process, and somehow still seems to like me, my undying gratitude and love. Susan has also graciously granted permission for the use of a photograph of her sculpture to appear as a cover illustration for the book. Thanks finally to the people at SUNY who helped make this book happen: James Peltz, who first read the manuscript; my acquisitions editor Jane Bunker; Katy Leonard, who kept me informed throughout the acquisitions process; series editor Emmanuel Eze; and Marilyn Semerad, who expertly steered this novice through the production process. I am grateful to them and all at SUNY Press for their professionalism and collegiality.

To these and many others who have assisted along the way, know that you have all in your way contributed to whatever virtues this volume may possess; its failures, to trot out yet another of those hoary yet unavoidable truisms, are all solely due to its author.

It is essential to create a jigsaw in which "pasts" and "presents" and likely or unlikely "futures" are the pieces that multitudes in the self employ in order to bridge chasms in historical memory.

—Wilson Harris, *Jonestown*

Introduction

I

It has become habitual in literary and cultural studies to hurl all that is troublesome or encumbering into the void of the 'post-': postmodernism, postcolonialism, postfeminism, and so on. It is a practice that come to be fantastically laden with meanings, but that also provides the soothing illusion that whatever is held to be really significant has either already happened or is yet to come. In the former case, such a reading casts the matter in question as aftermath or accessory, an appendix to that which the critic posits as already extant or formed, reified and arrested in the manner of that which can be studied and known in its finitude (e.g., postmodernism, as that field secondary to, because dependent upon, modernism); in the latter case, it becomes part of a safely theorizable 'future' whose true implications remain unconsidered, its impact blunted by the perceived lack of immediate impact upon the moment.

But living after the end of what has been a century of such 'posts'—what we might venture to dub 'the postcentury'—forces us to rethink these assumptions. Because that is precisely where the fearsome 'post-' (p)resides: *here,* in our actuality, with us. It is, as G. W. F. Hegel reminds us tirelessly in his preface to *The Phenomenology of Spirit,* not a matter of projecting or imagining a future but of seeing the future that is already before us.[1] In the pages that follow, then, I will be implicitly reading this sign of the 'post-' as that space or index of a future already glimpsed, coming into view in the form of an array of texts which, although not necessarily recognizable as a unified literary genre, style, movement, and so forth, together point to a horizon and a future.

One may of course already object here: "What future?" Or rather *which*—the immediate problem with such a theory being the very multiplicity of national colonial experiences, to say nothing of individual variations across the range of ethnic, class, and gender distinctions, and the manifold responses to colonialism that will inevitably proceed from these. Each of these instances of colonization, this line of reasoning goes, comes with its own historical and cultural contingencies, and leaves behind its own legacy for colonial subjects to repress or confront or work through. Thus not only does the plural 'futures' emerge as the more appropriate form, but "postcolonial" itself appears as a theoretical chimera: an at best unnecessary and at worst hindering nomenclature applied to a more or less randomly chosen and certainly incongruous group of discourses that would otherwise never appear together on a college syllabus, much less a bookshelf. Such critiques attack postcolonial studies as an ideology rich in abstraction but lacking in historical and cultural specificity. Postcolonial discourses, such critics assert, fail to empower precisely because of this drive to encompass all colonialisms within its polemic; thus Aijaz Ahmad regards 'postcolonialism' as a term that "designates far too many things, all at once."[2]

While recognizing these and other shortcomings in what has come to be known collectively as 'postcolonial studies,' we must also acknowledge the extent to which such unaligned, irregular responses to colonialism together constitute a critique of the manifold injustices perpetrated upon the once- and still-colonized Third World by Western colonial powers. To argue, given this, that postcolonial discourses fail to address this or that historical instance of a colonial occupation in its local specificity is to miss the point entirely. To argue for something called 'postcolonial studies' is not the same as claiming that all nations and peoples everywhere on the planet have collectively moved "beyond" imperialism in one fell swoop, or that there are not plenty of examples remaining in the world of colonial or neocolonial regimes. But conversely, to fail to see any structural relation or kindred ideological impulses among these myriad instances of colonial oppression and national-liberation struggles is to miss the postcolonial forest for the nationalist trees. On the other hand, it is simply implausible that the term 'postcolonial' is, as one recent conference speaker would have it, redundant or unjustified because "it quite erroneously suggests that something new and . . . too particularly depraved has taken place in human history."[3] On the contrary, it is precisely *because* Alexander the Great is not Napoleon is not the British raj that any postcolonial scholarship worthy of the name must be comparative, rather than ethnocentric or nationalist, in its approach.

Still, there remains for this contested ground of the postcolonial to name its referent. What exactly do we mean when we say that a given novel or painting or political theory is 'postcolonial'? How appropriate is it to apply the term to some or all of these things? As Padmini Mongia asks; "Does the term refer to texts or practices, to psychological conditions or to concrete historical processes?"[4] The response of this book to these and related questions, at the risk of seeming disingenuous, is 'all of the above.' What establishes the postcolonial as a unity or heading, however tenuously or provisionally, is not a specific method, thesis, or object of analysis but a condition; that is, the discourses collectively known as 'postcolonial' share, if not a common history of colonization, then a condition or state of having been or presently being colonized, as well as the problem of how best to think of and live with that condition. These shared concerns constitute a broad context or outline for postcolonial studies as it emerges at the intersection of discourses such as nationalism, class, ethnicity, gender, language, economics, and geography, and so on. All of these and more must enter any consideration of the postcolonial, even if no single overarching theory can hope to do them all justice. To focus on one of these at the expense of others, to argue for a formulation of postcoloniality that "is" this and not that, or that attacks such studies for not centering around a particular ideology or method, is to forget how far and in what diverse forms the discourses of imperialism have themselves trafficked through the centuries. The postcolonial is, in this sense, certainly a response to the brute facts of colonization; but beyond that it also represents an analysis of its own relation to colonialism, a reckoning or coming-to-terms with what has happened (and is happening) under the banner of the colonial.

The development of these diverse discourses that would 'speak to' the experiences of colonization and liberation obviously varies according to individual national and colonial histories, and within these by variations of class, gender, and so on. However, in terms of the organized study of these discourses we may identify a change in terminology that reflects an accompanying shift in their relation vis-à-vis the academy—a gradual but profound realignment of the epistemic categories within which such texts are taught and studied. As Meenakshi Mukherjee points out, the organization of courses and critical studies of non-English/non-American Anglophone texts under the heading of "Commonwealth Literature" dates back to the early 1960s, and allowed for the first time the study of such writers as Chinua Achebe, Ngugi wa Thiongo, and Wilson Harris under the auspices of the English Department.[5] In retrospect it is easy to see the limitations and inherent biases of such a categorization; aside from the obvious problem of the continued "conceptual centrality of England" implicit in the term (MM 6), such a framework only allowed for an oppositional approach in which the new writings always appeared within the context of a canonical colonial forerunner: Naipaul and Conrad, Narayan and Forster, and so on.

From this phase springs a scholarship that would abandon this implicitly subservient 'Commonwealth' relation for a more combative, but still oppositional approach that would privilege a text's culturally specific or indigenous elements over the influence of European aesthetics. While rightly demonstrating the role of postcolonial writings and writers in resisting and counteracting colonial domination, such approaches tend to privilege the more blatantly nativist or anticolonial texts and writers (Achebe and Ngugi) at the expense of those who take a more ambivalent or cosmopolitan stance (Naipaul and Rushdie). This type of nativist or anticolonial theory calls for a clean break with the West and all Europocentric discourses, and the recovery of what Frantz Fanon called "a national culture which existed before the colonial era."[6]

But such attempts to exhume a national identity prior to the forms left in the colonial wake are always limited to the reactive status of the anticolonial, at best reconstructions from the scraps of precolonial culture not destroyed by the colonizer, and at worst facile idealizations that belie the hybridizations and complicities that colonial encounters inevitably produce. As Michael Gorra points out, critics such as Edward W. Said and Abdul JanMohamed tend "to settle for a Manichaeanism of their own, a too-easy reliance on binary distinctions between the center and the margin, the canonical and the noncanonical, relying on the tired vocabulary they would nevertheless destabilize."[7]

A more recent phase of postcolonial scholarship attempts to move beyond easy binaries of colonizer/colonized, to an examination of such essentialized categories and roles and the extent to which they constitute representations designed to perpetuate the superiority of the West and the subservience of its colonized and once colonized others. Such theorists as Gayatri Chakravorty Spivak, Homi K. Bhabha, and Trinh Minh-ha, taking a cue from poststructuralist philosophy, have tended to focus their analyses on the role of language and writing specifically in the dissemination, of, and resistance to, colonial ideologies. Such studies as Bhabha's *Location of Culture* seek to apply this heightened awareness of the ambiguities and undecidabilities of Western thought and writing in general to interrogate the contradictions and inconsistencies inherent in colonial discourses. This type of analysis turns on what Bhabha calls "the separation from origins and essences" that characterize the postcolonial as it moves away from binary anticolonialism to a more nuanced examination of the ways in which the positions of both colonizer and colonized are inwardly conflicted.[8] Bhabha's work in particular tends toward terms such as 'hybridity' and 'mimicry' to help illustrate the inwardly split subjectivity that he asserts as the mark and legacy of the colonial encounter; for Bhabha, the essential dominant or subservient role that is outwardly performed by a subject can always be read against the grain to reveal the subject's troubling self-awareness of the speciousness of their fictive role, carried out either in the name of colonial authority or in obedience to that authority. George Orwell's self-conscious colonist in "Shooting an Elephant" perfectly exemplifies this colonial ambivalence: "A sahib has got to act like a sahib. . . . He wears a mask, and his face grows to fit it."[9] The colonized subject also wears a mask of acquiescence or resistance, love and identification, or hatred and resistance. But each of these essentialized "masks" deconstruct themselves upon the colonized subject's realization that they are neither wholly apart—from nor a part—of the colonizing regime; that is, the fact of colonization brings with it the inevitable intermingling of cultural discourses between colonizing and colonized groups, and the impossibility that either one will emerge 'uncontaminated' by the other.

The once-colonized subject's dilemma, then, is on the one hand the impossibility of a complete break from the language, cultural practices, political institutions, and so forth, of the former regime, and on the other the impossibility of ever achieving full identification with it. This "separation from origins and essences" renders the once-colonized subject forever hybrid, an interstitial subjectivity that constantly and ambivalently negotiates between cultural imperatives; for Bhabha the result is a subject who is, culturally and ethnically, *"a subject of a difference that is almost the same but not quite"* (HB 86). At best such a theorization would compel the once-colonized and -colonizing subject to turn away from reductive oppositions of self and other that would damn them to 'contaminated' or 'mongrel' status, and toward a formulation of postcolonial subjectivity that would allow for a more empowering view of these successful negotiations of multiple ethnic and cultural imperatives: not 'neither,' then, but 'both.' As Stuart Hall suggests, we must think in terms not simply of a multicultural society composed of multiple discreet identities, but rather of "new ethnicities"—multicultural individuals who embody the ongoing intermixture of cultural and racial identities that best defines the postcolonial world.[10]

The appropriation of such terms as 'hybridity' and 'syncretism' into the postcolonial nomenclature is itself telling as a reflection in the language of postcolonial studies' privileging of terms and subjectivities once shunned as signifying a secondary mongrel status. As Christopher Balme explains, as recently as the early twentieth century these terms signified a lack of racial or ethnic 'purity' as a consequence of 'contamination' with the subaltern colonized:

> In the conceptual world of the nineteenth and early twentieth century, clear cultural boundaries were essential for cementing identity, and expressed notions of difference and even superiority vis-à-vis other nations and cultures. In this world view, which encapsulates the essence of colonialism in both its paternalistic and aggressive, exploitive manifestations, any suggestion of mingling and interchange was synonymous with dilution, deracination and breakdown.[11]

By contrast, current academic usage of both 'syncretism,' 'hybridity,' and related terms indicates a more dynamic view of cultural interchange; while sometimes overlooking the stark history of colonial domination and present inequalities of power among cultural/national groups, Balme, Robert J. C.

Young, and others count the reinterpretation of such terms among the few positive results of the otherwise appalling history of European colonization and cultural domination.[12]

In literary terms, this new postcolonial discourse moves beyond both a subsidiary 'Commonwealth' status and a nativist anticolonialism to achieve a space within the erstwhile master's literature from which to write its own hybrid or syncretic identity. Such new postcolonial writings embody what Gilles Delleuze and Felix Guattari have, in their work on Franz Kafka, ironically called a "minor literature" that minority groups construct "within a major language."[13] Of course, Deleuze and Guattari bring their own poststructuralist sensitivity to bear on their opposition of the terms 'major/minor.' Their idea of a minority writer making a major contribution to the literature of their 'adopted' language (in their case, the Czech Jew Kafka writing in German) borrows liberally from Jacques Derrida's notion of the 'supplement'; for Derrida, the 'supplement' is that element of a structure which, although regarded as secondary or negligible, can be demonstrated to be actually indispensable to the structure's integrity (e.g.; slave labor as the 'supplement' within the structure of American and European capitalism). Deleuze and Guattari's concept of the "minor literature" as an irreducible supplement to the "major" language clearly applies to the position of colonial and postcolonial writings as well; although writers such as the Polish immigrant Joseph Conrad and the Anglo-Indian Salman Rushdie represent minorities within the Anglophone world, they could hardly have made more "major" contributions to English literature.

Although far from a unified movement, postcolonial studies can be said to demonstrate a certain trajectory in its writings and to share among its sundry manifestations certain ideas and concerns. This trajectory is not to be confused with any metanarrative of development or as any sort of prescription or poetics; it does not offer any sort of schedule or other measurement of a national literature's "progress" toward postcolonial status. Nor does the commonality of certain broad-based concerns assume that all postcolonial national/cultural groups face the same cultural or historical conditions in their respective postindependence moments, or apply the same ideological conclusions or political solutions to their individual national problems. In this book I seek to present this baggy monster of the postcolonial not as a finished product or reified object of study, but as very much a work-in-progress, a disparate group of cultural discourses that nevertheless ask some of the same questions and toil at similar tasks. In these pages I present the postcolonial as a condition, a set of historical and cultural contingencies; and I see postcolonial writings generally as less object than activity, a body of work that seeks to address these contingencies in the hope of finding ways of thinking and living in its unprecedented historical moment. In the broadest terms, then, the tasks of postcolonial writing are twofold:

a reckoning with the colonial past, which primarily takes two forms: (a) an acknowledgment and analysis of the cultural and historical pressures that colonization has brought to bear on once- and presently colonized societies, and the manifold ways that the colonial legacy (what some would call the 'neocolonial') lingers into the postindependence moment and beyond, in effect constituting the postcolonial nation's inheritance of colonialism; and (b) a revision or reenvisioning of the colonial history, through both a rereading and reinterpreting of canonical Western texts that produces a critique of their assumed "universal and transhistorical values" and exposes colonial literature's complicity in the building and maintaining of empire, thus allowing for interrogations of the colonizer's culture;[14] and

an analysis or articulation of postcolonial diasporas, or diasporic communities that result from the scattering of indigenous peoples around the globe through the machinations and processes of colonialism and its aftermath. In terms of the postcolonial, however, 'diaspora' signifies identities constituted not in relation to an idealized 'homeland' compared to which they will always play a secondary or diluted role (the diaspora as somehow inferior culturally inferior to the population of the home country), but to an ongoing dynamic of heterogeneity and diversity and difference. This postcolonial conception of diaspora marks the limits of the historical categories and concepts of identity—citizenship, the nation, the community, and so on—and signifies the onset of a new formulation based on multiple (and often conflicting) subject positions and allegiances based on race, gender, and ethnicity. As Michael Gorra points out, in postcolonial writings "the migrant is the emblematic figure of our times" (MG 171) because it is the transnational movement of displaced (and displacing) individuals and groups in the aftermath of colonization that has fueled the conditions now being recognized as postcolonial. In this postcolonial context the migrant's condition is not a lack of belonging, but rather an excess of allegiances and identifications not 'neither' but 'both.'

Within these broadly defined tasks, we may begin to read the multiplicity of nation- and community-specific objectives pertinent to their respective individual postcolonial contexts; and these readings necessarily run the gamut, from analyses of the material means of colonial and neocolonial domination to more abstracted explorations of ontological relations to mastery, the epistemological implications of the 'post-,' poststructurally informed studies of linguistic ambivalence, and so on. Due to the proliferation of possible objects of study under the heading of the postcolonial, along with the dispersed and irregular nature of this burgeoning body of texts, my own efforts here are already qualified by the knowledge that the appearance of this 'post-,' arising multiply from the ashes of colonial discursive regimes that are themselves multiple, runs the risk of never being established as a unity, of never being able to produce its referent, of never being able to write its poetics or methodology or announce itself as a self-contained, delimited field of study. Michel Foucault has described most succinctly this condition of dispersion, of criticisms not reducible to a single position or school of thought yet efficacious in their interrogation of a range of institutions, discourses, and so on. Foucault identifies the recent period of criticism (in his immediate context, roughly 1955–1975) as

> a period characterized by what one might term the efficacy of dispersed and discontinuous offensives. There are a number of things I have in mind here. I am thinking, for example, where it was a case of undermining the function of psychiatric institutions, of that curious efficacy of localized anti-psychiatric discourses. These are discourses which you are well aware lacked and still lack any systematic principles of coordination of the kind that would have provided or might today provide a system of reference for them. . . . I believe that what this essentially local character of criticism indicates in reality is an autonomous, non-centralized kind of theoretical production, one that is to say whose validity is not dependent on the approval of established regimes of thought.[15]

Lacking such a metanarrative discourse or overarching telos or rhetoric, we can nevertheless begin to read the arrival of the postcolonial in such an array of nonaligned critiques of colonial and neocolonial cultural imperatives: from the Guyanese novelist Wilson Harris and Jamaican writer Michelle Cliff, to the Martinican psychiatrist and revolutionary Frantz Fanon, to South Africans J. M. Coetzee and Breyten Breytenbach—as diverse a group of writings and writers as one could imagine, yet all inhabit in one way or another that ambivalent and contested index of the 'post-.'

II

Critiques of postcolonial studies have ranged from analyses of individual critics and theorists to interrogations of the concept of postcoloniality itself; the latter have ranged from questions about postcolonialism's usefulness as a category of literary study to charges of its complicity with the very discourses of Western colonialism and neocolonial domination that it purports to critique. As in any field of intellectual inquiry, there has been no shortage of facile, inadequate, or even sloppy thinking among both postcolonialists and their critics. Yet the polemic raging around postcolonialism has been remarkable for both the level of vituperation and the sheer amount of it, especially as so much of it comes from otherwise urbane, thoughtful scholars. At worst, such ad hominem attacks substitute but poorly for the careful reading and discussion of the texts and critics in question; at best, the ruse of applying such analyses to inferior "strawman" (-woman) texts rather than to the better texts/thinkers in the field elides the true complexity and significance of the issues that such texts address and the questions they raise. For a scholar as highly regarded as Arif Dirlik to stoop such a level of vitriol as to accuse Third World postcolonialists of using narratives of victimhood to advance their First World academic careers is disappointing in the extreme, a cynicism that attempts to make up in venom what it lacks in rigor.[16] Likewise, Kwame Anthony Appiah's assertion that postcolonialism is merely the contrivance of a "comprador intelligentsia" stands out as a cheap shot in his otherwise admirable writings.[17]

Worse still is the sustained level of invective in E. San Juan Jr.'s *Beyond Postcolonial Theory,*[18] a promising title that belies the poorly reasoned diatribe against postcolonial thought contained within its covers. Space considerations will not allow me to enumerate in their entirety all of the slippages and outright lapses of reason that San Juan commits in his eagerness to chastise postcolonial theory; beyond these, however (which I will address to some degree in my discussion of the more salient objections to postcolonialism), San Juan's book-length tirade is further marred by his constant ad hominem attacks on individuals, especially Bhabha and Spivak. San Juan dismisses their work collectivelly as "dilettantish" (ESJ 6), then respectively as a "cult of . . . ambivalence" and a "fetishism" (ESJ 22), and Bhabha is singled out for further abuse as postcolonialism's "most doctrinaire instigator" (ESJ 25). San Juan excuses these and many other such statements, and his apparent refusal to demonstrate more than the most passing acquaintance with Bhabha's or Spivak's writings, on the grounds that "plenitude of meaning or communicative 'good faith' is unwarranted here" (ESJ 25). Further, San Juan's attitude toward postcolonialism in general, and Bhabha and Spivak in particular, stems from a Marxist model of thought that would posit every text and critic not directly and explicitly engaged in a rhetoric of class struggle as abandoning history in favor of "verbal dexterity and ludic rhetorical games" (ESJ 25) that would elide its own complicity with the capitalist West: "Postcolonial discourse generated in 'First World' academies turns out to be one more product of flexible, post-Fordist capitalism, not its antithesis" (ESJ 25). And it is precisely because San Juan reads postcolonialism in such dialectical binary terms that he fails to see Bhabha's or Spivak's work as at all empowering or liberating. Thus he can blithely refer to such phantasms as "postcolonial doctrine" (ESJ 6), "orthodox postcoloniality" (ESJ 7), and even "deconstructive essentialism [whatever that is]"(ESJ 12), thus painting all postcolonial texts and writers with the same demonizing brush—as if there were no appreciable methodological or ideological difference between, say, Bhabha and Spivak and Said. In arguing for an increased awareness of historicity and social conditions in Third World studies, he paradoxically chooses to overlook these very elements in the theorists he savages; anyone who has actually read these and other postcolonial thinkers will verify the very different histories (individual and personal) of race, ethnicity, class, and gender that informs each of their work.[19]

Bad faith and gross misreadings aside, however, there remain significant areas of contention regarding postcolonial studies, which we may divide roughly into three camps:

objections to the term 'postcolonial' as a discreet epistemological category, which regard the term itself as at best unnecessary or redundant, and at worst as ignoring both the lingering effects of colonial and neocolonial regimes and denying its own proximity to (and even complicity in) hegemonic discourses. This latter objection would posit the 'postcolonial' as a misnomer whose very invocation prematurely announces the demise of imperialism and elides the continued domination of subject peoples in every part of the world. Much of the difficulty for the term 'postcolonial,' as I just alluded to, is its very 'post-ness,' or rather the very presence of the 'post-' and its ambiguous relation to the referent 'colonial.' The *Oxford English Dictionary* provides four general, and in some ways contradictory, significations for the prefix 'post-': that which follows or comes after; an answer to or refutation of a given referent; a higher or more advanced version or state of the referent; and a later stage of the referent.[20] The former two definitions imply a secondary, reactionary relation to the root word, while the latter two present 'post-' as an extension of the root; 'postcolonial,' in this context, appears as at best an aftermath or oppositional response to colonialism and at worst a continuation of it. As Ella Shohat points out, the term 'postcolonial' also occupies an ambivalent position in relation to an array of other 'posts':

> The prefix "-post," then, aligns "post-colonialism" with a series of other "posts"—"post-structuralism," "post-modernism," "post-marxism," "post-feminism," "post-deconstructionism"—all sharing the notion of a movement beyond. Yet while these "posts" refer largely to the supercession of outmoded philosophical, aesthetic and political theories, the "post-colonial" implies both going beyond anti-colonial nationalist theory *as well as a movement beyond a specific point in history,* that of colonialism and Third World nationalist struggles. In that sense the prefix "post" aligns the "post-colonial" with another genre of "posts"—"post-war," "post-cold war," "post-independence," "post-revolution"—all of which underline a passage into a new period and a closure of a certain event or age, officially stamped with dates.[21]

Shohat goes on to posit this tension between teleologies in 'postcolonial', that is, between an abstract philosophical periodization and a more temporally concrete historical one, as being partly responsible for the ambiguity of the term. Stemming from this basic slippage, 'postcolonial' has come to be applied in an immense range of temporal and geographic contexts, from Columbus's first landing in Cuba in 1492 to the British handover of Hong Kong over five hundred years later and half a world away. Thus for Shohat and others, postcolonial studies' relation to colonialism remains unclear;

questions of postcolonial agency and the subaltern, which focus on the status of postcolonial subjectivity in the aftermath of the colonial experience. The primary question here regards the relation of the colonized subject to colonial power and to the efficacy of individual and collective resistance. In this context 'agency' or the 'human agent' is understood in the broadest terms as the will of a unified subjectivity, the desire of a coherent entity to act with or against the forces that act upon her;[22] the term 'subaltern' is used to define all subordinated populations oppressed by hegemonic regimes, colonial and otherwise.[23] A range of critics have condemned postcolonial theorists for the production of a discourse that at best privileges cultural and linguistic difference over the historical and economic conditions of oppression, and at worst, as Benita Parry puts it, ignores "the voice of the native" and reduces "native resistance to [discursive] devices circumventing and interrogating colonial authority.[24] In her critique of Bhabha's and Spivak's writings, Parry asserts that such discourses deny the agency of the subaltern and the voices of the oppressed by ignoring the "enabling socioeconomic and political institutions and other forms of social praxis" (BP 43). Likewise, San Juan accuses Bhabha, Spivak, et al., and others of a "'posting' of reality" that "coincides [with] if not sanctions the metaphysics of the West's infamous 'civilizing mission'" (ESJ 266). Further, San Juan admonishes her for what he sees as her conviction that "the subaltern cannot speak or represent herself; she must be spoken for and represented" (ESJ 85). In this context, postcolonial writings would appear less the voice and product of once- and still-colonized masses than a critical platform for those who are to some extent already empowered by virtue of their positions within the First World academy, access to Western media, and so on. Thus the interrogation of postcolonial 'agency' centers on the question of whether postcolonial writings actually function primarily in the interest of a small group of Third World elites, and whether and to what extent they can credibly represent or 'speak for' the colonized subalterns of their respective cultures; and

questions of postcolonial hybridity and the critique of hegemony, which interrogate the efficacy of postcolonial studies as an oppositional anticolonial discourse and the limits of its resistance to—and complicity with—hegemonic colonial and neocolonial discourses of power. What is the once-colonized subject's relation to colonial power, to their nation's particular *legacy* of colonialism? To what extent can that subject and nation now refute, deny, or expel all that is colonial and Western? To what extent is that inheritance from colonialism (language, political systems or parties, education, etc.) an irreducible part of the postindependence nation—and where is the line that divides this cultural legacy from neocolonial political and economic dependence on the former colonizer? Bhabha's use of the now-ubiquitous terms 'hybridity' and 'mimicry' illustrate his ongoing attempt to read postcolonial culture within the context of modern anxieties: How, his essays ask, are we to understand the concept of 'culture' in a time of shifting, blurring boundaries and unstable identifications, a predicament that M. M. Mahood once identified as "the post-colonial crisis of identity"?[25] Bhabha's emphasis on hybridity, ambivalence, and difference in his writings represents an implicit rejection of modernist, progressive metanarratives of liberation and resistance, most prominently Marxism, in favor of the concepts and language of postmodernism. For Bhabha, postcolonial identity is less a coherent self-consciousness than a conflicted economy of desires and identifications, less a phenomenological reduction or framing of subjectivity than a "persistent questioning of the frame, the space of representation, where the image . . . is confronted with its difference, its Other" (HB 46). Throughout his writings, Bhabha finds this economy of difference and hybridity in texts, such as Toni Morrison's *Beloved,* and Rushdie's *Satanic Verses,* which similarly privilege this negation and displacement of identity in postmodern and postcolonial texts.

For many critics, however, such privilegings of grammatological difference over historicist resistance elide postcolonial studies' shortcomings as an oppositional discourse. Gorra laments in his otherwise appreciative discussion of Rushdie that the latter's emphasis on fluidity and hybridity in the portrayal of his characters "remains best suited for those most able to live with a sense of uncertainty and improvisation—*for the gifted and well-off,* those for whom shuttling between London and Bombay is the literal and not the figurative truth" (MG 172, emphasis added). That much postcolonial writing, from Rushdie's fiction to the theorizing of Spivak and others, can make for difficult reading even for skilled readers from other fields only compounds the suspicion that postcolonial studies harbors a certain elitism within its revolutionary rhetoric. Arif Dirlik is less charitable in his allegations that postcolonial critics emphasize cultural difference at the expense of a critique of Western colonial and neocolonial hegemony:

> However much postcolonial intellectuals may insist on hybridity and the transposability of locations, not all positions are equal in power, as Spivak's interrogators in India seem to recognize in their reference to the "wings of progress" that brought her to India. To insist on hybridity against one's own language, it seems to me, is to disguise not only ideo-

> logical location but also the differences of power that go with different locations. (AD 343)

Dirlik goes on to assert that postcolonial writings ignore not only power differences between colonized and colonizer but the continued presence of colonial domination, "as if the only tasks left for the present were to abolish its ideological and cultural legacy" (AD 343), a sentiment echoed in Ella Shohat's complaint that although the term 'postcolonial' "suggests a distance from colonialism," the unambiguous delineation of a "clear opposition" to colonial oppression remains conspicuously absent (ES 107). Most pointed of all, perhaps, is San Juan's postulation that in postcolonial thought "a transcendental politics of aporia and equivocation is substituted for a critique of hegemonic authority" (ESJ 30). What all of these criticisms share is the conviction that postcolonial studies unnecessarily privilege Western theorizations at the expense of a politics of resistance to colonial oppression in all of its concrete manifestations, or put another way, that the postcolonial is the playground of a "Third World cosmopolitan" elite whose ideological blind spot is its own inability to articulate a history of class struggle as part of its critique of colonialism. At best, such objections would have it, postcolonial writings are irrelevant to the true status of the historically and presently dominated peoples of the world; at worst, their neglect of present material conditions in favor of historical colonialisms constitutes a collusion and complicity with First World imperialism itself. As Dirlik puts it none too delicately, the rise of postcolonialism is both contemporaneous and complicit with "the emergence of global capitalism . . . in the sense that the one is a condition for the other" (AD 352), and remarks on the conspicuous lack of postcolonial studies of its status in relation to post-Soviet global capitalism (AD 331 and 352).

More specifically, this critique of postcolonial hybridity constitutes a rejection of postcolonial studies' comparative, global approach in favor of a critique of hegemony in its material and local manifestations; such methods would substitute the poststructuralist penchant for analyses of linguistic or cultural representations, psychological ambivalence, and so on, with a more explicitly Marxist specificity of historicized conflict and struggles against imperial domination. Variations of this critique include the repudiation of the concepts of multiculturalism and diaspora for, respectively, discourses of racial/ethnic difference and nationalist struggles against global capitalism. Examples of the former include Eva Cherniavsky's depictions of the United States as an inwardly or "internal" colonial power by virtue of its history of subjugation of its nonwhite others and the endeavors of a "New Americanist" studies to expose "American exceptionalism" to its own colonial and racial unconscious;[26] and Allen Chun's use of the Chinese diaspora as an example of the ontological and ideological slippages that grow among terms such as 'diaspora,' 'ethnicity,' and 'identity,' and the limitations of postcolonial theory in addressing not only the interactions of the terms within the context of Chinese nationalism but the "huge gap in our understanding of the local historical-sociological framework that produces local cultural discourse."[27] Cherniavsky and Chun consider extant postcolonial theories inadequate for addressing, respectively, the United States' imperial impulses and the ideological struggles that created the Chinese diaspora; but both critiques shun postcolonial formulations of hybridity and global migrancy in favor of a discourse grounded in specific national and community contexts. Chun is particularly pointed in his assertion, shared by San Juan and Kyung-Won Lee, that "multivocality by itself does not insure the deconstruction of cultural hegemonies . . . one should not assume that *all* instances of decentering constitute active moments in a contest of power" (AC 129).[28]

Among the more instructive critiques of postcolonial notions of diaspora is Dirlik's admonition that the kinds of fluidity of peoples and national boundaries championed by postcolonial critics is actually explainable in terms of global movements of capital. For Dirlik these post-Cold War shifts in global capital bear an uncanny resemblance to those visible under colonialism:

> The situation created by global capitalism helps explain certain phenomena that have become apparent over the last two or three decades, but especially since the eighties: global motions of peoples (and, therefore, cultures), the weakening of boundaries (among societies, as well as among social categories), the replication in societies internally of inequalities and discrepancies once associated with colonial differences. . . . Some of these phenomena have also contributed to an appearance of equalization of differenceswithin and across societies, as well as of democratization within and among societies. What is ironic is that the managers of this world situation themselves concede that they (or their organizations) now have the power to appropriate the local for the global, to admit different cultures into the realm of capital (only to break them down and remake them in accordance with the requirements of production and consumption), and even to reconstitute subjectivities across national boundaries to create producers and consumers more responsive to the operations of capital. Those who do not respond—four-fifths of the global population by the managers' count—need not be colonized; they are simply marginalized. (AD 351)

In short, Dirlik asserts that global capitalism has essentially replaced colonialism, with transnational corporations as the new neocolonial agents of domination. In this ominous context, the transcending of national boundaries occurs simply in the interest of creating new and better markets, with little or no regard for the local national cultures subsumed and assimilated in and by the process; those national cultures not interested in participating are no longer colonized, but simply marginalized. Likewise, Masao Miyoshi argues that despite postcolonial theories' emphasis on the decentralization and dismantling of colonial hegemonies, under global capitalism power is heavily concentrated in transnational corporations that render national attempts to regulate the economy superfluous, if not entirely irrelevant. Miyoshi sees this phenomena reflected in the proliferation of global and regional organizations and treaties that attempt to cope with transnational capital's emergent power (NAFTA, GATT, the European Union, etc).[29] For these and other skeptics, the fluidity of peoples and borders that inspires Gorra to describe the migrant as "the emblematic figure of our times" (MG 171) and that Bhabha posits as the "separation from origins and essences" (HB 120) that defines the postcolonial subject actually signifies at best a continuation, and at worst a heightening, of Western domination of its others. San Juan takes this line of reasoning to a logical extreme by asserting that in its focus of the migration of Third World elites, postcolonial thinkers overlook the millions of migrants who come to the West as Overseas Contract Workers (OCWs) who labor largely without benefits or the protection of unions and constitute a key strategy in global capitalism's drive for profits: the deployment of cheap Third World labor in order to lower costs and to simultaneously undermine the stability of Western labor unions; for San Juan, OCWs represent "the dialectic between neocolonies and imperial metropoles" and exemplify the uneven development of economies under global capitalism, by which "the industrialized North grows richer at the expense of the underdeveloped South" (ESJ 221–222). For this group of Marxist-oriented critics, then, the postcolonial privileging of migrancy reflects less the lived realities of the world's workers than the exploits of a small group of privileged Third World academics.

Indeed, a prevalent variation on this objection to postcolonial portrayals of diaspora is directed precisely at diasporic academics in the West by indigenous Third World scholars. At a recent conference at the Indian Institute of Advanced Study, at which both of these groups were represented (as well as non-Indian postcolonial academics), one Indian panelist goes as far as to characterize postcolonialism as an unwelcome "importation" and a form of Western academic imperialism, and applies quotation marks in reference to diasporic "Indians" Bhabha and Spivak;[30] another avers that the relation of Third World literature to First World theory (which in the present context includes postcolonialism) "re-iterates the familiar town/country relationship between the empire and the colonies with the latter providing raw material to the former, to be made into finished shipped back for consumption" (MM 9–10); and a third chides Anglo-Indian fiction writers for "tak[ing] recourse to fantasy and fabulation" at the expense of social and political praxis: "But all this to what end is the question that bothers me [*sic*]. Is this a luxury we can afford? Is this not a wasted creative effort?"[31]

Apparently responding to these and other such attacks, Gareth Griffiths—arguably the most prominent postcolonialist at the conference—refers to such local critiques of postcolonialism generically as "a form of anti-theory" and warns against the "kind of fascist historiography" that in the name of nationalist resistance to global discourses would justify "the suppression of minority voices by an appeal to an imaginary necessary unity . . . which refuses to deal with the actual sociology and politics of the cultural formulations it invokes" in opposition to perceived hegemonic threats from the West. Finally, Griffiths acknowledges what he calls the "excesses" of colonial discourse theory, but remains firmly against "the more naive forms of nativist regression."[32]

Griffith's brief but spirited defense of postcolonial studies might serve as a useful point of departure for reading the efficacy of these and other objections to the proliferation of postcolonial studies within Western academia. Griffiths displays a certain sympathy for "local and recuperative" projects as an antidote to poststructuralist approaches with "their overconcentration on the discursive regime at the level of significatory system" (GG 23). But in both the essay in question and his better-known "The Myth of Authenticity," Griffiths warns against a reflexive rejection of all 'contaminated' discourses in the search of a mythical singular "authentic" voice of the indigene. For Griffiths such a homogenization or reduction to the "pure" voice that would speak for the indigenous threatens to "overwrit[e] the actual complexity of difference" of the group.[33] Such an insistence on 'authenticity,' with its corresponding erasure of difference under the sign of the authentic, paradoxically "may write out that voice as effectively as earlier oppressive discourses" (gg 237); that is, for Griffiths the fetish of authenticity may actually serve to suppress the true difference of indigenous voices by permitting only those that fit essentialized norms of 'nativeness'—those that are 'indigenous enough,' black enough,' and so forth, to be heard in the media, in government, and so on, thus eliding the true range of difference among indigenous others (differences of ethnicity, gender, etc). Such a sublation in the name of authenticity helps create what Griffiths variously calls a "privileged hierarchy" and a "local neocolonial elite," which can then continue to live uncritically under the banners of nationalism, racial identification, and so on, bequeathed to them by virtue of their inheritance of colonialism. For Griffiths, any responsible analysis of, and response to, colonialism must thus move beyond "the mere assertion of the archive of the local and specific" and toward a more in-depth understanding of "the complex processes of historical action on a multiplicity of sites in the period of imperial expansion and on to the present day" (GG 23). These historical interactions resulting from the colonial encounter constitute what Griffiths understands as Bhabhian hybridity: "a necessary, even inevitable 'hybridity' resulting from the impact of colonisation on both the colonised and, it needs to be said, on the coloniser" (GG 23). This understanding of cultural hybridity leads Griffiths to question not only the antitheoretical leanings of the local critique of postcolonialism, but also the facility with which such local voices would "speak for" or represent the indigenous subaltern; for Griffiths, this difficult theoretical problem complicates the discourses of local indigenous elites at least as much as those of the diasporic postcolonialists they so virulently oppose. Questions of hybridity and subalterity, it seems, obtain on the local intranational level as well as the diasporic international.

What follows is a closer analysis or reading of the specific critiques of postcolonial studies as I have outlined them, beginning with some general remarks which, I hope, will serve as landmarks of a sort; that is, I would like to frame my examination or 'critique of the critique' of the postcolonial within certain global parameters.

First and foremost, *the postcolonial is not simply an economic or historical phenomenon,* but encompasses class, gender, race, ethnicity, language, and geography—all of the discourses and identifications that go into the shaping of nations and nationalisms. To posit postcolonialism, as do Dirlik and San Juan, solely as a symptom of international capitalism and its imperatives, and to cast postcolonial intellectuals as so many Gunga Dins reaping the pecuniary benefits of their complicity with neocolonialism while turning a blind eye to their Third World "constituencies" is to miss the crucial point that colonial domination extended (and extends) well beyond mere economic subjugation and into the minds and bodies of the colonized (and colonizers). Such a reductive understanding of the postcolonial has its consequences for literary study as well: witness Frederic Jameson's infamous notion of Third World literature as "national allegories" akin to "outmoded stages of our own first-world cultural development,"[34] which would read Third World national literatures in terms of economic backwardness vis-à-vis the West. Jameson's essay is predicated upon a Marxist metanarrative of development and "progress" that does not allow for the multiplicity of local affiliations and intersections of forces other than economic that inform all cultural productions, Western or not. Thus Jameson's prescriptive metamodel would be unable to account for the culturally hybrid fictions of, say, Rushdie or Wilson Harris or Zoe Valdes, because these authors' works move precisely beyond the boundaries of the "national allegory" in their texts and toward a more nuanced representation of their characters' multiple subject positions and cultural identifications.

Second, *the postcolonial is not simply an idealism or an essentialism,* nor can it be facilely dismissed as another failed "end of either history or ideology" (ESJ 14) or as a neo-Enlightenment nominalism (ESJ 18), nor as a dialectical stage to be overcome per Jameson's "national allegory." What constitutes postcolonial studies today is the emergence of an irregular diasporic critique of precisely these kinds of categories or functions to which the postcolonial would be reduced. Yet this antipathy to taxonomy is seldom so automatic—even in the most self-reflexive writings of critics such as Spivak and Minh-ha—that it would become an anti-essentialism for its own sake. Beyond poststructuralist academic exercises, the best postcolonial writings share a desire for agency, a willingness to stand *for* something, even if that agency and its object or focus are more ambivalent and qualified than their critics let on.

Third, at its best *postcolonialism does not lack historical specificity,* nor does it avoid or "detour" around the world in its analyses of colonial discourses, nor does it attempt to escape from history into myth. The question here, as Jacques Derrida so aptly put it, is not whether to historicize but how to do so.[35] To the extent that postcolonial studies is concerned with the colonial encounter and its aftermath—its effects on colonized (and colonizing) subjects then and now—and with a rethinking and revision of colonial history as disseminated by the colonizing powers, it is an unavoidably historiographic project. This preoccupation with historical discourses and the writing of history is one point at which the postcolonial intersects with the postmodern; there is no shortage of postcolonial fictions that fit Linda Hutcheon's definition of 'historiographic metafiction,' which she affirms as the emblematic form of postmodern writing.[36] To reproach a writer such as Rushdie for "tak[ing] recourse to fantasy and fabulation" (KCB 211) at the expense of historical engagement is to misread his particular brand of historiography as an evasion, when it is actually an attempt to engage a national history filled with such ambivalences and undecidabilities as to render a more conventional account absurd.

But Rushdie is not an exception to the historiographic rule. All of the texts that I discuss in this book address to varying degrees the material conditions of their respective histories of colonization, and their reckoning with the continuing presence of the colonial within their specific national/regional contexts is one of the salient concerns of this book. To have somehow bracketed this crucial element of the postcolonial would have been a disservice to the evolving field of postcolonial studies, and an affront to those writers and texts and peoples who have suffered and suffer today under the heel of colonialism. On the other hand, to focus exclusively on "places in which an actual movement of resistance or opposition to imperial domination exists," as San Juan does (ESJ 17), is to overlook both the resistance to imperial regimes that are nominally postcolonial but continue to oppress their people (Cuba and apartheid-era South Africa come to mind) and the effects of the colonial legacy on peoples no longer directly under the colonizer's heel. Finally, most critiques of postcolonial historiography fail to account for the necessary work of historical rethinking and revision taking place in former colonial centers—for the United States, Great Britain, and so forth, as moving toward not only actual decolonization (Britain out of Hong Kong, the U.S. return of the Panama Canal) but a collective reckoning with their respective colonial histories and what those histories will mean to the futures of their respective nations.

Given this abiding concern with revising and reenvisioning the colonial past, the group of discourses known collectively as 'postcolonial studies' arrived at that term via their own institutional history of shifting and contending epistemological categories. While reflecting on the vagaries and difficulties presented by the rubric of postcoloniality, most postcolonial critics find the term less problematic than previously available nomenclatures. Aside from Meenakshi Mukherjee's remark that the appellation "Commonwealth Literature," while allowing for the entry into the Anglo-American academy of noncanonical, nonwhite writers, did so at the price of reinforcing the "conceptual centrality of England" (MM 6), both Gorra and Rajeswari Mohan prefer 'postcolonial' over its historical forebears. Gorra agrees to some extent with Shohat's assessment of the postcolonial as "imbued with an ambiguous spatiotemporality (ES 101) but differs with her contention that it does not offer a sufficiently concrete oppositional position vis-à-vis colonialism, and argues that in fact postcolonialism signifies a move beyond the strictly anticolonial and toward a more nuanced analysis of colonialism's effects upon its former (and current) subject peoples. Mohan, for his part, points out that 'Third World,' a term dating back to the 1955 Bandung Conference of Asian and African nation-states, has the advantage over "Commonwealth" of at least originating from former colonies rather than a former empire; nevertheless, he believes that in the absence of the Soviet "Second World," the term has deteriorated into a pejorative oppositional term signifying its inadequacies in relation to the developed West: "third rate" rather than "First World."[37] Mohan further asserts that 'postcolonial' has at least three advantages over previous terms such as 'Commonwealth' or 'Third World studies': it foregrounds the cultural and historical fact of colonial domination; it recognizes the ambiguities of decolonization through what he calls "the provisionality and precariousness of the 'post-' (RM 271); and it provides openings for oppositional readings of colonial discourses.

The question of just who 'is' postcolonial, however, remains a tricky one. Again, Shohat's charge that postcolonial studies, as codified by Bill Ashcroft,

Gareth Griffiths, and Helen Tiffin, "collapses very different national-racial formations—the United States, Australia, and Canada, on the one hand, and Nigeria, Jamaica, and India, on the other—as equally 'post-colonial'" is instructive for what it assumes about the methodologies and reading practices of postcolonial critics. Shohat further specifies her objection thusly:

> Positioning Australia and India, for example, in relation to an imperial center, simply because they were both colonies, equates the relations of the colonized white-settlers to the Europeans at the "center" with that of the colonized indigenous populations to the Europeans. It also assumes that white settler countries and emerging Third World nations broke away from the "center" in the same way. Similarly, white Australians and Aboriginal Australians are placed in the same "periphery," as though they were co-habitants vis-à-vis the "center." The critical differences between the Europe's [*sic*] genocidal oppression of Aboriginals in Australia, indigenous peoples of the Americas and Afro-diasporic communities, *and* Europe's domination of European elites in the colonies are leveled with an easy stroke of the "post-." (ES 102)

While the kind of conflation of colonial contexts Shohat critiques is certainly reductive (and at times, downright silly: India is, after all, not South Africa), she herself fails to reflect on the extent to which Ashcroft, Griffiths, and Tiffin qualify their own definition within the very paragraph she quotes in her chapter. Certainly the authors of *The Empire Writes Back: Theory and Practice in Post-Colonial Literatures* do not overlook the diversity of cultural and political contexts at work in postcolonial nations. While they do seemingly want to include the literatures of every colonized or once-colonized nation in their definition of postcolonial literatures at the outset of the paragraph Shohat cites, by its latter half they have tempered their enthusiastic inclusiveness somewhat:

> What each of these literatures has in common beyond their special and distinctive regional characteristics is that they have emerged in their present form out of the experience of colonization and asserted themselves by foregrounding the tension with the imperial power, and by emphasizing their differences from the assumptions of the imperial centre. It is this which makes them distinctively post-colonial.[38]

This is perhaps the best articulation extant of what a careful reader will find grouped under the category of 'postcolonial': a disparate group of cultural and other practices which, while maintaining their individual colonial histories and national identities, nevertheless share the experience, however far-flung and varied, of European colonization. What countries as vastly different as South Africa and India also irreducibly share is the multiple tasks of assessing the extent of the injustices committed under their respective colonial subjugations; recognizing, measuring, and reckoning with the impact of colonialism on their national cultures and its lingering influence in the form of language, political institutions, and cultural and economic practices; and seize the historical opportunity to revisit the colonial scene of the crime(s), in order to rethink both their learned histories (of dependence, inadequacy, and want of 'civilization') under colonialism and begin the project of revising—*reenvisioning*—these into an interrogation of the colonizer's cultural imperatives and a postcolonial horizon of national agency and empowerment.

Of course, this process of decolonization is seldom as effortless as some theoretical formulations make it seem; few postcolonial national projects meet (or even wish to meet) these goals in an unqualified way, and some arguably oppress sectors of their populations more viciously than the colonizers ever did. As Rosemary Jolly points out: "postcolonial liberation was a fact for Afrikaner nationalists before 1990, since independence from Britain was won with the 1961 establishment of the republic under the leadership of Hendrik Verwoerd."[39] Jolly goes on to explain that Afrikaners saw apartheid as immanent to their hard-fought independence from English rule, and thus accepted international condemnation and isolation from the international community as the price of freedom; thus Jolly argues: "Afrikaner nationalists have always seen themselves as true postcolonialists" (RJ 22). That this nominally postcolonial state systematically oppressed the majority of its population until its eventual demise in 1994 does not make it any less 'postcolonial' in the strict sense of the word. Neither do the atrocities over the last forty years of the Castro regime in Cuba assuage the fact that Castro's nationalist project grew out of a virulent anti-imperialism; Castro's revolution owes its success partly to his ability to situate himself as the inheritor of a long line of colonial patriots, going back to José Martí's nineteenth-century War of Independence against Spain. That Martí's struggle ended with his beloved island subjugated as a neocolony to the United States under the Platt Amendment of 1901, and that even after its abrogation in 1934 Cuba remained under the heel of a *de facto* dictatorship at the time of the Castro revolution, only strengthened his popular support.[40] That Castro has turned out to be another in the succession of dictators; and that his hold on Cuban sovereignty and qualifiedly successful opposition to Western imperialism have come at the expense of the personal freedom of his people and the democratic processes of the nation; and that his intolerance for dissent has created the greatest diaspora of Cubans in history, which grows with the boatloads that reach the shores of South Florida almost daily—none of these qualifying factors mitigate the irreducible fact that Cuban nationalists (as opposed to exiled Cuban-*American* nationalists, a crucial distinction) see themselves as citizens of a postcolonial state. The point in all of this is that postcoloniality, although bearing some of the marks of a utopian discourse, does not always or even necessarily have to be a good thing; to the extent that it is quantifiable as a temporality at all, we might think of the postcolonial as a period of struggle not only against colonialism *per se*, but against its lingering effects in the postindependence state and against the state's own struggles to achieve an appropriate vision of itself—and its people, in all their difference—as a nation. As we have learned from that ongoing social experiment in representational democracy known as the 'United States,' making one from the many can be the greatest of challenges.

To the extent that postcolonial studies seeks to affirm and empower the subject-positions of subaltern peoples suppressed by colonial regimes, this question of the other's representation—whether in revisionist historiographic discourses, in governing bodies, or in the media—comes to the fore. For Spivak, with whom the term 'subaltern' is arguably most commonly associated,[41] the term indicates a colonized underclass who are politically marginalized, yet whom possess a potential for a collective and oppositional agency that the subaltern historian can exhume through an interventionist critique of colonial and neocolonial relations cutting across class, ethnicity, and gender. For Spivak, subaltern historical studies represent an opportunity to produce a postcolonial historiography that reveals the previously discarded or suppressed role of the subaltern in maintaining the structures of colonialism; such a historiography would both reveal the true nature of the subaltern's relation to power as "histories of domination and exploitation" and signify "a functional change in sign-systems" that would return the subaltern to a place within the discourses of the postcolonial nation.[42] However, Spivak attempts to achieve this reinscription of the subaltern while maintaining the tension between the various, and often conflicting, feminist, Marxist, and poststructuralist discursive strands extant in her work. (Not for nothing does Colin MacCabe describe Spivak as a "feminist Marxist deconstructivist."[43]) Spivak remains critical of a Marxist metanarrative of collective class consciousness (what she calls "the great modes-of-production narrative" [IOW 197]), preferring a deconstructive approach that would highlight the more radical difference of the subaltern that would continue to be suppressed under a more traditional Marxist rhetoric of class struggle. Spivak also critiques the Subaltern Studies group to the extent that they seek to uncover a unitary 'subaltern consciousness' or will, a project that she contends belies the true heterogeneity of subject-positions within the field of colonial subjects. For Spivak, this emphasis of subject-positions allows for a more specific analysis of the ways in which class, ethnicity, and especially gender shatter the notion of a unitary field of undifferentiated colonial subjects, or class of 'subalterns.' Spivak argues for an understanding of subalterity that moves beyond traditional Marxist oppositional models of 'dominator/dominated':

> It is possible that it is not only "the relationship between the three domination systems [class, racial/ethnic, and sex/gender]" that is "dialectical" but that in the theaters of decolonization, the relationship between indigenous and imperialist systems of domination are also "dialectical", even when they are variously related to the Big Three Systems. . . . Indeed, the relationship may not be "dialectical" at all but discontinuous, "interruptive." (IOW 251)

Such an understanding of subaltern historiography as more a Foucauldian series of interruptive 'events' that emerge as scattered, unpredictable insurgencies within the field of colonial power—with a corresponding understanding of colonial power itself as such a series of epistemic 'events' also prone to renegotiation and violent rearrangement—leads Spivak to reject notions of any simple overturning or single reversal of subaltern subjectivity.

As a consequence of this ongoing awareness of both the tension between the "Big Three Systems" of postcolonial analysis and the precarious position of the critic who would negotiate among them, Spivak is arguably the most consistently self-reflexive of postcolonial theorists. Spivak tirelessly advises the historian against viewing the subaltern unproblematically as an 'object' of study, and advocates a careful attention to what Robert J. C. Young calls "the hidden ways in which nominally radical, or oppositional historians and often unknowingly, or even knowingly, perpetuate the structures and presuppositions of the very systems which they oppose."[44] This translates into a heightened awareness of her own position as a nominally 'Third World' academic working within the Western academy. Spivak constantly returns to this question of the position or "space" of the critic: her own, in relation to both the subaltern she champions and the Western academy; that of the 'native' Indian intellectuals who criticize her as an outsider posing as a Orientalist authority for the 'First World' academy; and that of the subaltern as a heterogeneous collectivity to be represented in academic discourse while simultaneously maintaining their power of insurgency and agency against hegemony. In short, the problem for Spivak is one of critiquing hegemonic power relations between imperialism and the subaltern *without* herself replicating that position in her function as critic-writer. Thus her constant, and often candid, foregrounding of her own difficulties in staking out a position from which to write/speak, as in this example from an interview with Indian intellectuals:

> I think the hardest lesson for me to learn—and I have not learnt it, one attempts to learn it every day—is that the word "woman" is not after all one for which one can find a literal referent without looking into the looking glass. And as you have yourself realized, what I see in the looking glass is not particularly the constituency of feminism. . . . And I am afraid of speaking too quickly in academic situations about the women—the tribal subaltern, the urban sub-proletariat, the unorganized peasant—to whom I have not learnt to make myself acceptable other than as a concerned benevolent person who is free to come and go.[45]

This ongoing tightrope of subject-positions that Spivak has walked over the course of her career and writings reaches its apotheosis in her formulation of the 'Native Informant,' a term she uses to describe both her own position as a Third World scholar working within the elite Western academy and the subject position occupied by many such scholars in similar (albeit less privileged) circumstances.[46] Structurally one might say that Spivak's 'Native Informant' is not far removed from Said's Orientalist; that is, both occupy the liminal position of cultural translator, one who enjoys the advantage of trafficking between worlds for the purpose of explaining to Western audiences the 'exotic' mysteries of colonialism's Others. The primary difference between the two figures is arguably one of allegiance and identification; for Said the Orientalist is at the end of the day, liberal rhetorics of tolerance and brotherhood notwithstanding, always and unproblematically a colonial agent,[47] while the present uproar regarding the Third World scholar at work in the West is precisely over their "fidelity," if I may be so simplistic, to a radical politics of anti-imperialism at the expense of their own comfortable positions within the elite academy. As S. Shankar asks: "If the presence of "Third World" scholars within the elite academy has had a transformative effect on literary and cultural study, what kind of effect has such a presence had upon the scholars themselves?"[48] Shankar's question, and his suggestion that any radical political project is always marked and delimited in advance by the fact of its production within a site of First World elite power, begs the question of whether the subaltern benefits at all from this apparent conflation of knowledge and power. Of course we know from Foucault that this conflation is not happenstance, that knowledge and power do not exist as discreet entities: "Relations of power are not in a position of exteriority with respect to other types of relationships (economic processes, knowledge relationships, sexual relations), but are immanent in the latter."[49] Thus the body of knowledge produced by Third World scholars in elite Western universities is to some extent shaped and marked by the fact of its emanation from the elite site. What is open to question is precisely to what extent such work is 'domesticated' (to use Shankar's unfortunate term) by the very academic institutions that facilitate it; and conversely, to what extent "[t]he institution itself is transformed by the struggles over knowledge taking place within it" (SS 486). This is not the same as asking whether and to what extent the postcolonial scholar can or should represent subaltern groups, or help create spaces for the subaltern to speak for themselves; but certainly the scholars' efficacy in such a project will be crucially affected by the boundaries that academic institutions wish to set for such oppositional discourses. Of course, this liminal relation between indigenous subaltern, Third World scholar, and First World academy is not lost on Spivak, arguably the most productively self-reflexive of postcolonial critics; for Spivak the position of the Native Informant is precisely that of "an unacknowledgeable moment" that lurks as a Derridean 'supplement' to "the great texts" (CPR 4) but remains in foreclosed or suppressed; one function of the Third World critic and reader of canonical Western texts of philosophy and literature is precisely to uncover and announce the Native Informant whenever possible. It is also significant that Spivak revisits the subaltern in her most recent book; in the chapter entitled simply "History," Spivak returns to the scene of her seminal essay "Can the Subaltern Speak?" and continues to refine her reading of the subaltern as "the sheer heterogeneity of decolonized space," rigorously distinguishing her own relatively privileged subject-position from the subaltern ("Simply by being postcolonial or the member of an ethnic minority, we are not 'subaltern' "), and calling for a "moral love" that would transcend both naive truth-claims of the scholar to "speak for" the subaltern and the "superficial utopianism" (CPR 310) of a undifferentiated class-based reading.

If it is true, as Benita Parry has asserted, that Spivak's and Bhabha's formulations "act to constrain the development of an anti-imperialist critique" (BP 27), it is only to the extent that Spivak eschews simplistic unitary formulations of anti-imperialist discourses in favor of a more embattled and self-critical assessment of the critic's position vis-à-vis both the subaltern and the elite site of enunciation. Spivak's point is precisely that the articulation of female subjectivity within the colonial context is already mediated by colonial power, or as Parry puts it in her description of the Spivakian project, that "the articulation of the female subject within the emerging norm of feminist individualism during the age of imperialism, necessarily excluded the native female, who was positioned on the boundary between human and animal as the object of imperialism's social-mission or soul-making" (BP 30). According to Parry, Spivak is so intent on demonstrating the subaltern's invisibility that she overlooks examples of insurgent subaltern agency, often within the very texts she uses to frame her arguments. Thus in her reading of Jean Rhys's *Wide Sargasso Sea,* claims Parry, Spivak passes over the native Christophine's open defiance of hegemonic and discriminatory discourses of power and constructs her reading instead around the Creole Antoinette/Bertha, positing her death as "an allegory of the general epistemic violence of imperialism, the construction of a self-immolating subject for the glorification of the social mission of the colonizer" (Spivak qtd. in BP 32). And indeed, Antoinette is a character better suited to Spivak's project of uncovering the liminality of subjects operating within or between the conflicting demands of race, class, and gender; certainly Christophine is a less embattled figure than Antoinette/Bertha in that respect. But at no point in Parry's essay does she make a persuasive case for why the kind of work Spivak and Bhabha do shouldn't make its own particular contribution to the critique of imperialism; certainly Spivak's reading of Rhys's novel is not far removed from the kind of contrapuntal or 'against the grain' readings of canonical English literature that Said provides in *Culture and Imperialism,* a text that even the arch-critic San Juan praises for its "committed" (ESJ 265) oppositional stance.[50] Further, at no point in the essay does Parry exhibit the kind of self-conscious analysis of her own position as critic, in relation to either the subaltern she chides Spivak for neglecting or the discourses of power mediating her own text at the site of production, which is always the precondition for Spivak's writings. If Spivak and Bhabha could be more explicitly oppositional in her work, then perhaps Parry and others could show greater awareness of the material conditions of institutional power and knowledge-production that permit her antihegemonic articulations in the first place. To assess questions of the subaltern in terms of representability and agency one must acknowledge and constantly foreground, as Spivak does, the distance between the privileged academic and the subaltern subject, a distance that Spivak measures precisely in terms of the former's privilege: "The postcolonial intellectuals learn that their privilege is their loss."[51] The point for the academic, Spivak explains, is not whether or how to speak for the subaltern, but to "learn to learn from them, to speak to them, to suspect that their access to the political and sexual scene is not merely to be *corrected* by our superior theory and enlightened compassion" (IOW 135). In other words, Spivak's work on the feminine subaltern and the Native Informant represents an important move toward precisely the "conception of the native as historical subject and agent of oppositional discourse" (BP 58) that Parry advocates, albeit one that respects what Spivak calls "the immense heterogeneity of the field" (IOW 136) and resists casting the subaltern in the role of unitary subject in an undifferentiated class struggle.

Certainly the figure of Antoinette, as a white Creole child situated uncomfortably between the black native and the English imperialist, serves as a useful illustration of Bhabha's key concept of 'hybridity'—a term which, as Simon Gikandi points out, is so crucial to Bhabha's modeling of the postcolonial "that it is difficult to see how he could exist without them."[52] In Bhabha's formulation hybridity is not entirely or even necessarily a racial or ethnic contingency but a condition of consciousness; it is a sort of "colonial doubling" that renders each side of the colonizer/colonized binary inwardly split, each locked into its own ambivalence about its relation to its other. Thus for Bhabha the colonial encounter does not take the form of a dialectic or a Freudian economy, but an interstitial "Third Space" or what he calls a "metonymy of presence" (HB 118–120) (akin to Jacques Derrida's concept of 'trace'/'*differance*') which problematizes binary models of colonization that cast the colonial encounter as a unilateral dismantling or subjection of the colonized. Rather, the entities act upon each other, albeit beyond and despite the obvious imbalance of power and in unequal ways; more specifically, the process of colonization always leads to elements of the oppressed culture surviving to infiltrate the dominant one, and combining with elements from the latter to form new formations and alignments of cultural practices that distinguish the postcolonial in all of its forms. That this cultural syncretism arises from the violence of colonial domination only emphasizes, for Bhabha, its viability over more sterile and contrived forms of cultural 'diversity' or 'multiculturalism':

> Cultural diversity is an epistemological object—culture as an object of empirical knowledge—whereas cultural difference is the process of the *enunciation* of culture as "knowledge*able*", authoritative, adequate to the construction of systems of cultural identification. If cultural diversity is a category of comparative ethics, aesthetics, or ethnology, cultural difference is a process of signification through which statements *of* culture or *on* culture differentiate, discriminate, and authorize the production of fields of force, reference, applicability, and capacity. (HB 34)

For Bhabha the concept of 'diversity' doesn't work because it approaches culture as a group of discreet, separately evolved essences that interact with each other in a series of oppositions: white/black, Jamaican/African-American, Cuban/Mexican, and so on; whereas true cultural difference—and thus true cultural hybridity—lies in the multiple identifications and allegiances that arise in the clash, often violent, of cultures and peoples that leads to the ambivalent, mixed identities *of individuals*. Thus creolization emerges as a condition not simply of European-descended whites native to the Caribbean, but of those whites taking on the cultural practices and formations that result from their interaction with the indigenous population, just as the natives take on the cultural practices (for example, language) of the white colonizers. That this process of creolization is, from the standpoint of the native, less than voluntary, only makes it more viable a historical model of cultural interaction. Hybridity as cultural difference also obtains within contexts of multiple racial or ethnic identifications; certainly the racial multiplicity of Latin American *mestizaje* owes its condition of hybridity to the originary rape of indigenous Amerindian women by the Spanish conquistadors. What begins as a myth of origins signifying oppression and violation emerges in the postcolonial context as a strength and a desirable feature of postempire cultural formations. Thus for Bhabha, cultural hybridity is desirable as a condition that "contains difference without an assumed or imposed hierarchy" (HB 4) of cultural imperatives: to identify, for instance, as English *and* black, or Indian *and* Trinidadian *and* Christian. Such a formulation of postcolonial subjectivity as a hybrid composed of multiple identifications that interpenetrate but do not coalesce into hierarchical oppositions, sublating, say, ethnicity under national identity, allow for a move beyond binary anticolonial nationalisms toward new formations of being that more appropriately capture the heterogeneity of the postcolonial world.

In response to charges that his concepts of hybridity and mimicry diminish the earlier efforts of anticolonial thinkers who sought a more resolutely oppositional stance toward imperialism, and that the ambivalence of his theory silences oppositional agency, Bhabha asserts that the hybrid subject (or for Bhabha, "subject-effect") possesses an agency more efficacious for its not being conflated into class struggle, what he calls "a contesting, antagonistic agency" (HB 193) not reducible to a single subject position and therefore not assimilable into the dominant culture. Further Bhabha does not himself fully historicize such a postcolonial subject in its encounters with imperial power, providing rather comparative readings across a broad range of discourses, he emphasizes that cultural hybridity is not incompatible with historical agency when deployed strategically to demonstrate the ambivalences and anxieties of colonial power (HB 208). For Bhabha, these "hybrid hyphenations" form the basis of open, contingent (rather than fixed) cultural identifications that defy any claim to a "singular sign of difference" (HB 219), thus impeding nationalist identity from coalescing around a single defining category of race, ethnicity, religious affiliation, language, or whatever else. Thus the multiple identifications of individuals as "neither One nor the Other" (HB 219) provides the basis for an interstitial "Third Way" of cultural difference that does not foreclose the national destiny but remains open (the future as an open question, as *Nachträglichkeit* [deferred action]) because it is not predicated on a fixed past or national myth of origins that would define forever the identity of its citizens. The postcolonial thus represents not simply an anti- or oppositional (comparative) position vis-à-vis colonialism but "another hybrid, 'inappropriate' enunciative site" (HB 241) of its critique. For Bhabha, the most provocative yet paradoxical articulation of such a "hybrid, 'inappropriate' " response to colonialism is his notion of 'mimicry'; here the colonial subject outwardly emulates the words, practices, and so forth, of the colonizer, yet retains their difference. The mimic man, who Bhabha describes as *"almost the same but not quite . . . [a]lmost the same but not white"* (HB 89), represents an unfinished representation of the colonizer, a repetition with a difference that displaces the latter's self-image and threatens the colonial order through a strategic imitation that Bhabha calls "the *metonymy of presence*" (HB 89). Although the mimic-man signifies on one level the colonized subject's complicity with the colonizer, he also represents a disturbance of the latter's unquestioned dominance; for mimicry, as Bhabha explains, is simultaneously resemblance and menace (HB 88–90). Agency, far from occupying a fixed point (the colonizer) in relation to power, now is uncannily transferred, however ambivalently, to the colonized subject. As Robert Young explains, agency thus enters "a process of circulation":

> the colonizer performs certain strategies in order to maintain power, but the ambivalence that inevitably accompanies the attempt to fix the colonized as an object of knowledge means that the relation of power becomes much more equivocal. Mimicry at once enables power and produces a loss of agency. (RY 147)

Young correctly reads Bhabhian mimicry as a hermeneutics of suspicion between colonizer and colonized: while the native's display of civility or cultural authority comes about as a condition of an assimilation of the colonial culture and thus a complicity with it, their remaining difference—a trace of an accent in otherwise perfect English, perhaps, or the brown face and hands protruding from the police officer's uniform—brings out the colonizer's anxieties about their own superiority. To the extent that the native becomes "almost but not quite," the colonizer's ability to continue to construct the native as essential Other is increasingly undermined; thus the colonizer's paranoia grows from the fear of the colonized's returned gaze, "where the observer becomes the observed" and the essentialized identities of colonizer and colonized begin to destabilize. This is not the same, I should note, as the figure of the native as 'trickster' who plays the master's game in order to gain the upper hand in their relations; Bhabha posits colonial mimicry as a much more subtle, even unconscious, slippage of the balance of power between colonizer and colonized based on the latter's (mis)appropriation of the master's signs of assimilation and compliance.

Bhabhian mimicry reaches its apotheosis in "Signs Taken for Wonders" with the figure of the Indian reading the English book of power, in this case the Bible. For although it is true that religious conversion played no small role in the 'civilizing mission' of colonialism, Bhabha maintains that if the arrival of the English book

> suggest[s] the triumph of the writ of colonialist power, then it must be conceded that the wily letter of the law inscribes a much more ambivalent text of authority. For it is in between the edict of Englishness and the assault of the dark unruly spaces of the earth, through an act of repetition, that the colonial text emerges uncertainly. (HB107)

Or put another way, the English book is transformed in the act of being translated for and read by the native; and if it imparts the law of the colonizer's regime, it also and irreducibly is transformed in the native's language, the native's mind and hands and voice, into something else that the colonizer can no longer control. Thus, in a different context, the melding of Afro-Cuban deities in the Caribbean with the saints of the Catholic Church: Our Lady of Mercy becomes the Yoruban god Obatalá, Saint Barbara morphs into Shangó, and so on. Later these African gods become imminent to the native's own systems of resistance, as they call upon their deities for strength and guidance in their struggles and uprisings against the colonizers.[53] Thus mimicry becomes, for Bhabha, a specific form of oppositional cultural practice, a more explicit act of subversion of the colonizer's cultural imperatives that engenders hybridities even as it opposes the categorical dictates of colonial power.

In order to better demonstrate these interactions of subalterity and agency, hybridity and complicity and resistance to colonial hegemony at work in the literature of the postcolonial, I turn now to a reading of an exemplary Caribbean novel that illustrates and embodies these forces in all their tangled beauty.

III

Robert Antoni's marvelous debut novel, *Divina Trace,* is a text especially significant for its representation of the most complex figures of difference, identity, history and myth within the multivoiced narrative of a single Caribbean family.[54] It is a text acutely aware of what Bhabha calls "the emergence of the interstices" (HB 3), those spaces or indexes located 'in-between' the primary conceptual and organizational categories (class, gender, and so on), categories which are inadequate to contain or apprehend the true complexities of both cultural difference and intersubjective relations on the level of the nation, community, and so forth. For Bhabha, reading the postcolonial is less a matter of cultural identity than cultural *difference,* less a question of subjectivity than of the various subject positions (or subject-effects) that already inhabit any claim of or allegiance to a unitary identity. In the case of *Divina Trace,* these interstices include the aggregation within geographic spaces (Trinidad, New York

City, and the rain forest of the Orinoco) of cultural differences that constantly overlap and displace each other in an ongoing negotiation of identities. For a writer as talented as Rushdie, it has arguably taken seven novels and over twenty years to reach this level of sheer global scope in postcolonial fiction; *The Ground Beneath Her Feet* does broach a sort of intercontinental postcoloniality, with a freedom of interaction between India, England, and the United States unprecedented in narrative fiction, with a protagonist, Vina Apsara, whose tri-continental acculturation reflects, however extravagantly, that of many Anglo-Indians in the United States.[55] *Divina Trace* lacks the astonishing array of pop culture references and globe-trotting characters that Rushdie commands like so many strands of an extraordinary tapestry of a novel; yet Antoni's debut displays a quantum sensibility of place and time that renders not only the interstitial positions occupied by the Domingo family, but also the specific historical context—however problematized by the events of the novel—out of which comes their own particular brand of cultural hybridity and difference.

Two early examples of this hybridity at work in the text are the very chair and desk at which Johnny Domingo, the primary narrator, sits as he tells his story. Both are irremediably infused with the interstitial conditions of postcoloniality:

> I am still a practicing physician, and as I sit here in this library, at this desk of my father's, of my father's father—lugged as a trunk of purpleheart wood *by six Warrahoon Indians out of the misty jungles of Venezuela,* floated down the Orinoco and towed across the Caribbean behind three rowing pirogues, my grandfather calling the cadence stroke by stroke in a language nearly forgotten. . . . (DT 3, emphasis added)

and:

> this absurd miniature Warrahoon-Windsor chair, carved from the same trunk of wood according to the diagram Barto had found in the Oxford dictionary, *but the little Warrahoon had sized the chair to fit himself and not my grandfather,* with its legs too short, its arms pressing uncomfortably into my sides, its saddle-seat shaped as though it were intended for the buttocks of a large boy. . . . (DT 26, emphasis added)

There is a remarkable movement of the signs "desk" and chair" between these passages, a trajectory from one to the other which, read outside of the immediate context of the novel, hint at the sort of cultural overlappings and displacements I have been discussing. The family in question in Antoni's text is Creole and Western-educated, a patrilineage of physicians; and the desk in this family's library is certainly a signifier of class or social standing, as is the fact of the library itself. What we learn of the desk's origins as "a trunk of purpleheart wood" carried from the Venezuelan rain forest by Amerindians, however, further marks the desk and chair as tropes of hegemony and neocolonial domination; the Creole family's polished desk, we reason, as a product of indigenous natural and human resources, is clearly symptomatic of the larger relation between privileged Creole family and marginalized indigenous peoples.

But something else happens in the latter description of the chair. What at first seems to be a simple binary relation of exploitation between civilized creoles and indigenous labor transforms into something much more ambivalent: "this absurd . . . Warrahoon-Windsor chair" that the indigenous worker, by an act not of supervised labor (as in "my grandfather calling the cadence stroke by stroke") but of active interpretation, has crafted into something different from what the master wanted. The anonymous artisan has in effect put his own "Warrahoon" *before* the intended "Windsor," and has superseded and hybridized irretrievably the object that is the product of his labor. The result is not a Windsor chair but a *parody* of one, and beyond that a powerful image of postcolonial hybridity; for the compound signifier "Warrahoon-Windsor chair" is no longer a unitary object but the result of a complex negotiation between subject positions of race, class, institutional power, and geographies. It is also a compelling metaphor of postcoloniality itself: hopelessly or hopefully polyglot, forever overdetermined by its multiple positionings in the interstices of cultural difference.

Here it is important to make a rigorous distinction between parody and satire on the one hand, and on the other between parody and mere imitation or aping. For the Warrahoon artisan's gesture is not one of either identification or rejection, but again of *interpretation* (however unfortunately for the Domingos); that is, parody in this context is as much imitation of inherited forms as it is a critique and refashioning of those forms, and not necessarily an act of mockery or derision. Linda Hutcheon suggests the efficacy of parody as a discourse of interrogation and inversion:

> It will be clear by now that what I am calling parody here is not just that ridiculing imitation mentioned in the standard dictionary definitions. . . . In fact, what is remarkable in modern parody is its range of intent—from the ironic and playful to the scornful and ridiculing.
>
> Parody, therefore, is a form of imitation, but imitation characterized by ironic inversion, not always at the expense of the parodied text. Max Ernst's *Pietá* is an Oedipal inversion of Michelangelo's sculpture: a petrified father holds a living son in his arms, replacing the living mother and

> her dead son, Christ. Parody is, in another formulation, repetition with critical distance, which marks difference rather than similarity.[56]

Within this context, then, the undersize chair and desk constitute an ironic (and very funny) inversion of neocolonial hegemonies, in this case at the expense (literal and figurative) of its relatively overstuffed patrons.

I will cite one more passage in order to make a few further points regarding this formidable Caribbean novel:

> Dis tale to take up, from da beginning of time,
> Future-past, past-future, now de present relate:
> Of Rama quick death, neath he selfsame strong hand,
> Of he meeting with Sita joyful in heaven.
> Of Sita rebirth, in dis statue of stone,
> Of a following, of a heritage slow make.
> Of petitionings bold, of a journey cross de sea,
> Of Sita home she return she fresh again.
> Of de passage of time, ever slow to turn,
> Of a child, of a burden now bear.
> Of dis, my child, my child now return,
> To take up, at long last, in dese waiting black arms! (DT 224)

The preceding passage functions as a microcosm, a summary or distillation of the larger text; in it, an apparition of Magdalena Divina, the island's unofficial patron-saint, narrates central events in the Domingos' family history in what we might call a 'mock-epic' or 'parodic verse style.' But more to the point is that (1) in this particular retelling of "dis tale" (as seen most clearly in the passage's second line: "Future-past, Past-future, now de present relate") an 'ancient originary past, distant in time as well as space—for this is, among other things, a Caribbean retelling of the *Ramayana*—merges through the act of narration with both a present *and* a projected present-to-be or future ("at long last"); and (2) in this translation the originary *Ramayana,* itself a text whose date of origin has never been precisely determined,[57] is again through narration altered in the act of telling to fit the history of a nineteenth-twentieth century Trinidadian family, in what we might call a 'becoming-past' of the present and a 'becoming-present' of the past. Thus the novel itself becomes not merely a historical accounting of, or witness to, historical events within a fictional frame, but a historiographic metafiction that emphasizes the family's (and the nation's) history of cultural and ethnic difference even as it draws attention to its own constructedness as a fiction and as an oral narrative subject to constant revision. The figure of Magdalena Divina reciting the Domingo family saga in a mock-epic parody of the *Ramayana* reflects Trinidad's identity as a nation that is

Hindu *and* Christian, English *and* African *and* Indian, and thus serves as a powerful reminder of the island's hybrid cultural reality; the fictional elaboration points to Trinidad's very real status as a site of multiple diasporic communities: Indian, African, and English. Yet the fact of its foregrounding its own intertextual relation to the Hindu legend, of the conscious shaping of the narrative in strategic and critical imitation of the epic poem, simultanously emphasizes the novel's metafictional quality as a self-conscious reckoning with its own colonial and precolonial past and the rewriting and revising of that past. Thus *Divina Trace* emerges as, among other things, a self-reflexive exploration of Trinidad's colonial history; its diasporic legacy; and its future as a heterogeneous, culturally hybrid nation.

Certainly the novel's primary character, Johnny Domingo, is an exemplary postcolonial figure. The novel's central conflict unfolds as the aged Domingo (he is ninety) tries to reach an understanding of his own cultural identity through a narrative that unravels family stories, local legends, and colonial history as told to him by six other narrators. And the central figure in turn of these multiple narrations is the statue of Magdalena Divina, whose growing myth encompasses Catholic, Hindu, Amerindian, and Afro-Cuban *santería* faiths as a highly syncretic icon whose own narration of the novel's crucial events (via the mock-*Ramayana* poem) renders her the text's most eloquent representation of the cultural hybridity that defines the postcolonial world. Magdalena's status as hybrid icon is further emphasized by the conflicting versions of her life that circulate through the novel; none of the narrators can agree on how old she was, whether she was raised by Amerindians or Hindus (she appears in the novel wearing a Hindu 'tilak' on her forehead), or was the illegitimate daughter of Johnny's grandfather Barto and Mother Superior Maurina (both white). She is further temporally skewed, and mythologized, as Johnny ponders what Magdalena's relation might be to the legend of Magdalena Divina memorialized in the form of the "Black Virgin" statue in the nearby church—a legend that he understands "belongs to a time much older than Mother Maurina. . . . She seemed as old as Corpus Christi itself" (DT 39–40). The mystery of Magdalena—and of the *crapochild,* the frog-like, amphibious baby that she may or may not have conceived with her own father, Barto—are never definitively solved, as befits a text and a national culture composed of such a marvelously entropic hybridity.

The point here—and what makes *Divina Trace* such an exemplary postcolonial novel—is that its many cultural and linguistic elements coalesce not in a neat synthesis or sublation of cultural discourses within a hierarchical whole, but in an agglomeration of cultural differences that exist in a provisional whole that nevertheless preserves its cultural heterogeneity. The impossible task of rendering all of this in a single ordered narrative is left to Johnny Domingo, fittingly, by Evelina, the Domingo family's black servant: "And if dere is anybody could explain all dis confusion to dose yankees, dat dey understand who we is and where we come from dat we can scarce even understand weself, it could only be you" (DT 313). We are left with Johnny Domingo in a position emblematic of the disaporic postcolonial intellectual: left to translate, to transcribe, a history, and legend and myth and story, from whose essences he is hopelessly separated, for an audience from whom there is also a cultural distance. Thus Johnny, in a Bhabhian formulation, by virtue of his "separation from [the] essences" of both history and identity as unitary objects of knowledge, remains a liminal figure occupying an interstitial position between/among the many cultures that have met and clashed and struggled in the Caribbean. Yet he also represents a newness; he embodies that unique syncretic heterogeneity that collectively points the Caribbean toward the possibility of a future or horizon beyond the neocolonial divisions of race, class, and so forth, and toward narratives of self-knowledge and empowerment. Thus is the postcolonial both and at the same time a summation of suppressive colonial pasts and a rewriting/revising of those histories toward a future or horizon of difference and diversity.

IV

The chapters that comprise the remainder of this book constitute in broad terms a theoretical framework, outlining critical concepts whose points of departure I have preliminarily addressed while also calling attention to certain historical moments and cultural conditions. In chapter 1, " 'The Other! The Other!': Conrad, Wilson Harris, and the Postcolonial 'Threshold of Capacity' " I argue that the "threshold of capacity" that Harris claims for *Heart of Darkness*[58] represents in fact a frontier or broken boundary through which postcolonial textuality has since grown and flourished.[59] *Heart of Darkness,* then, emerges as a vanguard or frontier text occupying an interstitial position between the categories of 'colonial' and 'postcolonial,' as it probes or encounters—yet finally shrinks back from—the generic and ontological boundaries that fictions such as Harris's *Palace of the Peacock*[60] have since transgressed more successfully. It is, in fact, precisely Harris's novel that I posit as representative of a literature that both surpasses and retains a debt to Conrad in its explorations of colonialism and its relations with its colonized others; more specifically, I argue that *Palace of the Peacock* succeeds where *Heart of Darkness* fails precisely in its ability to articulate a landscape and an ontological crisis that reduces Conrad's Marlow (and one could argue, Conrad himself) to silence. If, as M. M. Mahood has claimed, *Heart of Darkness* illustrates "the two minds in which Conrad found himself about colonization: the Polish mind which saw it as mere conquest and rapine masquerading in the guise of philanthropy, and the English in clinging to the faith that some work of real benefit could be done" (MM 34), then we can certainly read Conrad (very carefully, as whenever we attempt to make claims, however provisional, for an author's 'intentions') as an avatar of that emblematic figure of postcolonial split-subjectivity, the migrant (MG 171). But this is, finally, not enough, and beyond an apologia for a brilliant and conflicted novella, and what Mahood calls "the cultural predicament of its author" (MM 35–36), we must turn to the texts of the emerging postcolonial world that have more successfully confronted the pitfalls of the diasporic subject and their relationship to European culture and literature, and transgressed beyond these and into the "threshold of capacity"—of subjectivity and agency and self-representation, however problematized—that constitutes the postcolonial.

Chapter 2, "Specters of the Nation: Resistance, *Criollismo,* and the Ambivalence of the 'Neo-,' casts the Harrisian "threshold of capacity" as a temporality, or more precisely as a critique of the conventional understanding of linear temporalities that generally informs the creation and application of such categories as 'the colonial (period)' and 'the postcolonial (period),' according to which logic the former period declines and 'ends' as the latter 'begins.' Here I present the postcolonial in terms of the metaphoric form of the Derridean 'specter': that which is glimpsed and palpable within a given moment but not present as such. As I began to explain, I present the arrival of the postcolonial specter in terms of both a vision of the future and a reckoning with the past; that is, as both a 'memory in advance' of freedom of a life and world after colonialism, and a 'haunting of the colonial past' or the confrontation with, and acknowledgment of, the lingering legacy of colonialism, the cultural residues that remain as part of the postcolonial in both individual subjects and collective national identities. In the chapter I address this 'spectrality' of the postcolonial primarily through careful readings of two Caribbean poets: the Cuban martyr and icon José Martí and Edward Kamau Brathwaite of Barbados. Also and in keeping with Jacques Derrida's *Specters of Marx,*[61] from which I have applied the concept of the arrival of the specter, the appearance of the postcolonial specter is also and necessarily a moment of reckoning; that is, the ghost appears because it *wants* something; it would demand something of us as readers, as witnesses to its apparition. This arrival and demand of the specter becomes especially poignant within the specific context of Caribbean histories of colonialism; for if, as Mahood has argued, the postcolonial Caribbean was the most thoroughly colonized of all European possessions—if, as he avers: "in the Caribbean the societies are themselves the creations of colonial power, and will never escape their history" (MM 181)—then the new nations of the Caribbean must nevertheless learn to confront their legacy as "bastard offspring of European mercantilism" (MM 181), to live with [*Mitsein*] the ghosts of the colonial past in order to better conjure the necessary spirits [*Geist*] of nationhood and self-determination.

The next two chapters address, at greater length and from different contexts, this reckoning with the colonial legacy and the postcolonial subject's experience of colonization. In chapter 3, "Whiteness and the Colonial Unconscious," I advance the term 'colonial unconscious' to account for the suppression, on the level of both individuals and nations, of traumatic or otherwise unwelcome knowledges associated with colonialism and its legacy. I argue that these lingering traces or residues of colonial knowledge or discourses in the postcolonial psyche operate in much the same manner as mental products that the subject retains as part of their inventory of postindependence knowledge yet would repress as representing or symbolizing the memory of their own subjection or enslavement as colonial subjects; that is, the colonial discourses in question maintain their influence over the subject's (and by extension, the society's) conscious life despite—or perhaps even because of—their relegation to a space or index beyond the reach of the subject's conscious critical faculties.[62] I then go on to show the workings of the 'colonial unconscious' as they surface in the autobiographical narratives of the Jamaican novelist-poet Michelle Cliff and South African novelist J. M. Coetzee, reading their texts as articulations of the problematic and undertheorized subject position of postcolonial whiteness. I further argue that for the colonized subject, the traditional literary form of the bildungsroman—the narrative of the child or adolescent's 'progress' toward adulthood, culminating in the protagonist's embracing and mastery of their culture's norms of social maturity and material success—are always mediated in advance by the social limitations imposed by the colonial culture; that is, for the postcolonial memoirist only a "broken" or incomplete bildungsroman is tenable, because of the impossibility of their ever achieving racial and social identity with the colonial ideal of whiteness.

Cliff has herself commented on her work as a critique of whiteness and racism in general, and more specifically on the significance of the protagonist Clare Savage as a "crossroads character with her feet (and head) in (at least) two worlds.[63] As a character whose mixed racial identity places her in a liminal position vis-à-vis both white and black members of Jamaican society, and as her socioeconomic position within a middle-class family positions her equally interstitially between city and country, rich and poor, Clare perfectly illustrates the text's preoccupations with race as a cultural, political, and economic signifier. And the concept of whiteness figures prominently in Cliff's critique of colonially instituted racism, as she herself explains: "When the mythic idea of whiteness . . . is given a construct from which the myth takes its form—i.e., the philosophy of white supremacy—the result is cultural or institutionalized racism, contained in the politics, literature, art and religion of the dominant culture."[64] Likewise, Coetzee explains Afrikaaner writing in terms of the settler's quest for a relation with the land "that will allow him and identity better than that of visitor, stranger, transient" and the growing postindependence realization that the future of South African whites "was going to depend a great deal more urgently on an accommodation with black South Africans than on an accommodation with the South African landscape."[65] Thus in Coetzee's memoir *Boyhood: Scenes from Provincial Life,* the young subject's attachment is always mediated by his keen awareness that the land does not belong to him, but to the Hottentots—the same people that Afrikaaner rhetorics of white superiority had for so long denigrated as inferior, lazy ("idle"), and unworthy husbands for the land.[66] The function of Clare Savage and the child Coetzee in their respective bildungsromans, then, is to illustrate how young subjects living in racially divided societies are shaped by the cultural imperatives of whiteness—imperatives that inform every material aspect of their lives—and how nonnormative subjects (Clare as white *and* black, young Coetzee as a white non-Afrikaaner) must negotiate their heterogeneous positions vis-à-vis the dominant national identity. Thus whiteness directly mediates, on the individual level of developing subjects, the reckoning with the colonial past and the reenvisioning of oneself as part of the national postcolonial future.

Chapter 4, " 'Toward a New Humanism. . . .': Fanon, Hegel, and the Crisis of Mastery," interrogates the cultural imperative and ideal of whiteness from the more confrontational position of the revolutionary humanism (with all of the contradictions such an appellation entails) of Frantz Fanon. In this chapter I offer a response to John Mowitt's pointed question: "Why does Fanon continue to matter? Why does he matter *today?*"[67] by way of Fanon's oppositional, and even impertinent, reading and rewriting of the Hegelian "Lordship and Bondage " relation from the position of the slave's burgeoning freedom and (frustrated) demand for recognition from the erstwhile master. But the chapter finally focuses on the very act of Fanon as a colonized subject engaging in a critique of colonial discourses, or more specifically of the philosophies and knowledges that are so often invoked in defense of the colonization and "management" of subjugated peoples—"talking back," as it were, to the discourses and knowledge of colonial power, and thus representing an irreducible (and, as Jean-Paul Sartre recognizes in the preface to Fanon's *Wretched of the Earth,*[68] irreversible) turning point in the history of postcolonial agency and resistance to the domination of colonial discourses of power. As Lou Turner points out, it is a moment that continues to reverberate throughout the postcolonial world, rendering Fanon "an originary of Third World revolution" inspiring "Third World intellectuals as diverse as Iran's Ali Shariati and South Africa's Steve Biko."[69] Fanon thus serves as an originary founding figure of postcolonialism, one who envisions a future beyond the strictures of neocolonial subservience as the grasping of that "torch that was already there, waiting for that turn in history."[70]

Finally, chapter 5, "Reason, 'the Native,' and Desire: A Theory of 'Magical Realism,'" represents in a sense the culmination of the critical concepts and concerns of the first four chapters. The chapter's argument is twofold: first, that the term 'magical realism' is itself symptomatic of a colonial fantasy—the desire of a Western criticism to apprehend a literature utterly alien to it within the terms with which Eurocentric discourse historically represent its others; that is, in terms of the 'primitive,' the 'exotic,' and the "magical," as opposed to the 'developed,' the 'normal' or 'everyday,' and the 'real' or 'reasonable' (always the recourse to Reason as the dominion and mark of authority of the colonizing West); and secondly, that the literature of so-called magical realism constitute a textuality that gives the lie to such attempts at critical apprehension—as a disorganized, irregular group of texts which, through their sophisticated articulation of other realities that nevertheless reject and defy Western canons of "realism," both exceed and escape the best efforts of Western critical approaches to marginalize them through the restriction to categories of the 'primitive' or 'exotic'—in short, of the "magical." The bulk of this final chapter is a careful close reading of arguably the two most famous works of so-called magical realism: Gabriel García Márquez's *Cien años de soledad*[71] (One hundred years of solitude) and Salman Rushdie's *Midnight's Children*.[72] In each case I endeavor to reveal a narrative that shows an acute awareness of its precarious interstitial position between an indigenous-represented and a Western-representing culture, and the ways in which each narrative manages to both fulfill and frustrate the expectations of its Western audience that it will 'translate' the exotic world of the other for them. I go on to argue for the novels as representative of the ability of the larger body of "magical realist" literatures to represent a reality that nevertheless does not conform to the strictures of a Western mimesis while simultaneously exceeding and escaping, overflowing from within, as it were, the imposed-from-without boundaries of Western critical terminologies: so-called magical realism as the strategic technique of an oppositional literature which, as Rushdie puts it, tells "a kind of truth which you couldn't tell in other ways."[73] Finally, I reveal this oppositional relation between so-called magical realism and the cultural imperatives of Western literary criticism as an allegory of a more general economy of desire; that is, the desire to apprehend, understand, and master the other's 'exotic' or 'fantastic' literatures as symptomatic of the overarching and lingering colonial desire of mastery in general; and I offer, both through the example of my own reading of the texts and concluding comments thereafter, an approach to the literatures of "magical realism" that circumvents this neocolonial model and opens possibilities for a more empathetic intersubjective 'reading-with'—as opposed to a unilateral and objectifying 'reading-of'—our others.

The texts upon which I construct readings in the chapters to follow are not necessarily representative of any particular field of 'postcolonial literature'; I chose them not for their representative value but for their efficacy in illustrating the particular arguments I have wanted to make. The question of a 'postcolonial canon' and of what and which texts might constitute it, is not at all a concern for me here; we should, however, note in passing that by reading the postcolonial in the terms I have just described, we will need to necessarily and completely abandon a certain prevalent notion of postcolonial studies—one which, while zealously and somewhat pedantically clinging to politically correct notions of a (largely self-congratulatory) notion of 'cultural diversity,' defines in the same breath its object of study as "those literatures written in English in formerly colonized societies,"[74] as if all the formerly colonized people of the world spoke English and the name of that originary colonizer hadn't really been *Cristobal Colón*. Thus the reservations of critics such as Santiago Colás, who suspiciously asks: "What can the term *postcolonial* contribute to an understanding of the culture of Latin America?"[75] In my readings of Caribbean Hispanic and Latin American texts in the chapters that follow, I have tried to fashion a response that also takes in the inverted version of the question to which Colás returns at the end of his excellent essay, which is: "What can the culture of Latin America contribute to an understanding of the term *postcolonial*?" (SC 383). My response to this question differs from his, however, in that I have presented in these a vision of the postcolonial that is more affirmation than negation, more horizon than reproach; yet I concur with him wholeheartedly that until Latin American experiences of decolonization and revolutionary struggles receive their due, "a partial, false concept of postcoloniality will dominate postcolonial studies" (SC 383).

This book, then, is not solely or even necessarily a defense of the academic phenomenon that has come to be known as 'postcolonialism.' Rather, it is an attempt to bring critical attention to a term which, for all its being in fashion, remains overused and understudied. That this oft-cited yet undertheorized 'post-' stands in danger of a certain devaluation or inflation should come as no surprise to anyone who has even cursorily surveyed contemporary use of the term. Yet this inflation, this crisis of the 'post-,' is also a symptom. It signifies, even despite itself, that the historicometaphysical epoch known as the 'colonial' must come to closure, must determine as *post-* colonial the direction of its embattled horizon. It must do so not only because we are living in the historical moment in which the postcolonial has been able to begin to emerge, but because the very concept of the postcolonial—no longer designating a derivative, secondary form of its 'root word' (whether understood as accessory, appendix, effect, consequence, etc.), no longer indicating an afterthought—is beginning to go beyond the mere extension (and thus perpetuation) of the colonial. In short, postcolonialism thus *overwhelms* the colonial. It is not that the word 'postcolonialism' has ceased to designate a movement away from, and is thus grown out of, colonialism, but rather that it no longer occupies the space of a mere substitution or replacement; 'postcolonialism' defines rather the movement of a freedom, a *liberation*—one which, althoughin its infancy, can already be seen as effacing the originary supervening of its 'root' while simultaneously pointing toward a future already visible.

Certainly one might object, in the words of Shohat's now-ubiquitous interrogation: When exactly *is* the future; that is: "When exactly . . . does the 'postcolonial' begin?" (ES 103). I have alluded to the 'post-' as something already glimpsed, already in the process of its arrival. But is there a single moment to be awaited, one cataclysmic '*now*' after which we will all have been inhabited, from without as it were? Or is the 'post-' the trace of that which, emerging as the discourses of cultures suppressed but never entirely destroyed, always already there in the first smallest expressions of resistance? We must understand that just as colonialism is not limited to a single historical period with identifiable beginnings/endings, so is the postcolonial open to different formulations of time/place. Any colonial/postcolonial canon of texts, then, for example, which would limit itself to a given century or so, say, 1850 to the present, risks leaving out documents crucial to certain formulations of what has happened, *is* happening. That *The Log of Christopher Columbus,*[76] for instance, can be posited as a colonial text may be arguable on temporal or ideological grounds; but that this written account of his voyages lays bare the basic tenets and assumptions of what followed is much less so. Mapping the postcolonial along national lines is equally difficult: Is *Heart of Darkness,* authored by a white European, Joseph Conrad, univocally a *colonial* text? Or is Wilson Harris correct in seeing that novel as encountering and identifying a certain limit, a 'threshold of capacity' (Harris's term), to be traveled, exceeded, by others? It is questions such as these, which I will pursue in the following pages, which have compelled me to abandon such boundaries in my own analysis, in order to address in some preliminary way the true scope of the issues that must be addressed in any responsible exploration of the postcolonial.

CHAPTER ONE

"The Other! The Other!": Conrad, Wilson Harris, and the Postcolonial "Threshold of Capacity"

I am a king of oceans and skies," said Proteus to Rose. "I swam, flew the Atlantic through Middle Passage Africa, India, Greece, Rome, multiple Christian/Pagan motherhood of carnival. I reached the margins of the world, I came to El Dorado, all in jest. What a golden jest colonialism and postcolonialism are. What untold riches! He knows as he dreams in his cradle. What a gift for a newborn child. . . .

—Wilson Harris, *The Four Banks of the River of Space*

It is thus not a matter of opposing another discourse on the same "things" to the enormous multiplicity of traditional discourses on man, animal, plant, or stone, but of ceaselessly analyzing the whole conceptual machinery, and its interestedness.

—Jacques Derrida, "'Eating Well,' or the Calculation of the Subject: An Interview with Jacques Derrida"

I

In this chapter I will address at length a question frequently raised regarding emergent postcolonial discourses, but seldom more directly than in a recent essay by Ella Shohat: "When exactly . . . does the 'post-colonial' begin?"[1] a question that presupposes a certain type of antitheoretical or 'empirical' interrogation, a question that already posits the postcolonial as a sign contained by the customary signifiers used to denote first sightings ("when," "where"—time, place, and the notion of "origin" itself). What I offer here, however, is not an originary location or moment but what we might for now call a limit or *boundary*. The boundary at stake here is not a generic or historical demarcation (as the question would seem to allude) nor of national borders (a limit respected much more often, it is worth noting, by literary critics than guerrilla fighters), but of a certain kind of capacity or fullness—a "threshold of capacity"[2] from which we may begin to glimpse the emergence of a postcolonial textuality. It is such a boundary, then, which may provide a space from which to begin the task of reading the postcolonial.

My chosen point of departure for reading such a space, while in no way essential to the task, provides us with a particularly rich body of texts from which to begin. As I have indicated elsewhere, the work of Joseph Conrad is especially valuable as a writer credited in many circles with opening a door for writers of the so-called developing world, credited with finding, whether deliberately; that is, *consciously* or not, a sort of fissure in Western colonial thought through which postcolonial texts have since grown and flourished. And yet at this very moment of fissure, within this gesture through which the postcolonial achieves its apparent extrication or (as we must say provisionally, carefully—yet we must say it) "freedom," *something else* emerges. Something that has always already complicated, *contaminated* the higher (because ostensibly "purer") state of Being to which such a freedom aspires. Such a freedom is an irreducibly teleological one; it carries within it the righteousness of the inevitable, of the destined people and their God (this already, of course, a calculated and even strategic move, what we might call a *theo-logistics*), of progress, of an e-*man*-cipation (which in its very articulation betrays its own profound phallogocentrism); and yet despite all of this, it is a word we must write, if only provisionally and in the form of a 'freedom from—.' We must ask, then: Is this "freedom from—," which the careful analysis of the deconstructive gesture would enable the subjugated discourse to enact, a "freedom *to*" as well? And what would be its (national/international? ontological?) horizon or heading: freedom to . . . what? One possible response to such queries is that the deconstructive activity creates a space or condition of freedom without necessarily producing it in its presence, in the form of an acting agent (such, of course, is the archetypal hero or messiah or Leader-of-the-People, the one who would destroy all barriers, answer all questions, resolve all doubts and contradictions (or render them irrelevant), and generally establish his earthly kingdom, under the banner of which all would thrive—in other words, not only an onto-theology but the seldom-examined metaphor of the master narrative: philosophy as Final Solution). So that after the attentive reading, after the analysis that lays bare the hierarchies and unresolved tensions that always underlie the violence (epistemic and otherwise) of empire, there lies the task of *re*-positing, of *re*-constructing, however provisionally or advisedly, the structures of agency—of the active individual and collective subjectivity, the "I am" of a people.

This is because there exists a danger, or rather a question of responsibility, which arises whenever we "raise the banner" of deconstruction. When in the manner of those theorists who implore us to "Always!" do this or that, we invoke the efficacy or inevitability of the deconstructive activity, we always run the risk of uncritically turning motion into method, of reifying and delimiting the very play that we make possible: theory-as-*techne,* critical virtuosity performed for its own erudite sake. Let us say further, in a cautious and preliminary way, that this fissure is the space of this incipient freedom, of this possibility of agency and extrication from the exigencies (discursive and otherwise) of empire, if it is anything at all. It is this, or it is nothing at all.

Let us, then, give this fissure a name; let us say that it is more than an alterity or a margin. Let this fissure become for us, through a certain metaphoric displacement, something else: the mark or signal or index whose referent or exterior is that of a *frontier.* As for this loaded word being a fantastically overdetermined term, bearing a history of meanings of which we cannot but be suspicious, we can for now only say that it is itself a metaphoric displacement ("frontier" for "margin," "threshold" for "limit") which we use advisedly, and whose efficacy will become later on. Let us nevertheless, then, speak of a *frontier*, which one novelist encountered or defined and another (among others) has gone beyond. We may begin with this favorable introduction to the work of the former:

> Conrad's books, I say it without fear of contradiction, have no counterparts in the entire range of English literature. . . . The manner, as opposed to the matter, is even more striking, more original. [Conrad's work] is wholly unlike that of any writer who has hitherto used the English language as his vehicle of expression, and may indeed be regarded, in some sort, as embodying a discovery of yet another use to which our tongues can be put.[3]

Sir Hugh C. M. G. Clifford's assessment is less relevant for its praise of Conrad (he was hardly alone in his admiration) than for what it praises: "the *manner,* as opposed to the matter," more the language than any thematic or ideological element of the texts; it is clearly the language of the texts that Clifford finds innovative, even "exotic" (HC 12): "yet another use to which our tongues could be put." This early (and mostly specious) distinction between the discursive forms and thematic content of Conrad's fiction, with its implicit privileging of the former, may be found in even the harshest of his postcolonial critics. Chinua Achebe, whose ideological aversion to Conrad is well-known ("Conrad was a bloody racist"[4]), recognizes him, albeit grudgingly, as "one of the great stylists of modern fiction and a good storyteller into the bargain" (CA

120); and Edward Said is likewise compelled to admit that the language of Conrad's texts "was far in advance of *what* he was saying."[5] Whether Conrad's discursive talents functioned in the service of morally or ideologically questionable interests, whether he was a knowing accomplice in what Said calls "the duplicity of language" (ES 171), or indeed whether he could have done otherwise, is not of immediate consequence here.

Just as clearly, however, it is not enough for us to simply say "Conrad was not a racist," or "Conrad did not mean that," or worse, to wash our hands of the entire question and say "What if he was a racist, does that diminish the value of his work?" as if we were under some obligation to choose between two moral or ideological contents, each essential and unchanging. When Wilson Harris says that *Heart of Darkness* is a "frontier" novel, he is not so much creating a place for Conrad alongside postcolonial texts as he is acknowledging a space from which such texts emerged. This space is not a delimiting line, but rather a fissure or fracture of a line; it is the "threshold of capacity to which Conrad pointed though he never attained that capacity himself,"[6] a capacity, in the most general terms, for language—or more specifically, for a discourse with the capacity or capability of representing *difference*. In opposition to homogeneous cultural imperatives, radical critiques of colonial discourses—*postcolonial* discourses—must themselves be manifold, heterogeneous; that is, they must help create the structures of which they speak. This is what Harris tells us in "The Frontier on Which *Heart of Darkness* Stands," an essay in which he defends Conrad's "strange genius" against Achebe's aforementioned attack:

> As I weighed this charge in my own mind, I began to sense a certain incomprehension in Achebe's analysis of the pressures of form that engaged Conrad's imagination to transform biases grounded in homogeneous premises. By form I mean the novel form as a medium of consciousness that has its deepest roots in an intuitive and much, much older self than the historical ego or the historical conditions of ego dignity that bind us to a particular decade or generation or century. (Wha 161)

Harris amplifies this statement a little farther on: The capacity of the intuitive self to breach the historical ego is the life-giving and terrifying objectivity of imaginative art" (Wha 162). The undoing of homogeneous premises here is the undoing of a historical ego: "This interaction between sovereign ego and intuitive self is the tormenting reality of changing form, the ecstasy as well of visionary capacity to *cleave the prison house of natural bias within a heterogeneous asymmetric context* in which the unknowable God—though ceaselessly beyond human patterns—infuses art with unfathomable eternity and grace" (Wha 162, emphasis added).[7] The psychoanalytic terminology chosen by Harris for his analysis—this interrogation of a "historical" or "sovereign" ego—apparently corresponds with the absence of a fixed and "knowable" God, or of any otherwise stable center for this "heterogeneous asymmetric context" from which he reads *Heart of Darkness.*

By its appearance, such a context would posit the epistemological or ontological necessity of a center as a monolithic cultural imperative—that is to say, as a historical illusion belying the heterogeneity of the discourses it systematically suppresses. Two immediate consequences of such a reinscription of suppressed discourses merit particular attention:

1. The apparent opposition 'intuitive self/historical ego' signifies an attempt to establish a self (not necessarily a subject in the narrow sense) outside of a linear-historical temporality, one of the "heterogeneous asymmetric contexts" through which Harris seeks to disrupt Western colonial notions of center-origin-unity-History (and so on, terms or signs constituting the chain of signifiers that has always bound colonized subjects everywhere), with the novel form generally and *Heart of Darkness* specifically as both tool and space or index of that irruption (or in Harrisian terms, 'transformation').

2. The act of invoking colonial discourses in terms of a "historical ego" is a preliminary gesture that calls forth a deconstruction of the colonizing subject as constituted by a history, a governing principle—in short, a body of law, conditioned historically by a homogeneous cultural logic driven to identify natural justice (the self-presence to itself of the subject's "moral right"), and natural *justification,* for the actions of a culture.

The beginning of the dismantling of the historical-colonial ego is, for Harris, already glimpsed in *Heart of Darkness,* as manifest in a constant if implicit questioning of what Harris calls the "monolithic absolutes or monolithic codes of behavior" (Wha 162) that invariable govern imperialist discourses, thus opening or pointing toward a space or index through which the process of questioning may continue.

Before moving on to *Heart of Darkness* we should perhaps look a bit longer at Clifford's essay, as we seek traces or symptoms of this Conradian fissure in texts written about him; for once the irruption is written it creates a space or index (for Harris, a "doorway"), a destabilization that makes new subject positions possible—and which, once realized, will inevitably be read and written by others. Consider Clifford's reflection that "Mr. Conrad had seen [nonwhites] and known them, but he had seen as white men see—*from the outside.* He had never lived into the life of brown people" (HC 16). Clearly a recentering has already taken place here; for despite Clifford's comments later in this same essay about the Congo (including a reference to "the incomprehensible savage life upon its banks" [HC 18], he has qualified all such comments in advance with the acknowledgment of his own—and Conrad's—positional bias: both see "as white men see—*from the outside*." This, more than anything else, is the meaning implicit or latent in this fissure over which *Heart of Darkness* presides: the realization that whiteness is not all, that the colonized other cannot be explained away by a simple opposition of "civilized" subject and barbaric object. If Conrad's fiction cannot itself cross over the threshold, cannot itself achieve a parallel intersubjectivity with its others, it at least—to a far greater extent than colonial fictions (Forster and Kipling come to mind)—realizes this condition as being deeply problematic. In Conrad we see acknowledgment, however ambivalent or even latent, that colonial discourses not only severely limited the play of differences within the symmetrical form of a 'liberal' society; but they also provided the form from which to construct a mandate of conquest, a "civilizing mission" given the lie by the heterogeneous bodies and tongues of the conquered. It is to the expression of this problematic in *Heart of Darkness,* and Harris's transformation of it, that we will now turn.

II

William W. Bonney's assertion that Conrad's fiction "probes the limitations of the English language,"[8] which Bonney develops at some length in his poststructurally informed study of Conrad entitled *Thorns and Arabesques: Contexts for Conrad's Fiction,* is a useful enough place to begin; it is especially relevant both for its articulation of the "frontier" to which Harris refers and for its own inability to cross over into a postcolonial discourse. Seen in this context, Bonney's take on the phrase "heart of darkness" is particularly instructive, for its incompleteness; that the image is "founded not upon anything that exists empirically either for Marlow or the reader" but rather based upon a metaphoric vehicle ("heart") and tenor ("darkness") which are themselves tropes for a tenor that neither Marlow nor Conrad can produce (WB 195) is an observation which, while largely accurate, does not account for what that "heart of darkness" might be or Conrad's inability to articulate it. Like Conrad, Bonney probes the *frontier,* the limitations that inevitably surface in the language, without going beyond them.

Grammatically, it would be correct enough to say that "heart of darkness" is an absurdity—a metaphor without a referent, a contradiction only compounded by the phrase's position as the title of the novella. Conrad's text would reveal—or more literally *illuminate,* shed light upon—the "heart of darkness," that we may "see" it; but in literal terms, such an illumination is clearly impossible. To shed light upon darkness is necessarily to change its intrinsic makeup. To render it no longer that which it was; the darkness can remain dark only if untouched by light, making any attempt at illumination a contradiction in terms: darkness cannot be 'illuminated,' and neither Conrad nor Marlow can 'illuminate' the darkness for us. Rather, the text, paradoxically works against itself to reveal an *absence* of clarity, the impossibility of providing, on its own terms, such an illumination; *Heart of Darkness'* act of 'revealing,' then, lies paradoxically in the revelation of its own self-concealment—a revelation of the *absence* of light, of a matter that cannot be produced in its presence: *lichtung* (clearing, *clariere*) rather than Aufklärung (illumination, E/enlightenment).[9] That the phrase "heart of darkness" was nevertheless conceived as a metaphoric vehicle *for something*—something that neither the critical nor literary text ultimately illuminate (or illuminate ultimately)—is instructive not only of Conrad's limitations but also those of a particular kind of deconstructivist analysis. For it is not enough to say that "*Heart of Darkness* is absurd" or that it "is about an absurdity," or as Bonney more qualifiedly puts it, that in *Heart of Darkness* "only a process of indeterminate imaginative regression survives the suicidal figurative inflation of the original grammatical unit" (WB 195). Bonney's assertion that readers of the text must remain "bereft of direction and any possibility of fulfillment" and "are thus rendered even more powerless to achieve a definitive orientation than are his most sensitive characters" (WB 195) is finally inadequate, not only of the implied universality of such a claim but because of the suspect standard by which readers are being judged. It is significant, if arguable, that by Bonney's standard the closest thing to a "sensitive character" in *Heart of Darkness* is Marlow himself, however much his reliability may be qualified by the fact of his first-person narration (he is, after all, representing himself more directly than anyone else in the text). If we nevertheless provisionally accept Marlow as a "most sensitive character" despite this caveat, we would still have to account for his own biases, his own situatedness, as a character within the events of the narrative; or in other words, we would need to determine what kind of a standard Marlow represents, and critique in a rigorous way the kind of discursive structure that would claim him as a standard of judgment or center.

Marlow's character is generally referred to as a kind of modern English "Everyman"; and certainly the earnestness of his work ethic, and strong sense of what we might call an English 'order' or morality (he is, by his own account, "one soul in the world that [is] neither rudimentary nor tainted with self-seeking"[10]) are qualities constantly emphasized throughout the text. Also unquestioned by Marlow (at least before his tenure in the Congo) is his belief in the work of empire; even after all he experiences, he can still claim a belief in the "power of devotion, not to yourself, but to an obscure, back-breaking business" (*HoD* 65). Marlow's lengthy encounter with the ruthless, predatory realities of the imperialist project clearly do some damage to these sensibilities. But while he may recoil in horror from Kurtz's anarchic, avaricious thirst for power and the "unspeakable rites" (*HoD* 65) over which he may have presided, Marlow nevertheless remains safely within the confines of his English rationality. But although Marlow clings tenaciously to his 'Englishness' and his Europocentric vision, he cannot help seeing through the "hollow sham" of imperialism, a pose embodied by Kurtz as the voice of the empire's 'civilizing mission.' It is this ambivalence in Marlow—this discrepancy between what he sees and what he can allow himself to tell—which fuels the narrative tension in *Heart of Darkness.* More importantly, however, we can see Marlow's ambivalence as the realization of a certain *lack;* that is, as symptomatic of the irreducible inadequacy of his language when faced with a crisis of perception (a crisis shared, I think, by Conrad). Marlow, in his encounter with colonial Otherness, can intuit a threshold, a frontier, which, as we shall see, he cannot bring himself to cross.

Marlow hints at the ambivalence of his own moral distinctions between good and evil from the narrative's opening pages; from his opening words, he is already attempting to undo the implications of the text's title. Marlow's observation that "[England] also . . . has been one of the dark places of the earth" (*HoD* 19) clearly challenges the hierarchical oppositions around which imperialist civilizing missions are invariably constructed: binaries such as 'light/darkness,' 'civilization/savagery,' 'white man/black man,' the implicit privileging of the former terms over the latter, and the subsequent conflation of these and other oppositions under the mate-opposition 'Europe/Africa.' By invoking Europe's "dark" past, Marlow blurs the boundary between the opposing terms, thereby implicitly calling into question the validity of the other oppositions—views shared, no doubt, by his immediate audience on the ship: Europe as a place of civilization, E/enlightenment, and so on.

Soon after this initial interrogation of terms, however, Marlow qualifies himself; no sooner has he begun his comparison of ancient Roman and contemporary British empires than he constructs his own hierarchical opposition, apparently in the latter's defense:

> Mind, none of us would feel exactly like this. What saves us is efficiency—the devotion to efficiency. But these were not much account, really. *They were no colonists;* their administration was merely a squeeze, and nothing more, I suspect. *They were conquerors,* and for that you want only brute force—nothing to boast of. (*HoD* 21, emphasis added)

But this opposition of 'colonists/conquerors,' with its implicit privileging of a European 'civilizing mission' over the mere plundering of invaders, is one that

Marlow already knows to be inadequate; hence his immediate undermining of his own just-constructed terms:

> The conquest of the earth, which mostly means the taking it away from those who have a different complexion or slightly flatter noses than ourselves, is not a pretty thing when you look into it too much. What redeems it is *the idea only.* An idea at the back of it; not a sentimental pretense but an idea; and an unselfish belief in the idea—something you can set up, and bow down before, and offer a sacrifice to. . . (*HoD* 21, emphasis added)

Here Marlow effectively gives the lie to his own construction, to his own complicity in the lie of empire. By erasing the opposition between colonist and conqueror, Marlow reveals the only difference between the terms to be that of "an idea"; the sacking of another culture is "redeemed," in other words, only by the idea of the 'civilizing mission,' of spreading E/enlightenment to the "dark places of the earth"—in short, by the same hierarchical logics that he has just called into question. Thus the deconstructive double-bind: Marlow accepts the discourses of empire into his narrative *in the very act of denouncing them,* revealing a state of ambivalence that permeates the narrative.

Seen in this context, it is no wonder that Marlow's immediate audience shows little enthusiasm at the prospect of "hear[ing] about one of [his] inconclusive experiences" (*HoD* 21). It is perhaps in response to his circuitous style of storytelling that one listener (the nameless narrator) chastises Marlow for appearing "so often unaware of what [his] audience would best like to hear" (*HoD* 21); if so, then this passage from Conrad's preface to *The Nigger of the "Narcissus"* is worth reading carefully:

> My task which I am trying to achieve is, by the power of the written word to make you hear, to make you feel—it is, before all, to make you see. That—and no more, and it is everything. If I succeed, you shall find there according to your deserts; encouragement, consolation, fear, charm—all you demand; and, perhaps, *also that bit of truth for which you have forgotten to ask*[11] (emphasis added)

Without returning to previously mentioned contradictions inherent in this task of illuminating "darkness," we can nevertheless begin to understand the problematic of this task as it applies to Marlow's story. Certainly Marlow's "truth" in *Heart of Darkness* is at best a difficult one, rendered ambivalent as it struggles against the awareness that it is decidedly *not* that for which its audience has asked. Yet Marlow is nevertheless revealing something, if less an illuminating truth (*Aufklarung*) than an interrogation of his own self-concealment (unconcealment [*aletheia*]); that is, what Marlow's (and by extension, Conrad's) tale signifies is less a self-evident truth (*Enargeia*) than the opening of a space or index where such truths may yet be thought. Given the absence of the implicitly promised revelation, then, Conrad's awareness of the possibility of an antagonistic relation with his audience, and the representation of such a relation in the text, should not be taken lightly. It is significant in this regard that Marlow is often referred to as an "unreliable narrator," one whom a reader must be careful not to trust entirely. To the extent that any first-person narrator is always more or less situated within the text, thereby making their assumed authority as witnesses problematic, such a critical point is well-enough taken. But Marlow does not necessarily aspire to such trust from his immediate listeners on the boat, and is, at times, quite bewildered by his experience, a state apparent from his numerous admonishments to his audience about the opacity of his tale. It is, then, Marlow's self-reflexive, digressive way of storytelling that marks him as unreliable:

> to [Marlow] the meaning of an episode was not inside like a kernel but outside, enveloping the tale which brought it out only as a glow brings out a haze, in the likeness of one of these misty halos that sometimes are made visible by the spectral illumination of moonshine. (*HoD* 20)

Although this is among the most oft-cited passages in *Heart of Darkness*, it is especially relevant here as an illustration of the text's awareness of its own inability to deliver on the title's promise. There is no inner essence or "kernel" of truth, of darkness or otherwise, to be revealed or illuminated in the telling; it is, rather, precisely in the telling—on the level of signifiers, *of narrativity itself*—that the text gropes for a definitive meaning that continually escapes it, as the passage's reliance upon simile amply attests: the meaning is "not inside *like* a kernel but outside," appearing only "*as* a glow brings out a haze, *in the likeness of* one of these misty halos." Meaning in Marlow's tales is not merely indeterminate, but restless, never content to reside in a single metaphor but constantly moving on, as each successive image proves insufficient to reveal its referent in its presence; what illumination Marlow is able to provide is qualified: "spectral," we are told in a final metaphoric displacement, as is the "illumination of moonshine." The narrator's critique of Marlow's tales, then, might itself serve as a useful metaphor of the slippage that constantly occurs along the signifying chain throughout *Heart of Darkness,* as the text's promise of truth in the form of an illumination [*Aufklarung*] constantly falls prey to the impossibility of that promise. The resulting and unresolved tension between the text's force (what it moves toward asa referent, what it *would say*) and its signification (what it is *able* to say, the limits of its articulation as what it must leave out) is what disturbs and disrupts Marlow and his audience throughout the telling of his tale.

This assessment of Marlow's storytelling, shared by the text's narrator and by Marlow's immediate audience, emerges more forcefully in Marlow's various asides to the latter throughout the text. Marlow's interruptions of his narrative to directly address this audience accomplish little in terms of narrative progression or clarification, save to make explicit for readers of the text the "faint uneasiness" (*HoD* 42) the developing tale inspires in his immediate listeners, and thus to mark the space or index of a tension or symptom within the text requiring further attention. This economy or unresolved tension comes closest to antagonism, however, as Marlow grows increasingly frustrated over his audience's apathy: "Why do you sigh in this beastly way, somebody? Absurd? Well, absurd. Good Lord! Mustn't a man ever—"(*HoD* 63), and so on. Marlow is unable to satisfy their impatience with his narrative, however; all he can muster by way of protest is an exasperated "Absurd be—exploded!" (*HoD* 63), confirming, as Bonney correctly observes, Marlow's frustration at trying to share an experience that he cannot adequately articulate.

But beyond this apparent tension, however, Marlow's most profound sense of contradiction remains internal, locked as it is within the confines of his discourse—or rather, of his growing realization of its inadequacies when faced with the nightmare of empire. Marlow's belief in the 'noble cause' of the imperialist project, already qualified from the text's opening pages, becomes increasingly complicated as Marlow attempts to articulate his experiences. Even before his arrival in the Congo, Marlow already feels ambivalent about the prospect, explaining his own "slight uneas[iness]" at entering what he sees as "some conspiracy—I don't know—something not quite right" (*HoD* 25). Caught between his complicity in "the possession of such a magnificent dependency" (*HoD* 26) and his aunt's errant enthusiasm for the 'civilizing mission' of empire ("weaning those ignorant millions from their horrid ways" [*HoD* 26]), Marlow grows increasingly uncomfortable with a rhetoric he already suspects of being delusory.

Marlow's suspicions about the imperialist project—and his own complicity with it—intensify with his increasing proximity to the 'dark' continent. Additionally, Marlow's ambivalence about the 'noble cause,' and his own role as an agent of it, becomes full-blown upon his first close encounter with the indigenous other:

> A slight clinking behind me made me turn my head. Six black men advanced in a file, toiling up the path. They walked erect and slow, balancing small baskets of earth on their heads, and the clink kept time with their footsteps . . . but these men could by no stretch of the imagination be

> called *enemies.* They were called *criminals,* and the outraged law, like the bursting shells, had come to them, an insoluble mystery from the sea. (*HoD* 30, emphasis added)

For Marlow, the discrepancy between signifier and signified is irreconcilable. The terms 'enemies' and 'criminals' are clearly inadequate to describe what is happening, what is being done to the black men in the name of the 'noble cause'; yet he cannot bring himself to comment on the scene other than elliptically, and not because he lacks the appropriate words: terms such as 'slavery' and 'oppression,' although certainly known to Marlow, represent concepts that cannot enter any discussion of empire without the necessity of confronting its true nature—a truth which, if the imperialist project is to succeed, must be suppressed. Having thus encountered this frontier of language and empire, Marlow's ambivalence here hints toward his complicity. And then he sees this:

> Behind this raw matter one of the reclaimed, the product of the new forces at work, strolled despondently, carrying a rifle by its middle. He had a uniform jacket with one button off, and seeing a white man on the path, hoisted his weapon to his shoulder with alacrity. This was simple prudence, white men being so much alike from a distance that he could not tell who I might be. He was speedily reassured, and with a large, white, rascally grin, and a glance at his charge, seemed to take me into partnership in his exalted trust. After all, *I also was a part of the great cause of these high and just proceedings.* (*HoD* 30, emphasis added)

As regards his uncritical or naive view of empire, this moment is for Marlow the beginning of the end; this moment of self-reckoning, in which he was caught in the knowing gaze of the "reclaimed" guard, confirms his fears: not only is the business of empire, this "conquest of the earth," as monstrous as he had suspected, but his own synonymity with it is unmistakable—whether or not he believes himself so, he is clearly seen by the guard as "a part of the great cause." Marlow's insight here, his recognition of the law as a legitimating discourse for exploitation and violence, is all the more terrifying for his own complicity with it; he has, after all, been identified as an agent of the "outraged law" come from the sea, a force only thinly veiled by its authenticating discourse of "high and just proceedings"—and a discourse more or less inaccessible to those subjected to the force of the "bursting shells," those for whom the law is little more than a wielding of power.[12] Seen in this context, the bitter sarcasm of Marlow's final words (especially the emphasized words) is palpable; it is the self-mockery of one who has seen not only the monstrousness of the hollow sham of empire but his own unwitting role as accomplice. It is this moment of self-discovery, this realization of his own coincidence with the "flabby, pretending, weak-eyed devil of a rapacious and pitiless folly" (*HoD* 30), the necessity of articulating his intuition of the imperialist horror combined with the impossibility of exposing it outright, which fuels Marlow's growing sense of ambivalence. Small wonder, then, that his immediate response is one of paralysis: "For a moment I stood appalled, as by a warning" (*HoD* 31): to acknowledge the horror explicitly would be, for Marlow, to completely undermine not only his sense of moral propriety—of good and evil—but the entire system of discourses upon which those beliefs are based. Despite Marlow's self-professed hatred of lies, then (significantly, he hates lies because they "appall" him [*HoD* 41]; hence his moral dilemma here), the "merry dance of death and trade" (*HoD* 28) continues unabated, as does Marlow's ambivalence—a psychic paralysis that is paradoxically also an oscillation, the ceaseless tracing of a movement between poles of a seemingly insoluble contradiction. It is the space or index of this oscillation, of this failed gesture of illumination that succeeds in revealing only its own complicity of concealment ('unconcealment,' *aletheia*)—it is this space or index (so troublesome to Conrad) which comes to constitute the clearing *(lichtung or clariere),* which in turn makes possible the emergence of the postcolonial, the possibility of thinking such a thing. What is for Marlow/Conrad a limit becomes, for Harris and others, a *threshold.*

III

There is much in Wilson Harris's prefaces to his novels that may prove useful as we begin to read the postcolonial frontier, that "threshold of capacity" to which *Heart of Darkness* points yet does not itself attain. We can begin to understand what Harris values about Conrad's "strange genius" (Wha 161) by reading the former's prefaces and criticism, in which he is primarily concerned with the ontological and metaphysical questions addressed in his fiction; the prefacing note to *Palace of the Peacock,* his first novel, is especially relevant for his notion of the "mixed metaphysic,"[13] a concept that stands in sharp opposition to the monolithic prerogative of Marlow's outlook. The dismantling of oppositional logics that is so problematic in *Heart of Darkness* is for Harris a condition to be desired, as he seeks to constructs a fiction "that seeks to consume its biases through many resurrections of paradoxical imagination" (*PP* 9). For Harris, then, to seek paradox is to invoke contradiction without surrendering to the reconciling impulse, without attempting to account for it in terms of oppositions and hierarchies; it is, in other words, to find a space within the monolithic categorizations and taxonomies of Western thought in which to reinscribe the alterity always suppressed with such systems—to find a place, in other words, in which to begin to address the Other.

The question may be suspiciously raised at this point: But what is the object that Harris wishes to illuminate, to render *present?* Or more crudely: What precisely is it that Harris "sees" and can tell, which Conrad cannot? Is this "threshold of capacity" to reveal, paradoxically, the 'absence of light,' that is, empire, to expose imperialism as a simultaneously self-affirming and self-concealing method of justification for its laws and cultural imperatives? Or is it rather in illumination (Aufklärung) of an essential or universal truth, that of the Other, of Other-ness itself, in opposition to the hegemony of colonial discourses, thus perpetuating the oppositional colonial model?

We will address these and other questions primarily by looking closely at both Harris's texts and *Heart of Darkness,* and examining their situatedness in relation to both a history of Western empire and dominion and a certain space or index of fissure (or by now, *clearing*) of writing. In order to better articulate our inquiry, however, I will make two preliminary statements:

1. This gesture of clearing implied in the first question is not a simple clearing of presence, allowing what is posited as presence (exploitation, slavery, etc.), to appear in its presence, as self-evident. Rather, it is an *unconcealment (aletheia),* a clearing not of presence as such but of presence *concealing itself,* or in Heideggerian terms "the clearing of a self-concealing sheltering" (MH 448); and

2. Implicit in this critique of colonial discourses as homogeneous constructs and imperatives is the reinscription of heterogeneity, of the radical alterity of the Other. Given the relative ease with which we could construct an entire history of Western domination as constituted through the comprehension and incorporation of its others, we might also produce another more recent (one might call it an 'alternative' or 'subaltern') history as constituted by a series of attempts to reinscribe a space or clearing or index for the Other *as Other,* to be written outside the oppositional logics of 'mastery/slavery,' 'colonizer/colonized,' and so forth, and thus implicitly beyond metaphysics in general—thus, for instance, Harris's positing not only of "multiple existences" but of an "unknowable God" who is only revealed outside the realm of "symmetrical contexts." For Harris, then, the threshold in question is one of 'freedom' (again, we will use the word advisedly, in spite of the ideological baggage inherent in this loaded word); not only freedom from an imperialist oppression, one that would perhaps simply substitute one dominant ideology with another (this is, e.g., the quandary in which traditional Marxist accounts of a single 'world history' invariably find themselves; the 'Third World' in such cases becomes itself a homogeneous entity, an unassimilable surplus or supplement to

Western narratives of empire), but a 'freedom *to*'—, in this case, a freedom to construct forms of being and knowledges that celebrate Otherness without absorption into or of the same.[14]

A useful enough way to begin reading this disruption of the discourses of empire, this fundamental shift from the problematic paradoxes of Conrad's fiction to the *meaningful* paradoxes of Harris's, is to look closely at the differences in narration between two otherwise very similar series of events. By way of a general introduction to Harris's novel *Palace of the Peacock* (which, like *Heart of Darkness,* is often considered a novella because of its relative brevity), I will attempt to present it alongside *Heart of Darkness* in precisely such a strategic manner, as a text that portrays a journey into the unknown territories of a jungle (in Harris's case, it is the Guyanese rain forest), for purposes of business and trade, a journey undertaken by a crew of mixed ethnic and racial backgrounds.

Soon after Marlow's first encounter with the African other comes this well-known passage, Marlow's description of native workers dying in a grove:

> They were dying slowly—it was very clear. They were not enemies, they were not criminals, they were nothing earthly now—nothing but black shadows of disease and starvation, lying confusedly in the greenish gloom. . . . These moribund shapes were as free as the air—and nearly as thin. (*HoD* 31)

Clearly this is, for Marlow, a horrible sight. But more relevant for our purposes here is the way in which the dying figures are described: they are "nothing earthly," but rather mere "black shadows" of life that are as free and thin as air. Life is, in this context, represented as being *earthly,* as having a certain vigor of substance that the "moribund shapes" in the grove clearly lack; the binary logic at work here, represented by the oppositions 'substance/shadow,' vigor/listlessness,' active/passive,' and so forth, again implicitly privilege the former terms over the latter, culminating in the conflation of oppositions under the overarching binary 'life/death.' Under this model, then, what horrifies Marlow is not only the physical condition of the workers but also their deviation from a state he, a European, would associate with life.

In this context, Harris's portrayal in his fiction of extra-earthly manifestations of life, his depiction of various transubstantiations and transmutations of life-forms considered by conventional Western logics to be "nothing earthly," is representative of his project of moving beyond the logic of empire, of crossing the Conradian frontier in search of a suitably "mixed metaphysic." To illustrate this point more concretely, we might turn to descriptions from

Palace of the Peacock of events not far removed from Marlow's experience in the grove:

> In this remarkable filtered light it was not men of vain flesh and blood I saw toiling laboriously and meaninglessly, but *active ghosts* whose labour was indeed a flitting shadow over their shoulders as living men would don raiment and cast it off in turn to fulfill the simplest necessity of being. (*PP* 33, emphasis added)

And later:

> [Vigilance] rubbed his eyes since he felt he saw what no human mind should see, a spidery skeleton crawling to the sky. . . . Vigilance could not make up his bemused mind whether it was Wishrop climbing there or another version of Jennings' engine in the stream. He shrank from the image of his hallucination *that was more radical and disruptive of all material conviction than anything he had ever dreamt to see.* (*PP* 82, emphasis added)

I have cited two separate passages here to illustrate a difference, not only between Harris's description and Conrad's but also between moments in the former's own text. As regards the first passage, we can say that its imagery bears a more than passing similarity to that in *Heart of Darkness,* with one strategic difference: unlike Conrad's listless shadows, Harris's ghosts are "active"; that is, Harris's figures, however unearthly, are not only not (yet) casualties of work but also carry a certain sense of agency—they retain the ability to "cast off" the burdens of labor, apparently at will. That the crew members retain the properties of active life in their otherworldly state serves to effectively undermine the oppositional logic prevalent in *Heart of Darkness.*

The second passage represents a more radical departure, yet also illustrates a certain relation to Marlow's appalled narration. Arguably what Vigilance sees—a hallucination (maybe) of his dead coworker's skeleton "crawling to the sky," is more shocking than even Marlow's vision of shadowy death in the grove. Let us note here also that even the name of Harris's character, Vigilance, already signifies a different posture or attitude toward events than shown by Marlow: namely watchfulness, a *willingness* to see; and that this watchfulness also stands in opposition to Marlow's own reluctant observation—and halting narration of—events (and certainly this trait would also separate Vigilance also from Conrad's audience, upon whom the author assumes he must force such vision: "to make you see"). Yet given the opportunity, Marlow would likely contend that he too experienced something that "no human mind should see"; and indeed, the horrific nature of events in *Heart of Darkness* is to a great extent what fuels Marlow's ambivalence and that of the narrative. Once again, however, there is an important strategic difference: whereas in Conrad's text the lack of "earthly" substance is a sign of weakness, exhaustion, and defeat, in *Palace of the Peacock* Wishrop's metamorphosis into a "spidery skeleton" is depicted as a "transubstantiation" (*PP* 83), if not a triumph, then certainly an escape or liberation from the physical trials of the journey into another existence, another realm of possibility. Additionally, this blurring of boundaries between the dead and the living is not limited to Wishrop; by this point in the text, not only has the first-person narrator inexplicably disappeared, but other characters are experiencing profound transformations as well: Vigilance's "immateriality and mysterious substantiality" (*PP* 82), Donne's suspicion that he is no longer "in the land of the living" (*PP* 83), and the crew boat's transformation into a "skeleton craft" (*PP* 83) are all representations of a reality alien to Marlow and, by extension, to *Heart of Darkness* itself—the frontier of a world whose multiple existences are hopelessly beyond the bounds of Marlow's English rationality. Harris's novel, then, emerges as less another entity among entities that we could simply oppose to *Heart of Darkness,* than a signpost of possibility for the multiple or quantum realities of the postcolonial. Which is not to say that Marlow as a character is in any way static; as we have already seen, however much in passing, the processes by which he encounters the frontier of Otherness; but while Conrad, through the experiences of his characterized narrator, steps back from the brink, Harris takes us across, fissuring oppositional lines as we breach the multiple realities of a postcolonial world.

To better understand the nature of this frontier, this opening into the postcolonial, we might consider Harris's own first encounter it; the passage is from Harris's own account of his first expedition into the interior of Guyana:

> I had penetrated 150 miles. It seemed as if one had traveled thousands and thousands of miles, and in fact had traveled to another world, as it were, because one was suddenly aware of the fantastic density of place. One was aware of one's incapacity to describe it, *as though the tools of language one possessed were inadequate.*[15] (emphasis added)

Certainly the resemblance to the crisis of language we see in *Heart of Darkness* is striking; like Marlow, Harris here lacks "the tools of language" to adequately contain the reality of his experience. Yet faced with this and other encounters with the Guyanese interior, Harris is eventually able to construct fictional narratives that can begin to represent the "fantastic density," what for Marlow is clearly the daunting difference, of this other reality. Which is not to say that Harris's fiction can remotely be called 'realism'; on the contrary, it is paradoxically to the extent to which Harris's fiction diverges from Western conventions of realism that it succeeds in representing Guyana's reality of place: "All this seemed less to do with the medium of place and more to do with the immediate tool of the word as representing or signifying 'place'" (Whb 58).

The impossibility of homogenization or suppression of the Other, then, can sometimes be seen as threatening and sometimes as liberating, depending of course upon context, subject positions (who is doing the suppressing or liberating or whatever), and so forth; and both of these possibilities coexist more or less simultaneously in *Heart of Darkness*. There are, accordingly, at least two ways to articulate this limit, this threshold of 'same/Other': in the empirical sense, the taxonomic sense of a field or area that is too large or unwieldy to adequately address under a given heading; and in a poststructurally informed sense of play, in which totalization is meaningless not because of the inadequacy of a finite discourse to cover or delimit and infinite area or field, but rather because of the infinite substitutability of a finite field. Or in Derridean terms, totalization is useless not because an area is too large, but because it is *missing* something: a center or transcendental signified that would arrest and limit the play of substitutions/differences. It is precisely this burgeoning realization in *Heart of Darkness* of a decentering of the discourses of empire, and the subsequent oscillation between desire and fear, interrogation and withdrawal, which places the text on the postcolonial frontier of Harris's title.

In the essay from which I cite this passage, Harris goes on to discuss his interest in critiquing what he calls the "static cultural imperative" (Whb 65) of Western thought; what this project entails, he tells us, is the constant calling into question of established (or rather imposed) modes of thought, structures that deny the polyglot nature of postcolonial reality. There is much in this very valuable essay (much more than I am able to include) that could be usefully discussed here; the passage I will cite, however, is especially relevant for Harris's reference to texts that contain the seeming roots or origins, if we may be given leave to make provisional use of such a problematic term, of such a cultural critique:

> One would have to turn to Melville to sense the beginnings of this kind of thing in the novel, to a poet like Coleridge, *or a novelist like Conrad.* It is something that is impertinent to the homogeneous novel, though immensely consistent with the subjective crisis of twentieth-century man [*sic*]. (Whb 61, emphasis added)

Here we may begin to read, if not anything so naively fixed as an essential origin (a "without-Conrad-none-of-this-would-come-to-pass" type of origin, with its implicit privileging of Conrad's fiction at the expense of those postcolonial writers who followed), then at least a place or instance where a frontier may have been breached; we may, that is, begin to glimpse the general location or event where this rupturing of the ontological frontier of the postcolonial may have occurred. If this is so, then questions of homogeneity and those elements that might be "impertinent" to it assume a most radical significance: Why, for instance, assuming the existence of such a thing as a "homogeneous" novel (for even in Harris's example of Jane Austen a case may be made for any number of subsumed others), is a critique of this type of fiction equated with crisis?

An answer to such questions may lie in the very terms 'impertinence' and 'heterogeneity,' in what such terms might imply. In Austen, to return to Harris's example, we find Otherness very carefully bracketed, subsumed within the patterns and premises of the narrative; by so doing, the text achieves a kind of sophistic homogeneity, specious because the monolithic exigencies of such texts attempt to belie or mask the existence of others who nevertheless are always already there. The success of any act of "impertinence," then, lies precisely in its interrogation of purportedly homogeneous texts, in its ability to call into question texts that attempt to conflate their others under the oppositional logics of sameness; it is a question, in other words, of *exhuming* difference, of producing or finding a fissure in the construction of sameness through which its previously interred others may emerge.

The fact that such fissures are more readily apparent in texts such as *Heart of Darkness* is illustrative of their latent heterogeneity—of their proximity, to the margins/frontiers of Otherness that the literatures of postcolonialism are now beginning to attain. It is, in short, simply not enough to say that "*Heart of Darkness* is overdetermined" or "*Heart of Darkness* is too 'loaded' to work with"; that is, it is not a simple matter of opposing some other, more contemporary or less studied discourse to the 'less enlightened' work of a Conrad or Kipling (to name another similarly maligned body of work) in the name of a postcolonial canon or aesthetic, but of rigorously and constantly interrogating the concepts and conditions from which such texts arose. In order to better understand the situatedness of these texts, where they stand in relation to both each other and their shared frontier of Otherness, we might look to this instructive passage from another of the writers mentioned in Harris's essay, one whose engagement with Otherness, however inexpert, predates Conrad's:

> As it must not, so genius cannot, be lawless: for it is even this that constitutes it genius—the power of acting creatively under laws of its own origination. How then comes it that . . . whole nations have combined in unhesitating condemnation of our great dramatist [Shakespeare], *as a sort of*

> *African nature,* rich in beautiful monsters, as a wild heath where islands fertility look the greener from the surrounding waste, where the loveliest plants now shine out among unsightly weeds and now are choked by their parasitic growth, so intertwined that we cannot disentangle the weed without snapping the flower?[16]

Without embarking on a detailed dismantling of oppositions here (and there are plenty: 'nature/culture,' 'domestic/exotic,' 'civilized/barbaric,' etc.), we can see how far removed this language is from Harris's postcolonial sensibilities (and even from Conrad's own colonial aesthetic). The most damning thing we can say about such a statement, from Samuel Taylor Coleridge's well-known defense of Shakespeare, is that it denies Africa a teleology; that is, the most striking opposition at work here is one privileging Shakespeare's 'ordered' (i.e., homogeneous: better because, contrary to the critics, Coleridge implies, Shakespeare's discourse is *all* ordered green and flowers and *no* chaotic waste or weeds) cultivated representations of a Western nature over an allegedly aimless, entropical African wilderness. The obvious premise, the subtext behind Coleridge's analogy, is of Africa as a wilderness lacking order, wanting for the 'disentanglement' of an enlightened (because European) civilizing plan; and it is precisely this kind of rhetoric that contributed to the founding of the notion of the 'civilizing mission' of European imperialism, the "great cause" of which Marlow, however sardonically, believes himself a part.

Upon confronting the wilderness himself, however, Marlow finds it to be less passive than he may have originally believed:

> Going up that river was like traveling back to the earliest beginnings of the world, when vegetation rioted on the earth and the big trees were kings. An empty stream, a great silence, and impenetrable forest. . . . And this stillness of life did not in the least resemble a peace. *It was the stillness of an implacable force brooding over an inscrutable intention.* (*HoD* 48–49, emphasis added)

Marlow goes on to describe the jungle's "vengeful aspect" (*HoD* 49), a dimension of silent rage that is coherent and palpable; for him, then, the jungle *does* have a sense of purpose—and it is decidedly malevolent. That Marlow experiences the force of an African nature in this way, moreover, aptly illustrates both his realization of a representative Otherness and his perceived oppositional relation to it. Because although Marlow has, by this point, realized a margin/frontier of Otherness, he remains wedded to one side of an oppositional 'rational' mentality, and thus cannot but shrink back in foreboding at the possibility of rupture.

Finally, we come to Harris's Guyanese forest, where the vital multiplicity of Marlow's fears (and of which Coleridge cannot even conceive) begins to manifest. This passage comes relatively early in the text, before the boat crew's own experiences of transformation:

> The solid wall of trees was filled with ancient blocks of shadow and with gleaming hinges of light. Wind rustles the leafy curtains through which masks of living beard dangled as low as the water and the sun. My living eye was stunned by inversions of the brilliancy and the gloom of the forest in a deception and hollow and socket. (*PP* 28)

And:

> A sigh swept out of the gloom of the trees, unlike any human sound as a mask is unlike flesh and blood. The unearthly, half-gentle, half, shuddering whisper ran along the tips of graven leaves. Nothing appeared to stir. And then the whole forest quivered and sighed and shook with violent instantaneous relief in a throaty clamour of waters as we approached the river again. (*PP* 28)

Clearly there is a profound transformation, one of both mimesis and teleology, which takes place between Marlow's narration and this one. Unlike both Coleridge's perception of mere disorder and Marlow's vision of a monolithic brooding, Harris's depiction reveals a multiplicity of life that contains the previous descriptions as it surpasses them; for while this forest is, certainly, at least as perilous as the one portrayed in Conrad's text, it represents with equal clarity the possibilities for a new and heterogeneous community—one that surpasses binary perceptions of the world in order to embrace all manner of paradoxical realities. Indeed, the characters' reactions of "surprise and terror" (*PP* 29) are fleeting ones, and by the text's final pages they embrace "the inseparable moment within [them]selves of all fulfillment and understanding" (*PP* 116) that comes with the overcoming of fears and the crossing of frontiers. To call this an 'ending,' however, would be misleading; for the breaching of frontiers—and the accompanying irruption or emergence of discourses once kept suppressed—is always a provisional, open-ended business, and we must, after all, continue to resist the monolithic imperatives of completeness and closure. What now remains addresses, however cursorily, is the future of the frontier, of this postdeconstructive moment of fissure.

Let us end with a more informed, a more useful pair of questions than the question with which we began: What form(s) can this postimperialist literature yet take? Can we, after all, write and read a new and radical postcolonial literature that moves beyond the oppositional logic of the Western *natio,* which escapes the self-defeating reductions of 'us' and 'them'? We can begin to address these questions by saying that the fissure to which I have been referring must begin not in the center (as the center is infinitely substitutable) but on the margins. But even this is not enough, for what has in the history of empire been written and read as the margin must come to be known as something else:

> To think of ourselves as marginal or marginalized is to put us forever at the edge and not center stage. The word *margin,* however, has another meaning which I prefer to think of when it is used as a descriptive term for managed peoples—it also means frontier. And when we think of ourselves as being on the frontier, our perspective immediately changes. Our position is no longer one in relation to the managers, but we now face outward, away from them, to the undiscovered space and place up ahead which we are about to uncover—spaces in which we can empower ourselves.[17]

The substitution of 'frontier' for 'margin' seems, as Marlene Nourbese Philip points out, harmless enough; it would seem, additionally, to represent a mere continuation in what has been an endless series of substitutions of center for center. The implications inherent in such a radical shift, however, are both profound and inescapable; for what it implies is nothing less than a complete reinscription of positions, literally a *turning away* from the homogeneous totalizations of the past. And if we cannot yet see where the frontier may lead us—what this "undiscovered space and place up ahead" might turn out to be—we have at least found a place to begin, a space or index from which to start reading and writing a future for Africa, the Caribbean, and the rest of the postcolonial world which may reconcile Harris's term 'meaningful paradox' to its contradictorily coherent parts.

CHAPTER TWO

Specters of the Nation: Resistance, *Criollismo,* and the Ambivalence of the "Neo-"

> Qué más, qué más laurel? Cuándo el martirio
> No fue en la frente la mejor corona?
> —José Martí, *Poesias completas*

To begin, then: What does Martí's question mean? Contained as it is within a poem, within a volume entitled *Versos Libres,*[1] a book of poetry written during a time of revolution and upheaval (much as is our own), is it a question that requires an answer? Is it a simple rhetorical gesture, requiring of us (or his contemporaries: not the same thing) an equally simple affirmation? Or does it somehow interrogate the future; that is, does the poet project his question, blindly, into a future, from which he hopes against hope for a reply, a *return?* To begin, then: What does the poet's question ask *of us?*

"What more, what greater laurel?" A question asked of us by a poet, a nationalist, a *revolutionary.* And finally, by a *martyr,* who in the name of the revolution died in the Battle of Dos Rios, Cuba, in 1895: "When has martyrdom / Not been . . . the finest crown?"

Alone, out of its context, Martí's question remains unanswerable, almost unintelligible. Again, we are apprehensive, suspicious of the possibility of our own implication, of what this dead-yet-living specter of a revolutionary poet might be asking us to do: "What more? . . ."

There is, as ever, the hint of violence, the fear of what the ghostly voice might want. Perhaps we, too, wish to ask: "What more? . . ." We are addressed by a voice that is not 'of our time,' which asks impertinent questions about the future—about struggle, about death. And we must hesitate in our response.

What would this revolutionary specter demand of us: Sympathy ("We feel for you in your struggle")? Education ("We know of your struggle")? Worship ("We love and admire you for your struggle")? Or *action* ("We, too, struggle with you")? Or put another way: Would the specter be satisfied with our admiration and approval? Would it be pleased to know of our reading and writing of it, our willingness to spread the word, to bear witness to its message? Or must we, too, struggle, fight, possibly become martyrs as well?

To understand, to better hear this demand or call of a voice not of our time yet strangely here, speaking to us, we must stand 'between knowns'—between, as it were, life and death. Between (1) our present-life and the ghost's long-ago death (past event, yet 'present' to us as a fact); (2) the ghost's past-life and our own death; that is, our knowledge of it as a future event, even if perceived only dimly or distantly (as a sort of specter itself); and most importantly (3) the ghost's own existence as an entity between life and death, which experiences *(knows!)* death yet appears to us, in order to call, to require. To require *what?* We do not know; the ghost must be *addressed.* So Jacques Derrida, who also speaks to/about ghosts,[2] would exhort us in this instructive passage:

> So it would be necessary to learn spirits. Even and especially if this, the spectral, *is not.* Even and especially if this, which is neither substance, nor essence, nor existence, *is never present as such.* The time of the "learning to live," a time without tutelary present, would amount to this, to which the exordium is leading us: to learn to live *with* ghosts, in the upkeep, the conversation, the company, or the companionship, in the commerce without commerce of ghosts. To live otherwise, yet better. No, not better, but more justly. But *with them.* No *being-with* the other, no *socius* without this *with* that makes *being-with* in general more enigmatic than ever for us. And this being-with specters would also be, not only but also, a *politics* of memory, of inheritance, and of generations. (*SoM* xviii-xix)

To live, then, with ghosts, with that which is not of our time, not present as such. To converse with ghosts, to keep an open ear to what they might ask us to bear witness to or do ourselves. And we must understand this as an irreducibly political task—our *inheritance,* whether we desire or even know of it—from other generations, past and future. Hence Derrida's reference to ghosts in the plural: generations of ghosts. Also, to do so not out of mere reciprocity or courtesy, but in the name of *justice* ("not better, but more justly"): justice not only or even necessarily for ouselves in the here and now, but for others who are, like the specter, not present as such, who are here and yet not, not yet here, no longer here. To speak of both past and future, and of our *responsibility* in and for them.

And so, to return: there is a ghost, the ghost of a dead poet named Martí, who asks us a question, a question for which we must take some responsibility: Is it not the greatest honor of all to die a martyr? To die 'for the revolution'? And we–what would we do 'for the revolution'? It is not easy to answer. We hesitate, as we must, not because the ghost's impertinant inquiry could be any clearer (indeed, it could not) but because, as Derrida has stated, there are other ghosts, *other voices.* It is not a matter of simply choosing this or that one; no, the apparition never comes but by its own design, it is independent of our machinations, our manipulations of this or that history, this or that political calculation. The argument of this chapter, then, is precisely this: that to know the postcolonial, to inhabit the space or index of the 'post-,' is to be forever surrounded, enveloped, by the generations upon generations of specters, both of lives that have been and lives to come; and that the postcolonial is both a past and a future inhabited, *haunted,* by them all.

And there are other ghosts, other spectral apparitions, to be read; and they, too, have their demands, would bring their voices to bear upon us. They ask: "Where to?" "What now?" "Whither?" To invoke, to conjure them all, it is true, each in its context and desired place, would no doubt be an endless task; and there are certain of these spirits that in one way or another inhabit us all. For now, then, I will take the liberty of privileging from this ghostly genealogy (a chain of spectral signifiers of ghosts chained to ghosts) two such hauntings, which are of particular interest for a future that would call itself 'postcolonial,' a future that would be free of the shackles and specters of a colonial past. (Before reading them let us note, however briefly, that although haunting is historical it is not linearly, reductively so; that is, it does not correspond [respond] to history as telos, it will not take its place in the chain of events as so many ducks in a row. As I have intimated earlier, the specter does not arrive simply when and where it is summoned, it is not at the beck-and-call of the sham psychic, the historian as *faux*-shaman. It is, in a word, 'untimely': alterity, other, but always there, the condition for the very existence or even possibility of a future.[3])

First example, from an essay by V. S. Naipaul:

> To be a colonial was to know a kind of security; it was to inhabit a fixed world. And I suppose that in my fantasy I had seen myself coming to England as to some purely literary region, where, *untrammelled by the accidents of history or background,* I could make a romantic career for myself as a writer. But in the new world *I felt the ground move below me.* The new politics, the curious reliance of men on institutions they were yet working to undermine, the simplicity of beliefs and the hideous simplicity of actions, the corruption of causes, *half-made societies that seemed doomed to remain half-made:* these were the things that began to preoccupy me. They were not things from which I could detach myself.[4]

The remainder of the essay is dedicated mostly to crediting Conrad and his fiction as a model for Naipaul's own work; yet the qualities for which he praises Conrad are themselves marked by a certain anxiety, a certain ambivalence.[5] What are we, readers of a 1974 apologia for a turn-of-the-century colonial novelist, to make of Naipaul's obvious uneasiness? We might, understandably enough, write off his apparent loathing of postindependence politics and predilection for colonial literatures as symptoms, signs of certain latent fears: the ambivalence of the 'neo-.' Yet in what he writes, as well as and especially in what he does not write about the ghosts that haunt him, Naipaul illustrates for us three distinct and distinguishable moments:

1. the desire to "inhabit a fixed world," and the illusion of identifying a posteriori—of *having lived*—a time before the appearance of the specter, as if the ghost did not replace and displace itself in the very movement of this history, as if haunting did not, as I have argued, did not mark the very existence of the colonial, of the postcolonial, of the West itself. But there is more: Naipaul's idyllic world is not only fixed, but also a "purely literary region . . . *untrammelled by the accidents of history or background*" (emphasis added). And what of this "purely literary" refuge? Is it not nostalgia itself, a longing for an old way of reading, an invoking of certain words spoken in a certain way with the professed intention of conjuring away—of *exorcising*—some dangerous spirit? A place of the dead letter, where such frightening ghosts may be dehistoricized, de-cultured (what is culture, after all, but "accidents of background" in their various configuratons?), where one may live in peace, untrammeled (read "unhaunted") by them. A romance, to be sure—and by Naipaul's own admission;

2. the realization of the haunting, and the eruption described in an almost dreamlike way, of the other's imminent arrival: "But in the new world *I felt the ground move below me.*" It is, for the colonial, the end of substance, fixity, permanence—in short, of a time that is set right, in step with itself. Also, we cannot make enough of Naipaul's chosen metaphor: *"I felt the ground move below me."* Is this not literally (and more than literally a shaking of security, a shattering of what was believed to be irreducible, of an illusory essence broken down beyond itself? And what of the metaphor's spiritual dimension? There is certainly an element here of the spectral, and even the apocalyptic; something has happened, the ground is *moving* below one's feet. Yet this is not the joyful epiphany of the converted; it is, rather, the fear and foreboding, the quaking-in-the-boots of the unbeliever confronted suddenly and without warning by the fact of the other's arrival. It is a comeuppance of sorts, and it is clearly dreaded.

Before moving on to the passage's last two sentences, we might attempt to indicate the space or index of a certain fear, an ambivalent experiencing of 'newness' as dangerous, of 'the new' as cataclysm.

First, and obviously enough, is the experience (and tacit acceptance) of the colonial as order (telos); note the words 'security,' 'fixed,' 'ground.' All of these are indexes of a colonial order accepted as stability, reason (or Reason [Logos]), even sanity, of which Naipaul clearly believes the formerly colonized nation to be quite incapable: "half-made societies that seemed doomed to remain half-made." We should note at this point, if only in passing, that Naipaul's exposition of himself as a colonial subject contrasts markedly with Frantz Fanon's frightening exegesis of colonial alienation and self-estrangement in *Black Skin, White Masks*. Why is it that Naipaul's acknowledged moment of ambivalence comes at the moment or even prospect of liberation, of *freedom?* Is not his situatedness as a colonized subject, a subject constituted between and among cultures of colonizer and colonized, already problematic for him in the "fixed world" of the colonial, where for Fanon "The Negro is not. Anymore than is the white man"?[6] I suspect that any useful reading of these texts would necessarily include a reconstruction of subject positions, which would in turn involve a more rigorous reading of the intersections or interstices of race/class/geopolitical location/and so forth, than we will have time to do here.[7] And yet we can begin to address the question in a preliminary way, when we ask of one of Naipaul's more curious turns of phrase:

3. Why "half-made"? What is the ontological status of a 'half-madeness,' the implications of it for a reading of the colonial's fear of chaos? How is it different from invoking, say, a 'transition' or translation,' or even a 'paradigm shift'?

I am reminded, even as I ask these questions, of certain formulations and interrogations of the subject: the subject as an instance, a 'who' always already divided within itself, besieged by its own trace, its own difference; 'who' as an indeterminate pronoun, one without a referent ("What is its name?"); this 'who' also as a sign which, à la Saussure, is determined by the signs around it and by its own difference from them—and transgresses that determination of its own meaning as soon as it is situated or placed differently. What or how, then, does Naipaul's statement signify in relation to such formulations? We might say, for now, that at the beginning of the passage in question the subject "Naipaul" in the terms of the economy of a 'who,' remember—finds itself determined by its proximity, its supposed *identity,* with the referent "colonial," a referent that grants it a certain determination of meaning, a certain destination or teleology. This being the case, can we not read Naipaul's ambivalence as a fear of losing its referent, of being placed differently or *différant*-ly—the deconstruction of a subject that now finds itself situated in, determined by, an entirely new set of surrounding signifiers: "independence," "citizen," "sympathizer," "traitor," and so forth. Which brings us again, finally, to a description of a subject besieged by its own difference, its own *différance.*[8] We can, then, within this context of shifting subjectivities/positions, read *différance* as a limit, the interrogation/interruption/frustration of the Hegelian *Aufhebung (relève),* the subject's drive to overtake, to apprehend otherness within its own boundaries; hence the neocolonial's comfort at the thought of "inhabit[ing] a fixed world" that 'fixes' them in an unchanged relation of mastery and the mastered, and their chagrin at the encounter with any element of alterity, of otherness, of that which will not be assimilated.

And yet: "half-made societies that seemed doomed to remain half-made; . . ." that is, the mourning for the unraveling of an order (telos), and the profound disappointment at being unable to ontologize the remains or remnants, to keep alive, if not the body itself, than at least the illusion of vigor, the maintaining through artificial means of the bodily signs. As I have already intimated, it is thus not a matter of the social corpus moving from one state to another: a translation of dialects or recognition of this or that "official" state language, a transition between administrations, paradigms, the endless substitution of center for center that belies the unchanging status of the neocolonial structures. No, this is not an ontology; it is not life nor death, as such. There is the appearance of the shape, of the apparition, of that-which-is-there-yet-not-there. It is, in fact, "half-made" precisely because it is that-which-is-not-there; one sees it, can *envision* it, yet it is not. It is the specter as endless *possibility,* as that ghost that would be followed but also persecutes, pursues: "They were not things from which I could detach myself." This is ever the state, the very condition, of the 'neo-': half-made, forever lingering between ghosts of empire and of the future, ever apprehensive and ambivalent when faced with the excess that is freedom, with the blind and terrible and cataclysmal justice of the 'post-.'

Second example, this time an interrogation, even an impertinent one, of specters. Of the specters of an empire, of a history of colonization, of that from which the questioner would detach himself even as he engages it, that which he would conjure in order to send it away. Edward Kamau Brathwaite addresses a ghost; or more precisely, he speaks about a ghost to an audience, in an academic setting, likely composed of writers, critics, and so on, who perhaps share the speaker's sense of haunting, of "things from which I could [not] detach myself." The speaker asks: How can we as Caribbean writers come to terms with our experience, how can we retrieve a sense of history *"in spite of and beyond the metropolitan English education we were given?"*[9]

The immediate problem, what we might recognize as the most obvious possible objection, revolves around the plural of "we as Caribbean writers" and the singular of "our experience." Given that Brathwaite's "we" is the product of an utterance spoken in a certain place to a certain audience, and transcribed, edited, and otherwise prepared for publication elsewhere and by others,[10] one might well object that such a claim to a common 'experience' could not credibly embrace all such writers, that it would be more than irresponsible to conflate under "our experience" the nationalist fervor of a José Martí and the neocolonial ambivalence of a V. S. Naipaul. And yet: What is being claimed here, or reclaimed? Is it not precisely "a sense of history"? And is not history, understood here as a means of documentation, as an ordering discourse of experience, precisely what creates the "our" of the question? The question that would posit such an "our" already and in advance lays bare the premise of its response: the "we" of the "our" would seek itself, or more precisely its 'origins,' in the ordering discourse of a history, and would uphold its own construction as its own validation.

But as we have seen, a conjuring is often also a conjuring away, a pursuing as well as a being-pursued; and in the case of Brathwaite's question the invoking of a certain historical *spirit* is also and at the same time the conjuring (away) of certain other specters, unwanted yet stubborn and tenacious in their haunting. (And here we begin to see a destination for the specter: for at what point does the specter become 'spirit' ['Spirit,' *geist*]?) Brathwaite would call upon certain specters—in the name, let us not forget, of a certain spirit (or Spirit)—and eschew others, embrace these and exorcise those; he would distinguish very carefully between desirable and undesirable hauntings. And yet, what of this remnant of empire, this inheritance of a colonial past—this "metropolitan English education we were given"? Whither to conjure such a thing, where to banish it, so that it will no longer be an obstacle to be gotten 'beyond'? Indeed, where to locate it at all, that it might be summoned forth and done battle with—or at least resisted, that this haunting of empire would no longer have its way with us? And finally, how to get beyond the naïveté of a simple belief in conjuring (away), the belief that the ghost will finally play by the rules, will respect and not cross lines of alterity, of resistance (and resistance to otherness), of the nation-state itself?

Much of what has come to be associated with nation-formation, with a nation-consciousness or what is often referred to as the national spirit *(Geist)*, is identified by resistance or struggle against an opposing force or ideology.[11] In terms of structure, this equation of nation-forming with resistance can be seen as part of the process of giving the nation a center, of establishing for it a point of presence through the notion of a fixed origin. (This is, of course, the romance of the birth of the State, the myth of [national] origins and corresponding origin of [national] myths.) Such a resistance, once acknowledged a posteriori as a point of origin, would then not only serve as a center around which notions of national identity may be organized, rallied, and so forth—it is, in fact, extremely difficult to conceive of a national movement not structured around some unifying form of resistance: "no taxation without representation," "Let my people go," Yanqui go home," and so on—but would also work to define the organization of that identity—and to insure that the nation will be defined in terms of its already-established 'origins.' Or to put it another way: the establishment of resistance as a point of origin simultaneously makes possible the formation of national identities and establishes the limits or boundaries of such identities. For what is resisted is always formulated as that which lies *outside* the nation; it is always perceived as that other that oppresses, enslaves, threatens, or is simply in the way of the nation- or empire-building project.[12] This concept of a national resistance, however, although it represents the nation itself, the condition of the *natio* as a common identity, is contradictorily coherent; for although the resisted other is perceived as being outside the nation, it is nevertheless also imbedded within the structure of the nation as a necessary counterpart to any national resistance, an indispensable object to the national subjectivity, literally a receiver of the action of resistance. Any notion of a national project of resistance, then, is always already imbricated with its others, because it must always presuppose that which is resisted; one cannot in fact conceive, for example, of a Caribbean nation without a former colonizing power anymore than we can an ancient Greece without its barbarians, or a British or Spanish empire without their respective Barbadoes or Cubas. Clearly then, these otherwise incompatible nationalisms, along with so many others, have this much in common: they are all structurally dependent upon some unifying notion of resistance, and consequently upon the play between resistance and what is resisted. We find a useful illustration of this play of the resisting and resisted in precisely national terms, in the famous analogy in Sigmund Freud's *Civilization and Its Discontents* of ongoing enmities between states with common borders. In his example of the Spanish and Portugese peoples, Freud concludes that "it is always possible to bind together a considerable number of people in love, so long as there are other people left to receive the manifestation of their aggressiveness."[13]

I do not mean by this that the nation is always reducible to the play of these particular opposites; on the contrary, it is precisely on the basis of such oppositional structures of nationalism, that a limitless series of substitutions, variations, and transformations of center for center can take place, all of which would serve the same functions within the structure. These substitutions are, in turn, always taken from a history of meanings *(sens)*; that is, from a history, whose origins may always be reawakened or whose end may always be anticipated in order to reinforce and perpetuate the particular needs of the state. The concepts of 'resistance' and 'resisted,' then, then, can receive any number of other forms or names; thus 'resistance' permutates into 'patriotism,' 'civilization', 'the True Faith,' and its resisted other into 'treason,' 'savagery,' heresy'; that is, in short, *difference.*

As we have seen, the notion of resistance is sufficiently common to the history of nationalisms as to have become impossibly overdetermined; that is, it has been charged with so many meanings in so many different contexts that it is no longer possible to use the term in any meaningful way (i.e., it means, paradoxically, too much). If we nevertheless accept the term provisionally, despite this knowledge, we would still need to ask: What is the nature of this particular resistance, this resistance of the postcolonial Caribbean, which invokes and effaces itself within the gesture of an "our" ("our experience")—what could we say constitutes it? And then: What precisely is being resisted, assuming for the moment the simplicity of an 'it' and not a 'those'? We could begin to address the former question by positing 'resistance' as on the one hand a kind of *rupture*—an attempt to break with/from structures that are already established. On the other hand, however, and at the same time, it is the attempt to escape the irreducible, to exorcise and conjure away the inheritance of a colonial past. To paraphrase Brathwaite, it is the desire to "retrieve a sense of history"; that is, to retrieve a history of meaning despite and beyond its relation to, or haunting by, another one.

It would be easy enough to present the problem as a simple opposition, in which the resisting literature, in this case that of a burgeoning postcolonial nationalism, would be set off against an established, oppressive colonial order. Such a model would, as we have seen, certainly provide us with an origin, and thus a causality, for this resistance; it would, to the extent that we need to know, provide a reason why the resistance is necessary. However, when the model is carried out further, we invariably find that the resistant literature is, from its originary founding to its present oppositional meaning, irreducibly dependent upon the very order it seeks to displace. Let us forget, for example, that the very word 'nation' is as old as the Latin *natio,* the idea of a community or state of belonging; that is, at least as old as Western philosophy itself. This is not happenstance, nor can it be entirely fortuitous that this specter (or in this case, this *Spirit*) of ancient Greece lingers over the very site of its challenge, and makes possible both its invocation and its professed abandonment.

To better understand what this could mean for postcolonial discourses in general, and a specifically Caribbean discourse of resistance in particular, we might return to Brathwaite's question: "How can we as Caribbean writers come to terms with our experience, how can we retrieve a sense of history *in spite of and beyond the metropolitan English education we were given?*" More instructive than even this provocative question, however, is Brathwaite's description of his native Barbados in two remarkable passages, the first of which I cite in its entirety:

> You have to begin with me in the small island of Barbados, this little island, this coral island of coral in the Atlantic where we have this tremendous landscape *which has no word attached to it, no word, no sound, no touch, no history.* And, like all of us growing up in the Caribbean, my responsibility was to try to find words for this amazing landscape which is awesome not only in its magnificence and the range of its architecural beauty, *but because it is so absent of words.* This is a landscape where the original population was destroyed within thirty years of Columbus' crunch upon the sand. Therefore there was in fact no native tradition, no tongue spoken, no whisper, no memory coming out of these islands. And we who inherited these islands had the responsibility of finding a way of speaking, finding a way of remembering *and finding a way of projecting that memory into a future.* (HCW 25, emphasis added)

And in the next paragraph:

> [Barbados] was colonized by the English very thoroughly, and whatever memories it had of itself were eroded by their English in their desire to establish their own colony and their own Empire. So Barbados became "Little England," and those of us who had to learn the history of Barbados did not learn the history of our landscape or the memory of that landscape or the memory of those people who lived there before us or who had come across the water towards us. We had to learn the history of the English kings and queens. *We had to behave as if we were born in England.* "Little England" became a very appropriate symbol for the island. (HCW 25, emphasis added)

In light of Brathwaite's references to what he calls his "eroded sense of history" (HCW 25), there are at least three significant historical contingencies that we should address, if only in passing:

1. because of a certain slippage of terms in Brathwaite's discourse here, a tendency toward the conflation of 'Barbados' and 'the Caribbean' already glimpsed in his question ("we as Caribbean writers"; again we must ask: Martí too? Naipaul? Errol Barrow?), it becomes necessary to ask: Which "Columbus' crunch upon the sand"? According to his own ships' logs, Columbus's travels to the Caribbean brought him to the Bahamas, Hispaniola, Cuba, Jamaica, and

the Venezuelan coast. Columbus never makes any mention of the island of Barbados, which it is unlikely he ever saw;[14]

2. there is no record or mention of Barbados by any European navigator until 1600, when a group of Portugese "adventurers" (read "pirates") landed on an island they named Las Barbadas. The island was first claimed for England in 1605, and was not settled until 1625, over a hundred years after Columbus's death;[15] and

3. according to colonial historians, both the Portugese and first English visitors claimed to have found the island deserted, *uninhabited.* Not wishing to read such assertions naively but nevertheless compelled to acknowledge their existence, I offer as an example this curious (and amusingly apologist!) passage from one early nineteenth-century text:

> In reviewing this early period of our colonial history, every liberal mind must glow with conscious satisfaction on reflecting, that the settlement which we have been contemplating, was quietly effected without the perpetration of those atrocious acts of cruelty and injustice which marked the progress of the Europeans in every other part of the new world. *Abandoned by its aboriginal inhabitants, if any such there were, for some cause wholly unknown to us,* Barbadoes, according to every principle of natural law, became the rightful and legitimate property of the first occupants. (JP 7–8, emphasis added)

Without entering into protracted discussions over historical accuracy, the credibility of certain colonial discourses, and so forth, we must already ask: If Columbus's "crunch upon the sand" is not, in the case of Barbados, a literal one, then what does his name signify here? For what purpose is he being invoked, conjured, only to then be conjured away? For is not knowledge of Columbus, of that name originary and foremost among the great colonizers of the so-called New World, an integral part of Brathwaite's own "metropolitan English education," of which he would be relieved in order to retrieve an-other history?[16] As we have seen, this act of conjuring away is in many ways the pursuing of the pursued; that is, one would summon for the purpose of an exorcism precisely those specters that trouble, which haunt. The poet's project, then: to "retrieve a sense of history in spite of and beyond. . . ." Beyond what? The specter, the remnant of an originary "crunch upon the sand," which renders it still troubling and painful for so many to speak and hear the name "Columbus" five hundred years after the (historical, *visceral;* let us not forget, the ghost seems to say, let us hear it, *feel* it: "crunch") fact.

And what of this "original population . . . destroyed" by the primal "crunch" of the colonizer? They are silenced, their history rendered irretrievable: "no native tradition, no tongue spoken, no whisper, no memory coming out of these islands." Their death is the death of a language, a memory. The land is itself silent(ced): "this tremendous landscape which has no word attached to it, no word, no sound, no touch, no history," which "is so absent of words," would yet be remembered, interpreted, represented; its remains would be eulogized even as the mourners strive to deny death and affirm, cling to the memory of life. This task of mourning is the responsibility of the living, of the living-present, not only to remember but to actively bear witness to life no longer here. Responsibility: "And, like all of us growing up in the Caribbean, my responsibility was to try to find words for this amazing landscape. . . ." And again, as if an echo: "And we who inherited these islands had the responsibility of finding a way of speaking, a way of remembering. . . ." And this is in fact the demand of the inheritance, *inheriting* as another part of the task of mourning: not just a passive acceptance or receipt, but the active taking on of a responsibility. A responsibility to speak, to remember, to preserve for the sake of generations to come, to follow (pursue) ghosts of the future. Here again what seems to be to-come comes back in advance, from the past: *"finding a way of projecting that memory into a future."*

We should also note the more-than-passing resemblance of such a postcolonial project, of the concept of the recovery or retrieval of a colonized culture, to the Derridean 'trace,' the notion of the radically other within the structure of the sign. For Derrida, the sign is precisely such a structure of difference, bearing within it the trace or track of what it is not. Read in a certain way, such concepts may prove to be efficacious for the reading of postcoloniality; reading for the trace within the structures of colonial sign-systems, for example, would enable us to uncover the persistence of the indigenous and the supposedly vanquished within the purportedly univocal colonial text.[17] For Brathwaite, then, the structure of the trace manifests as a recourse to an originary "voice" (specter-as-trace-as-voice), the project of recovering a discourse usurped—but not destroyed—by the colonizing power of the British Empire.

Finally we return to the question of resistance, this action that is also always a reaction, an attempt to rupture and exorcise. A resistance to 'erosion' that contradicts and deconstructs itself; because it posits (i.e., professes, claims *to know*) on the one hand an originary, pristine, 'preerosion' state that existed before the colonizers' "crunch upon the sand," and on the other hand the utter annihiliation of that state by the invaders. What is thus being invoked in Brathwaite's "eroded sense of history" is, again, a memory that is there yet not, which is his by *inheritance,* inaccessible except by a conjuring of that which is no longer there: "the original population was destroyed within thirty years. . . ." And yet, what is it that is being inherited here, where there is "no native tradition, no tongue spoken, no whisper, no memory coming out of these islands"—

where, indeed, all of this has fallen before the originary onslaught of the conqueror? Again, an apparition, and that uncomfortable Derridean moment of *being-with* that which is yet is not—in short, with *ghosts.* All memory—and especially that which assumes the status of a collective memory—must in some way know this moment, this reckoning with ghosts.

Even beyond the historical and other contingencies involved, certain key terms stand out: the destruction or 'erosion' of a non-Western 'tongue,' 'tradition,' 'memory,' and its replacement or displacement by Western language, history, and knowledges. This state of affairs is not, of course, unique to Barbados; displacement of indigenous cultural institutions is to varying degrees a precondition of any imperialist enterprise, a task made less problematic by the extermination of the native cultures and, if necessary, population. Nor is Western cultural domination of colonial possessions anything new to postcolonial writers, to the extent that they seek to construct discourses in response to an lingering Western hegemony. Rather, my point here is precisely the difficulties involved in addressing that hegemony, these ghosts and residues of empires past. For what Brathwaite is in fact fighting against is not merely the legacy of British colonialism, nor even the institution of imperialism itself, both of which he could arguably locate somewhere 'outside' of himself as a binary other; rather, the object of engagement for Brathwaite's work; that is, what he needs to rupture, to exorcise, is a totality of European thought and its unavoidable impositions upon any would-be discourse of resistance: in effect, the very basis of his "metropolitan English education."

It is not, then, simply a matter of "going beyond" the languages and cultures of empire, of somehow escaping a hegemonic discursive regime in order to interrogate it. Because those discourses, and the models of thought upon which they are based, are themselves the precondition of any such critique; thus for Brathwaite there is no language or resistant discourse that is not already contained within the form, the logic, and the implicit conventions of precisely what he wishes to subvert. Resistance, then, can never be based on simple Manichaean oppositions; for the postcolonial thinker, there must be something more. Rather than a "going beyond" or otherwise naive gesture of oppositional critique—a move that ultimately fails to account for the critic's own implication within the structure—the construction of a postcolonial discourse of resistance must begin with an examination of its own relation to Western thought and, and even more reflexively, to the forms and concepts inherited from it. The objection might certainly be raised that poets such as Brathwaite are less interested in resisting Western cultural institutions than in creating new Caribbean ones, and that beyond my own privileged examples there are others whose work is more important for their advocacy of a uniquely Caribbean language than for their rejection of Western forms or concepts; it might further be objected that such a history of the structures of nationalism as I have cursorily pointed out can always be suspected of stemming from a state of neocolonial dependence, from the desire, in the words of a colleague, to keep the Englishes of the world forever wed to British or American standards.[18] It is certainly true that English, as Salman Rushdie has observed: "no longer an English language, now grows from many roots; and those whom it once colonized are carving out large territories within the language for themselves"[19]; but what is equally true, what is, in fact, irreducible, about these non-English Englishes is their relation to the 'English Englishes' from which they emerged.

Such a discourse, then, as would define the postcolonial in terms of a resistance to hegemonic models of thought must, to be critically responsible, also problematize the ways in which it borrows from Western thought the tools necessary for that resistance. For the Caribbean writer, the construction of nation-forming literatures is always a problem of strategy, a question of what Linda Hutcheon calls "the postmodern paradox": namely, the strategy of working within conventions in order to subvert or interrogate them.[20] For Hutcheon, such a strategy involves more than merely opposing another discourse of resistance or contestation to the traditional hegemonic ones, but of continually analyzing the whole conceptual machinery by which structures of resistance, nationalist and otherwise, come about. Despite its apparent contradictions (or perhaps precisely because of the critique that makes the contradictions apparent), such a critique could prove to be an important first step toward new and radical postcolonial discourses, which by their very existence would contest not only specific historical colonialisms or even the entire institution of imperialism, but also the Western models of thought that make these contingencies possible and even efficacious. Such discourses, while not precisely free of the forms and concepts of empire, will at least be able to read its own paradoxes without crisis. The possibilities of such a radical critique arising from the ashes of colonial exploitation and dependence, as we shall see, depend from the outset on its ability to break away from the tyranny of Western oppositional logics—the ability, as Brathwaite states in another article to which we will now turn, to move "from imitation to invention";[21] what is at stake is nothing less than the future of what we call 'diversity,' the future of the postcolonial Caribbean and of the 'post-' itself. As we shall see, these futures are inextricably and irreducibly linked.

For the postcolonial entity known as 'Creole society,' the path to resistance paradoxically begins with mimicry—or what *appears* to be mimicry—of the dominant culture. For as Brathwaite observes, what may appear to be imitation nevertheless involves, in the case of the Creole, "a significant element of creativity, while [their] creativity in turn involves a significant element of imitation" (*CO* 16). Thus mimicry can be said to be imitation with a difference, both a mimetic acculturation (the enforced imitation of a dominant culture) and a semiotic interculturation: for Brathwaite, "an osmotic [lateral] relationship proceeding from this yoke" (*CO* 6); but for our purposes here also an appropriation of that culture and its sign systems—literally the permutation of the dominant culture into the Creole, the transmutation of the dominant culture's discourses into a set of similar yet distinctly Creolized signifiers and signifieds. The resulting 'Creole society,' then, can neither stand in simple opposition to a dominant culture from which it emerges (conceived as it is from an act of repetition) nor identify fully with it (since it always repeats with a difference). Such paradoxes are, as Homi K. Bhabha has observed, always an ambivalent part of the colonial presence:

> It is this ambivalence that makes the boundaries of colonial "positionality"—the division of self/other—and the question of colonial power—the differentiation of colonizer/colonized—different from both the Hegelian master/slave dialectic or the phenomenological projection of Otherness. It is a *différance* produced within the act of enunciation as a specifically colonial articulation of those two disproportionate sites of colonial discourse and power: the colonial scene as the invention of historicity, mastery, mimesis or as the other scene of *Enstellung*, displacement, fantasy, psychic defense, and an "open" textuality. (*LoC* 108)

For Bhabha, such logics of opposition and confrontation fail to account for this distinctly colonial (for Brathwaite, "Creole" or "Creolizing") articulation of *différance:* a subjectivity both *different* and *deferred*, neither distinct from nor identical to the colonizing 'original.'[22]

Brathwaite's poem "Negus" critiques this postcolonial paradox of creolization as well as any scholarly paper, from its recognition of the ontological inadequacy inherent to European acts of so-called emancipation ("it is not enough to be free / of the red, white, and blue"[23]) to its acknowledgment of the need to create a body of knowledge—of *languages*—other than those of empire. The tension between these seemingly complementary drives; that is, between the independence of national sovereignty and the 'in-dependence' upon the knowledge of empire, an ontological malaise symptomatic of a nation still(un)born, a (mal)formed (per)mutation of its master's image, is nevertheless undermined by the repeated phrases "it is not enough" and "I / must be given words." The words for which the speaker asks, however, are clearly not those of the poet's "metropolian English education"; these are words already in the poem, already in the poet's possession (or which, the speaker has perhaps realized, already possess him), words which, the speaker tells us, are "not enough." Rather, what he would have is another language, one that would allow him to "refashion futures" beyond those of his inherited tongue(s). To "refashion" in this context, however, is not necessarily to oppose or destroy, or even entirely to reject; it is rather to reconstitute, to revise from materials already at hand. To "refashion" is, for Brathwaite, to find words with which to think and speak *otherwise:*

Attibon Legba
Attibon Legba
Ouvri bayi pou' moi
Ouvri bayi pou' moi

Aside from the obvious invocation of a non-European entity (of which more presently), these lines are remarkable for their refashioning of a Caribbean future from the words of a colonizing power; the Creole "Ouvri bayi pou' moi," although based in the French, is clearly a Caribbean (per)mutation, not only for its manipulation of a European language, but for what that language is now being made to signify. The colonized subject who was once taught to say "Vive L'France," "God save the Queen," and "Thou shalt have no other gods before me" has now, much to the master's chagrin, now also learned to say "*Ouvri bayi pou' moi,*" to call upon "*Attibon Legba*" to open doors Europe could not have foreseen.

This *Legba,* or *Papa Labá,* or *Elegua,* this latter as he is known by worshipers in the Afro-Cuban tradition of *santería,* is the god of the gateway *(bayi)*; he is a specter in the literal sense, and a link to otherness: other languages, other knowledges, other times, other places, other gods. That *Legba/Papa Labá/Elegua* is aged and walks with a limp illustrates both the spatial and temporal nature of the gateway; he walks, as legend would have it, with one leg in each world, as a trafficker or negotiator. *Legba/Papa Labá/Elegua,* then, embodies not opposition but mediation, literally a channeling or interstice—a model whose duality is at least as old as the oppositional 'either/or' telos of Western logic; that he is known by many names also intimates the many guises or channels or spaces through which that otherness might be negotiated, from which the ghosts might be summoned. To invoke this many-named god of the gateway, then, in the language of a colonizer—even in (or rather, especially in) a creolization of it—is to both rupture and redouble, to conjure and beckon—to speak, as Derrida would have it, to ghosts. By an apparently simple act of mimicry it is possible to forever alter the colonizer's illusion of a mono-language; it is an act of subversion for which the implications, the many repercussions and returns, are yet to be read and written.

The term 'Creole,' although partially defined in Brathwaite's *Contradictory Omens: Cultural Diversity and Integration in the Caribbean* (*CO* 10), might nevertheless be addressed in yet another context. I have elsewhere defined Cuban Creoles (from the Spanish *criollo,* literally meaning "to have been bred or founded in a certain place") as people of Spanish ancestry born and/or bred in Cuba;[24] in the specific and typical example of José Martí, *criollismo* was defined literally on the basis of one's birthplace, a standard akin to the one applied in Brathwaite's text: "*criollo:* born in, native to, committed to the area of living, and . . . used in relation to both black and white, free and slave" (*CO* 10). What is significant about both this nineteenth-century Cuban *criollismo* and twentieth-century colonial Barbados as described by Brathwaite, however, is that in both cases those who counted themselves *criollos* were not at all related to the island's indigenous population; that group, the Taino and the Siboney Indians, had been for all practical purposes exterminated soon after Columbus's arrival in 1492, the referent for Brathwaite's spectral "crunch upon the sand." What, then, can we say about the Creolism, the resistance, of Martí's revolutionary efforts? And what genealogy of ghosts, however provisional, an we begin to glimpse, from these generations of Caribbean *criollismos* and their inheritances: inheritances of resistances, rebellions, and nations? We might begin to address these questions with a look at this untitled poem from Martí's *Versos sensillos*[25]:

> Por la tumba del cortijo
> donde está el padre enterrado,
> pasa el hijo, de soldado
> del invasor; pasa el hijo.
>
> El padre, un bravo en la guerra,
> envuelto en un pabellón
> álzace, y de un bofetón
> lo tiende, muerto, por tierra.
>
> El rayo reluce; zumba
> el viento por el cortijo;
> el padre recoje al hijo
> y se lo lleva a la tumba.[26]

The question of both specter and spirit *(Gespenst* and *Geist),* the construction of national identities, and the situatedness of those identities in relation to an extranational other becomes extremely complicated in this poem, and not only because of the father-son relationship of the characters (although the metaphor of the nation as 'fatherland' is certainly significant—more on this presently); rather, what is most immediately relevant here is the space, literally the geographic *location,* because the concept of a national community assumes its most tangible form in the pages of atlases, where resistance takes place. Until now I have spoken of the exterior form of the nation as ideological and discursive. But we must remember that the nation also has a topographical reality; that is, its existence, or lack of same, on the world's maps is undoubtedly part of what constitutes the structures of national identity. By saying this I do not mean to privilege the geographically recognized nation-state over other nationalisms, for it is often precisely that lack of topographical existence that becomes the *raison d'etre* of a burgeoning national identity (much of what we now know as the Palestinian nation, to passingly cite one such example, has its 'origins,' structurally speaking, in a national resistance based precisely on this lack of a homeland). For Martí, it is the physical entity of the national space that is being contested, or more specifically, what is at stake is precisely the question of which national identification, Spanish empire or Cuban Creole society, will be identified with the geographic space known as 'Cuba.' But read in a certain way, we might also glimpse in these verses the poet's understanding of a coexistence beyond the moment of reckoning, beyond this Hegelian struggle for (national) recognition—the understanding that, besides and beyond this struggle to the death, there is the never-ending reckoning with the specter, with that which recourses and returns and lingers, always demanding, wanting to question, to accuse, or redress.

The father-son relationship in the poem only makes explicit the problematic that exists implicitly in any so-called civil war. Indeed, the term itself is paradoxically appropriate here because although the Cuban Revolution of 1895 was ideologically fought against an extranational colonial other, a significant part of the colonial population counted itself on the side of the Spanish colonizers; as a result, much of the actual fighting unavoidably occurred between the rebels and Spanish sympathizers (known as *voluntários*) who were also *criollos,* also Cuban-born, also fighting in the name of one or another nation. Martí clearly portrays the encounter between rebel-father and *voluntário* son, then, as a microcosm of the clash of national identities battling for control of the land. That the setting for the poetic confrontation is a graveyard, then, is of particular relevance; the metaphor of the father's tomb as the site of the son's death has an almost visceral impact, not only the image of death as the bloody price of constituting the national corpus, but also a reminder of the burden—of the *responsibility*—of an inheritance, of a past and future that would return to demand accounting for the wrongs committed against it. A demand, in short, for responsibility and for *justice:* this is what the ghost would have, the final business of any haunting. The actual landscape, then, becomes a space of contestation between nationalisms, the object of conflict being to attempt by violence what cannot otherwise be done: the banishment or deportation of the (perceived) extranational other to the margins, to a place safely outside the borders of the nation. The demographic makeup of the nation, according to such a line of reasoning, must correspond to its geography, which would in turn parallel the model of a logocentric oppositional resistance as I have just outlined: the national 'we' within our borders, the extranational 'they' outside. This deconstructive moment (or rather the moment at which we realize how this opposition of nationalisms deconstructs itself) has enormous implications for the future of nationalism, too many to be adequately addressed here. We can, however, allow for this observation: that the structures of the nationalist 'we/us' deconstruct themselves at the point at which they intersect with other, supposedly supplementary constructions of 'we/us' situated within them—the 'we,' for instance, of the family unit, the culture, and the "race." And these intersections of birthplace and "race" and culture and sovereignty are what constitute the Creole society, that conglomeration of interstices that both escape and exceed the binary constructions of nationalism.

This postdeconstructive process of creolization, then, is a fundamentally radical one, shaking the nation to its mythical foundations before building anew. I should, additionally, emphasize that poems such as this one are the exception in Martí; that is, much of his poetry is concerned with constructing images of both an ideal *patria* (fatherland) and an opposing other, the absolute enemy of the nation as personified by the evil *tirano* (tyrant). To the extent to which Martí's work seeks to rally the nation's sense of resistance around such a model, it renders itself unable to account for the many others within its borders, others which, as Brathwaite points out and Martí's poem intimates, are nevertheless part of the Creole society. This inescapable slippage between *patria* and *tirano* is part of the ambivalence of the Martían legacy; it is, moreover, precisely this slippage in Martí's work that has made possible the existence of such widely divergent, and mutually hostile, Cuban nationalisms. And yet in these stanzas of Martí's verse there is opened up a space or index, an instance of possibility, within which can be reclaimed or "refashioned" a future, one in which the living-present might find ways to live with both the ghosts of a colonial past and our various and respective inheritances from them—that which comes to us neither by right nor request, but is ours all the same. It is our collective inheritance as *heirs,* of the revolutionary poet, of the expatriate conqueror, of an entire genealogy of events for which, despite their occurrence beyond or before 'our time,' we must nevertheless assume a responsibility. We are called upon, not only but also as readers and thinkers of the Caribbean, of the postcolonial world (postcolonial, post-Martí, and post-Columbus) *to answer for these things.* One cannot simply go naively about as if "Columbus's crunch upon the sand" had never happened, as if the question of the martyred poet, and so many others like him, had never been asked. For in the end this is precisely what the ghost would demand of us; it is the very reason for and condition of the apparition: an accounting, a reckoning in the name of responsibility. In the name of *justice.* And finally, again: "What more? . . ." It is a question which, like the specter itself, is beyond life, beyond death: beyond, therefore, the living-present in general; and like the specter, we may address it only by inhabiting the interstices ourselves. We must enter as we are called into the spectral *socius,* this strange and unsettling being-with ghosts, this blind and excessive justice of the 'post-' that comes in the name of others who are no longer here, who are not yet here. It is there where our question must finally be directed, as the poet who addresses and projects his own ardent query, blindly beyond his own time and into our own, in hopes of obtaining in return not only the manner or form of a future but its very condition, its very possibility. "What more? . . ." The specter would demand of us an accounting in the name of responsibility, in the name of justice.

We cannot answer. We must answer.

CHAPTER THREE

Whiteness and the Colonial Unconscious

I

> I envision "whiteness" in a nostalgic way. . . . I believe there must have been a sense of security, knowing that they were among a privileged race, backed by a powerful country, complete with armies, taken treasure, strategies and plans for advancement.
>
> —Anonymous

> Whiteness is a lie. . . . Whiteness is nothing more, to me, than the absence of pigment. Yet, the centuries-old rule of my homeland by Europeans has left a permanent mark on the way people are looked at.
>
> —Anonymous

These epigraphs are excerpts from two separate statements, written and submitted anonymously by undergraduate students, in fulfillment of an in-class assignment: "Complete the following sentence: 'Whiteness is. . . .'" As they were given no other instruction or guidance, and as this was their very first assignment on the first day of my course bearing the title "Whiteness after Empire," the range of responses was understandably quite broad; they described whiteness as everything from a code of conduct (behaving "like a white person") to spiritual enlightenment and purity (souls ascending into heaven, "where everything around [is] white") to a feared and hated symbol ("Whiteness is evil"). The two responses I have selected stand out, however, for their thoughtful articulation of whiteness as a sort of cultural fiction—on the one hand as a category devoid of meaning ("a lie," or "the absence of pigment"), on the other as a historical determinant of power and prestige, the glorious 'once-upon-a-time' of security and progress that lingers only as nostalgia: the 'good old days,' as it were, of empire and a white-dominated world.

But in the act of denying or rejecting whiteness as a relevant cultural entity; that is, by the act of distancing themselves temporally, geographically, and even epistemologically ("Whiteness is a lie. . . .") from whiteness and its relation to colonialism, and by the most naive and untenable defenses: "I wasn't around back then," "I wasn't there," "It has nothing to do with me," and so on, such responses also point to the respondents' wish, conscious or not, to dissociate themselves from whiteness as it applies to their own lives. Such a distancing mechanism is symptomatic of an entire culture's larger aversion to whiteness, particularly in its association with global colonial oppression. I will use the term *colonial unconscious* to denote this suppression, on both an individual and collective level, of traumatic or otherwise unwelcome knowledges associated with colonialism and its legacy. These colonial knowledges or discourses, which I will define broadly for now as ideological in nature,[1] operate in much the same manner as thoughts or ideas that the Freudian subject banishes, by the mechanism of repression, to the unconscious; that is, they maintain their influence over the subject's (and by extension, the society's) conscious life despite—or perhaps even because of—their relegation to a space or index beyond the reach of the subject's critical faculties.[2]

Although the contents of this colonial unconscious necessarily vary among individual subjects within a given postcolonial situation, we may nevertheless make a rough distinction between that of the white colonizer and nonwhite colonized, and a further distinction within each between what is suppressed during the colonial and postcolonial stages. For the colonizer(s), all knowledge that does not cohere with the stated official purposes of colonization—or in other words, any impulse or desire on the colonizers' part that clashes with the more elevated rhetorics of the economic mandate or the "civilizing mission"—must be suppressed. In the *late-colonial* and *postcolonial* context, however, within which the true violence of the colonial regime is to some degree exposed, denounced, and reproached (but seldom really avenged), repression continues less successfully to censor feelings or suspicions of national guilt and individual complicity.

For the colonized subject, we may likewise further distinguish between two phases or stages of repression: a *colonial* stage, in which both the cultural memory of the moment and circumstances of colonization and the memory of a precolonial cultural history are suppressed, for the sake of submission to the colonizer—or more to the point, success or even survival within the colonial context; and a postcolonial or "postindependence" stage during which the colonized culture's previous complicities with the colonizer—and present acceptance and internalization of the colonizer's cultural values and knowledge—

come to light and are, again less successfully, suppressed. Perhaps I may best convey the overall structure of this model, with its distinct yet interrelated stages, by the following table:

	COLONIZER	**COLONIZED**
Colonial—Late Colonial	*"Civilizing Mission"* aggression, desire to dominate	*submission, "assimilation"* pre-colonial history, trauma of colonization
Neocolonial—Postcolonial	denial of wrongs, "recognition" of postcolonial subjects, guilt over colonial oppression, injustices	anti-colonial aggression, nationalism, "emancipation" from colonial power, guilt over complicity w/ colonizer, internalization of colonial value

In each quadrant, the dividing line between terms separates what I take to be the primary discourses or conditions of each stage; the conscious articulations sit above the line, and the suppressed contents of the colonial unconscious below.

I should clarify here that by "desire to dominate" I do not mean any particularized national project of domination or conquest, of the type generally justified in terms of some mandate, some "national interest," or another (economic gains, international prestige, or competition with other imperial powers); I refer rather to the primal drive or need for aggression, on both the individual and collective level, which is so integral to the Freudian view of human nature.[3] As both Freud and Homi K. Bhabha point out, a major factor in the nation's cohesion lies in its ability to displace aggression by turning its potentially destructive internal tensions outward toward its others: "So long as a firm boundary is maintained between the territories, and the narcissistic wound is contained, the aggressivity will be projected onto the Other or the Outside."[4] But Bhabha also questions whether such a boundary remains tenable in the postcolonial context; that is, whether the Freudian "narcissism of minor differences" does not in effect become a divisive, destructive mechanism at the point at which former Others become fellow citizens:

> The problem is, of course, that the ambivalent identifications of love and hate occupy the same psychic space; and paranoid projections "outwards" return to haunt and split the place from which they are made. So long as a firm boundary is maintained between the territories . . . the aggressivity will be projected on to the Other or the Outside. But what if, as I have

> argued, the people are the articulation of a doubling of the national address, an ambivalent *movement* between the discourses of pedagogy and the performative? (*LoC* 149)

With his interrogation of "the narrative address of the nation," Bhabha effectively carries the Freudian model to its subjective limit. What, indeed, happens to the nation's image of itself after the Other of the Outside finds her way in—when former colonial subjects return to London or Paris as citizens of the Mother Country, when whites of the former oppressing class in South Africa choose to remain behind in the postapartheid state, to live and work alongside the newly empowered black majority? What happens to whiteness, in other words, after it loses its colonial privileges?

In each of these quadrants, we may generally characterize what is suppressed as a transgressive desire that would undermine or give the lie to the officially mouthed purposes of the colonial mission on the one hand and the anticolonial rhetorics of the postindependence state on the other. Or more to the point: each lies about its true relation to its respective other, then engages in a vain effort to repress and bury (and ultimately, forget) the reality of this fundamental relation. As with any such mechanism of repression, however, there are always memory-traces, residues of uncomfortable truths that remain to be uncovered and deciphered, then traced back along their paths to their originary pathogenic sources. In chapter one I discuss more specifically the psychic limits and implications of the colonial unconscious from the colonizers' position;[5] for present purposes, however, I will limit my focus here to the colonial unconscious as it applies to the postcolonial, specifically postindependence context; that is, it is the argument of this chapter that what emerges in the relation between former colonizers and colonized, now fellow citizens in a postindependence state, what now begins to be glimpsed through the cracks of the flawed repression-mechanism is their common dependence upon—and complicity with—the ideology of whiteness, or more specifically of white (hence Western) superiority. Each must now face the unpleasant truth of their own complicity in the telling and believing in the cultural lie of colonial whiteness. Indeed, I argue that such a bitter epiphany is indispensable for the future health of the postindependence state in particular and the postcolonial world as a whole. As Michelle Cliff tells us, such a facing-down of colonial ghosts is immanent to the task of constructing an integrated postcolonial subject:

> To write as a complete Caribbean woman, or man for that matter, demands of us retracing the African part of ourselves, reclaiming as our own, and as our subject, a history sunk under the sea, or scattered as potash in the canefields, or gone to bush, or trapped in a class system no-

> table for its rigidity and absolute dependence on color stratification. *On a past bleached from our minds.*[6]

To continue Cliff's analogy, much of the process of psychic decolonization depends upon a sort of "repigmentation" or "unbleaching" of suppressed cultural histories to reflect both the precolonial past and the ugly truths of colonial violence and oppression. I also find telling Cliff's metaphor for this process of repression: it is "a past bleached from our minds." Whiteness, then, represents for Cliff not only the contents of the Jamaican colonial unconscious but the very agent of its own repression; it is, in short, that which would simultaneously recast everything else in its own image and banish the scene of the recasting into an originary myth—thus displacing or "bleaching" the precolonial past and replacing it with its own cultural imperatives. Jacques Derrida is emphatic about this irreducible relation between colonial domination, racism, and cultural tyranny, a relation that for Derrida serves as a founding fiction for Eurocentrism:

> Metaphysics—the white mythology which reassembles and reflects the culture of the West: the white man takes his own mythology, Indo-European mythology, his own *logos,* that is, the *mythos* of his idiom, for the universal form of that he must still wish to call Reason. Which does not go uncontested. . . .
>
> White mythology—metaphysics has erased within itself the fabulous scene that has produced it, the scene that nevertheless remains active and stirring, inscribed in white ink, an invisible design covered over in the palimpsest.[7]

"Palimpsest" best illustrates Derrida's vision of this process by which whiteness establishes its colonial myth-of-origins: a surface that has been written upon many times, and that still bears the incompletely erased traces of previous inscriptions, rendering those traces still visible. The image of "white ink" complicates and enriches the metaphor still further, as it conceals the originary inscription of the myth-of-origins (or what Derrida cogently calls "onto-theology") that would expose it as a text constructed for the purpose of a dominating culture's need for self-validation; in other words, it is the moment of the myth-text's *invention* that must be erased or "written over," along with the colonized culture's myths, values, and so on, in order for the colonizer to credibly posit their own myth-of origins as preeminent. But as the metaphor of the "palimpsest" indicates, the traces of always imperfectly concealed discourses remain legible, rendering always possible the task of "reading past" the imposed surfaces to glimpse the contents, however fragmented, of what has been suppressed. Thus the Derridean concept of Europocentrism as a "white mythology" that suppresses within itself "the fabulous scene that has produced it " yet cannot completely conceal the traces of those suppressed discourses owes much to the Freudian model of repression and to the unconscious, and the superficial exteriority of consciousness that nevertheless always bears the memory-traces of repressed knowledges. This ongoing and unresolved tension (what Freud would call an "economy"), between what the colonial ego must banish from its sight for the sake of its functioning and the residues or memory-traces of an entire inventory of colonial acts of aggression, domination, violence, and so forth—between, in other words, manifest white denial and latent white guilt—continues to fuel the ambivalence of relations between whiteness and its others in the postcolonial world. Thus do the contents of the colonial unconscious remain active as the pathogenic nucleus—the very *crux*—of this postcolonial quandary of whiteness.

Returning to the student respondents, the former (R1) goes on to describe their vision of just who the privileged members of this once-prestigious 'whiteness club' must have been, and what their lives might have been like:

> I envision "whiteness" in a nostalgic way, based on what little knowledge I've gained from books, TV, etc. I imagine "whiteness" at a high point, which would be colonialization [*sic*]. Flashes of images of British soldiers and high society fellows living it up with grand lifestyles in tropical settings [and] being served by uniformed natives come to mind. Power, prestige, privilege are some of the words that come to mind. *I believe there must have been a sense of security, knowing that they were among a privileged race,* backed by a powerful country, complete with armies, taken treasure, strategies and plans for advancement. *It must have been a feeling of pride* [*sic*], *back then, to be part of such a country*, pushing forward, opening the world to new places.
>
> I think it is this same pride that kind of still lingers on in some, a feeling of once being part of an Empire. It is something to feel proud of, though much of the integrity of the once powerful country(s) [have] dwindled in giving up colonial held power. (R1, emphasis added)

Read in this fuller context, we can see R1's envisioning of the cultural fiction of whiteness as, more specifically, a cultural *romance:* an ideal of colonialism as a historic "high point" of civilization, a mission of which any who had the opportunity (by way of racial qualification, of their whiteness) would have been proud to be a part. More significantly for R1, however, it is also a bygone era, a time about which some might feel nostalgic; there "must have been" a feeling of security and cultural and/or national pride among those so fortunate as to have been members of the colonial mission of progress and advancement. One also gets R1's sense here that the party is now long since over, and that the sense of security and pride that "must have" once accompanied membership in the colonial 'whiteness club' (R1 wouldn't know personally) has now largely dissipated, more or less in proportion to the decline of the Western empires that once enabled it. Nevertheless, R1 can still identify traces or residues of that supposedly long-gone world of white-European cultural dominion in the present tense, *here and now*, although the material grounds for its persistence may be diminished by the relinquishing of colonies ("though much of the integrity of the once powerful country(s) [have] dwindled in giving up colonial held power"). So that for R1, a sort of cultural memory, or more precisely, the *inheritance* or legacy of a memory, of the prestige of whiteness and the nostalgia of white-European colonial power lingers in residues within the formerly colonizing culture. Whiteness may have lost something of the material basis of its power, but within the psychic life of the Western subject, it retains much of its allure.

A further look at the latter respondent's text (R2) will also show an awareness of the lingering traces of a colonial regime as manifest in notions of whiteness. R2, however, does not share R1's relatively benign view of them:

> Whiteness is a lie. I come from a society, an ethnicity, which regards the blond-haired, blue-eyed as part of an elite class. I have felt within my own family the pain caused by the color of skin. When the founding fathers of my country freed us from European rule they also liberated the slaves, yet [the] structure of [our] society has been slow to change. I still hear [of] sections classified by the color of the residents' skin. I have [heard of] members of my own family be[ing] put up on pedestals or chastised because of how they appear.
>
> Whiteness is nothing more, to me, than the absence of pigment. Yet, *the centuries-old rule of my homeland by Europeans has left a permanent mark on the way people are looked at.* When I go home I see the foundation culture of my country, the one that was there before Columbus came, in everything. These are things which are taken for granted by the people who make their homes there. *There is no more whiteness or brownness or redness, but I don't think they've realized that yet.* (R2, emphasis added)

In this respondent's statement we may read a sense of ambivalence about the remains of empire that is strikingly similar to R1's, however different this respondent's subject position. We are perhaps not surprised at R2's less hospitable view of the colonial legacy, given the latter's subject position as a member of a once-colonized culture and nation. But the statement is nevertheless striking for its articulation of the postcolonial subject's psychic and ontological double bind when confronting the legacy of its colonial past: Europe and whiteness are gone, yet they remain. Nominal and political sovereignty do not coincide with the instantaneous emergence of a postcolonial subjectivity, full-blown, bursting forth from beneath the colonial regime that once held it submerged. Rather, the physical absence of Europe and whiteness belies, for R2, the enormity of a cultural legacy, one product of which is a postcolonial society that has taken on the colonizer's gaze and turned it collectively upon itself: "the centuries-old rule . . . has left a permanent mark *on the way people are looked at.*" Or more precisely: the way people of a formerly colonized land look at each other. A way of looking that persists for lack of another way (an *other*'s way) of seeing themselves and each other: "There is no more whiteness . . . but I don't think they've realized that yet."

My simple prompt thus appears, in retrospect, to have been a somewhat cruel existential trick: "Whiteness is. . . ." Yet it is not. Yet we behave as though it is; thus it is. It is my argument in this chapter that our featured respondents are in agreement, and rightly so, on at least one point: that among the many things that "Whiteness is, . . ." it is a strategic component of the colonial legacy, of the remains of empire retained within the structures of emergent postcolonial societies and subjectivities. For just as colonial regimes are seldom entirely successful in their attempts to cleave colonized peoples from their precolonial cultures, so is life after empire not a clean break. However the burgeoning postcolonial society strives to unlearn the ways of their former masters, the best that may be achieved is a colonialism *sous rature*—a palimpsest in which one can always read the traces of empire, however faintly.

This is, of course, not to say that the emergent postcolonial society is doomed to forever be an accessory or apprentice culture, that its status as 'post-' cements its position into perpetuity as a 'prefix' cultural entity to the dominant 'root' culture of the erstwhile colonizer. Yet is independence the proposition of a simple reversal of terms? Europe is gone, yet it remains. Whiteness remains, often in the form of whites who do not follow the retreat of their (former?) country's ships and the descent of its flags, but remain as citizens of the new nation. So then we must pose the two questions that I will pursue for the remainder of this chapter: (1) What happens to whiteness—to the former imperialist, erstwhile colonizer and oppressor, perhaps still "settler," of a colonized nation or people, *after* emancipation or independence? And (2) What is the relation between the postindependence state and the residues, legacies, traces of whiteness—a language, educational system, religious practices, and so forth—that linger within its borders?

I pose the first question not on a broad, political level, in terms of the officially sanctioned rhetorics of power sharing: "peaceful transition," "truth and reconciliation," "reconstruction," and so forth, but on the level of individuals both white and nonwhite, all who either remain as part of the "new" nation or have significant interactions with it; that is, I am not primarily interested here in accounting for the official processes by which a new state invariably attempts to redress empirically the imbalances between racial or cultural groups left behind in the wake of the colonizer's nominal departure. These are both legion and easily enough identified in the period immediately following independence: the returning of lands taken, redistribution of wealth in general, suffrage for newly enfranchised citizens, equal-opportunity laws regarding education, employment, and so forth; and they often represent a new regime's attempt to both consolidate power and persuade the newly enfranchised former colonized, now citizens—those with the collective power, however dormant or underdeveloped, to choose the nation's new social and political horizons—that they are in fact earning their keep as leaders, that something momentous and irreversible has in fact happened and that "from now on"—beginning with the magical and arbitrary moment of official independence—nothing will be the same.

The problem with this idyllic myth-of-origins of the postcolonial nation is that it begs my second question; that is, it fails to account for the existence within its borders not only of the continued physical presence of former colonizers, now fellow members of the national corpus, partners with their former victims not only in the immediate political processes of national "transition" but in the nation's long-term fortunes, what some would call the 'national destiny'; but also the residual legacy of empire, the colonial inheritance of all the members, white and nonwhite, former colonizers and former colonials alike, of the new state. Setting aside for the moment the particularities or contingencies at work in individual national contexts, we might pose the overarching question this way: What are the dynamics of this new relation between the former colonizers and the once-colonized—what could we say characterizes such a relation? The relation itself is structurally the product, the remainder, of colonization, and is thus unique to this, our century of decolonization. It is the argument of the following pages that achieving an understanding of this vexed relation between former adversaries, now fellow citizens, is crucial not only to the fate of individual postcolonial states but to the future of the very concept of postcoloniality. So it is not only the formerly colonized who must account for the residues of empire within the new nation; whiteness, too, must learn to live with its others in an unprecedented way. For the white postcolonial subject, the relation with the other in the postindependence state is now irrevocably intersubjective.

In the following pages, I will consider this question of the status of "whiteness after empire" by way of certain categories or conditions that together point to a whiteness in crisis:

1. *the concept of whiteness as cultural history,* as part of what is now, in the postcolonial moment, a group of new national histories that must be written in such a way as to reinscribe all that colonial regimes once chose to exclude in the interest of "colonial management." How much, then, of this occluded, perhaps embarrassing or even painful part of the new national history should be kept, be remembered? Much of this is a matter of governmental decree: national dates of remembrance, official apologies to wronged groups, the amending of school curricula to reflect new national values, and so on; and on a socioeconomic level such official or legislated acts would necessarily include the redistribution of power and capital to reflect the new status of the postcolonial citizenry.[8] Yet both collectively and individually, publicly and privately, this process takes the form of a national ritual of repentance and forgiveness, or what the South African government of Nelson Mandela calls "Truth and Reconciliation."[9] What is at stake here, then, more so than the official doctrine of a new administration, is nothing less than the national *conscience,* or what, to paraphrase Fredric Jameson, we might call the national 'political unconscious' of the new postcolonial state;

2. *the concept of whiteness as cultural aesthetic,* as a cultural ideal now suddenly under examination, which now finds itself under interrogation or scrutiny by those who once subscribed to it more or less uncritically. That this whiteness appeared and imposed itself as an immanent part of the colonial mission, that whiteness as a cultural ideal is in fact inseparable from the "civilizing mission" of empire, under the terms of which the colonized subject is invariably viewed by a colonial administration as one of "those ignorant millions" who must be "wean[ed] . . . from their horrid ways"[10] and learn to live as a member of a civilized society—or, as one might more rudely put it, "like a white man."

As we have seen from the examples of R1 and R2, we can identify two attitudes common to this relatively new critique of colonial whiteness: on the one hand a *nostalgic* view, in which the subject sees abstract whiteness as a cultural ideal no longer efficacious for the contemporary white subject (it "must have been" nice, says R1); and on the other a more *contemptuous* or accusatory view, in which the subject sees whiteness as a cultural norm forced upon the native population by the colonizer; such a process of asymetrical (or even unilateral) cultural inscription also has the effect of suppressing or outright crushing the colonized population's own cultural beliefs and values, and imposing assimilation to the colonizer's cultural norms as a precondition for social and material achievement The immediate benefit for such assimilation or submission on the part of colonized subjects to the cultural norm of whiteness is often the promise of economic and class mobility; to be closer to whiteness is also, in this context, to achieve closer proximity to where the social, economic, and political power of the colonized state lies, with the white colonizers. Thus for the colonial subject whiteness becomes synonymous with material success and class mobility, a relationship that does not dissolve, either perceptually or materially, with the coming into statehood of the former colony. The ideal of whiteness, then, emerges as an indispensable component of a colonialism that would establish itself upon arrival as the universal standard of civilization, to which colonial subjects are compelled to aspire.[11] Never mind that even those colonial subjects who most sincerely and earnestly attempt to emulate the white ideal, however skilled their performance or astonishing their transformation, learning to speak the colonizer's tongue, to dress, walk, even think "white," can never really attain it, as an ontological if not a physical fact (to "be white").[12]

It stands to reason, then, that the demise of colonialism brings with it the beginning of the end of whiteness as well; but it is also true that one of the cultural residues left in the wake of empire is precisely this ideal of or aspiration to whiteness, what we might call a postcolonial 'will to whiteness' that lurks in the burgeoning state's national racial unconscious, as an unacknowledged, because unexamined, national aesthetic. To carry the metapsychological analogy a bit further, it is precisely what we might call the 'trauma' of national independence, and the ensuing realization of the absence of the colonial father, which forces the former colony's preoccupation with whiteness into the blinding light of the national conscience.[13] It is thus paradoxically the departure of the white colonizer that brings the realization that whiteness remains, not only in the physical form of white and mixed-race citizens but in the more insidious and abstract form of a *desire,* and a tacit standard against which all who remain as part of the new postcolonial state are measured; such an unwelcome realization produces an inevitable ambivalence in the psychically divided postcolonial subject, a sense of guilt often fueled by depressed social and economic conditions in the postindependence state, and bordering for some even on self-hatred (or "auto-racism") for the impossibility of reconciling the desire for whiteness with the impossibility of achieving it. It is this "will to whiteness," and the ambivalence immanent to its realization by the postcolonial subject, which makes necessary a national reckoning, a collective examination, of the new state's cultural-racial aesthetic.

3. *the concept of whiteness as an ontological relation,* no longer between master and slave or colonizer and colonial subject, but an *intersubjective relation between citizens.* This is the most telling moment for postcolonial whiteness on the most basic and individual level—and more instructive than the official rhetorics of emancipation or the public behavior of the colonial administration

during the ritual of the handover ceremony, because the latter is never reenacted; it is, on the contrary, the daily encounters between whiteness and its others on the street, in cafés, at work, which will determine the political future of the former colony, now postcolonial, multiracial nation. Such encounters are unavoidably complicated by consideration of socioeconomic class in individual cases; the ambivalence of a poor white patient encountering a black doctor for the first time is certainly not the same as the white middle-class professional's fear of being mugged by poor blacks in a now-integrated neighborhood, and both of these pale in comparison to the collective white trepidation at the prospect of a nonwhite majority going to the polls for the first time.[14] Indeed, Ting-Lao Yuo's question, posed in the immediate aftermath of South Africa's 1994 elections, seems especially prescient here:

> What relevance does it have to continue to ask the meaning of whiteness when blackness promises to be no longer the underdog, when the imposed supremacy of whiteness has already begun to fade out, when, in view of the "rowdiness" among the myriad "native tribes" shown in the first democratic election ever, blackness can no longer be made to signify the same homogeneous absence or homologous silence?[15]

What I am concerned with, however, is the ability, and willingness, of a white subjectivity to adapt to this new relation of relative equality with its formerly colonized others.[16] Whether the collective attitude of whiteness toward its others manifests as abject fear and loathing; or as a civility born of guilt that is nevertheless a veneer for such fears; or as the resentment and anger that would grow from the repression on a national level that such a false civility would necessarily set in motion; or on the other hand, whether white subjects can overcome their fear of the other's retribution and take their place in the collective dialogue of the new postcolonial society—this is, much more so than official rhetorics of tolerance and race-blind patriotism, what will largely determine the future of the new postcolonial state. The new nation will either learn to see itself as polyglot, and choose its multiple identity as a necessity and a strength, or it will finally collapse under the weight of its interminable quarrels over privilege, capital, power, land among its embittered cultural and racial combatants.[17]

In the remainder of this chapter, I will examine each of these categories or conditions of whiteness as they surface in the work of key writers occupying a range of postcolonial contexts and subject positions. To continue our analysis of postcolonial whiteness—"Whiteness After Empire," as it were—we will turn to the work of Michelle Cliff and J. M. Coetzee, whose texts articulate the complexities of this postcolonial reckoning with whiteness in its historical, aesthetic, and ontological manifestations.

II

> The Coloured were fathered by the whites, by Jan van Riebeeck, upon the Hottentots: that much is plain, even in the veiled language of his school history book. In a bitter way it is even worse than that. For in the Boland the people called Coloured are not the great-great-grandchildren of Jan van Riebeeck or any other Dutchman. He is expert enough in physiognomy, has been expert enough as long as he can remember, to know that there is not a drop of white blood in them. They are Hottentots, pure and uncorrupted. Not only do they come with the land, *the land comes with them, is theirs, has always been.*
>
> —J. M. Coetzee, *Boyhood: Scenes from Provincial Life*

The autobiographical texts of Cliff and Coetzee represent two such reckonings with whiteness, as variations on the bildungsroman: the trials and struggles of the young protagonist as she or he grows into adulthood, the coming-of-age and coming into (self-)knowledge of the young subject as she or he negotiates a position in relation to a society that has mediated—and often hindered—their personal progress. A defining element of this 'narrative of progress' is that by text's end, the protagonist is able to claim for themselves not only social and material success,[18] but more importantly a measure of *agency;* that is, of empowerment over, or at least happy coexistence with, the larger forces that acted upon them over the course of the text.

Crucial to the narrative structure of the bildungsroman, then, is the intertwining or interpenetration of historicizing discourses—or more precisely, between the narrative of the subject's personal history and that of the cultural and historical context in which that life story unfolds, the latter of which constantly acts as a mediating factor upon the former, with or without the subject's knowledge. Both Cliff's *Abeng,* an autobiographical fiction,[19] and Coetzee's *Boyhood: Scenes from Provincial Life,*[20] a fictionalized memoir, feature child protagonists coming of age in their respective postcolonial societies (Jamaica and South Africa) under the influence and power of larger forces that shape their lives. Further, each text narrates the struggle and coming-to-terms of the child-subject with a colonial legacy—or more specifically, with a colonial history—of whiteness, conquest, and racial and cultural stratifications. And in each text, the extent to which the subject succeeds in this reckoning with historical whiteness largely determines their sense of self-empowerment as a subject; that is, of an individual *agency* that exists in relation to both a colonial history and its legacy.

Another significant commonality between the texts is the narration of the protagonists' nascent realization of a desire for their respective others, a desire that invariably runs contrary to the official dictates and unofficial norms of racial and gender stratification, and that would reject the colonial legacy and cultural imperative of whiteness; in each case, it bears the more or less explicit mark of a sexual desire. This desire remains ambiguous and somewhat muted, one might say suppressed, in Coetzee's memoir, and takes on a more explicit, and more singularly focused, property in Cliff's novel; yet it is undeniably present in both. So the question arises: What does the narration of a light-skinned Jamaican girl's innocent attraction to a dark-skinned girl, of a white boy's friendship with his family's "Coloured" servant boy mean within the larger context of their respective cultural moments? And more pragmatically: What is the function of such events, within both the narrative bildungsroman and the reckoning with the colonial legacy of whiteness?

One possible answer, as we have already seen, is that such narrated events show the extent to which the postindependence subject—especially, each text seems to emphasize, at a formative age—is acted upon by, or "subjected to,"[21] not only larger discourses or conditions of the actual moment (economic status, a rigid class system, officially sanctioned or tacitly condoned racism and heterosexism, etc.) but also and especially an entire history of the establishment and employment of these discourses and conditions in the service of a colonizing regime that systematically oppressed ("managed") its colonized subjects. These discourses and conditions are now left behind as part of the colonial legacy, colonial weapons no less debilitating than soldiers and guns, now left for a postindependence state and people to use on itself and each other.

But also, and more pointedly in the case of the autobiographical texts in question, there is the attempt by the colonial subject to rewrite ("retracing" and "reclaiming," says Cliff) the history of the nation in such a way as to write/narrate themselves back into it; that is, such postcolonial autobiographical texts would inscribe or reinscribe a space or index for the subject within the postcolonial nation that does not render them hopelessly and irremediably other. What is at stake in this struggle over the nation's past, in other words, is precisely its future, or more to the point, who is and is not welcome to participate in it. This epigraph from Coetzee's memoir is laconic yet unequivocal in its articulation of this struggle for the nation's past/future; we can see it in the child-protagonist as he grows to perceive the irreducible discrepancy between what "his school history book" says and what he himself observes and intuits about the "Coloured" boy and his race. But more crucially, the child's bitter epiphany is about the discrepancy between the place in South African society that the official (school) history would ascribe to him, and another, as yet (for the child) not fully envisioned place or index *that he would wish to negotiate for himself,* possibly within a very different social and cultural structure. There is no question in the child's mind that the official and convoluted rhetoric of whiteness as articulated in the history book, that the "Coloured" boy is part white, and that his partial whiteness also makes him an imaginary descendant of the original Dutch colonizers, thus creating a metonymic sense of identification between whites and the land, is utterly incompatible with what his eyes (and, let us not forget, his knowledge of physiognomy) tell him: "They are Hottentots, pure and uncorrupted." And thus: "Not only do they come with the land, *the land comes with them, is theirs, has always been.*" The presence before him of the "Coloured" boy gives the lie to the carefully crafted ("veiled") rhetoric of whiteness contained in "his school history book," and brings the troubling realization: my whiteness does not mean what the schoolbook says it does. And: the "Coloured" boy belongs here *("the land . . . is theirs, has always been"),* and (he suspects, he fears) I do not.

Thus *Boyhood* does and does not fulfill the structural requirement of the bildungsroman; that is, the protagonist does move experientially through the narrative from ignorance (or passivity) to knowledge (or active awareness), but that knowledge will not necessarily help him reconcile himself to South Africa's post-1948 apartheid culture or to find "his place" within it. To the contrary, it is precisely in spite of their society's professed values and norms that the protagonist must find what they need to know about their position as a subject within that culture. The protagonist's growth into a final and unproblematic identification with his culture, as the structure of the bildungsroman would require, is here frustrated or stunted; there can be no final, felicitous union with the national Spirit, no achievement of coincidence or "oneness of Spirit" in the Hegelian sense,[22] because difference remains unexplained, unaddressed. Or to put it more bluntly, what the postindependence subject does not know or is not told, especially about whiteness and its imbrication within the nation's cultural history, can and does hurt them. And further, that this gap or chasm that lies between what the subject knows and does not know—or suspects but cannot articulate—is analogous to the boundary between the postindependence state's manifest official discourses and its latent conflicts, fears, and anxieties. Or put more tersely: between the national consciousness and its colonial unconscious.

The opening lines of *Abeng* already reveal Cliff's theme of empire as it impacted the island of Jamaica, colonialism as a 'presence' in both time and space:

> The island rose and sank. Twice. During periods in which history was recorded by indentations on rock and shell.
>
> *This is a book about the time which followed on that time.* As the island became a place where people lived. Indians. Africans. Europeans.[23]

The "indentations" of colonialism upon the land and people of Jamaica come to preoccupy much of the novel. The term "indentations" proves especially telling as a metaphor of the temporal and spatial effects of colonialism upon the island and its people: first, the term implies a power imbalance between an active "indenting" agent and a more-or-less passive "indented" subject;[24] and second, because of the lasting effects of such "indentations" upon both individual colonial subjects and the postindependence state's collective memory. Further, the memory, individual and collective, of that originary "indenting" (what Edward Kamau Brathwaite has called "Columbus's crunch upon the sand"[25]) becomes itself one of the lasting and traumatic effects of the Jamaican colonial experience. The rest of *Abeng* strives to illustrate how both the landscape and the colonized subject's body become the primary spaces or indexes on which colonial discourses leave their psychic "indentations." Foremost among these lingering marks or imprints of colonialism is the legacy of whiteness as what Cliff calls *"a past bleached from our minds"* (*LB* 14); that is, as it eclipses the histories of both the true violence of the colonial encounter and all that came before it. Part of the task of a truly *postcolonial* literature (and criticism!), then, must be precisely to bring such suppressed knowledges into the light of conscious deliberation.

Thus the prominent narrative strategy of *Abeng* is the interweaving of personal and national histories; the narration constantly shifts between the experiences of the characters and past events that they either have forgotten or never knew, but that nevertheless exercise a lingering influence upon them. Or more specifically, the colonial past remains within the characters' present as a material and psychic condition or *contingency* that establishes both the terms and limits of the characters' actions, thoughts, and decisions throughout the narrative. It is this tension within the narrative, always implicit, often explicit, between what the characters know and do not know, which fuels the narrative; and at the center of this narrative tension lies the personal drive toward knowledge, the postcolonial bildungsroman, of the protagonist Clare Savage.

The novel's first three chapters do not immediately focus on Clare, but on the land and the colonial history that it both contains and conceals from its inhabitants. It is in fact the islanders' near-total ignorance of the history of colonialism, and the narrator's controlled rage at both that history and its suppression from and by the present (1958) inhabitants, which stand out as the central elements of the novel's early chapters, a tension that culminates in this astonishing passage that begins Chapter 3. Such is the significance of the passage for both the development of the narrative and a proper reading of it, that I must cite it in its entirety:

> The people in the tabernacle could trace their bloodlines back to a past of slavery. *But this was not something they talked about much, or knew much about.* In school they were told that their ancestors had been pagan. That

> there had been slaves in Africa, where Black people had put each other in chains. They were given the impression that the whites who brought them here from the Gold Coast and the Slave Coast were only copying a West African custom. As though the whites had not named the Slave Coast themselves.
>
> The congregation *did not know* that African slaves in Africa had been primarily household servants. They were not seasoned. They were not worked in canefields. The system of labor was not industrialized. There was in fact no comparison between the two states of servitude: that practiced by the tribal societies of West Africa and that organized by the Royal African Company of London, chartered by the Crown. *These people did not know* that one of the reasons the English Parliament and the Crown finally put an end to the slave trade was that because of the Victorian mania for cleanliness, manufacturers needed West African palm oil to make soap—soon the trade in palm oil became more profitable than the trade in men and women and the merchants shifted their investments.
>
> *No one had told the people in the Tabernacle* that of all the slave societies in the New World, Jamaica was considered among the most brutal. *They did not know* that the death rate of Africans in Jamaica under slavery exceeded the rate of birth, and that the growth of the slave population from 1,500 in 1655 to 311,070 in 1834, the year of freedom, was due *only* to the importation of more slaves, more people. *They did not know* that some slaves worked with their faces locked in masks of tin, so they would not eat the sugar cane as they cut. *Or that* there were very few white women on the island during slavery, and so the grandmothers of these people sitting in a church on a Sunday evening during mango season, had been violated again and again by the very men who whipped them. The rape of Black women would have existed with or without the presence of white women, of course, but in Jamaica there was no pretense of civility—all was in the open. (*Ab* 18–19, emphasis added)

The narrator presents all of this historical information as discourses that remain as active presences within the lives of the people in the Tabernacle, regardless of their awareness or lack thereof; or more precisely, the historical events the narrator describes are ones that actively shaped the structure of the society in which the people in the society now live. The structure of the narrative *did not know* serves to emphasize this asymmetrical—not to say unilateral—relation between the active "indenting" discourses of colonial history and its passive "indented" recipients. This relation of ignorance becomes further compounded by the mediation of the British colonial school system, which actively misinforms Jamaican children and misrepresents colonial history: "in school they were told. . . ." Indeed, in *Abeng* the colonial educational apparatus, with its systematic suppression of uncomfortable truths and dissemination of more comforting colonial fabulations represents one of the primary obstacles Clare must overcome on her path to self-knowledge.

There is in fact much that Clare does not know during Part I of the novel, about not only her country's history but her family's. Clare's visit with her father to Runaway Bay, the erstwhile family plantation where her family once owned slaves as part of their sugar business, is the first of many instances in the novel in which the Savages' "carefully contrived mythology" of "color, class, and religion" (*Ab* 29) fails to correspond with her experience as a mixed-race Jamaican child. Boy and Clare enter the run-down site of the family's colonial glories, to find only the merest remnants—faded wallpaper, some broken chairs, and a dusty old mantelpiece—of their opulent past. Boy tries, with little success, to conjure up a fragment of the family history, "filling in the room for his daughter" (*Ab* 25); but Clare sees only rubble: "The only objects to be seen were a few broken-down chairs stacked in one corner, and these were uninformative as to origin" (*Ab* 25).

As Clare stands facing the backyard and outbuildings, the narration moves to what is by now a familiar strategy in *Abeng:* a detailed, lengthy explanation of the historical significance of the site and the activities that once occurred there—knowledge of which the experiencing characters remain ignorant, and that would serve to undermine their already tentative sense of identity, as this short passage illustrates:

> These buildings out back, only a few yards from the great house, had once contained molasses and rum and slaves—the points of conjunction of the system known as the Triangle Trade. They contained these things and they contained the paraphernalia of day-to-day existence on a sugar plantation. . . .
>
> *The traces in the earth which Clare could now see* indicated where the slave cabins had been. Little more than huts, really, twenty to twenty-five feet long and twelve feet wide, made of wattle and plaster, with dirt floors and palm-thatched roofs. . . .
>
> The outbuildings on which the livelihood of the plantation hinged were these cabins, and the sugar mill and the boiling-house. The cane was cut—after it had reached past the height of a human being—tied into bundles, and carried from the fields to the sugar mill on the backs of cattle or mules or slaves. . . . (*Ab* 26)

The remainder of the passage goes on to describe the sugar-making process and the slaves' role in it, and the transportation of the final products (sugar, molasses, and rum) back to Britain (*Ab* 26–27). The narrative returns finally to Clare, still standing in the backyard among the buildings, "noting the existence of the foundation stones and the gullies in the earth, *but not knowing the former life they represented*" (*Ab* 27). Thus does the Jamaican landscape in *Abeng* both contain and conceal not only an entire history of slavery and oppression, but the Savages' participation in it. Clare's light-colored skin and green eyes, the most prominent markers of her whiteness, function as signifiers of both her privilege within Jamaican society and her complicity with the oppression of Jamaicans of color. Yet this knowledge is available to Clare only in the visible residues, the "traces in the earth which Clare could now see" but does not recognize as bearing any latent meaning, because she (unlike the narrator) does not know how to read them.

For the young protagonist of *Boyhood,* on the other hand, the act of reading national history—especially the officially disseminated history of his schoolbooks—serves only to deepen his sense of alienation from the national *Geist.* The young Coetzee is a schoolboy in the immediate aftermath of the pivotal 1948 elections, in which the heavily Afrikaans, pro-apartheid National Party defeated the more moderate, English-speaking United Party. As a primarily English-speaking child from a "United" family, he feels little consonance with the fiery nationalist vision of the school's history books:

> Although, in examinations, he gives the correct answers to the history questions, *he does not know,* in a way that satisfies his heart, why Jan van Riebeeck and Simon van der Stel were so good while Lord Charles Somerset was so bad. Nor does he like the leaders of the Great Trek as he is supposed to. . . . Andries Pretorius and Gerrit Maritz and the others sound like the teachers in the high school or like Afrikaners on the radio: angry and obdurate and full of menaces and talk about God. (JMC 66, emphasis added)[26]

Here the protagonist's aversion to the Afrikaaners' nationalist fervor does not seem to be driven by any quarrel with their version of South African history; that is, the young Coetzee does not directly question the veracity of such events as the Great Trek, and in fact knows little about a moment as significant as the Boer War;[27] his primary knowledge of it comes in the form of a story that his grandmother had told his mother: "When the Boers arrived on the farm, . . . they demanded food and money and expected to be waited on. When the British soldiers came, they slept in the stable, stole nothing, and before leaving courteously thanked their hosts" (JMC 66).

This anecdotal evidence weighs at least as heavily in the young protagonist's mind as does the more authoritative discourse of the schoolbook, so much so that despite the boy's limited awareness of the Boer War as a struggle for liberation from British colonial rule, and thus a "War of Liberation" (JMC 66), he nevertheless persists in his sympathies for the British:

> In stories of the War one is supposed to side with the Boers, fighting for their freedom against the might of the British Empire. However, he prefers to dislike the Boers, not only for their long beards and ugly clothes, but for hiding behind rocks and shooting from ambush, *and to like the British for marching to their death to the skirl of bagpipes.* (JMC 66–67, emphasis added)

Young Coetzee's allegiances here are clearly informed by something other than concern over the representations of a national history. Rather, what drives the protagonist's Anglophilia is something akin to, but larger than, an admirable code of conduct or honor, or the romantic image of marching to martial strains of bagpipes; likewise, his loathing of the Afrikaaners is largely informed by their alleged conduct on both the battlefield and the family farm, as well as their unwholesome appearance ("long beards and ugly clothes"). Further, the young protagonist's aversion to all things Afrikaans and attraction to "Englishness" persist even after his own counterintuitive experiences with an Afrikaaner farmer, who withholds punishment after the boy and his friends trespass on his farm (JMS 70–71), and Trevelyan, the very English ("through and through") lodger who volunteers to beat the indentured servant after an attempted escape: "Trevelyan . . . snorted with every blow, working himself into as much of a rage as any Afrikaner. How does Trevelyan, then, fit into his theory that the English are good? (JMC 74–75)

The truth is that he doesn't, anymore than the forebearing Afrikaaner farmer "fits into" the boy's theory of "Afrikaners as people in a rage all the time because their hearts are hurt" (JMC 73). Young Coetzee's distaste for Afrikaaner culture as a whole extends to his Afrikaaner classmates' behavior (JMC 69), the Afrikaans language (JMC 124–125), even the unattractiveness of Afrikaaner women (JMC 126); in fact "[t]he thought of being turned into an Afrikaans boy, with shaven head and no shoes, makes him quail" (JMC 126). Conversely, his predilection for English culture encompasses not only language (JMC 126) and historical exploits and legends that he finds admirable (JMC 108 and 128), but also the romantic and attractive figure of Robin Hood "with his longbow of yew and his suit of Lincoln Green" (JMC 128)—all counts on which he finds the Afrikaaners wanting. Given the choice, by virtue of his bicultural, bilingual upbringing, between white cultures, between, as it were, competing versions or visions of whiteness, the boy's preference is unequivocally for "England and everything that England stands for, to which he believes he is loyal" (JMC 129). "Englishness" in this context represents whiteness at its apex, a nostalgic cultural ideal that the young protagonist transforms, through his fetishization of traditional English icons (the Light Brigade, the Victoria Cross, Robin Hood, "God Save the King") into a cultural *aesthetic*—a cult of English whiteness whose grace and beauty would protect him from the debased, guttural whiteness of the Afrikaaners.[28]

But the young Coetzee also realizes that, as with any fetish, the act of enshrinement is itself the index or measurement of the idol's inaccessibility; that is, the worshiper creates the ideal's unattainability in the very act of idealizing it. Thus the boy reflects that more than loyalty is required before he can "be accepted as truly English: tests to face, some of which he knows he will not pass" (JMC 129). As Ross Chambers explains, the maintenence of the cultural ideal of whiteness demands that it appear as an abstract paradigm, the better to distinguish it from its "knowable others":

> It is as if the system encompassed two mythic (or incomparable) categories, blank whiteness and absolute blackness, each of which is held to lie outside the sphere of examinability. One is unexamined "norm," and the other is unknowable "other" (or extreme of otherness), and between them lies the pluralized area of the multiple categories that come under scrutiny, constituting the knowable others of whiteness as the domain of the examinable.[29]

As a result of his positing the fetish "Englishness" as the white ideal, the young protagonist always finds himself wanting; that is, because of his own pluralized status as half-Afrikaaner, half-English, he remains in a perpetual relation of inadequacy to the abstract, unexamined (and specious) norm of true whiteness (being "truly English").

In *Abeng,* that normative ideal of whiteness rules Jamaica in the form of Queen Elizabeth, whom the novel's narrator dubs "[t]he whitest woman in the world" (*Ab* 5). But unlike the young protagonist of *Boyhood,* Cliff's narrator looks upon the ubiquity of the queen's image with a more acute awareness of the disparity between the white icon and its black subjects:

> The portrait of the white queen hung in banks, department stores, grocery stores, schools, government buildings, and homes—from countryside shanties to the split-levels on the hills above Kingston Harbor. A rather plain little white woman decked in medals and other regalia—wearing, of course, a crown. Our-lady-of-the-colonies. *The whitest woman in the world.* Elizabeth II, *great-granddaughter of Victoria,* for whom the downtown crafts market—where women came from the countryside to sell

> their baskets and Rastafarians sold their brooms and old Black men sold their wood-carvings to the passengers of cruise ships and Pan-American Clippers—was named. (*Ab* 5, emphasis added)

Unlike the young Coetzee, who "subjects himself to . . . the standard of the VC, the Victoria Cross" (JMC 108) as a desirable if unattainable ideal, the narrator of *Abeng* sees the legacy of Victoria as apparently irrelevant to the daily lives of the primarily black vendors; yet the image and its assumed (because unexamined) position of superiority nevertheless presides over the market, as it does over other activities of daily Jamaican life: "banks, department stores," and so on. The passage, then, indicates the unbridgeable chasm of race and class that separates "the large working class, and class of poor people, [which] was Black" (*Ab* 5), from the colonial icon of "the white queen."

For Clare, however, that chasm is markedly "less unbridgeable" than for her fellow Jamaicans in the market, or perhaps it would be more accurate to say that in Clare's case the gap is closed in an inadequate or incomplete way. Because Clare is fair-skinned and middle-class, she enjoys the privilege of a *proximity* to whiteness denied her darker, poorer fellow subjects; that is, she stands to benefit from a "gradation of shading" that places her nearer the normative colonial ideal which, as exemplified by the queen and denounced by R2, values whiteness "as part of an elite class."

But as in the case of *Boyhood*'s young protagonist, partial adherence or eligibility is insufficient for complete identification with the unexamined ideal. In Clare's case, finances, straight hair, and light skin help, but alone are not enough; she must also learn and practice; that is, she must *internalize,* a code of behavior appropriate to her (actual or aspired-to) social position. In short, Clare must learn to act as a 'lady,' a term that the child already recognizes as a more or less transparent euphemism for acting 'white':

> To Clare's mind a lady was someone who dressed and spoke well. A lady was a town creature. A lady often had people in her home where they talked about the theater or books. Above all, a lady was aloof—Clare knew all of these criteria from the Hollywood movies she saw and the lessons of her teachers. They did think they were ladies. They taught her to drop her patois and to speak "properly." *Proper* was a word they used very often. . . . Ladies, Clare had been taught, did not speak in a familiar manner to people beneath their station. Those with the congenital defect of poverty—or color. (*Ab* 99)

'Lady' thus emerges as a term that Clare already rightly associates with race and class—whiteness and a certain social "station." Clearly, however, adopting the conduct of a "lady" is but a secondary requirement, a position to which one may realistically aspire only after meeting the more fundamental condition of skin color and class; because of her light-colored skin and middle-class status, then, Clare enjoys opportunities for social and material advancement that "[t]hose with the congenital defect of poverty or color" do not. Clare is "a lucky girl" because she is light-skinned "in a world where the worst thing to be—especially if you were a girl—was to be dark" (*Ab* 77). Later, when Clare's parents send her to live with a white aunt, her mother explains to her the social and material stakes involved in this task of becoming a "lady":

> Look here, you have a chance someday to leave Jamaica behind you. When you are grown you can be anything you want. You can be anything you want to be. A doctor. A teacher. *But to get there you have to learn the rules*. . . . Girls like you have a better chance at life than other girls. I know what I am talking about. What I would have given to have the chances you are going to have. Mrs. Philips can teach you to take advantage of who you are. (*Ab* 150)

In this further context "lady" emerges as a higher form of whiteness, restricted in its access not just to a certain race or class but to those observing a certain code of conduct. A "lady" fits into the colonial class-hierarchy somewhere between the unexamined norm of the white queen at the one pole and the unexaminable other of the black market-vendors at the other. Each is equally inaccessible to Clare because of the rigidity of the structure, and because of her own "gradation of shading"; but although Clare can never realistically aspire to the cultural ideal embodied by the white queen, her achieving the status of a "lady" would nevertheless place her both markedly closer to the society's white norm and further from its disdained black masses. Thus would Clare achieve, through her effective emulation of whiteness, the "success story" of the bildungsroman: affluence, social status, and a certain consonance (if not a complete identification) with the norms of the society.

Such an unqualified "happy ending" is rendered impossible, however, by Clare's burgeoning awareness of herself as a being for others; that is, it is in the realm of Clare's relations with her racial and social other that the abstract ideal of whiteness comes to crisis. Before the appearance in the text of her friend Zoe, Clare's nascent interrogation of the meaning of whiteness occurs largely on the abstract level of textual interpretation: she reads *The Diary of Anne Frank* (*Ab* 68); engages Boy in a discussion of *Ivanhoe* and the relative virtues of its central female characters, the Jewish Rebecca and Saxon Rowena (*Ab* 72); and scours the local library for books on "the extermination of the Jews of Europe" (*Ab* 75). But it is Clare's realization of the concrete existence of the other in the form of her friend Zoe—and of herself as an object for that other—that finally shatters the hermeneutic circle and brings Clare into an intersubjective relation with Zoe's active blackness. Indeed, Clare's desire for a relation analogous to that of Anne Frank's with her diary, and her realization that her own mother cannot be that friend, ends chapter 11 and dovetails neatly into Zoe's introduction in chapter 12 (*Ab* 80–81).

Clare's growing intimacy with Zoe is the primary focus of the novel's next five chapters, and their blossoming friendship thrives during the summers they would spend together as playmates in the countryside. But the circumstances and setting of the girls' bond serve to cast their individual differences into the background, and creates a temporary, idyllic insulation from the discourses of race and class that elsewhere act upon them as individuals:

> Their friendship over these years was expanded and limited in this wild countryside—the place where they kept it. It was bounded by bush and river and mountain. Not by school or town—and felt somewhat free of the rules of those places. . . . They did not yet question who each was in this place—if the need to question was there, *it remained in the back of their minds.* (*Ab* 95)

Clearly, if "place" serves to strengthen the girls' bond, the landscape also marks its limit; or in other words, the "wild countryside" on which their friendship is structured both enables and delimits the play of that structure.[30] So that if the girls' countryside-bound friendship is "somewhat free of the rules" of school and town, it only remains so within its own preset boundaries of "bush and river and mountain." Further, if the idyll cannot penetrate the discourses of race and class that rule the school and town, it proves to be itself vulnerable—and it is here that the 'inside/outside' opposition between country and town proves specious. For the passage's binary logic deconstructs itself in the paragraph's final phrase: if the differences of race and class seldom intrude on a manifest level, they nevertheless remain in a latent state *in the back of their minds.* The girls' awareness of the divisive discourses of school and town may be pushed, suppressed, into the background for the purposes of their play, but their knowledge of and subjection to, these discourses in a sense precede them. These discourses, the product of a colonial legacy and contents of their own and of their society's colonial unconscious, exert their unacknowledged influence over the girls' every thought and action; and their "background" or unconscious status enables them to operate in a more or less unexamined manner, abridged but relatively unchallenged by the critical faculties of consciousness. In this context, the narrator's assessment of Clare would apply equally to both girls: "She was a colonized child, and she lived within certain parameters—which clouded her judgment" (*Ab* 77).

Yet the fact remains that the narrative implicitly presents Zoe as an answer to Clare's unarticulated desire for a friend like Anne Frank's diary, in whom she may have "complete trust." The immediate context of this trust, which in turn constitutes the relationship with Zoe, is Clare's inhibited relationship with her mother. Clare's mother Kitty shows un unwillingness to discuss matters of a sexual nature openly with her daughter, at a time (approaching puberty) when Clare's curiosity and desire for knowledge about such matters is growing; Clare thus resolves to "not tell her mother anything which was close to her" (*Ab* 80) and seeks her special friend elsewhere.

Enter Zoe:

> When the wispy hairs began to grow between Clare's legs and under her arms—slowly, slowly—it was only Zoe she told, only Zoe she showed them to. And Zoe showed her own hairs. Quick glimpses. And then giggles as the parts were covered over. (*Ab* 81)

It is not surprising, then, after this revelation to learn that "Clare considered Zoe her closest friend" (*Ab* 81); the structure of the narrative indicates that Zoe is indeed the friend Clare was seeking at the end of the previous chapter. The girls' friendship thus grows steadily through the novel's next five chapters; the narrative of the strengthening bond between them is interspersed with episodes from their lives that serve to emphasize the girls' perceptions of their respective social positions or "stations" (*Ab* 81–82 and 96–100).

What becomes increasingly apparent in the narrative, however, is the tension between "the differences-already-there" on the one hand (*Ab* 100) and Zoe's growing consciousness—and Clare's increasingly untenable denials—of them on the other. This tension leads to Zoe's admonishing Clare for her childish plan of hunting down a wild boar, and a further warning, over protests from Clare, of how the (race-based) expectations that come with adulthood would finally separate them:

> "Me not town gal. And me not buckra. Me jus' want to do something so dem will know we is smaddy."
> "Wunna is town gal, and wunna papa is buckra. Wunna talk buckra. Wunna leave here when wunna people come fe wunna. Smaddy? Wunna no is smaddy already? Gal smaddy. Kingston smaddy. White smaddy. Dis place no matter a wunna a-tall, a-tall. Dis here is fe me territory. Kingston is a fe wunna. Me will be here so all me life—me will be marketwoman like fe me mama. Me will have fe beg land fe me and fe me pickney to live

> pon. Wunna will go a England, den maybe America, to university, and when we meet later we will be different smaddy. *But we is different smaddy now.*"[31] (*Ab* 118, emphasis added)

Clare "fought hard not to believe all that Zoe had said" (*Ab* 119), because admitting the truth of her friend's statement would have the effect of allowing the discourses and material contingencies of the "outside world" to become a permanently manifest element in their relationship, thus qualifying their union once and for all. By "union" I do not mean a strictly sexual bonding, partly because the narrative takes great pains to depict the relation as bearing a greater emotional and psychic significance, but also because their relationship is not an explicitly sexual one.[32] Nevertheless, Clare's desire for a more complete identification with Zoe; that is, her desire to achieve an ontological *unity with her perceived other,* is frustrated by the latter's introduction to the relationship of the contingencies of race and class that would always delimit and eventually end their friendship.

It is significant in this regard that Clare's immediate reaction to Zoe's declaration is to feel "split into two parts—white and not white, town and country, scholarship and privilege, Boy and Kitty" (*Ab* 119). This reveals finally the true nature of Clare's psychic and ontological dilemma: by acting out her desire for the other, Clare seeks *to unite or heal what she perceives as the "split" ruptured sides of her own subjectivity*. Clare's fantasy of union with Zoe is thus her own unconscious attempt to "heal" herself, render herself coherent as a subject, to render whole a subject "split" by the divisive discourses of colonialism. The true source of Clare's psychic suffering, then, is the colonial discursive regime that not only alienates her from the object of her childhood desire, but also and more damagingly creates a subjective chasm between those "parts" of Clare that cohere with buckra "ladyhood"; that is, with the normative ideal of whiteness, and those that do not.

Clare nevertheless enjoys a final idyllic moment with Zoe, as they bathe nude in the river and bask together afterward on the rocks (*Ab* 120–121); however, it is a moment that ends disastrously for Clare, as she accidentally shoots her grandmother's bull and is subsequently separated from her childhood friend (*Ab* 122–123 and 134). After this irreversible moment, Clare still reflects on Zoe's words and on the significance of her own desire: "She had never thought before about losing that friendship until Zoe spoke to her and the vectors of Zoe's anger threatened to cross out their closeness. Clare held on by the river *that the two of them could erase difference*" (*Ab* 124). This, with the revelation that Clare "had wanted to lean across Zoe's breasts and kiss her" (*Ab* 124) before they were interrupted, constitutes the novel's most acute depiction of the relation between physical longing and the desire for *psychic* unity—with both the forbidden other and those subject-positions or fragments that do not conform to the demands of a white subjectivity. In this context, then, Clare's desire for Zoe is finally symptomatic of her longing for psychic union within her own "split" colonial subjectivity.

For the young protagonist of *Boyhood,* the psyche is the site of a submerged tension between unspoken desires and the fear of punishment. Unlike Clare's attachment to Zoe, young Coetzee's desires are decidedly not focused on any single object: "He likes to gaze at slim, smooth brown legs in tight shorts. Best of all he loves the honey-tan legs of boys with blond hair" (JMC 56). The boy is also more intensely conscious of his desires, however unfocused, as something to be suppressed:

> Of all the secrets that set him apart, *this may in the end be the worst.* Among all these boys he is the only one in whom this dark erotic current runs; among all this innocence and normality, he is the only one who desires. (JMC 57, emphasis added)

More than simply "disturbed by the feelings" (JMC 56) sparked in him by the boys' legs, the protagonist realizes that his desire is one that the greater society would condemn; his understanding of this psychic splitting between individual desires and societal demands is far more acute than Clare's passing sense that her feelings for Zoe "should be guarded from family" (*Ab* 127), or the vague parallel she (and the narrator) draws between her own situation and that of her gay cousin Robert and his dark-skinned "dearest friend"(*Ab* 124–127). But for both young protagonists, it is the desire for their respective others that finally enables a critique or interrogation of the colonial cultural-imperative of whiteness.

In *Boyhood,* there is no single object of desire on which the narrative focuses; rather, it is only through the narration of a range of fragments or impressions from the boy's life that the larger pattern of desire and identification emerges.[33] Two such "scenes," however, stand out, depicting in composite the boy's incipient consciousness not only of his relation to his Afrikaans and nonwhite others, but also of himself as an object for those others. These are the protagonist's momentary glimpsing of a "Coloured" boy in the street, which occupies the whole of the brief chapter 8; and his brief friendship with Eddie, his family's "Coloured" indentured servant, which provides the primary "scenes" of chapter 10 (with one crucial exception). In each case, as we shall see, young Coetzee's desire coincides with a sense of guilt or shame—not only on a sexual level as in this example, but in the more generalized sense of his own privilege as a white subject and the nonwhite other's subjection to that privilege. That these emotions coincide in the narration (and in the protagonist); that is, that the memory-trace of white guilt accompanies every thought or gesture of white desire, points beyond the immediate context of South Africa and apartheid to the irreducible role of white guilt in the workings of the colonial unconscious, and as an unignorable part of the colonial legacy to the postcolonial condition.

The event of the "Coloured" boy's brief appearance in the public ground is "important beyond all measure" to young Coetzee, "not because of who he is . . . but because of the thoughts that are going on in his head, that burst out of him like a swarm of bees" (JMC 59–60). In the immediate aftermath of the boy's passing, the protagonist's sense of shame at his own longings resemble closely his thoughts of the previous chapter, even to the point of echoing that passage's language with the reflection that "only dark and guilty souls know such secrets . . . he, ruled by his dark desires, is guilty" (JMC 60). Yet in the presence of the dark-skinned boy there is a further refinement of this guilt, a guilt that focuses not on sexual desire as a projection into future of fantasies but on the protagonist's realization that the other's body is already subjected to him to an extent that he finds disturbing:

> So this boy . . . who is slim as an eel and quick as a hare and would defeat him with ease in any contest of swiftness of foot or skill of hand—this boy, who is a living reproof to him, *is nevertheless subjected to him in ways that embarrass him so much that he squirms and wriggles his shoulders* and does not want to look at him any longer, despite his beauty. (JMC 61, emphasis added)

Significantly, the young white boy is embarrassed not entirely or even primarily by the sexual nature of his desire, but by the fact of his attraction to someone who is "subjected to him" as a privileged white subject—whom his mother could call upon to do her any menial service ("carry her shopping basket, for instance") and who would be grateful to be paid with "a tickey in his cupped hands" (JMC 61).

This tension or economy between desire and guilt in the young protagonist of *Boyhood* extends to his birthday celebration at a local café, which is "spoiled by the ragged Coloured children standing at the window looking in on them" (JMC 72). The encounter triggers a chain of associations in the narrative that culminate in the remembrance of Eddie, "a seven-year-old Coloured boy" brought to work for his parents as a domestic servant, and the budding friendship cut short by Eddie's attempted escape and subsequent beating and dismissal (JMC 73–75). The young protagonist remembers his friend's helping him master the bicycle as "a debt he still owes Eddie" (JMC 75); he also fondly recalls "wrestling with Eddie on the lawn" and the smell of, and taste of, his body during these bouts (JMC 75–76). But for present purposes the most telling recollection of Eddie is of watching his friend bathe:

> Every weekend Eddie had to give himself a bath, standing in a footbath in the servant's lavatory and washing himself with a soapy rag. He and his brother hauled a dustbin below the tiny window and climbed up to peek. Eddie was naked but for his leather belt, which he still wore around his waist. Seeing the two faces at the window, he gave a big smile and shouted *"Hê!"* and danced in the footbath, splashing the water, not covering himself.
>
> Later he told his mother: Eddie didn't take off his belt in the bath.
>
> Let him do what he wants, said his mother. (JMC 76)

Although more elliptically narrated than the blunt declarations of desire elsewhere in the text, when combined with young Coetzee's interest in "the smell of Eddie's body" this passage reveals his fascination with his friend's body, and the focusing of his desires in the direction of that body. Equally muted but equally active in this economy of desire is the cryptic expression of guilt and trepidation: "One thing he knows for sure: Eddie will have no pity on him" after his beating at Trevelyan's hands (JMC 77).

These instances or "scenes" of the protagonist's encounters with active blackness share a certain structure—desire followed by guilt—and the realization of the other's body as both an object of desire and as a site of white domination. The scenes also share a recourse to two tropes or motifs which, properly read, point to the residues or memory-traces of colonial anxiety in the postcolonial context: (1) the recourse to the other's 'innocence' and the inversion of the opposition 'white/black' or 'light/dark,' by the terms of which it is the "Coloured" other who embodies "the path of nature and innocence" (JMC 61) and the white observer who casts himself as a "dark and guilty soul" (JMC 60); and (2) recourse to 'the land,' or more specifically to the land as the other's rightful possession of which they are deprived by the white minority ("the land comes with them, is theirs, has always been").

The protagonist's casting of the nonwhite other as a sexual "innocent" is, read in this context, allegorical of his larger perception of the other's nescience of the discourses of whiteness that oppress them. Or more specifically, the *gaze* of whiteness: the "Coloured" boy in the street "is absorbed in himself, he does not glance at them" (JMC 60), and Eddie is troubled not at all by the white boys' voyeurism ("he gave a big smile and shouted *'Hê!'* and danced in the footbath"). This 'innocence of the other' stands in opposition to white guilt, along a well-traveled chain of signifiers that "returns to accuse him":

> Beauty is innocence; innocence is ignorance; ignorance is ignorance of pleasure; pleasure is guilty; he is guilty. This boy, with his fresh, untouched body, is innocent, while he, ruled by his dark desires, is guilty. (JMC 60)

The passage goes on to cite the word 'perversion,' which young Coetzee understands to define both his own "dark" desires and the fact of the boy's being subjected to his mother's most frivolous whims. Likewise, Eddie's "beauty" lies in the fact that he shows no guilt to the intrusive white eyes that gaze at him (again: "he gave a big smile . . . not covering himself") and no sense of rage or apparent awareness of the desires of that gaze or the structure of domination and subjection immanent to it.

Whiteness's power over its others extends, of course, to dominion over the land; and this relation between white domination of the other's body and their land, and the latent guilt and shame that become manifest only in the later postcolonial ritual of repentance, crystallize in young Coetzee's reflection upon glimpsing the nameless "Coloured" boy that "the land comes with them, is theirs, has always been." The protagonist's memories of Eddie lack such straightforward revelations; but a careful reading will reveal seven direct references to Eddie's hometown of Ida's Valley, three of them within the final two paragraphs. Although young Coetzee has never been to Ida's Valley, he imagines it "as a cold, sodden place" where "the rain is always falling" (JMC 76–77). Despite the protagonist's conviction that the land "is theirs," Eddie's only chance of escaping the squalid corner of the land to which whiteness has banished him is to work for a white family. This strengthens young Coetzee's sense of shame upon learning of Eddie's attempted escape, and subsequent beating and dismissal (JMC 74–75); but although he is not personally responsible for any of it, he wonders apprehensively what treatment he would receive from his erstwhile friend should they meet again (JMC 77). The boy conjures an image of Eddie that confirms his anxiety over his own passive complicity, and his fear of the other's retribution:

> At this moment, in the leaky house in Ida's Valley, curled under a smelly blanket, still wearing his blazer, he knows that Eddie is thinking of him. In the dark Eddie's eyes are two yellow slits. One thing he knows for sure: Eddie will have no pity on him. (JMC 77)

Although the passage does not reveal precisely *what* Eddie "is thinking of him," the protagonist can allow no possibility of the other's compassion or sympathy for him: "Eddie will have no pity on him." Young Coetzee can expect no benevolence, no "pity" from one who has received such blows and who is consigned to such a life; this insight applies specifically to his family, who has participated in the boy's oppression by returning him to Ida's Valley, and especially to himself. But why to himself, since he had no part in Eddie's punishment and treated his playmate as a relative equal? Of what can the boy accuse himself that would render him worthy of Eddie's contempt?

One answer, which has constituted part of the argument of this chapter, is that the boy's guilt and foreboding grow from the same source: they are the traces or residues of a colonial legacy that manifests in the former colonizer as collective guilt over both the colonial desire to dominate and the lengths to which whiteness has gone to maintain its ascendancy. Let us not forget the Hegelian subject, for whom knowledge is always a matter of mastery in the form of a dialectical overtaking (*Aufhebung*): of an abstract principle of reasoning, of a body, of a territory. It is all one to the knowing subject, for whom all the world's contingencies represent only so many intermediate positions he must overcome on his way to the apex of Absolute Knowledge. To "know" the world, then, is for such a subject analogous to the will to an ever higher and more elaborate form of mastery. Thus the subject's guilt, at the eventual realization that his desire or the other and his domination of the other are inherent to the same gesture and structure of want, and the perpetual frustration of the subject's desire for complete union with the other; for such a union would constitute for the white subject the encompassing within itself of its own difference; that is, by embracing the other whiteness would reclaim as good that "dark" part of itself that is always cast away, "split off" under the cultural imperatives and prohibitions of colonialism. Yet such a union can never be complete, because of the very nature of the white subject's desire and of desire itself; that is, the desire for the other paradoxically sparks a consciousness of the other that becomes the ground of the frustration of that desire. The young man knows he cannot have what he wants, cannot even bear to articulate it, because he has begun to glimpse how his desires are complicit with the drive for domination that has enslaved them both. The desire and the guilt are thus together bound; the boy can neither enjoy his desire without the intrusion of the knowledge of shame, nor can he wholeheartedly confront, and thus be rid of, the destructive feelings from which he derives a 'perverse' pleasure and to which he is nevertheless, in the face of everything, still attached.[34]

As revealed through the boy's meditations on land and place that occur simultaneously with his thoughts on the other, there is in young Coetzee's, as in Clare's, desire for the other a latent attachment for—and fear of losing—the land itself. The longing for the body of the other thus emerges as analog or allegory to a desire for union with the land itself—a drive for identity with the land that would undo its exploitation—or at least provide the impetus for a wish-fulfillment for a seductive but specious return to a nature "untouched" by colonialist expansion; and this corresponds, in turn, with the wish for a relation with the other uncontaminated or uninformed by the oppression of empire. Thus, we return briefly to Cliff's novel, Clare's passionate attachment to both Zoe *and* the landscape, the *place* where their friendship unfolds. The structure of young Coetzee's attachment is somewhat different, but nevertheless characterized by the same metonymic displacement: *Boyhood*'s narrative shifts seamlessly from the boy's loss of his friend Eddie to the memoir's longest chapter by far, an extended and wistful elegy to the family *veld* (farm). Young Coetzee's suppressed desire for Eddie is thus deflected or modulated into a longing for an idyllic *place,* on to which he will project his latent sense of loss and guilt, and his elliptically articulated demand for identification and union with both the external other and his own dissociated or "split" subjectivity.

This nostalgic fetishization of the land is sharply distinguishable as a psychic category from the marked position of disdain or even contempt for the other's landscape that permeates the "expatriate" fiction of writers such as, say, Paul Theroux or Hilary Mantel, in which the narrator and/or protagonist has no desire to identify with a landscape they see as bleak at best and foreboding or outright threatening at worst;[35] and it also stands in stark opposition to the depictions in the colonial fictions of Conrad and Kipling of the other's landscape as both beautiful and dangerous, as paradoxically both inviting and threatening (*Heart of Darkness* being the archetypal example). This difference is quantifiable to the degree that the respective narrators-protagonists feel themselves *invested* in the land; that is, there is a level of identification or even devotion to the land in Cliff's and Coetzee's texts that is far less evident in Theroux, Mantel, and others. Which is to come upon a crucial distinction between this postcolonial whiteness of identification and allegiance, however ambivalent, and all whitenesses that came before: this new whiteness strives, however contradictorily, for *an identification or union without mastery;* that is, they would to some degree submit or "give themselves over" to the new cultural imperative of difference and the other in exchange for the sake of maintaining their stake in the land and its future. And yet this love is already qualified and undermined by a sense of guilt that stems from the suspicion that the land is not, and has never been the rightful property of whiteness, that the land is in some essential way "other." Thus, we witness young Coetzee's passionate attachment and poignant sense of loss when he visits the family farm:

> He must go to the farm because there is no place on earth he loves more or can imagine loving more. . . . *Yet since as far back as he can remember this love has had an edge of pain.* He may visit the farm but he will never live there. The farm is not his home; he will never be more than a guest, an uneasy guest. Even now, day by day, the farm and he are traveling differ-

> ent roads, growing not closer but further apart. One day the farm will be wholly gone, wholly lost; already he is grieving that loss. (JMC 80, emphasis added)

The structure of the tension or economy between desire and guilt, and love and pain is again evident in this passage, and finds explicit expression in the narration where Eddie and his fate did not. The boy's attachment to the farm, and his keenly felt sense of its imminent loss, are especially poignant for his identification of the farm with his family; in this context, the farm represents his family's final direct link not only with the land but with a nostalgic vision of the nation from which young Coetzee feels all but disconnected in the visceral world of Worcester and the ruder, coarser Afrikaaner boys in the school. The idyllic atmosphere of the farm extends, in fact, to the language spoken there:

> Greedily he drinks in the atmosphere, drinks in the happy, slapdash mixture of English and Afrikaans that is their common tongue when they get together. . . . It is lighter, airier than the Afrikaans they study at school, which is weighed down with idioms that are supposed to come from the *volksmond,* the people's mouth, but seem to come only from the Great Trek, lumpish, nonsensical idioms about wagons and cattle and cattle-harness. (JMC 81)

The boy's experience of the *volksmond*—and of the *volk* itself, for that matter—clearly does not coincide with the official "version" of Afrikaans language and culture that the school would have him learn and emulate. As in Clare's Jamaican countryside, the boy's family farm is a place from which the discourses of apartheid are apparently banished. Yet it is the boy himself, whose presence on the farm is always provisional and qualified; he can say *"I belong to the farm"* but not *"The farm belongs to me"* (JMC 95–96). *"Belong"* is thus "[t]he secret and sacred word that binds him to the farm" (JMC 95); it is, however, a relation of identification without mastery: "Voëlfontein belongs to no one. The farm is greater than any of them" (JMC 96). Thus the young Coetzee short-circuits the white cultural imperative of mastery by capitulating in the manner of Hegel's bondsman: he recognizes Voëlfontein unconditionally, without demanding recognition in return. The boy wishes only to *"belong to the farm,"* to forfeit mastery and submit himself to the land—and in the process to the higher workings of the dialectic of belonging and not-belonging that is the nation. Thus in *Abeng* Clare's dismay at Zoe's denouncing of Clare as a "town gal" and claiming the countryside as "fe me territory," it is not that Clare would dispute Zoe's claim in terms of her own ownership (Clare's grandmother owns the land that Zoe and her mother live on), but a denial or exclusion of Clare's identification with the land. And in fact, the novel goes to considerable length to draw a sharp distinction between Clare's love for the land and her ancestors' rapacious drive to acquire property as wealth. There is, however, a final crucial point to make regarding this drive of the excentric "split" subject to recenter or recohere itself via a bonding with the land: namely, that it is also immanent to the subject's impulse in both these texts to narrate, to write—to (re)inscribe for itself a space or place in the discourses of the postcolonial nation.

III

> How will he keep them all in his head, all the books, all the people, all the stories? And if he does not remember them, who will?
>
> —J. M. Coetzee, *Boyhood: Scenes from Provincial Life*

> Her diary was in her lap, and she was writing about what she had woken to.
>
> —Michelle Cliff, *Abeng*

The young Coetzee's rhetorical question, to which *Boyhood* is one possible answer, is in a sense anticipated or even preempted by Clare's resolve to write it all down. Having been successively denied the objects of their respective desires and the displaced or aim-inhibited devotion to the land, the final site of contestation in both *Abeng* and *Boyhood* is writing itself. The struggle of each young protagonist with the meaning of their own whiteness in the postcolonial context, and the negotiation by which this new whiteness might aspire to a new intersubjective relation with otherness, finds itself displaced one more time into the pages of Clare's diary and Cliff's novel, and Coetzee's memoir and works of fiction. Thus writing itself becomes, by this metonymic displacement of attachments from body to land to text, the frontier or 'site' of contestation where the future of whiteness remains to be written and read.

Read in this context, then, the incomplete or broken bildungsromans of Clare and the young Coetzee become instead exemplary fragments of a larger 'narrative of progress' for whiteness itself, the coming-of-age narrative of a cultural imperative that learns to live and coexist within a postcolonial world of many colors. The challenge that remains for such a narrative would thus come not from without, in the form of an angry, avenging other; rather, the final and most damaging obstacle to the psychic maturation of a postcolonial whiteness remains its own will-to-mastery—the lasting legacy, in short, of a colonialism that has left its ineffaceable mark on the postcolonial world, which continues even now to function as unacknowledged ideology. To systematically uncover and interrogate such colonial traces wherever they may surface is the proper work of a postcolonial discourse; thus the highly self-conscious narrations of both *Abeng* and *Boyhood,* which subject their respective protagonists to the most exacting inquiry into the meaning of whiteness in its relation to the colonized other, present an efficacious balance between aesthetic praxis and ethical concerns. For above all what such writers as Cliff and Coetzee do in their work is to unceasingly interrogate the very psychic machinery that works to suppress their most crucial insights, which produces a tactical resistance to the ascendance into consciousness of the most painful self-recriminations, the most chafing of truths locked away in the colonial unconscious. But to interrogate whiteness does not, can never mean to *undo* it, either in its historical indentations or in the memory-traces of empire that remain; one cannot glibly declare that "[t]reason to whiteness is loyalty to humanity"[36] as if there were only a single cataclysmical battle to win against a clearly marked and utterly othered enemy, as if undoing the entire history of colonial whiteness were a simple matter of negation. It is thus less a matter of abolishing or otherwise erasing whiteness for the purpose of recovering some chimeric originary "native essence," or of plunging blindly into a future based on the facile platitudes of "color blindness" or "multiculturalism," than of moving toward the inscription of a new script or narrative of a postmastery whiteness, a whiteness that can enter into a relation of mutual recognition with its others without admonitions, without fear, without shame.

CHAPTER FOUR

"Toward A New Humanism. . . .": Fanon, Hegel, and the Crisis of Mastery

> As I have often pointed out, I don't much like hearing that we have *gone beyond* Hegel, the way one hears we have *gone beyond* Decartes. We go beyond everything and always end up in the same place. Hence, an ever more elaborate mastery.
>
> —Jacques Lacan, *The Seminar of Jacques Lacan*

I

If the diversified and dispersed group of criticisms known collectively as 'postcolonial' can be said to have a single unifying principle or project, it is a general interrogation of Western culture in its power structures, its assumption of superiority over its marginalized others, and, most importantly, the discourses that underlie those structures and suppositions. The editors of *The Postcolonial Studies Reader,* for instance, state that postcolonialism is primarily a critique of European colonialism "as a civilizing mission which involved the suppression of a vast wealth of indigenous cultures under the weight of imperial control";[1] Padmini Mongia's finely edited collection of postcolonial theoretical essays also offers the perspective that "the term postcolonial refers not to a simple periodization but rather to a methodological revisionism which enables a wholesale critique of Western structures of knowledge and power, particularly those of the post-Enlightenment period."[2] Whatever the detectable variations of critical method or ideology between these editors' introductory statements that a more in-depth reading might reveal, they agree in defining postcolonialism as the study and analysis of the complex interactions between the cultural imperatives of colonialism on the one hand and the wide range of the colonized's cultural practices—including, but not limited to, acts of anticolonial resistance—on the other. One instructive example of this endeavor, although not postcolonial in the strictest sense, can be found in the oft-cited passage from Henry Louis Gates Jr:

> Current language use signifies the difference between cultures and their possession of power, spelling out the distance between subordinate and superordinate, between bondsman and lord in terms of their "race." These usages develop simultaneously with the shaping of an economic order in which the cultures of color have been dominated in several important senses by Western Judeo-Christian, Greco-Roman cultures and their traditions.[3]

Gates's statement seamlessly combines capitalist exploitation, racism, and colonialism with Western historiography and, most tellingly, the structure of the Hegelian master-slave dialectic. But what is most striking about the passage is not the reference to Hegel itself; what rather begs the question here, as Robert Young has pointed out,[4] is the act of invoking Hegel, along with a Western model of "History," within the same discourse that would attack the hegemonic Western discourses that oppress and enslave. My point here is not that Gates necessarily undermines himself with his reference to Hegel, anymore than does any oppositional reading practice that shows a healthy awareness of its own complex and often vexed relations with a dominant discourse; rather, it is that Western discourses, and their accompanying assumptions of Western privilege and superiority, are pervasive even, even perhaps especially, within the discourses that would resist and oppose them. It cannot be mere happenstance that the Hegelian dialectic serves as a legitimizing reference for Gates's interrogations of Western culture, even as he points out Hegel's own disparaging remarks about African culture only a few pages later (HLG 11); nor is it mere contingency that the master-slave dialectic remains an efficacious way of discussing the structures and effects of racism and colonialism.

Indeed, at least two recent texts by leading postcolonial thinkers, Paul Gilroy's *The Black Atlantic* and Lewis Gordon's *Fanon and the Crisis of European Man: An Essay on Philosophy and the Human Sciences,* specifically address the implications of Hegelian philosophy for a postcolonial cultural theory. Both of these, along with Homi K. Bhabha's *Location of Culture*, are discussed in a recent review article by Simon Gikandi, who sees the texts, despite their diverse cultural and theoretical concerns, as focusing on questions "about how the colonized can reread their temporal and spatial geographies within the culture of the modern West now that the categories that invented modern occidentalism can no longer sustain their universal authority."[5] It is a group of questions that we might paraphrase thus: How can/should the formerly colonized reinscribe their place in the world in the aftermath of the authoritative master-narratives of knowledge and power that colonialism once imposed? And: How can/should the formerly colonized come to terms with the lingering residues of colonial knowledges that remain in the form of postcolonial desires and anxieties?

Both Gikandi's article and the texts under review address Hegelian historicism to some degree as part of their respective explorations of these questions. Significantly, Bhabha's text lacks any substantial direct exposition of Hegel's work, and Gikandi inexplicably refers to Hegel only in the title of his article; both Gordon and Bhabha, however discuss Hegelian philosophy primarily within the context of their work on Frantz Fanon, the Martinican psychoanalyst and postcolonial polemicist.[6] While the theorists employ very different methodologies—Bhabha's poststructurally informed approach seems to be incongruous next to Gordon's more Sartrean brand of phenomenology—each casts Fanon in more or less the same ideological light; that is, as an oppositional voice raised powerfully and eloquently against Western colonialism and its structures of knowledge and power, and as a thinker who, however problematically, sets precedents in his writings for much of the subsequent work that has come to be known as 'postcolonial.'

But as both Bhabha and Gordon point out, Fanon's engagements with Western culture, particularly his encounters with philosophy and that most Western of discourses, psychoanalysis, does not come without its complications, its moments of ambivalence. One such moment in Fanon's writings stands out as a singular intervention in the history of readings of Enlightenment philosophy, because it signals the onset of a new and transgressive kind of reading, one in which the colonized subject has the temerity to read the Great European Books and come to his own conclusions, and to decide for himself what meaning these texts might hold *for him*. Fanon, in this context, emerges as an allegory for all the reading and writing to follow that would call itself 'postcolonial': a figure situated at an intersection or interstice between a postcolonial horizon and a colonial legacy, between the desires of the formerly colonized and their lingering anxieties. Fanon thus emerges as a revolutionary in more than the narrow sense of one who would take up arms against an oppressor; rather, as a reader and writer of texts he enacts the originary postcolonial scene of the colonized other's "reading back" at the colonial discourses of knowledge and power in general, and Western philosophy and psychoanalysis in particular. It is in Fanon that we begin to glimpse the possibility of a specifically postcolonial *poetics* of oppositional reading, one in which the texts imposed upon the colonized other in the name of a latently ideological "knowledge" are read in the spirit of interrogation, of *impertinence*, an act from which the other emerges with an understanding far removed from any officially sanctioned interpretation.

The moment of postcolonial transgression in the act of reading to which I have been referring appears in a brief but momentous discussion of Hegel in *Black Skin White Masks* ("The Negro and Hegel"). For Fanon, what short-circuits the slave's fulfillment within the master-slave relation is the untenability of a mutual recognition between the two. The "Negro" remains frustrated in his desire for recognition from the white master, because the master has released him from servitude without the necessary moment of conflict in which the slave returns to demand the recognition denied him in his enslavement—thus denying the slave the moment in which he would *take* his freedom: "There is not an open conflict between white and black. One day the White Master, *without conflict*, recognized the Negro slave. But the former slave wants to *make himself recognized*."[7]

For Fanon this is the Hegelian dialectic's undoing; for by freeing the slave without a struggle, the master has denied the slave the chance to act upon the master's consciousness and thus establish his own:

> At the foundation of Hegelian dialectic *there is an absolute reciprocity* which must be emphasized. It is in the degree to which I go beyond my immediate being that I apprehend the existence of the other as a natural and more than natural entity. If I close the circuit, if I prevent the accomplishment of movement in two directions, I keep the other within himself. Ultimately, *I deprive him even of this being-for-itself.* (*BSWM* 217, emphasis added)

Clearly for Fanon, this depriving of the slave's desire for recognition fuels the slave's sense of alienation or "invisibility" in relation to the master. It is thus not only the fact of colonization that brings such a psychic impact upon the colonized, but the ease with which the master can turn away afterward without what the native considers a necessary and rightful moment of reckoning: "The former slave wants to *make himself recognized*." It is not simply a matter of acting out a reciprocal violence upon the former master, although this certainly constitutes an element, whether manifest or latent, of the slave's desire for recognition; after all, it is primarily through violence that the colonizing power imposes and maintains its power over the colonized and exacts the native's recognition of its authority. For Fanon, however, there must be something further: an "absolute reciprocity" that makes each party in the dialectic responsible for the other's being-in-itself. Without such a relation of reciprocity, the former slave's newfound freedom is meaningless, because it lacks the mediation of an other who would recognize him *as a subject:* "The only means of breaking this vicious circle that throws me back on myself is to restore to the other, through mediation and recognition, his human reality, which is different from natural reality" (*BSWM* 217). The difference between "natural reality" and "human reality" here is reducible to the former master's recognition of the native as an equal participant, in both an intersubjective relation and the larger social and political context of the postcolonial state.

However much Fanon's analysis is informed by Jean-Paul Sartre in particular and the existential critique of phenomenology in general, his introduction of racial and cultural difference to the master-slave relation sets an important precedent for later appropriations within the postcolonial realm. Read in this context, *Black Skin White Masks* emerges as a rethinking of Sartrean existentialism in terms of race; as Sartre attempts in *Being and Nothingness* to fracture the hermeneutical circle of the master-slave relation by viewing it through G. W. F. Hegel, Edmund Husserl, and Martin Heidegger simultaneously,[8] so Fanon strives for "the elimination of the vicious circle" (*BSWM* 10) by viewing master-slave as part of a much larger racial and cultural framework. The issue in Sartre of the master's indifference toward the enslaved other and the slave's subsequent marginalization, discussed later, becomes for Fanon the dispossession and displacement of an indigenous people under the mastery of a colonizing power; as such, we may usefully think of *Black Skin White Masks* as an exegesis of one man's radical alienation, in which the experience of the colonized is mediated entirely by the colonial power—and in which the slave, having had his own indigenous cultural identity all but annihilated, nevertheless identifies to a troubling degree with the very master who marginalizes and humiliates him: "For twenty years they poured every effort into programs that would make the Negro a white man. In the end, they dropped him and told him, 'You have an indisputable complex of dependence on the white man' " (*BSWM* 216). A careful reading of Fanon's reading of Hegel will reveal the inescapable paradox of the colonized other's subject position in relation to the discourses of knowledge and power to which he is ceaselessly subjected: the colonized as perpetually 'developing,' always emulating but never achieving the ideal of ontological equality with Europe, whiteness, and empire. Further, the official rhetorics of emancipation do nothing, in Fanon's eyes, to dissipate the colonized sense of an Adlerian inferiority, both psychically and ontologically, to the colonial ideal of 'civilization' in the wake of which they must now build both individual postcolonial subjectivities and a national identity. This quandary, of a lingering colonial unconscious and its continued impact upon postcolonial anxieties about the formation of a postindependence national culture, is perhaps best summarized by Lacan's notion of "an ever more elaborate mastery" as cited in the epigraph; for Lacan, the naive insistence of a "going beyond" of Hegel signifies at best an aversion to confronting the unpleasant truths of empire, and at worst a willing ignorance of repression of the persistence of the structures of empire in the postcolonial world. Fanon's great contribution to postcoloniality is precisely the insight, gleaned from psychoanalysis, that for the colonized subject the only way out is *through*, that it is only by confronting the psychic specters of the colonial past, and a rigorous examination of those traces of empire that remain in the postcolonial psyche and even within the very articulation of the resistance to, or repudiation of, the colonial, that the subject and the nation can begin the work of reconciling the fragmented pieces of the colonial psyche into a new coherence. For now, however, we have Fanon reading and writing about Hegel, about the slave reading the master's books and finding within them (within himself?) his own desire for recognition, and the beginnings of his own struggle against mastery. Before returning to this portentous and beautifully impertinent act of reading, however, let us turn to Hegel himself, to see what exactly it is that Fanon has read that has caused him to "write back" to the Great Book, to Europocentrism, and to mastery.

II

From its origins in the Hegelian system, the master-slave dialectic has been among the most protean of philosophical warhorses; since its first substantial exposition as "Lordship and Bondage" in *The Phenomenology of Spirit,* it has been subjected to reformulations and revisions across a wide range of critical and philosophical discourses.[9] Through all of these, the master-slave dialectic not only appears as the basis of a useful strategy for analysis of power relations and the ways in which power is constituted, but remains an implicit—and not always acknowledged—part of the methodologies behind the strategies of empowerment advanced by contemporary postcolonial critics. Since the project of the postcolonial critic seems in part to be committed to an undermining of any such closed systems of analysis—or more specifically, to refute such model as would assume a governing structure of self-realization in *all* historical processes—it would, I think, be useful to historicize the model itself; that is, to trace a history of the Hegelian "Lordship and Bondage" relation in its various critical applications and appropriations, if not in a comprehensive manner (which would constitute a much larger project than the focus of the present work will allow) then at least in a more selective overview that would follow the Hegelian model from its originary source to some of its subsequent applications. My aim in addressing these different approaches is not, as is an all-too-common practice, to formulate some overarching metaposition from which to comfortably comment; rather, what I hope to do here is provide some sense of the critical dialogue that has grown around the Hegelian master-slave relation, in order to uncover some of the ways in which Hegel, far from having been "gone beyond" or otherwise rendered obsolete, remains (as Lacan alludes in the epigraph) an immanent part of the discussion.

The first striking thing about reading the "Lordship and Bondage" chapter of the *Phenomenology* is Hegel's assertion that it is only through interaction with another that we may aspire to self-consciousness in any concrete way. The chapter opens with Hegel's statement that "Self-consciousness exists in and for itself when, and by the fact that, it so exists for another; that is, it exists *only in being acknowledged.*"[10] The ability to make self/not-self distinctions, to desire to possess another, is, in this context, not enough; self-consciousness requires the recognition of another self-consciousness. Significantly, Fanon chooses an opening statement from "Lordship and Bondage" as the epigraph for his own discussion of "The Negro and Hegel"; and he follows it with his own opening remark that paraphrases Hegel's statement: "Man is human only to the extent to which he tries to impose his existence on another man in order to be recognized by him" (*BSWM* 216–217).

Clearly, then, self-consciousness as posited by Hegel and echoed by Fanon does not—cannot—exist in a solipsistic vacuum. This concept of self is modeled upon, and directed toward, others; that is, consciousness can only be aware of itself as such because it encounters other consciousnesses. Self-consciousness, then, means first of all to be one consciousness *among others.* Or to put it another way, to not be recognized as a consciousness by other consciousnesses means simply not to belong, to not be recognized in this context is to be ignored, within a given community where such concepts have their meaning. Within the Hegelian dialectic: "Action by one side only would be useless because what is to happen can only be brought about by both" (PHN 112); consequently, self-consciousness is necessarily the result of a social interaction and cannot be a one-sided or individual activity.

The master-slave dialectic, then, emerges from this mutual drive for recognition as self-consciousness, which in turn leads to a struggle in which each tries to obtain recognition from the other. Hegel describes this struggle as a fight to the death, in which each seeks the death of the other; indeed Alexandre Kojève tells us that within the Hegelian model "Man can appear in Nature or create himself as Man . . . only if a fight to the death for the sake of Recognition *(Anerkennen)* leads to a relation between a free man and a man who is enslaved to him" (AK 224). In this scenario, the combatant who is truly prepared to die for the sake of recognition emerges as master, and the one who fears death, who recognizes without being recognized rather than face death, as his slave.

True to the dialectical nature of the relation, however, this victory of one self-consciousness over another is provisional, and indeed carries within it the seeds of its own undoing in the next stage. The slave exists for the comfort and convenience of the master, and provides services and goods for the master's enjoyment; however, the slave also achieves self-consciousness—and thus, independence from the master—by recognizing his own worth in that which he produces; that is, the slave realizes self-consciousness in what he has produced. This new self-consciousness is both different from the master's and inaccessible to him, since it comes into being independently of the master's gaze, and as it is achieved through work, which the master does not perform.

But for Hegel, the final undoing of the master-slave relation comes not with the slave's realization of his work through self-consciousness, but rather with the *master's* realization that he has not gained what he sought after all; the slave's recognition is not, after all, the recognition of another self-consciousness, because the slave had forfeited, as it were, his claim to self-consciousness when he submitted to recognizing the master without being recognized by him in turn. Recognition from the slave, then, cannot satisfy the master, simply because the slave does not recognize him freely. Such is the double bind of the master's position within the Hegelian dialectic: what he really wants is for the other to recognize him *freely;* that is, with the other having, *but not exercising,* the option of not recognizing him. It is only through each one's freely chosen acknowledgment of the other that mutual recognition between free consciousnesses can occur. Neither the Lord nor the Bondsman in his burgeoning self-consciousness finally gains what he needs in the relation: the slave's coerced recognition of mastery is inadequate to the master's for *unconditional* recognition, and the slave's inability to achieve recognition from the erstwhile master—or as Frantz Fanon points out, to force a second confrontation with the master in which the slave would *make himself* recognized—leaves him with an Unhappy Consciousness that taints his newfound freedom. Hegel's exposition of the former slave's Unhappy Consciousness as "the consciousness of self as a dual-natured, merely contradictory being" (PHN 126) anticipates what Fanon, Lacan, and any number of postcolonial critics would later refer to variously as a 'split' or 'divided' colonial subject, torn between its hatred of, and identification with, its erstwhile colonial master:

> This *unhappy, inwardly disrupted* consciousness, since its essentially contradictory nature is for it a *single* consciousness, must forever have present in the one consciousness the other also; and thus it is driven out of each in turn in the very moment when it imagines it has successfully attained to a peaceful unity with the other. (PHN 126)

Thus the former slave experiences himself in Hegelian terms as an "*inwardly disrupted* consciousness"; that is, as a being-for-itself that remains radically alienated from both its identification with the former master and its own desires to be rid of him.

In *Being and Nothingness* Sartre problematizes and develops this element of the master-slave relation, particularly Hegel's notion of recognition from the other as a necessary element in the establishment of a self-consciousness. Sartre explicitly affirms with Hegel that self-consciousness (Sartre's "Being-for-itself") is born of the struggle to the death for the other's recognition, and that this need for the other's recognition amounts to a constant mediation of us by others: "Thus Hegel's brilliant intuition is to make me depend on the Other *in my being*. I am, [Hegel] said, a being-for-itself which is for-itself only through another"(*BN* 321); in this respect, Sartre's conception of the master-slave relation closely resembles the confrontational nature of the Hegelian model, with master and slave always exerting consciousness upon each other and acting upon each other's freedom.

Sartre also makes explicit the notion, implicit in the Hegelian model, that mastery and slavery are not "*given or innate* characteristics" (*BN* 224); that is, rather than simply act out the master-slave scenario according to an essentially "free" or "slavish" nature, Sartre's master and slave *create* themselves (or come into being) freely through their actions. For Sartre, the only thing that is different between master and slave is precisely their actions—what they did or did not do: the master is the one who was willing to risk his life in the struggle, the slave the one who, fearing death, submits rather than risk being slain. For Sartre, this notion of freedom is indispensible to understanding the master-slave relation:

> Freedom coincides at its roots with the non-being, which is at the heart of man. For a human being, to *be* is to choose himself; nothing comes to him either from without or from within himself that he can receive or accept. He is wholly and helplessly at the mercy of the unendurable necessity to make himself be, even in the smallest details of his existence. Thus freedom is not a being, it is the being of man, that is to say his non-being. . . . Man cannot be at times free and at other times a slave; either he is always and entirely free or he is not free at all. (*BN* 420)

Freedom, as Sartre presents it, is the nonnegotiable foundation of being; it is, in fact, the one thing we cannot choose away; that is, we can never choose *not* to be free. Additionally, the freedom to choose our own being is also the one thing of which the other can never deprive us; in this respect Sartre, much more than Hegel, emphasizes the freedom of the other. Elsewhere in the book, and in a different context, Sartre explains that while the sadist (read "master") aims to appropriate the other's transcendent freedom, that freedom "remains on principle out of reach" (*BN* 525) more so as the other is objectified as a slave or instrument of the master's will. As in the Hegelian model, here the master is again frustrated in his desired goal of apprehending the other's freedom and exerting his own consciousness upon it; that is, the master realizes that the slave's recognition cannot satisfy him, because what he wanted was for the slave to recognize him *freely*. This last moment of recognition (or more specifically, the master's recognition of his own error) is of particular importance here, for it brings us to Sartre's break from the Hegelian model.

Within Hegel's *Phenomenology*, the master-slave relation is part of a much larger dialectical movement. The relation is thus, as with all conflicts within the dialectic, brought to resolution; that is, the relation between thesis (Lordship) and antithesis (Bondage) is brought to synthesis (*Aufhebung*, 'resolution') through the mediation of a third party (variously referred to by Hegel as the 'mediator', 'minister', and 'third term'), subsequently bringing about the mutual recognition of self-consciousnesses: "thus this middle term [mediator] is one which presents the two extremes to one another, and ministers to each in its dealings with the other" (PHN 136). Within Sartre's model, however, this resolution does not and cannot happen; unity within the master-slave relation (or for that matter, any self-other relation) is for Sartre an unresolvable opposition, as he explains in "Concrete Relations with Others":

> We have seen that this contingency is insurmountable; it is the *fact* of my relations with the Other, just as my body is the *fact* of my being-in-the-world. Unity with the Other is therefore in *fact* unrealizable. It is also unrealizable in *theory*, for the assimilation of the for-itself and the Other in a single transcendence would necessarily involve the disappearance of the characteristic of otherness in the Other. (*BN* 477)

We can see here that, for Sartre, the impossibility of transcending the master-slave opposition stems from the very structure of the relation. Sartre is at pains in this section to establish the link between Being-for-itself and *Being-for-others*, in which each for-itself (or consciousness) attempts to recover its own being by making an object out of the other; a mediation or synthesis of these two by any "third term," then, is unacceptable both in fact and theory for Sartre because it would involve a Being-for-itself without a Being-for others—clearly a contradiction. Or put another way, for Sartre there is no mediating force or agency that can transcend *difference* as the irreducible ground of all relations with others. This insight of Sartre's is in turn crucial to such postcolonial theories as Bhabha's formulation of "cultural difference," which the latter posits as the dialogic basis for a heterogeneous postcolonial society; and significantly, for Bhabha any sublation of such difference, or recasting of it into an inert "free play of polarities and pluralities in the homogeneous empty time of the national community" (*LoC* 162), is finally inadequate as a cultural interpretation of "[t]he jarring of meanings and values" that exist simultaneously within postcolonial nationalisms.

For Sartre, then, the master-slave relation does not move toward eventual resolution, but remains in a state of radical alienation; each one defines and mediates the other's being, with neither able to apprehend that being or even fully understand it (*BN* 473). What emerges, then, is a mutual objectification of self and other, a mutual *estrangement*. For Sartre, as for Hegel, to enslave the other is to effectively undermine one's own desire for recognition, for to act upon the other's freedom is to simultaneously and irreducibly destroy any chance of gaining their *freely given* recognition. In a move strongly informed by Marx's theories of the worker's radical alienation under industrial capitalism,[11] however, Sartre posits a mechanism by which the accosted master can circumvent the slave's demand for recognition or confirmation of his self-coonsciousness gained through work; although frustrated in his attempt to gain the other's freely given recognition, the master always has the option of objectivizing the other entirely, reducing the enslaved other to their function in an attitude Sartre calls "indifference toward others":

> Those "people" are functions; the ticket-collector is only the function of collecting tickets; the café waiter is nothing but the function of serving the patrons. . . . In this state of blindness I concurrently ignore the Other's absolute subjectivity as the foundation of my being-in-itself and my being-for-others, in particular of my "body for others." (*BN* 496)

Sartre's use here of the word 'blindness' is significant, particularly for its use not as a state or condition but as a form of being: "I *am* my own blindness with respect to others" (*BN* 495), Sartre tells us and this term, combined with the use of parentheses around the word "people" later in the same paragraph, illustrates most chillingly the fate of the slave within the Sartrean master-slave scenario. The master, faced with both the slave's burgeoning self-consciousness and the impossibility of ever really possessing the slave's freedom, can simply make the slave ontologically disappear; indeed the master can, as Sartre tells us, maintain this psychic marginalization of the inconvenient or disturbing other indefinitely, for "as long as [his] fundamental bad faith desires" (*BN* 496). And the notion of bad faith as a determining factor in the master's ontological "blindness" is especially significant for our understanding of master-slave relations as a collective; for this "invisibility" of the slave translates, for Sartre, into mass displacement of the former slave on the societal level.

In the Hegelian model, the slave achieves the self-consciousness that eluded him in the struggle with the master through his relation to, and identification with, that which he produces. For although the slave exists for the sake of the master and works for the master's enjoyment, he also achieves self-consciousness, and thus independence from the master, by perceiving his own value in what he produces; for Hegel, then, the slave's escape from bondage lies precisely in his labor and the sense of independence that is established through it. Sartre (as informed by Marx),[12] however, problematizes the slave's escape through work, partially through the "indifference toward others" mentioned previously; but more significantly, Sartre calls into question the whole notion of work as a transcending agent by bringing the individual master's indifference toward the slave's emerging self-consciousness to bear upon slaves as a collective, whose identity and works are looked upon by the class of masters, when at all, as an object. As I will explain in this chapter, it is this same "indifference toward others" as practiced by the formerly colonized upon their erstwhile colonial masters that Sartre mistakenly attributes to Fanon in *The Wretched of the Earth*: "his work—red-hot for some—in what concerns you is as cold as ice; he speaks of you often, never to you."[13]

For Sartre, it is others who make known to us not only our own being (in the sense of our Being-for-others) but also our membership and standing within groups, which Sartre refers to as "our belonging to a subject-community, especially the existence in the world of manufactured objects" (*BN* 547). And it is in this relationship, of the individual to both the work they do and the group of workers to which they belong, that Sartre problematizes the master-slave relation. For Sartre, what the worker experiences in work is their own reduction to the status of function, which Sartre calls "his being an instrument for others" (*BN* 549); that is, the worker's subjectivity is negated in that he or she is working for a nameless, faceless "they" who can neither know nor recognize them. Work done for another's enjoyment, in this case, is for Sartre a mode not of transcendence but of alienation (*BN* 548); that is, whatever potential satisfaction the worker may find in what he or she produces is negated, not only by the other's indifference but by the concrete and irreducible *undifferentiatedness* of the other, the depersonalization of the "they" that rules over them and enjoys the worker's production.

And this "invisibility" of the slave in Sartre, this alienation of the worker from what he or she produces on the one hand and the faceless master who consumes it on the other, looms even larger within the subject-community of workers; for it is here that the individual slave's alienation becomes "a common shame and a common alienation" (*BN* 537) in the slave's recognition of himelf as an undifferentiated object among a group of other such objects. In the terms of a Marxist formulation that at least informs Sartre's model, this translates into the "we" of a working class, aware of being looked-at or apprehended collectively as an object by the "they" of a ruling class. Sartre further posits this relation as a radical difference between a We-as-subject (conscious of being active or looking-at) and a We-as-object (being-looked-at) that he calls, respectively, the 'We-subject' and 'Us-object.' In this scenario, the us-object becomes aware of being perceived or apprehended as an objective collectivity (workers, the working class, etc.) by a collective "they" who are, nevertheless, not aware (because of its own collective indifference-toward-others) of itself as a We-subject being looked-at in return by the group they objectivize (*BN* 554–555). Sartre does allow for the possibility of the workers' Us-object to become a We-subject; for Sartre, however, such an entity would be constituted not by the work experience per se, but by a common *apprehension* of that experience as defined by common structures of perception:

> In the "we," nobody is the object. The "we" includes *plurality of subjectivities* which recognize one another as subjectivities. Nevertheless this recognition is not the object of an explicit thesis; what is explicitly posited is *a common action or the object of a common perception.* "We" resist, "we" advance to the attack, "we" condemn the guilty. (*BN* 535, emphasis added)

The words I have emphasized in this passage are especially significant in that they point to how, for Sartre, an oppressed group or Us-object comes to know itself, recognizing within its plurality of subjectivities the common perception of: (1) work as a means not of transcendence, but of alienation; and (2) their marginalization or "invisibility" as a result of the indifference-toward- others brought to bear upon them by an oppressing or ruling group. The latter is especially significant, for much post-*Being and Nothingness* oppositional criticism is informed by Sartre's construction of a collective under- or object-class, constituted through a common perception of marginalization or "invisibility" in relation to a dominant group or culture.

Sartre's revisionary ideas on the master-slave relation are themselves taken up, pointedly if sporadically, in Jacques Lacan's "Freud, Hegel, and the Machine." In this published lecture, Lacan hints toward a reading of the *Phenomenology* as being itself positioned within the dialectic *as the master's own discourse,* or more specifically, that the *Phenomenology*'s professed end—the attainment of Spirit as the embodiment of Absolute Knowledge, and the ability to reconstruct the whole of human history from the standpoint of scientific philosophy—represents the perfection or completion of discourse, which in turn embodies "the instrument of power, the sceptre and the property of those who know" (*SJL* 71). Seen in this context, both the master-slave relation and the *Phenomenology* as a whole (and beyond that, the phenomenology of Spirit itself) becomes "the forward march of . . . an ever more elaborated mastery" (*SJL* 70). This in itself is an important observation on the *Phenomenology,* for it both advances the notion of European discourse and ideology as tools of a Western mastery and places the Hegelian dialectic firmly within that discourse; and this in turn amplifies appropriations of Hegel by oppositional or anti-Western critiques and—more importantly—complicates the relation of such critiques to Hegelian models precisely to the extent to which they are informed by them.

Sartre's notion of indifference-toward-others also finds its place, if not an explicit one, within Lacan's lecture on Hegel. For Lacan, this attitude of indifference toward the enslaved other was made possible by what he calls "the advent of the world of the machine" (*SJL* 74); this of course echoes Marx's insight that only after the onset of an industrialized capitalist culture can the slave really be reduced to their function, because it is only with the introduction of the machine that the master can think of them as such. Certainly the advent of industrialization in the West made of the worker an anonymous entity (and in the postindustrial era, an ever more dispensable one), a faceless, nameless drone distinguishable from others only, as Sartre points out, by their immediate function (ticket taker, café waiter, etc.); but unlike Sartre, whose approach focuses on relations between individuals (for even his formulations of the We-subject and Us-object are ultimately reducible to a plurality of individual subjectivities) and therefore eschews direct reference to a larger social or political context, Lacan makes explicit the link between industrialization and the slave's "invisibility" left implicit in Sartre's model.

Lacan illustrates his 'slave-as-machine' analogy through a look at what he calls the "energy myth" and its bearing upon the biologic view of the human body as a machine; specifically, he is interested in how the introduction of the machine made it possible for us to view the slave in terms of energy:

> Energy, I had you observe last time, is a notion which can only emerge once there are machines. Not that energy hasn't always been there. Except that people who had slaves didn't realize that one could establish equations for the price of their food and what they did in their *latifundia*. . . . It took machines for us to realize [slaves] had to be fed. And more—they had to be looked after. But why? Because they tend to wear out. (*SJL* 75)

Lacan's use of the word "equation" is significant here, because it illustrates perfectly Sartre's notion of work as a mode of alienation. In Lacan's industrialized master-slave relation, the slave is not only marginalized but *quantified;* that is, there is nothing about the slave that is not entirely knowable as, or reducible to, his function. But beyond this, the idea of the slave's quantification is useful for its exposition of the industrial master's agenda regarding the slave-machine: to formulate the correct equation by which to calculate how much is needed to keep it running—and no more. Such a scenario, in which the slave is merely a machine-object to be maintained for the master's enjoyment, at best negates the slave's freedom, and at worst renders such questions irrelevant; consequently, the slave as self-consciousness is, by not being recognized, indeed made "invisible."

Compounding this problematic of the colonized subject's ontological "invisibility" and alienation on a societal level is the former slave's continued identification with the former master, or rather with the former master's cultural imperatives. The resulting inwardly split subject, which for Hegel takes the form of the Unhappy Consciousness,[14] occupies an interstice between its dual desire to destroy and replace—or rather, *emulate*—the former master. This for Hegel constitutes the double bind of the Unhappy Consciousness:

> [T]he duplication which formerly was divided between two individuals, the lord and the bondsman, is now lodged in one. The duplication of self-consciousness within itself, which is essential in the Notion of Spirit, is thus here before us, but not yet in its unity: the *Unhappy Consciousness* is the consciousness of self as a dual-natured, merely contradictory being. (PHN 126)

This Hegelian Unhappy Consciousness, or for Hegel the "*unhappy, disrupted* consciousness" of the former slave (PHN 126), finds itself constantly mediated by the discourses and cultural imperatives of mastery, as figure 1 illustrates:

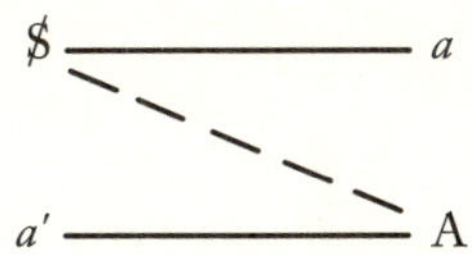

In this illustration, *a* signifies the ego or self, *a'* the ego-ideal (what/who the subject perceives it may become; and what it may aspire to be, or how it imagines itself in the future), and A the colonizing entity that mediates the *a-a'* relationship. $\$$ represents the "split" subject, alienated from itself as a result of its interstitial position between the 'colonizing' and 'colonized' elements, as it were, of its divided psyche; and the dotted line depicts the psychic trajectory of the mediating discourse itself (in Lacanian terms, the *symbolic*), intersecting the relationship between the ego and the ego-ideal; that is, mediating both the subject's idea of itself in the present moment and its idea of what it might aspire to as it perceives its own future. Hegel explains further this radical disruption of the former slave's consciousness:

> This *unhappy, inwardly disrupted* consciousness, since its essentially contradictory nature is for it a *single* consciousness, must for ever have present in the one consciousness the other also; and thus it is driven out of each in turn in the very moment when it imagines it has successfully attained to a peaceful unity with the other. (PHN 126)

In true dialectical fashion, Hegel sees the Unhappy Consciousness as already containing within itself the makings of a new intersubjectivity; that is, it "itself *is* the gazing of one self-consciousness into another, and itself *is* both, and the unity of both is also its essential nature" (PHN 126)—but does not know itself as such, experiencing itself rather as a radical alienation. This moment of inward rupturing of the colonized subject, and its struggles to reformulate itself in terms of an intersubjective relationship with whiteness and with Europe—in short, with an entire history and legacy of mastery—is both the *raison dê'tre* and the exegesis of Fanon's work. It is from the tortured ontology of the Hegelian Unhappy Consciousness that Fanon constructs a "revolutionary humanism"[15] that would resolve or transcend the economy of colonial oppression. Thus does Fanon in *Black Skin, White Masks* dedicate his remarks from the first page "[t]oward a new humanism. . . ." (*BSWM* 7) that would enable the kind of transgressive reading and writing of a humanism *against* Europe, against colonial oppression, which his work embodies. Fanon would resolve the contradictions of the postcolonial Unhappy Consciousness by constructing a humanism *against* Europe, one that would narrate, interrogate, and finally expose colonialism as the lie that lurks behind European rhetorics of a humanist "civilizing mission." And it is finally to Fanon as a revolutionary reader and interpreter of Europe and its contradictorily coherent humanism, a humanism that can schizophrenically speak of "Understanding among men. . . ." and "Our coloured brothers. . . ." on the one hand and "Race prejudice. . . ." on the other, that the rest of this chapter will turn.

III

> When it does happen that the Negro looks fiercely at the white man, the white man tells him: "Brother, there is no difference between us." And yet the Negro *knows* that there is a difference. He *wants* it. He wants the white man to turn on him and shout: "Damn nigger." Then he would have that unique chance—to "show them. . . ."
>
> —Frantz Fanon *Black Skin, White Masks*

> Let us waste no time in sterile litanies and nauseating mimicry. Leave this Europe where they are never done talking of Man, yet murder men every-

> where they find them, at the corner of every one of their own streets, in all the corners of the globe. For centuries they have stifled almost the whole of humanity in the name of a so-called spiritual experience.
>
> —Frantz Fanon; *The Wretched of the Earth*

Between these epigraphs, we can trace the problematic of the colonial subject's radical alienation as it oscillates between ontology (or as Lewis Gordon would have it, a critique of ontology[16]) and epistemology, or more specifically moves between the being or experience of individual subjects on the one hand and the ways in which the collective nation comes to know itself—and the sources of that knowledge—on the other. The slave in *Black Skin, White Masks* seeks to confront the master and actively demand his freedom, only to find that again he has been acted upon: "The white man, in the capacity of master, said to the Negro, 'From now on you are free' " (*BSWM* 220). Thus is the now-former slave negated in the very act of gaining his freedom, for he has failed in his bid to be finally recognized as a consciousness. As Fanon points out in an important footnote to the sentence just cited: "I hope I have shown that here the master differs basically from the master described by Hegel. For Hegel there is reciprocity; *here the master laughs at the consciousness of the slave.* What he wants from the slave is not recognition but work" (*BSWM* 220). As I have already argued, the master evades the confrontation and thus the slave's desire for an intersubjective relation; and he does so as an act of bad faith, extending his dehumanization of the slave from the fact of slavery into what Sartre calls "indifference toward others" and Lacan calls "the slave-as-machine"—both a fundamental negation of both the other's subjectivity and the master's own responsibility for their actions in having enslaved and oppressed that other. The day of reckoning that Hegel would posit in the absolute reciprocity of the dialectic is thus short-circuited by the master's bad faith in his continued denial of the slave's demand for recognition.

On the level of colonialism this is the moment of the negotiated withdrawal of the occupying colonial army, the peaceful handover or "transition" to national rule. Fanon describes this abrogation of mastery as far from altruistic, however; for Fanon the colonial retreat is motivated not by goodwill but by a wish to avert the wrath of the colonized:

> This is why a veritable panic takes hold of the colonialist governments in turn. Their purpose is to capture the vanguard, to turn the movement of liberation toward the right, and to disarm the people: quick, quick, let's decolonize. Decolonize the Congo before it turns into another Algeria. Vote the constitutional framework for all Africa . . . but for God's sake let's decolonize quick. . . . (*WE* 70)

In Fanon's writings, then, there is a strong correspondence between the individual slave's desire to take his freedom by violence and "the atmosphere of violence, that violence which is just under the skin" (*WE* 71) which permeates the virtually every page of *The Wretched of the Earth* and that Fanon posits as the prerequisite for the armed uprising that alone can drive out colonialism and, more importantly, colonial influence, from the colonized land. Fanon does not equivocate in the least on this point; it is clearly in the armed, violent overtaking of the colonizing entity that the colonized people recognizes itself as a nation in the process of asserting itself as such. The violent overthrow of the oppressor, in this context, is the nation's first collective act: "We believe that the conscious and organized undertaking by a colonized people to re-establish the sovereignty of that nation constitutes the most complete and obvious cultural manifestation that exists" (*WE* 249). Reading this relation between an individual's and a nation's respective demands for recognition and the mutual desire to impose this recognition through violence upon the erstwhile master, it becomes clear that on the one hand it is the native's *threat* of violence that brings about change; but on the other hand, and equally as irreducible, is the fact of the besieged colonizer's ability to short-circuit the dialectic by negating its reciprocity, by simply saying "uncle" and walking away without a fight, thus frustrating the colonized's desire to finally be recognized. There lies largely unacknowledged in Fanon's writings, then, the parallel between the former slave as a divided or "split" subject who can neither destroy nor achieve recognition from his erstwhile master and the epistemological schism of a nation that remains collectively torn in terms of its ethical, political, and socioeconomic horizons.

In Fanon's writings, this epistemic economy of the postindependence state reaches its fullest articulation in his alternating and contradictory meditations on humanism. In the conclusion of *The Wretched of the Earth,* after nearly three hundred pages in which Fanon tirelessly advocates violent revolution as the truest route to national solidarity and postcolonial cultural identification, he reaches an impasse: he would on the one hand "[l]eave this Europe," thus making a great show of turning his back on a master—and a humanism—that is well into the process of abandoning the game, if the phenomenological exposition of "The Negro and Hegel" is to be believed (and I would argue that it is); yet the text's remaining pages call for a new humanism and "a new man" which/whom, Fanon's professed repudiations of Europe to the contrary, nevertheless preserves implicitly within the new nation at least elements of what the colonized had contested—indeed, fought to the death against—as the culture that the colonizers had violently imposed upon the colonized in their drive to dominate as thoroughly as possible. Fanon makes clear earlier in the text that what is at stake in the colonizer's cultural impositions upon the colonized is no less than a fight for the identity of the nation:

> Colonial domination, because it is total and tends to oversimplify, very soon manages to disrupt in spectacular fashion the cultural life of a conquered people. *This cultural obliteration is made possible by the negation of national reality,* by new legal relations introduced by the occupying power, by the banishment of the natives and their customs to outlying districts by colonial society, by expropriation, and by the systematic enslaving of men and women. . . . Every effort is made to bring the colonized person *to admit the inferiority of his culture* which has been transformed into instinctive patterns of behavior, *to recognize the unreality of his "nation,"* and, in the last extreme, the confused and imperfect character of his own biological structure. (*WE* 236, emphasis added)

The diagram with which I illustrated the colonized subject's relation with colonial discourse and culture also applies in this collective scenario; that is, the postindependence nation in *The Wretched of the Earth* faces the same psychic double bind as the former slave in "The Negro and Hegel" and *Black Skin, White Masks* generally: having already recognized the colonizer's cultural superiority—and correspondingly, "the inferiority of [its own] culture"—and having internalized the colonizing culture along with the preexisting "instinctive patterns" of its own indigenous cultural practices, the new nation finds itself in the position of being thoroughly mediated by the culture that once oppressed it and still denies it recognition.[17] Such a nation finds itself in the contradictory position of wanting simultaneously to destroy the master and replace him; it both rejects and emulates Europe, it both *is* and *is not* European. Curiously, this problem does not escape Fanon's attention in his discussion of the development of a "national" art:

> In the sphere of the plastic arts, for example, the native artist who wishes at whatever cost to create a national work of art shuts himself up in a stereotyped reproduction of details. These artists who have nevertheless thoroughly studied modern techniques and who have taken part in the main trends of contemporary painting and architecture, turn their backs on foreign culture, deny it, and set out to look for a true national culture, setting great store on what they consider to be the constant principles of national art. But these people forget *that the forms of thought and what it feeds on, together with modern techniques of information, language, and dress have dialectically reorganized the people's intelligencesand that the constant principles which acted as safeguards during the colonial period are now undergoing extremely radical changes.* (*WE* 226–227, emphasis added)

Clearly Fanon reads the producing of a postcolonial culture as less a return or "exhumation" of indigenous cultural practices than an ongoing interaction, a dialectical "reorganization", of native and European cultural elements. Read in this context, Fanon's comments on national culture apparently contradict his later dictum of "leav[ing] Europe"; neither the former slave nor the former colony can "leave Europe" because, through the various acts of violent cultural impositions that accompany colonization, European cultural discourses remain dialectically as an irreducible part of the new nation. Fanon's numerous admonitions against a return to a specious precolonial cultural "essence," along with his impassioned calls for the creation of a new humanism and a "new man," provide ample testimony to the lingering influence of the colonial cultural legacy. Thus, to paraphrase Gordon, Europe is not the postcolonial nation's other; it is *Europe*'s other (LG 6). The new state finds itself linked to a Western culture which, while not explicitly rejecting it, nevertheless turns away from a part of its own history that it would rather forget. The call for a new humanism paradoxically both denies and affirms that which is European in Fanon's model of a revolutionary and postcolonial national identity; thus does the Fanonian nation act out on a collective level the contradictions of the Hegelian Unhappy Consciousness.

Since the Unhappy Consciousness takes the form of an economy, or what Hegel calls "only the *immediate unity*" (PHN 126) of discourses, it experiences them as unresolvable opposites; in the case of the colonial subject, this economy would take the form of a specious opposition between a precolonial "essential" element and colonial "unessential" element. Although within the Hegelian model such a conflict would be dialectically resolved by the subsuming of both entities into a new synthetic whole, the Unhappy Consciousness suffers precisely because it fails to recognize both of these cultural entities, the European and the indigenous, as irreducible elements of his own subjectivity, and sees itself as the conflicted, incoherent unity of incompatible cultural forces: "But it is not as yet explicitly aware that this is its essential nature, or that it is the unity of both" (PHN 126). The colonial subject thus struggles within its own cultural contradictions as it works toward a resolution which, within the Hegelian model, it already embodies; it is only its lack of awareness of itself as such a bridge between cultural entities that perpetuates its struggles and miseries.

Read in this context, Fanon's depiction in *The Wretched of the Earth* of the ideological struggles of the native intellectual are as instructive as they are self-reflexive, as he comments from a position of knowledge on the stages of intellectual development that he believes others will follow. Fanon describes this "evolution" of the native intellectual as a dialectical movement, consisting of three phases: first, a "period of unqualified assimilation" of the culture of the colonizing power; then, a corresponding opposite "immersion" in the exterior forms of the indigenous culture; and finally what Fanon calls the "fighting phase," in which the native learns to produce "a revolutionary literature and a national literature" (*WE* 222–223). For Fanon, the awakening of the native intellectual to his role in the national struggle is what finally allows him to overcome the demands of conflicting cultural imperatives to create a genuinely national literature; this implicitly already signifies the retention, even within the native's "fighting literature" (*WE* 223), of an element of "his opposite numbers in the mother country" (*WE* 222). After the successful struggle, however, the native intellectual, along with the people generally, find that the colonizer's "techniques of information, language, and dress" (*WE* 225) that informed the subject culture during colonization are now dialectically part of the epistemological inventory (aesthetics, ideologies, etc.; knowledge in general) of the new nation—and no credible nationalist discourse can ignore such knowledge, or parse them out of the new nation's identity. A nationalist discourse that espoused such a view of the new state would clearly, in Fanon's terms, be guilty of the same fundamental bad faith as its colonial predecessor.[18]

At this point a crucial objection might be raised: Isn't the revolutionary who passionately calls for a "new humanism" in the same breath within which he cries "Down with Europe!" also guilty of acting in bad faith? What of these "Western values," this humanism whose invocation on the one hand produces in the native "a sort of stiffening or muscular lockjaw" (*WE* 43), inspiring the native to reach for his knife and "laugh . . . in mockery when Western values are mentioned in front of him" (*WE* 43), yet later in the same book inspires the same native intellectual to aver that "[a]ll the elements of a solution to the great problems of humanity have, at different times, existed in European thought" (*WE* 314)? What exactly is it in Western thought that Fanon continues to posit as the new heading or horizon of a postcolonial humanism? Is such a term, 'postcolonial humanism', even intelligible, given the Western values that Fanon rightly sees as serving as a tool in the service of colonial oppression and violence? We might begin to respond to such an objection, as Fanon implicitly does, by pointing out that it carries within it an unexamined assumption of humanism and its professed values as essentially European; the problem with such a formulation would thus be the irreducible linking, even identification, of "humanism" with "Europe," an assumption that implicitly if unexaminedly opposes European civilization with its barbaric, inhuman Others. Thus positing the analogy "European: human as non-European: nonhuman." It is precisely in the face of such ontological denials that Fanon's reading and "writing back" to Western philosophy would fly, to deny the Eurocentric assumption that the colonized is incapable by definition of reading and writing himself—*constructing himself*—in a manner that both critiques and affirms European humanism, that in other words embodies not simply a passive consumption of so-called Western values but an active engagement with IT. Thus does Fanon transgressive, even insolent reading and writing of the West and its humanism ("Who dares to speak thus?" asks Sartre. "It is an African, a man from the Third World, an ex-'native'" [*WE* 9]) represent a crisis of European reason and point the way toward both its fall from predominance and its preservation, however residual, within a new postcolonial philosophy. The revolutionary humanist might ask, rather contentiously: Because there was once a European Enlightenment, can there never be an enlightenment that is *not* European? Must Europe forever be the intellectual master, graciously bestowing its light upon the rest of us, who are compelled to bask in but a passive, imitative manner? Why must not Europe's others also say, as Europe itself once did: "we must invent and we must make discoveries" (*WE* 315)? Fanon's provisional, divided yet hopeful responses to such questions come in the form of a "new humanism," the "new man," which/who both is and is not European but who is entirely postcolonial. It is finally Hegel who reminds us that the Unhappy Consciousness will not always be so, that it is but a moment within a larger movement of cultural forces; it is so now only because it does not know that it is always already that which it seeks, and thus the resolution of its own alienation. For Fanon, then, the crisis of European colonialism is thus an opportunity to wrest that abused, overdetermined signifier "humanism" away from Europe once and for all, to gear it toward a philosophy for *all* humans, what Lewis R. Gordon calls "a radical approach to the study of human being" (LG 87). And as Fanon's writings pointedly remind us, the responsibility for such a project is shared by all, whether conscious of it or not, whether willing or not. Such a formulation of a revolutionary postcolonial humanism leaves nothing and no one unexamined. On this crucial point, let Fanon himself have the final word:

> No one has clean hands; there are no innocents and no onlookers. We all have dirty hands; we are all soiling them in the swamps of our country and in the terrifying emptiness of our brains. Every onlooker is either a coward or a traitor. (*WE* 199)

CHAPTER FIVE

Reason, "the Native," and Desire: A Theory of "Magical Realism"

I

> Pero que es la historia de América toda sino una crónica de lo real maravilloso?
>
> —Alejo Carpentier, *El reino de estes mundo*

'Magical realism.' A European term applied to a 'non-European' literature, a literature which, despite the assimilating effects of the "Third World cosmopolitan" status bestowed upon its originary authors, retains its irreducible difference, its mark of a radical alterity, which only begs the question: What of this act of *naming,* of the boundary or mark of a text written by, say, a Latin American author, imposed upon it from without, in a futile European attempt to categorize and thus 'understand' it by this process of naming—which is already itself an act of appropriation, a bid to harness the wild, 'exotic' text within a reasonable European critical framework—to 'master' the other's difficult text? Here the act of naming emerges as the allegory of a colonial fantasy: the mastery of reading as a reading of mastery.

There is, happily, no need to circulate this inflated term 'magical realism' any longer, in light of critics as estimable as Roberto González Echevarria, having both dismissed the term decades ago and begun the necessary task of reading so-called magical realism within a postcolonial context. It is the intention of this chapter to contribute to this inevitable and important critical project.[1] But we need hardly lift a finger to show this overdetermined yet hollow "magical realism" self-destructing, to show it consuming itself, Sphinx-like, in its own shame and anger at having been found out. Even the originary coiner of the phrase, the Venezuelan literary critic Arturo Uslar Pietri, who first applied the term to Latin American literatures in 1947,[2] recognized the term as an oxymoron, which is to say that it constitutes a binary opposition: 'magical/real.' But an oxymoron is also, as we shall see, an *economy,* in this case the economy of what certain critics have attempted to reduce to a narrative technique, to explain away as Otherness or political allegory or a naive 'nativism' the movement of a literature which, as I will explain shortly, is not apprehended by a neocolonial desire that lies latent in Western practices of reading and classifying texts. "Magical realism," then, emerges as a Eurocentric attempt to apprehend within a Western criticism—and to graft a Western ontology upon—a body of texts that continually exceeds and escapes it. "Magical realism," then, is the mark of both a desire and its frustration. 'To be,' if we remember the Hegelian definition of the subject as that which can apprehend its Other as its own; 'to be,' then, = 'to have,' to *overtake,* appropriation of a literature as the colonial symptom of an imaginary (in the Lacanian sense) relation—the desire to apprehend, to consume or overtake on the way to, and in the name of, a 'higher unity,' the illusion of a transcendental totality that variously calls itself 'comparative literature' or 'world literature' or 'the Western Canon.' And the insiduous movement of this dialectic of mastery can take unawares even those who would question its validity; Carpentier's prologue, despite its critique of a European-imposed totality, is itself caught up in its relation of mastery: the 'Third World' author as interceding author-*ity,* interpreting for a mostly Western readership the "marvelous reality" of Haiti: the Other-as-travelogue. To better see this point we might turn to the Derridean critique of "the Preface," which reduced to analogy would look something like this: 'preface/text' = 'signifier/signified,' which for Derrida is the movement of the Hegelian *Aufhebung (relève).*[3] I will return to this point in the next section.

I will begin with Carpentier's article, the prologue to his novel *El reino de este mundo.*[4] Carpentier's prologue proposes the term *lo real maravilloso* (marvelous reality) to counter the more common (then as now) "magical realism." Carpentier posits "marvelous reality" as a radical alterity that continually exceeds and escapes its neocolonial signifier: "magical realism" on the one hand as an unwitting oxymoron, a contradictory coherence, and "marvelous reality" on the other as a knowing or self-aware paradox: a reality *of* marvels that always slips beyond its imposed-from-without boundaries.

I will begin with the prologue's opening paragraph, in which Carpentier remarks on his travels in Haiti:

> A fines del año 1943 tuve la suerte de poder visitar el reino de Henri Christophe—las ruinas, tan poéticas, de Sans-Souci, la mole, imponente-

> mente intacta a pesar de rayos y terremotos, de la Ciudadela La Ferrière—y de conocer la todavía normanda Ciudad del Cabo—el Cap Français de la antigua colonia—, donde una calle de larguísimos balcones conduce al palacio de cantería habitado antaño por Paulina Bonaparte. *Después de sentir el nada mentido sortilegio de las tierras de Haití, de haber hallado advertencias mágicas en los caminos rojos de la Meseta Central, de haber oído los tambores del Petro y del Rada,* me vi llevado a acercar la maravillosa realidad recién vivida a la agotante pretensión de suscitar lo maravilloso que caracterizó a ciertas literaturas europeas de estos últimos treinta años. Lo maravilloso, buscado através de los viejos clisés de la selva de Brocelianda, de los Caballeros de la Mesa Redonda, del encantador Merlín y del ciclo de Arturo. Lo maravilloso, pobremente sugerido por los oficios y deformidades de los personajes de feria—no se cansarán los jovenes poetas franceses de los fenómenos y payasos de la *fête foraine*, de los que ya Rimbaud se había despedido en su Alquimia del Verbo? Lo maravilloso, obtenido con trucos de prestidigitación, reuniéndose objetos que para nada suelen encontrarse: la vieja y embustera historia del encuentro fortuito del paraguas y de la máquina de coser sobre una mesa de disección, generador de las cucharas de armiño, los caracoles en el taxi pluvioso, la cabeza del león en la pelvis de una viuda, de las exposiciones surrealistas. O, todavia, lo maravilloso literario: el rey de la *Julieta* de Sade, el supermacho de Jarry, el monje de Lewis, la utilería escalofriante de la novela negra inglesa: fantasmas, sacerdotes emparedados, licantropías, manos clavadas sobre la puerta de un castillo. (AC 1–2, emphasis added)[5]

In this passage, Carpentier explains that he has settled upon the term "marvelous reality" after *"experiencing the very real sorcery of the lands of Haiti, having witnessed magical symbols . . . having heard the drums"* along the riverbanks. And so already, this claim to a firsthand experience (and thus author*ity*, an authority to represent: to speak for) begs the question: What is this if not a Third World cosmopolitan's encounter with an irreducible alterity, an entity not apprehendable, not subject to the sublations of a Western desire to know. The landscape resists this attempted *Aufhebung;* it is not contained within the rigors of the close reading or any other more-or-less naive move to capture it within a system of representation. Analogous to Carpentier's position here, although not entirely so (Carpentier being, of course, much less shocked or paralyzed by what he sees; he is thus better able to articulate Haiti's irreducible difference) is Marlow's position in *Heart of Darkness*: both are faced with a reality—for Carpentier a "marvelous reality," for Marlow/Kurtz "The horror! The horror!"—that is simply not apprehendable or comprehensible in the terms of a simple overtaking.[6]

Carpentier also refers in this first paragraph to "ruins," the "still-Norman," and other architectural residues/scars of "the ancient colony" (at one point referring to Cap Haitien by its erstwhile colonial name: "the Cap Français of the ancient colony"), while simultaneously speaking of the country's "marvelous reality" as, for him, "recently experienced." The allusion is twofold: (1) to elements of Haitian culture that—however many and systematic the attempts to obliterate them—remain, having withstood in an apparently passive, almost stoic manner the invasions and violent superimpositions that are always part of the imperialist mission (and not just cultural, institutional ones; these are not mere metaphors, for who knows, even now, how many grand old colonial-era Catholic churches in Mexico—built largely by indigenous hands—were built directly—*strategically*—upon the ruins of Aztec temples and other places of worship? It would be prudent in this context to remember Frantz Fanon's assertion that "[a] national culture under colonial domination is a contested culture whose destruction is sought in systematic fashion"[7]); and (2) to the fact that these cultural elements not only survive but do so *beyond the grasp of the Western observer's understanding,* and thus beyond assimilation. For all Carpentier's talk of "sorcery" and "magical symbols," any real understanding, and therefore any apprehension within a Western cultural taxonomy, of Haiti's "marvelous reality" remains beyond his grasp, as distant as the sound of the drums along the river.

Carpentier goes on to compare Haiti's "marvelous reality" to the "marvelous element that has characterized certain European literatures of the past 30 years," specifically citing "the old clichés of the forests of Britain, of the knights of the Round Table," of Merlin and King Arthur, dismissing these and other examples in terms such as "poorly suggested," "tricks of sleight-of-hand," and "surrealist expositions"; he also includes narrative devices of the English Gothic novel: "ghosts, ministers entombed behind stone walls, werewolves, mysterious hands knocking on a castle door." For Carpentier this is all sham, a cheap, contrived imitation of what he posits as "real" marvels and a parasitic appropriation by Western literatures of what he considers, because of his privileging of his own discourse of "experience," of one who may bear expert witness in the manner of an authority, the "very real" marvels of Haiti. It is crucial to Carpentier's argument here that his readers understand that "Haiti" represents not only the geographical/cultural/and so forth, space of a particular island nation-state, but by a series of metaphoric displacements becomes an index for the whole of the Caribbean, indeed of the non-Western or 'Third World.' And that these, too, in turn come to be read in this manner, and so on, so that Carpentier's opposition of the terms 'Europe/Haiti' comes by this process of associations and displacements to signify 'Europe [Old World]/America [New World].' But this is, as we know, never such a simple matter as all that; for we must remember that Marlow has seen, has 'witnessed' too, and yet delivers a narration remarkable precisely for its epistemological *limits*, in short, for what it does not, cannot tell us about "The horror! The horror!" All of which yet again places the text, however fiercely it champions its cause, in a deconstructive moment or double bind: (1) on the one hand, this privileging of the "very real" marvels of Haiti over the "poorly suggested ones" of European arts and literatures perpetuates the opposition, with its chain of infinitely substitutable signifiers and signifieds (in itself a relation of hegemony, of mastery) of Self and Other in the very act of reversing it, with the previously dominant culture now cast in the role of dependent. González Echevarria has also noted this problematic gesture in Carpentier's prefaces:

> To assume that the marvelous exists only in America is to adopt a spurious European perspective, since it is only from the other side that alterity and difference may be discovered. . . . [I]t may very well be that magic is on this side, but we have to see it from the other side to see it as magic. (RGE 128)

It is not at all difficult, in this context, to recognize Carpentier's positing of the marvelous as an exclusively American category as a gesture of *legitimation*, with the problem of its corresponding and implicit (and naively causal) notion of an originary state of the Other's pristine (because 'uncivilized') 'purity' and its subsequent dissolution at the hands of the 'sophisticated' colonizer; and (2) on the other hand, this gesture is rendered doubly problematic by Carpentier's own position as one of what Timothy Brennan calls "Third World cosmopolitans," writers who occupy an inwardly split, interstitial position between Western and 'Third World' cultures.[8]

The imaginary relation between a sophisticated, knowing colonizer and an innocent, uncivilized other goes back at least as far as Columbus's so-called discovery of the New World, as even a cursory of ships' logs from the first voyage will reveal. Columbus's positing of the newly acquired lands as markers of a pristine 'innocence' and 'purity' emerges most pointedly when one takes into account the overwhelming number of references is the text to the people and landscape in precisely such terms. I will cite only three of a great many such statements:

> [*Tuesday, 6 November 1492*] All that these people have they will give for a very ridiculous price; they gave one great basket of cotton for the end of a leather strap. *These people are free from evil and war*. All the men and women are as naked as their mothers bore them. It is true that the women wear a cotton swatch only large enough to cover their private parts and no more. *They are modest, nevertheless*. . . .

> [*Sunday, 11 November 1492*] I see and know that these people have no religion whatever, nor are they idolaters, but rather, *they are very meek and know no evil.* They do not kill or capture others and are without weapons. They are so timid that a hundred of them flee from one of us, even if we are merely teasing. They are very trusting; they believe that there is a God in Heaven, and they firmly believe that we come from Heaven. . . .
>
> [*Tuesday, 27 November 1492*] As I went along the river *it was marvelous to see the forests and greenery, the very clear water, the birds, and the fine situation,* and I almost did not want to leave this place. I told the men with me that, in order to make a report to the Sovereigns of the things they saw, a thousands would not be sufficient to tell it, nor my hand to write it, *for it looks like an enchanted land. . . .*[9]

I have emphasized the points in these passages where Columbus articulates this imaginary relation of knowing other and innocent indigenes that goes on to become such an immanent element in colonial discourses of the next five hundred years. Two prevalent characteristics of such discourses are already evident in Columbus's logs: (1) the description of both the land and its inhabitants by a series of signifiers that are finally reducible to the category of the 'unspoiled,' a term that operates both literally and metaphorically; and (2) the ambivalence of the colonizer at the implicit realization that the process of "civilizing" the natives will irreversibly alter their pristine state, that in short, it is the knowing, decadent colonizer that comes to "spoil" the indigenous idyll. Whether and to what extent such early manifestations of colonial guilt are presciently symptomatic of what is to some—of what the colonizer knows will be done to the colonized in the name of "civilization"—is a question that is beyond the scope of the present chapter. More to the point here is that in each of these passages, the claim of the other's 'innocence' works to reveal the precise contents and extent of the colonizer's barely repressed (for now) desire for, respectively, the indigenes' bodies (particularly the women's), their recognition of the colonizers' authority, their land, all desires which, as we know all too well, were acted upon not long thereafter. Carpentier's opposition of a genuine, unselfconscious reality of marvels in America to the contrived, cultivated marvels of a European surrealist painting or an English Gothic novel thus retains the traces, however sublimated by way of the most labyrinthine of cultural displacements, of an entire history of mastery and cultural domination.

Carpentier's own position as "Third World cosmopolitan," an interstitial translator between cultures, further complicates his gesture of championing an 'authentic' American marvelous over a European artifice of marvels. Here Carpentier fills, despite himself, a role analogous to that of Said's Orientalist: that of an expert faced with the task of interpreting the object of study for a largely Western audience, a task simultaneously limited and enabled by his own relation to—and distance from—the cultures among/between which he operates.[10] Thus Carpentier's well-intentioned intervention on behalf of a misrepresented and marvelous 'Third World' reality is itself caught up in the conventions of appropriation, desire, and mastery.

As my remarks here are intended as an introduction to other texts, and thus as preliminary ones, I will limit my comments here to one more significant moment in Carpentier's prologue, this one in the closing paragraph:

> Sin habérmelo propuesto de modo sistemático, el texto que sigue ha respondido a este orden de preocupaciones. En él se narra una sucesión de hechos extraordinarios, ocurridos en la isla de Santo Domingo, en determinada época que no alcanza el lapso de una vida humana, dejándose que lo maravilloso fluya libremente de una realidad estricta mente seguida en todos sus detalles. Porque es menester advertir que el relato que va a leerse ha sido establecido sobre una documentación extremadamente rigurosa que no solamente respeta la verdad histórica de los acontecimientos, los nombres de personajes—incluso secundarios—, de lugares y hasta de calles, sino que oculta, bajo su aparente intemporalidad, un minucioso cotejo de fechas y de cronologías. Y sin embargo, por la dramática singularidad de los acontecimientos, por la fantástica apostura de los personajes que se encontraron, en determinado momento, en la encrucijada mágica de la Ciudad del Cabo, *todo resulta maravilloso en una historia imposible de situar en Europa, y que es tan real, sin embargo, como cualquier suceso ejemplar de los consignados, para pedagógica edificación, en los manuales escolares.* Pero qué es la historia de América toda sino una crónica de lo real-maravilloso?[11] (AC 5–6, emphasis added)

Carpentier's insistence that despite the "fantastic nature" of events, his novel is based on "extremely rigorous documentation" that "respects the historical truth" of events and characters ("even secondary ones"); he further defends the text as a "meticulously detailed assemblage of dates and chronologies. Yet despite this, Carpentier finally (and inevitably) relents, calling his novel a "magical history" which, for all its historical veracity, "would be impossible to situate in Europe," yet is as historically "real" as any other historically based narrative, as real, he claims, "as any successive chronicle consigned, for pedagogic edification, to the scholarly journals." Again, the deconstructive moment or double bind emerges as Carpentier would have it both ways: in his intermediary position as a Caribbeanist authority having to intercede, interpret, and translate an exoticized "magical" culture for an audience alien to it, he presents Haiti as an object both worthy of scholarly study and beyond it, both within and without his grasp possible and impossible to understand and apprehend as a knowledge (*Logos*). Here again is the slippage to which I had earlier alluded: the irregular and diversified movements of a literature (which is to say a group of texts or knowledges) which both exceeds and escapes the impositions of a critical discourse that would strive to know it—to reconcile its difference with what is already known as 'literature,' to apprehend and retrieve its radical difference and return it to the Western reader—thanks in no small measure to the intercession of the interstitial 'Third World' critic, whose erudition helps to render the exotic text palatable to domestic tastes—as the known. To read the history of "magical realism" in this way is to read an entire history of colonial and neocolonial desire, of nativist interpretation, the allegory of an ever more subtle and elaborate mastery.

But what is there, then, about the "marvelous reality" of a text that refuses to allow itself to be situated or captured in such a manner, *staged,* one might say, in or by this Europocentric desire? What would the reading of such texts, with their insistence on narrating worlds neither governed by the cultural imperatives of Western rationality nor dismissable as mere fabulation or exoticism, contribute to the study of postcolonial literatures? It is with these and related questions in mind that we will turn to two texts widely privileged as being representative of the best of this "marvelous" literature, this literature of marvels.

II

> Poetas y mendigos, músicos y profetas, guerreros y malandrines, todas las creaturas de aquella realidad desaforada hemos tenido que pedirle muy poco a la imaginación, porque el desafío mayor para nosotros ha sido la insuficiencia de los recursos convencionales para hacer creíble nuestra vida. Este es, amigos, el nudo de nuestra soledad.[12]

"This, friends, is the crux of our solitude": so Gabriel García Márquez says to his audience in his Nobel acceptance speech, from which I cite the epigraph. The phrase speaks of a crux, which is also a knot,[13] a hindrance; but García Márquez is singular in his emphasis on *this* crux, *this* one, which is the knot of 'our' solitude. And this 'our'? It is part of a predicate which speaks of a solitude, one that belongs to an 'us'; and because the phrase is part of a spoken address, a speech delivered before an audience, there is also an implicit 'you' to which this solitude does not belong, and to whom the speaker can only metaphorically, incompletely explain his solitude. Already, this contrived situation, this staging of an acceptance speech for that most European of literary prizes, the Nobel, awarded to a non-European, unveils an alterity, an unreachable entity: "Look, see here," the Latin American writer seems to be telling the Award Committee, "this is our solitude, which you would know but cannot."[14] Certainly the writer's statement begs the question of the Award Committee's credibility; they have, after all, chosen to award this literary prize based on the assumption that, as discerning, discriminating readers, they *do* understand, have mastered, the complexities of this writer's texts. But no, the Latin American writer says to the European Award Committee: you don't get it. Thus emerges again, as in Conrad, the Heideggerian moment of *Lichtung:* not a revealing or enlightenment *Aufklärung,* but the always uneasy moment of *unconcealment;* the knowledge of that which, as in the "heart of darkness," is not to be illuminated.[15]

But to return to this predicate, which speaks of solitude in the present of the verb 'to be' ("This, friends, is. . . ."): although this 'you' to which the predicate speaks immediately belongs to the time of the moment of the speech, back 'then' in 1982, to members of a physical audience, we as Western readers as nevertheless also part of this 'you' to which the Nobel laureate (half-mockingly, but not without a certain wistfulness) speaks of an ontological state irreducibly alien: to know another's solitude? How is it that we are already being spoken to, before our arrival or being-present *(Gegenwart):* How are we already being apparently both discouraged from and seduced into wanting to understand the crux, the tangled "knot," of the other's solitude? What is it that the writer of this "exotic" literature, this literature of magic and marvels, is asking us as its readers to do, think, and feel? Perhaps that we not foreclose on the text's messages, that we allow its textuality of difference to speak and be heard on its own difficult, impertinent terms. It is with this structure of reading in mind, this task of reading otherness that promises no final felicitous union but holds out unerringly for its own radical difference

The events in *Cien años de soledad* take place in a world utterly alien to its Western readers, a world of prophesies and magic carpets, and levitating priests and cursed children born with pig's tails. This, for García Márquez, is the crux of so-called magical realism: the movement of a literature that arrives as almost pure alterity, so beyond the grasp of the most radical European fictions that it must be singled out. And given a name: "for our problem has been a lack of conventional means to make our lives believable." And so the rendering of a history, the narration of a history of solitude, begins. And we begin to read:

> Muchos años despues, frente al pelotón de fusilamiento, el coronel Aureliano Buendía había de recordar aquella tarde remota en que su padre lo llevó a conocer el hielo.[16]

"Many years later . . . remember that distant afternoon. . . ." Already an alterity, something to 'understand': a time out of order, so to speak, a time that is clearly not our time, not present to us as such *(Anwesen)*. It is the mark of this "magical" literature, this writing-of-the-other-who-will-not-be-absorbed, to efface itself temporally, that is, to exceed and escape from its very first words the bounds of the linear narrative, of the tyranny of a certain rigid temporality. What many readers interpret as a mere blurring or "distortion of traditional time/space boundaries"[17]—which is already an imposition, the betrayal of a desire to apprehend within "traditional" (Western canonical) boundaries of the literary—can be more tellingly read as the movement of an alterity, of an-other textuality that arrives when it will, beyond the grasp of a criticism bent on knowledge, on mastery of the text.

A text, then, which effaces itself as it is written, and certainly as it is read: Many years later . . . Colonel Aureliano Buendía was to remember that distant afternoon. . . ." An effacement, even a denial, of the infinitive 'to be,' to be present, of anything, in short, which would allow us to locate the text in anything like a 'here and now.' Within a single remarkable opening sentence we may read the span of a lifetime, from a child's memory to an adult's mortal peril. What would it mean to read such a sentence critically, then, to aspire to pick up the 'right signals' from a narrator in order to produce an interpretation? And what would be asked of us in such a project of reading: Are we to abandon our Western prejudices and give ourselves entirely over to the "magical realist" illusion (the other-as-fantasy, a world of colorful but irrelevant "magic" or "marvels" or "exotica"), or rather should we aspire in our reading to a certain 'disinterestedness,' an illusion of critical impartiality or distance from the object of scrutiny, what one critic has condescendingly called "a mixed reaction of sympathy and comic detachment"?[18] Neither course is finally adequate; this distinction between dogmas however, is nevertheless significant as we begin to glimpse a similar polarization among the characters in the novel; that is, between those characters who live naively in a magical world that ultimately consumes them, and those who nurture links, however tenuous, to an outside (modern, Western) world and escape the cataclysm that befalls Macondo and the Buendías. That such a reading perpetuates the binary model by which texts of so-called magical realism (and to a large degree, postcolonial texts in general) are read and ignorantly judged, on the one hand the belief in magic, a dead nostalgia;[19] on the other, notions of linearity and progress, especially as concerns the construction of a history, the colonial fantasy of 'innocence/sophistication' (as just discussed), 'Magic/Reason,' and so on, should not surprise anyone. And while we are faced with a narrative in which the recourse to such oppositional logics is ceaselessly frustrated and questioned,[20] *Cien años de soledad*'s narrator is clearly a distanced observer, viewing the "magical" folk-beliefs of the characters from his 'First World' perspective, the narrator-as-anthropologist, whose discourse is always privileged, always inscribed more-or-less violently as difference. González Echevarria comments at length on precisely this kind of problematic relationship between the Latin American novel and the discourses of anthropology:

> The truth-bearing document the novel imitates is the anthropological or ethnographic report. The object of such studies is to discover the origin or source of a culture's own version of its values, beliefs, and history through a culling and retelling of its myths. Readers of anthropology are aware that in order to understand another cuulture, the anthropologist has to understand his [*sic*] own *to the point where he can distance himself from it,* and in a sense disappear in the discourse of method. Distancing, a process whose counterpoint can only be found in modern literature, *involves a kind of self-effacement.*[21]

For both the anthropologist and the "anthropological novel," then, this is precisely the point of the narration: the representation of a culture and the self-effacement of the mediating figure, constructed as an "objective"opposition of cultures, most often in the form of an "our" culture and an "other" culture. González Echevarria cites Lévi-Strauss's *Tristes Tropiques* as an especially illustrative discussion of this kind of self-effacing movement of the anthropologist; and Jacques Derrida also comments extensively in *Of Grammatology* on the writings of Lévi-Strauss in particular and European anthropology in general (*OG* 101–140).

Read within this context, then, the choices of a writer carry implications, bring consequences: to narrate in this particular way and not another, to begin the novel with these events and leave those for later (or not at all). García Márquez's decision to begin *Cien años de soledad* with the gypsy's visits and Jose Arcadio Buendía's journey into the swamp, then, tell us less about Macondo than about what he would have us know of it. And again, there emerges in this most basic of narrative decisions, one that all writers have to make but that is complicated by the interstitial position of a writer astride two cultures: what and how much to tell a Western audience of a Latin American novel, how best to narrate a reality that runs the risk at every turn of being mistaken for the merely fantastic. It is again the insoluble double-bind of the "Third World cosmopolitan": to write in the name of an other and be othered oneself, to write in the spaces in between.

Jose Arcadio Buendía's search for "civilization" is the text's first major reinforcement of the 'Magic/Reason' opposition (which we might also write as 'nature/culture'); convinced that Macondo suffers from its isolation, Buendía and his men set out to establish contact with the outside world, only to be nearly overwhelmed by the strange, the exotic, or "primal":

> Luego, durante más de diez dias, no volvieron a ver el sol. El suelo se volvio blando y húmedo, como ceniza volcánica, y la vegetación fue cada vez más insidiosa y se hicieron cada vez más lejanos los gritos de los pájaros y la bullaranga de los monos, y el mundo se volvió triste para siempre. Los hombres de la expedición se sintieron abrumados por sus recuerdos más antiguos en aquel paraíso de humedad y silencio, anterior al pecado original, donde las botas se hundían en pozos de aceites humeantes y los machetes destrozaban lirios sangrientos y salamandras doradas. Durante una semana, casi sin hablar, avanzaron como sonámbulos por un universo de pesadumbre, alumbrados apenas por una tenue reverberación de insectos luminosos y con los pulmones agobiados por un sofocante olor de sangre. No podían regresar, porque la trocha que iban abriendo a su paso se volvía a cerrar en poco tiempo, con una vegetación nueva que casi veían crecer ante sus ojos. <No importa—decia Jose Arcadio Buendía—. Lo esencial es no perder la orientación.>[22]

The most striking thing in this passage, more remarkable than the narrative description of the scene itself, more stunning than the ashen ground, or the supernatural vegetation growing before the men's eyes, more disorienting than even the visceral encounter with "luminous insects" and the "suffocating smell of blood," more remarkable than any of this is the rhythm with which it is all narrated, and the release of tension that comes with Buendía's authorizing statement; it is a narration by accumulation, with item after item of the most alien sensory stimuli imaginable, until Buendía breaks the narrative spell, releases us from its grip, with an astonishing nonchalance: "It's all right . . . [t]he main thing is not to lose our bearings." Buendía's reaction to his surroundings (It's all right") fails to indicate that there is anything at all extraordinary happening. When later in that same journey, "surrounded by ferns and palm trees, white and powdery in the silent morning light,"[23] Buendía and his men find a Spanish galleon, no one seems particularly shocked; no one, in fact, thinks to even ask how a Spanish warship got that far inland.

With no indication from characters that anything fantastic is happening, and in the absence of an authoritative narrator—an interpreting "Latin Americanist" who would translate this other's world *à la* Said's Orientalist—the Western reader[24] is left to assume that these events are simply reasonable within the context of the narrative, that such events are reasonable *for the characters who populate the world of the text.* And a certain critique of "magical realism," let us call it a 'formalist' one for lack of a more useful description, would leave it at that, would find it sufficient to say: "The reader is *defamiliarized,* is rendered unable, because of certain narrative techniques, to make any automatic assumptions about this text or its events." This type or method of theoretical approach to "magical realism," which has enjoyed something of a vogue in recent years, is based on the Russian formalist notion of defamiliarization *(ostranenie),* originally coined by Victor Shklovsky in the famous essay "Art as Technique." The idea, as developed by Shklovsky, is to do away with habitual or "automatic" perception, the reliance on stock, time-worn images or symbols, in favor of a rigorous and ceaseless analysis of "the characteristic thought processes compounded from words." The desired result, of course, is to generate new interpretations, new significations: as Shklovsky would have it, to once again "make the stone stony."

But although this is, to be sure, a vast improvement over the poetic simplicities of the Russian Symbolist school (with the image as fixed, as "far clearer than what it clarifies"), it still belies certain assumptions regarding relations with others and the relations of such relations in general.[25] Such a critical framework also begs the question: What exactly is this 'defamiliarization'—what can we say is its *referrent?* Its prefix 'de-' signifies reversal, an undoing of the root word. This is clearly not the same, then, as simply being *un*-familiar with a given object; the word's very structure, then, denotes a reversal—more an *erasing* of familiarity or knowledge. The thing in question, then, has escaped our grasp—it is no longer known to us, in the same way that a tamed circus animal is no longer considered a known quantity when it escapes from its bounds, and is suddenly considered dangerous. But what can it mean to 'reverse' an act of cognition, of knowing? If we have learned anything from Freud and psychoanalysis, it is that forgetting is a myth of the mind, that one never 'forgets' anything:

> Since the time when we recognized the error of supposing that ordinary forgetting signified destruction or annihilation of the memory-trace, we have been inclined to the opposite view that *nothing once formed in the mind could ever perish, that everything survives in some way or other, and is capable under certain conditions of being brought to light again,* as for instance, when regression extends back far enough.[26]

If, however, we take such criticism at its word when it declares its intention to interrogate "the characteristic thought structures compounded from words" (VS 151), then our inquiry takes on a different set of possibilities: 'defamiliarization' thus becomes a critique of the signified itself, or rather of its relation to a given signifier. We are 'defamiliarized' precisely because of the inadequacy of a given structure, a given signifier, to apprehend what is happening, or rather because the signifier does not correspond to anything that we would identify as an appropriate signified. Thus the term 'magical realism' represents the mark or space of a confrontation with a literature that would exceed and escape, which would be known to us only as 'alterity,' as other. Subsequent encounters with "fantastic" events in the text bring us no closer, and arguably distance us further: the epidemic of amnesia, Remedios the Beauty's ascension, the various ghosts and specters that populate the pages of the novel—all events revealed or cleared *(Lichtung)* but not illuminated *(Aufklarung)*, glimpsed but not understood, all signs of an encounter with otherness.

A further glimpse of this arrival of an other, this unveiling that paradoxically distances as it reveals, is Jose Arcadio Buendía's "discovery" of ice. We are confronted with a description as mystifying as the object is to the character:

> Al ser destapado por el gigante, el cofre dejó escapar un aliento glacial. Dentro sólo había un enorme bloque transparente, con infinitas agujas internas en las cuales se despedazaba en estrellas de colores la claridad del crepúsculo.[27] (*100Y* 74)

Read outside the context of the novel this would seem to be an intelligible enough, if not exactly straightforward, description of ice: "glacial exhalation . . . enormous, transparent block". And it would take very little to show that, even after reading descriptions of mystical gypsies and alchemy experiments in a prehistoric world in which "many things lacked names"[28] (100y 11), despite whatever blurring of binary oppositions might be taking place ('real/fantastic,' Magic/Reason,' and so on)—that is, despite our so-called defamiliarization, our privileged position as readers who assumedly know what ice is gives us, unlike the character, the ability to recognize the mysterious object as ice. And this knowledge clearly creates an irreducible distance between reader and character that makes it impossible for us to share the latter's magical perception of the object; we simply know too much to believe such a thing, and it is precisely this knowledge, that is, this body of knowledges and of contexts that constitutes each of us as a Western (or at least Western-informed) reader, which renders us unable to share the character's magical worldview. Our relation with the character, then, is one of *distance* and *alterity*.

After the gypsy's comic disclosure, moreover, we can read even more clearly the text's sense of distance, of irreducible alterity. Arcadio Buendía's declaration that the ice is "the great invention of our time"[29] (100y 26) is believable to the degree that it is mimetically credible for a character who has just discovered ice to feel that way. But again we cannot share in that response, because the gypsy's correction illustrates all too clearly the chasm between Buendía's awestruck innocence and our own privileged, more informed position. Remedios the Beauty's ascension into heaven works in much the same way; although the town's inhabitants (and those readers entirely receptive of the text's "magic" at the expense of its "realism") may believe it to be true, our response as Western-informed readers would likely be analogous to the town's "outsiders," who "thought that Remedios the Beauty had finally succumbed to her irrevocable fate of a queen bee"[30] (100y 223)—and for a similar reason: our status as outsiders, with a corresponding knowledge of worlds and contexts outside the confines of Macondo, makes us supposedly less susceptible to such tales of magical ascensions.

And yet such a naively oppositional interpretation of events serves only to further obfuscate matters, to further perpetuate the radical alterity of our relation to the characters; it also limits our ability to read beyond that alterity and toward other possibilities. I am reminded of the comical but telling contextualization of Remedios's "ascension" related to me by a colleague at a Mexican university; according to the anecdote, it was once quite common among Mexican families whose daughters had eloped or otherwise run off (or had become pregnant and been quietly sent off to a convent) to tell the neighbors that she had bodily ascended into heaven, thus saving the family honor with a minimum of explanation. This tactic was apparently not without its risks, however, as the reappearance of the daughter in question was a possibility to be dreaded indeed.[31]

Aside from its comic value, of course, the anecdote illustrates the very slippery nature of reading the "marvelous" events in this and other texts of so-called magical realism, and especially the dangers of reading such events and texts as merely and oppositionally counterfactual. This reading of alterity is, I would argue, largely an analysis of misrecognitions of various sorts—a reading composed of recognitions-of-misrecognitions, as it were—a game that becomes obvious only once it's pointed out. Once read in this way, however, the act of reading moves beyond the simple opposition of '(active) representer/ (passive) represented' to become *play,* the playing-out of a game of masks, of mirrors: the uncanny *(Unheimlich)* sensation of simultaneously reading-and-being-read, the glimpsing behind the mask of the-other-who-reads-and-is-conscious-of-being-read, which sees us in the act of seeing and is an agent of its own representation.

Having said all that, however, we must return to the recognition of this distance between knowledge; that is, between the knowledge of the text's characters and those of the Western-informed readers and narrator. This distinction is perhaps best illustrated by the arrival of the railway in Macondo, and the characters' reactions to advancements that we take for granted (although of course there was once a time when we, too, shared the Macondans' astonishment at such things, and we live even now in a world where we are daily confronted with such "marvels" as genetic engineering, or manned space-stations).

It is certainly an exasperated and bewildered group of inhabitants that witnesses the introduction of such "marvels" as the cinema, telephone, and phonograph:

> Era como si Dios hubiera resuelto poner a prueba toda capacidad de asombro, y mantuviera a los habitantes de Macondo en un permanente vaivén entre el alborozo y el desencanto, la duda y la revelación, hasta el extremo de que ya nadie podía saber a ciencia cierta dónde estaban los límites de la realidad.[32] (*100Y* 268)

To return to the (somewhat insufficient) term introduced earlier, it is now the characters, the inhabitants of the town, who seem to be thus 'defamiliarized,' as they can no longer distinguish between natural and supernatural events in their own lives; having been denied what Arcadio Buendía calls "the benefits of science"[33] (100y 21), and their only previous exposure to the outside world having come through the gypsies, it is perhaps not surprising for native Macondans to regard the new arrivals as somehow magical. And yet we must wonder just what it is that Buendía posits as "the benefits of science"; that is, what kind of 'civilized' and 'civilizing' discourses are being privileged by his anguished lament. Let us remember that Buendía and his party embark on a journey *in search of civilization,* in the name of knowledge, of science; and that before this expedition their only contact with these discourses come through Melquíades and the other gypsies. Does this not mean that, as this text constructs them, these 'civilizing' discourses are always located elsewhere, and thus that they are the exclusive property and domain of another more 'civilized' culture? Read in this way, we can begin to see the most profound and naive Eurocentrism at work, latent in Buendía, in his aspirations, his journey, and his dealings with the gypsies (agents of progress that he perceives them to be).

And yet it is Buendía's uncritical embrace of scientific and pseudoscientific discourses that makes the townspeople's later examination and rejection of Western advancements all the more significant. Rather than perpetuate Buendía's stance as a passive receptacle of science, the Macondans who encounter these "marvels" of the West emerge as active readers and interpreters of their (and our) culture. And although they are understandably awestruck at their first encounter with such items as electric light bulbs and telephones, they are also able, as exemplified in this astonishing passage, to adopt an interpretive and *critical* attitude toward other such developments:

> Se indignaron con las imágenes vivas que el próspero comerciante don Bruno Crespi proyectaba en el teatro con taquillas de bocas de león, porque un personaje muerto y sepultado en una película, y por cuya des-

> gracia se derramaron lágrimas de aflicción, reapareció vivo y convertido en árabe en la película siguiente. El público que pagaba dos centavos para compartir las vicisitudes de los personajes, no pudo soportar aquella burla inaudita y rompió la silletería. El alcalde, a instancias de don Bruno Crespi, explicó mediante un bando que el cine era una máquina de ilusión que no merecía los desbordamientos pasionales del público. *Ante la desalentadora explicación, muchos estimaron que habían sido víctimas de un nuevo y aparatoso asunto de gitanos, de modo que optaron por no volver al cine,* considerando que ya tenían desventuras de seres imaginarios. Algo semejante occurrió con los gramófonos de cilindros que llevaron las alegres matronas de Francia en sustitución de los anticuados organillos, y que tan hondamente afectaron por un tiempo los intereses de la banda de músicos. Al principio, la curiosidad multiplicó la clientela de la calle prohibida, y hasta se supo de señoras respetables que se disfrazaron de villanos para observar de cerca la novedad del gramófono, *pero tanto y de tan cerca lo observaron, que muy pronto llegaron a la conclusión de que no era un molino de sortilegio, como todos pensaban y como las matronas decían, sino un truco mecánico que no podía compararse con algo tan conmovedor, tan humano y tan lleno de verdad cotidiana como una banda de músicos.* Fue una desilusión tan grave, que cuando los gramófonos se popularizaron hasta el punto de que hubo uno en cada casa, todavía no se les tuvo como objetos para entretenimiento de adultos, sino como una cosa buena para que la destriparan los niños.[34] (*100Y* 267–268, emphasis added)

A moment beyond opposition, beyond simple reciprocation or mutual misunderstanding, here are the objects, the artifacts of a modern Western civilization being encountered, warily approached, carefully examined, and critiqued by an ostensibly naive, unsophisticated other who assumedly lacks the skills of interpretation and reason *(Logos)* to undertake such an impertinent, interrogative project—skills that are associated with, are the very requisites of, the privileged scientific discourses that they have been denied. Thus again emerges the deconstructive moment: to feel the interrogating gaze of subjects never recognized as such, to be seen in the act of seeing, to catch a glimpse of an other, who-reads-and-is-conscious-of-being-read, not a passive represented but an active interpreter of artifacts and discourses.

Further evidence of the Macondans' active engagement with the discourses of knowledge and power that swirl around them is their resistance against the town's colonio-industrial plundering at the hands of Mr. Herbert and his banana company, which comes in the form of a strike led by Arcadio Segundo. The subsequent crushing of the workers' insurrection, culminating in their massacre, is to be the final attempt at political agency by the Buendías; the massacre, and Arcadio Segundo's self-imposed exile to Melquíades's room, mark the onset of the town's terminal decline. Yet as thoroughly decimated as Macondo becomes at the hands of its colonizers, and as seemingly total their domination of the town, there is a space or index that remains beyond the grasp of the oppressors' reign of violence. It is Melquíades's room that provides for Arcadio Segundo a literal place of refuge and escape.

Read in this way, within the context of a movement that exceeds and escapes the grasp of mastery (discursive and otherwise), Melquíades's room becomes the very index of so-called magical realism, and certainly exemplifies its overdetermination and inadequacy as a critical term; the single room functions in effect as a ceaselessly floating signifier, whose signification shifts and moves with every character who encounters it. After Melquíades's death, the room stands empty and abandoned until Aureliano Segundo's curiosity leads him to unlock it; upon opening the room, he finds that "there was not the slightest trace of dust or cobwebs, with everything swept and clean, better swept and cleaner than on the day of the burial"[35] (100y 175–176). Ursula goes to clean the room weeks later, only to find that "there is nothing for her to do"[36] (100y 176). But the room does not appear so to everyone; to Colonel Aureliano Buendía "an unbearable smell of rotten memories floated" in the air[37] (100y 227). Fernanda del Carpio is indifferent to the room and its long history; she finds it an appropriate place to store her chamber pots, after which the room is known as 'the chamber pot room.' The colonel considers this

> el nombre más apropiado, porque mientras el resto de la familia seguía asombrándose de que la pieza de Melquíades fuera inmune al polvo y la destrucción, él la veía convertida en un muladar.[38] (*100Y* 302)

There is a further circulation or slippage of the sign "Melquíades's room" as Jose Arcadio, after his failed attempts at activism, takes refuge there. While in the room he is invisible to the soldiers who come for him; moreover, the officer who opens the door not only overlooks his quarry sitting in plain view, but sees a room completely different from the one described by the narrator on the same page. Narrator and character 'see' the room simultaneously, yet offer contradictory versions of it:

> [Narrator:] Había la misma pureza en el aire, la misma diafanidad, el mismo privilegio contra el polvo y la destrucción que conoció Aureliano Segundo en la infancia. . . . (*100Y* 349)
>
> [Officer:]—Es verdad que nadie ha estado en este cuarto por lo menos en un siglo. . . . Ahí debe haber hasta culebras—.[39] (*100Y* 349)

After escaping the soldiers, Arcadio Segundo abandons completely all notions of engagement or agency, denouncing his activist uncle the Colonel as "nothing but a faker or an imbecile"[40] (100y 289) and retreating to the solace of Melquíades's room:

> En el cuarto de Melquíades, en cambio, protegido por la luz sobrenatural, por el ruido de la lluvia, por la sensación de ser invisible, encontró el reposo que no tuvo un solo instante de su vida anterior. . . . [41] (*100Y* 349)

Melquíades's room emerges here as a sort of shelter, a refuge from enemies and the vicissitudes of an oppressive, violent history. Yet it is also more than that, and certainly more than any single description offered within the text. We could say that "Melquíades's room is the space or index in which Arcadio Segundo withdraws from the world," or "finds solace" or "takes comfort" or some such thing. And such a statement would, in the most narrowly literal of ways, be correct: Arcadio Segundo does in fact take refuge in the room, where he is "magically" delivered from his oppressors. And he does thereafter abandon all attempts at engagement with the social and political contingencies of his surroundings—or more to the point, with a Western historicist model of activism or agency. And yet: Is not a withdrawal (when successful) also an *escape?* Must withdrawal always signify defeat, the flight of neurosis from a 'real world' for which the neurotic is psychically ill-suited? Or can we, as I believe we must, read such a move toward invisibility as a strategic one, read Melquíades's room itself as a site of resistance and refuge? Certainly for the inhabitants of Macondo, to allow oneself to be labeled or 'known' in any finite way—to be associated, say, with a given politics, whether Liberal or Conservative, or a given family name, as in the Buendías—is to be marked for death; we find the clearest illustration of this in the murders of the 17 sons of Colonel Aureliano Buendía, whose killers identify them by the indelible cross of ashes on each of their foreheads (*100Y* 282–283). The classification of such a withdrawal on the part of Arcadio Segundo as a flight from rational activism and into the comforting mental constructs of the neurotic is informed indirectly by Freudian ideas about the neuroses, which has metamorphosed into the contemporary notion of mental illness as a 'flight from reality':

> The asocial nature of neuroses has its genetic origin in their most fundamental purpose, which is to take flight from an unsatisfying reality into a more pleasurable world of phantasy. The real world, which is avoided in this way by neurotics, is under the sway of human society and of the institutions created by it. To turn away from reality is at the same time to withdraw from the community of man [*sic*].[42]

This is certainly one of Freud's more concise, and hence more definitive, descriptions of the neurotic subject. Nevertheless, there are two points worth raising within the context of Melquíades's room and its occupant:

1. the circularity of Freud's model: the subject in question is neurotic because of their apparent rejection of the 'real world' as constituted by his social and cultural surroundings, and is determined to be in flight from those surroundings because he exhibits asocial symptoms of neurosis. The symptom and the diagnosis, then, are mutually determining and determined, foreclosing upon any possibility or escape; and

2. the privileging within this opposition 'real world/neurotic' of the former term as 'real,' setting in motion a socially constituted mimesis against which all who rebel are judged mentally wanting, and simultaneously denying both the status of both terms as discursive structures within a sociopolitical context *and* any claim the subject might have to critique that 'reality.' (To be fair, Freud was himself aware of the neuroses as social structures, seeing them as a deviation from, or caricature of, the social instinctual elements of a given culture.)

One need only reflect upon certain moments of recent medical history—Nazi doctors and Soviet psychiatrists diagnosing dissenters as "insane" and confining them to mental hospitals; American psychologists conducting highly questionable experiments under the auspices of the CIA; and Michel Foucault's estimable studies of the mental asylum as a place of imprisonment for the poor, the undesirable, and the politically dangerous—to begin to glimpse the more troubling implications of this model uncritically applied.[43] Read in this context, Arcadio Segundo's disappearance into Melquíades's room is not a simple matter of withdrawal from historical responsibility into a more-or-less naive or self-delusory world of magic, as would seem to be the interpretation most common among a wide range of the novel's critics;[44] it is, rather, a matter of strategy and of survival.

The last five chapters of the novel chronicle the Buendías' (and Macondo's) final retreat into invisibility, beginning with the torrential rains that last "four years, eleven months, and two days"[45] (100y 291). All attempts at historical agency or activism having invariably ended in failure, the surviving Buendías and others who escape the government's wrath now seem to have become victims of their own strategy of withdrawal. What begins as a defense against certain and violent death proves to be itself a dead-end of circularity and self-marginalization. And as Melquíades's room best represents this strategy of escape, so do Melquíades's parchments, a text of both history *and* prophesy, which contains the history of the family and the town, including their future and eventual fate, now emerge as a counterdiscourse that is deterministic and self-destructive as the imposed-from-without discourses of the town's erstwhile colonizers.

There are, however, characters who do not share the Buendías' fate, who escape the grasp of both the Banana Company and the oracular parchments of Melquíades. In the novel's penultimate chapter, as Macondo continues its apparently irrevocable slide into magical self-reference, several characters appear for the first time, among them Gabriel Márquez and the old Catalonian. The latter serves as a sort of 'anti-Melquíades' figure; the Catalonian is also an author of mysterious pages, yet his own attitude toward his text seems markedly different from the gypsy sage's: "His fervor for the written word was an interweaving of solemn respect and gossipy irreverence. Not even his own manuscripts were safe from that dualism"[46] (100y 368). But what the text calls 'dualism' is also more than that, more than a simple antithesis or alternative to Melquíades's monolithic oracle. For what is attributed to the old bookseller in this brief passage is nothing more or less that *a mode of reading,* one that moves beyond the self-referring tyranny of Melquíades's parchments and the absolute authority that Aureliano Babilonia invests in them.[47] The Catalonian's "dualism," then, is what enables him to read beyond both colonial hegemonies and self-referring parchments—and thus to escape the town's destruction.

The Catalonian is thus the first of the new group of characters to leave Macondo, and it is he who sounds the alert for others to abandon the town. Having thus awakened from "his marvelous sense of unreality"[48] (100y 370), the Catalonian explicitly rejects both the comforts of nostalgia and the magical consciousness engendered upon the town by the gypsy Melquíades. Again, it would be tempting to read this counterfactually, a simple and categorical rejection of magic in all its forms. Yet to do so would require certain presuppositions about this literature called 'magical realism' that we need hardly raise a finger to expose as mean-spirited and ignorant: that this is a literature of exhaustion or nostalgia, that memory is a mere cowardly escape from history, that desire is always and only a lapse from rationality into "unreality."[49] To read so-called magical realism in this manner is to deny the movement of a text and a literature that would escape and exceed the logics of opposition, a literature that moves beyond the structures of mere 'anti-' or 'counter-' discourses.

Other characters follow the Catalonian's lead, most notably the authorial namesake Gabriel Márquez. Aureliano Babilonia, however, never makes that escape. He is by now too attached to Amaranta Ursula, to Melquíades, and to the pronouncements of the gypsy's deterministic parchments, to measure meaning by any other than his own self-referential yardstick. Before the Catalonian's departure, Gaston correctly observes that Aureliano "did not buy the books in order to learn but to verify the truth of his knowledge, and that none of them interested them more than the parchments"[50] (100y 352). The obvious self-referentiality of Aureliano's mode of reading makes him an ideal reader—and a perfect prey—for the cataclysm that ultimately consumes his family, his text, and himself.

The novel comes to closure through the deciphering of Melquíades's parchments, specifically at the moment when Aureliano Babilonia simultaneously sees his child carried off by "all the ants in the world" and decodes the meaning of the parchments' epigraph: *"The first of the line is tied to a tree and the last is being eaten by ants"*[51] (100y 381). Consistent with not only the technique of defamiliarization that runs through the text but also the narcotic self-referentiality of Aureliano's reading, he is struck not by horror or shock but by his breakthrough of understanding the parchments[52] (100y 381). And who would argue that this mode of reading, this reading as an ultimate act of self-absorption and self-annihilation, is not in fact terribly exciting, even seductive? Are we as readers not just as absorbed by our desire to understand the parchments—to finally achieve our own *mastery* over the mysteries of the text? Are we not, as is Aureliano, concerned less with "the wrath of the biblical hurricane"[53] (100y 383) blowing outside than by the need to finish deciphering the text before us, to find the resolution and closure that we desire?

Finally, we must confront the will-to-mastery that lies latent in our own act of reading, as a compulsion to apprehend the ever-elusive object of a desire and a demand. What desire? Simply put, the desire *to know*. What demand? That the object of our scrutiny yields to us, that it neither exceeds nor escapes our gaze: in short, *that it allows itself to be known*. This is not merely the misguided reading of a character, Aureliano Babilonia's tragic flaw, and our catharsis and absolution. No, it is also the measure of our own complicity in Aureliano's reading, and the ways in which that reading becomes an allegory for an ever more elaborate mastery. Aureliano places himself at the epicenter of the parchment narrative, reading it as a preordained chain of events leading up to the fulfillment of the parchments' final prophesy:

> Sólo entonces descubrió que Amaranta Ursula no era su hermana, sino su tía, y que Francis Drake había asaltado a Riohacha solamente para que ellos pudieran buscarse por los laberintos más intrincados de la sangre, hasta engendrar el animal mitológico que había de poner término a la estirpe.[54] (*100Y* 447)

Yet this must not, as Aureliano Babilonia so fervently believes, be the only way, the only possible outcome for the only possible history of colonization and conquest and incestuous self-referentiality and death. Because the parchments of Melquíades are in fact *not* the novel *Cien años de soledad*, because Aureliano Babilonia deconstructs his own suicidal fatalism by choosing both to skip eleven pages of the parchments and to read the end—acts that are not determined by the parchments (*100Y* 447–448 and 100y 383)—we can read in the very moment of Macondo's apocalypse the mark of possibility, the movement of a text and a literature that does in fact allow for endless second opportunities on earth. We now turn to one such opening or space of such a 'second opportunity,' a text that writes and effaces a history and projects a future despite all.

III

> India, the new myth—a collective fiction in which anything was possible, a fable rivalled only by the two other mighty fantasies: money and God.[55]
>
> —Salman Rushdie, *Midnight's Children*

The events of *Midnight's Children* occur in a setting that is in many respects analogous to that of García Márquez's novel: a world in which prophesies, magic carpets, and children born with magical powers are, if not commonplace, then at least within the realm of the plausible. Saleem Sinai also presides, as does the narrator of *Cien años de soledad,* over a text that engages in a narrative technique that we have called 'defamiliarization'; in effect, the undermining and implicit interrogation of Western notions of the real. The significant differences between the respective narrators, then, is one not of function but of engagement; rather than adopt the spurious stance of the detached, objective observer, Saleem is an active participant in the events of the narrative. Saleem is, in fact, the central character in his own 'autobiographical' narrative, which is contained within the novel *Midnight's Children*. Aside from and beyond the novel's ostensible subjects, then, *Midnight's Children* is also the story of how Saleem tells his story; that is, how he sees himself in relation to an entire history of stories, generated both within and beyond the boundaries of the novel. And certainly *Midnight's Children* has been labeled variously as a 'historical novel' or 'postmodern historiography' and so on, because of its acute engagement with both a national history and the ways in which those histories are constructed and reconstructed.[56] Such assessments, however, do little to account for the movement of a text (and an entire body of such texts) that both writes and erases, posits and undermines a history of empire and postempire.

Saleem's narration pervades the text with a self-conscious anxiety that is also a sort of narcissism, which some psychoanalytic approaches to the text would consider symptomatic of full-blown paranoia;[56] he is, additionally, acutely aware of narrative techniques and of what we might call the *narrativity* of his own story and of Indian history. This dimension of Saleem's narration is already clear from the novel's opening paragraph:

> I was born in the city of Bombay . . . once upon a time. No, that won't do, there's no getting away from the date: I was born in Doctor Narlikar's Nursing Home on August 15th 1947. And the time? The time matters too. Well then: at night. No, it's important to be more. . . . On the stroke of midnight, as a matter of fact. Clock-hands joined palms in respectful greeting as I came. Oh, spell it out, spell it out: at the precise instant of India's arrival at independence, I tumbled forth into the world. There were gasps. And, outside the window, fireworks and crowds. A few seconds later, my father broke his big toe; but his accident was a mere trifle when set beside what had befallen me in the benighted moment, because thanks to the occult tyrannies of those blandly saluting clocks I had been mysteriously handcuffed to history, my destinies indissolubly chained to those of my country.[57]

Saleem hems and haws about the circumstances of his birth before finally revealing them; he is apparently preoccupied with the question of how much to tell; that is, how much he needs to tell non-Indian and other Western readers in order to illustrate the significance of his birth; Indian readers, assumedly, would not need to be told that August 15th is Indian Independence Day. But why is he so ambivalent on this point—thinking out loud, as it were, about whether to divulge what emerges as a crucial element of his own story—and why the very cryptic pronouncement that follows it? What does it mean to be "handcuffed to history"? And in what sense is this a "benighted moment," and for whom?

In the most narrowly literal sense, the adjective's meaning is clear enough: Saleem is born at night, on the stroke of midnight of India's first day as a nation-state. Yet the word carries another, more ominous signification; 'benighted' in this other sense is not a mere temporal designation, as in 'denoting nighttime,' but an *ontological* one, the index of a state of *being:* to be caught or surrounded by darkness, in a moment of moral or intellectual darkness, the very opposite of enlightenment. Read in this context, Saleem's opening revelation becomes contradictorily coherent: as in Conrad's untenable metaphor, the paradoxical illumination of darkness, less a revelation than the unveiling of that which may not be revealed: less *Aufklärung* than *Lichtung*. The narration's opening gesture, despite its carefully built-up tension and air of 'announcement,' apparently turns up empty: as in Marlow's fitful and inconclusive exposition of darkness, the opening of *Midnight's Children* paradoxically works to reveal an *absence* of clarity, the revelation of its own self-concealment and the clearing *(clarière)* of a space or index for that which cannot be revealed in its presence. Such a clearing is what Heidegger called *Lichtung,* an act of clearing or opening-up of a space in which things may be revealed in their presence *(Anwesen):*

> Speculative dialectic is a mode in which the matter of philosophy comes to appear of itself and for itself, and thus becomes present *[Gegenwart].* Such appearance necessarily occurs in luminosity. Only by virtue of some sort of brightness can what shines show itself, that is, radiate. But brightness in its turn rests upon something open, something free, which it might illuminate here and there, now and then. . . . We call this openness that grants a possible letting appear and show "clearing." *[Lichtung]*[58]

And so it is possible to read in Saleem's (and India's—more on this presently) "benighted moment" a metaphoric displacement by which a narrator's ostensible exposition is rendered untenable, almost absurd: the 'illumination' of that which remains 'benighted.' But that cannot be all. Surely the phrase "benighted moment" signifies, is a metaphoric vehicle for, *something;* and the text's inability to ultimately 'illuminate' the elusive referent is itself instructive, and not only of the limitations of a particular narrator or mode of analysis. For if what is at stake here is the question of presence, the relative credibility or instability of a text, then we must recognize that the closest thing to a credible witness remains Saleem, however reluctant his narration or ambivalent his language. Having nevertheless accepted Saleem as a "most credible witness," we still have to account for his instability—his own situatedness—as a character within the text; that is, we must determine what kind of position Saleem occupies within the novel as a narrating character, and critique rigorously the theoretical structures that would privilege him as a standard of judgment—in short, as an *authority.*

Certainly, Saleem is not the most stable of narrators; it would hardly be revelatory to say that he fulfills the modus operandi and general profile of the typical 'unreliable narrator,' as his instabilities both narrative and psychic are emphasized throughout the novel. Yet part of that instability or ongoing crisis within the text is precisely Saleem's obsessive self-reflexivity, or what we might call his 'compulsion-to-order'; he is, after all, writing a narrative of his own life (a text not to be confused with the novel *Midnight's Children,* a distinction I will discuss more fully later), and seems constantly preoccupied with his own self-positioning within that memoir, an anxiety made clear from the novel's second paragraph: "I must work fast, faster than Scheherazade, if I am to end up meaning—yes, meaning—something. I admit it: above all things, I fear absurdity" (*MC* 4). At stake, then, in Saleem's self-conscious history of India, and his significance within that history, are both (1) his reliability as a witness to important events; and (2) his *authority* to translate and/or represent those events for a largely non-Indian audience, a task which, as for Said's Orientalist, is simultaneously enabled and limited by his own relation to, and more importantly, distance from, the cultural discourses among/between which he operates. It is precisely through such self-reflexive gestures that Saleem takes on the role of unwitting Orientalist himself: his "benighted moment" takes its place alongside "the veils of an Eastern bride" and "the inscrutable Orient" as testimonials to the Western-informed scholar's inability to apprehend the Indian other (ES 222). Again, as in the earlier example of Carpentier's prologue, an authority's attempt to 'give us' an-other culture is itself caught up in the ever more elaborate trappings of mastery: the compulsion to discover, to apprehend, to know.

Clearly, Saleem's many generalizations about India, from the (admirable, he tells us) state of Indian dental hygiene to observations of old men in the pawn-shop playing hit-the-spittoon, are credible because of his own subjectivity as an Indian; he observes the culture 'firsthand,' and is immersed in a way that would be almost impossible for any Western reader. Yet that very position of the privileged observer who would study and 'translates' Indian culture and history is also what allows Saleem to assert his mastery over the object of his representation. So that when Saleem claims to be "mysteriously handcuffed to history, [his] destinies indissolubly chained to those of [his] country," the association becomes metonymic: Saleem *is* India, his narrative, life, and even body transformed into the very battleground upon which his country struggles for a future beyond empire. And when Saleem claims that he has been "buffeted by too much history" and that he is "literally disintegrating" (*MC* 37), he speaks for—*as*—a nation; but the very fact of his privileged and knowledgeable intervention also and at the same time confirms the appropriation of that nation's cultural and historical discourses within the context of his own narrative, which in turn seeks to assert its hegemony over those discourses, and by extension over the nation itself. In this claim to metacultural supremacy Saleem's text would appear to be indistinguishable from that of empire, becomes synonymous (albeit unwittingly) with an entire machinery of domination, an entire history of colonial discourses and strategies.

And yet there is the "benighted moment," "occult tyrannies," a "mysterious" handcuffing to a history. The privileged would-be chronicler and interpreter of modern Indian history never quite masters his object, never apprehends India as more than myth or dream: "a collective fiction in which anything was possible, a fable rivalled only by the two other fantasies: money and God" (*MC* 130). Again, the unceasing movement of a textuality that *exceeds* and *escapes*, is always already just beyond the grasp even of those who would be 'inside' it, who would understand its complexities and render it knowable.

Thus does *Midnight's Children* emerge as less an explanation or representation of a 'magical' or 'exotic' India than the self-reflexive playing-out of its own inability to deliver such a representation: *Lichtung* rather than Aufklärung. And Saleem is certainly not the only character caught in this double bind of cultural displacement, the alienation of 'Westernized' subjects from their sense of a indigenous cultural and national identification; indeed, the text is full of characters equally stranded, 'defamiliarized' by their own national cultures precisely because of their increasing distance from them. True to the novel's preoccupation with this theme of cultural estrangement, Aadam Aziz's return to Kashmir—and his ensuing crisis of faith—is the first incidence of that character's "altered vision," his inhabitation of the "strange middle ground" between belief and disbelief. Aadam's inability to sincerely say his morning prayers creates the text's first major instability:

> "Guide us to the straight path. The path of those whom You have favoured. . . ."—But it was no good, *he was caught in a strange middle ground, trapped between belief and disbelief,* and this was only a charade after all—" Not of those who have incurred Your wrath, nor of those who have gone astray." My grandfather bent his forehead towards the earth. And now it was the tussock's time. At one and the same time a rebuke from Ilsa-Oskar-Ingrid-Heidelberg as well as valley-and-God, it smote him on the point of the nose. (*MC* 6, emphasis added)

In an aside leading up to the fateful moment, Saleem reveals that "the tussock of earth, crucial though its presence was as it crouched under a chance wrinkle of the prayer-mat, was at bottom no more than a catalyst" (*MC* 5). But for what? To ask what the ground, or for that matter, the event itself, is a catalyst for is, of course, to question the event's significance within the narrative. But if we also choose to read the event as a possible incidence of so-called magical realism within the text we might productively revise the question this way: Why is this 'magical' event presented as a catalyst, and what is it a catalyst for?

To address this point adequately, it is necessary to remember who is speaking. Certainly we may read the event as just another example of Saleem's intrusiveness as a narrator; the intervention is in this sense unnecessary, as the event itself as narrated is illustration enough of Aadam's cultural dilemma. But remembering Saleem's stake within his autoiographical narrative: that is, his preoccupation with position within his story in a certain way and for certain reasons, both the intervention itself and his choice of words within it take on another significance. Why then "catalyst"? Or more to the point: Why would Saleem want his readers to read the event as "at bottom *no more than* a catalyst"? It would seem that the 'magical' nature of the event is being downplayed here, undermined by a narrator who would have us read it as a mere preamble to his own life of between-ness, or what we might call Saleem's 'internal exile' within his own national culture. "The years in Germany," Saleem tells of

Aadam, "had turned him to a hostile environment" (*MC* 5); it is to a large degree the same "environment" that he believes constantly assaults him, to the point where he claims to be "literally disintegrating" (*MC* 37). And the referent of this catalyst, this "hostile environment" that would destroy its Westernized prodigal sons? Its function now seems to be strictly anecdotal; it makes its enigmatic appearance in what we might call 'The Parable of the Raised Tussock' and is left, never to return. It would appear to be discarded by Saleem, who within the context of his narrative certainly has larger concerns. But that tussock of earth nevertheless remains unsolved, as 'inscrutable' as before its fleeting employment within the progression of events. Its representation, to put it another way, does nothing to demystify it; it remains the cryptic vehicle for a Western-informed narrator's ambivalent tale of disbelief. If we do read this as the 'magical' or supernatural element within the event, then, we are again forced to bear witness to its utter evaporation within the narrative: once again, an index of so-called magical realism that escapes and exceeds (for it does turn out literally to be excessive, an element both peripheral to and beyond the grasp of the narration) a text's best attempts to apprehend it.

The boatman Tai further serves as a foil or "catalyst" for Aadam's burgeoning struggle, confronting him with a resistance to his new Western-informed self that borders on violence:

> The old man is clearly furious about something, possessed by an incomprehensible rage that appears to be directed at his erstwhile acolyte, or, more precisely and oddly, at his bag. Doctor Aziz attempts to make small talk. . . . "Your wife is well? Do they still talk about your bag of golden teeth?" tries to remake an old friendship; but Tai is in full flight now, a stream of invective pouring out of him. The Heidelberg bag quakes under the torrent of abuse. "Sistersleeping pigskin bag from Abroad full of foreigner's tricks. Big-shot bag. Now if a man breaks an arm that bag will not let the bone-setter bind it in leaves. Now a man must let his wife lie beside that bag and watch knives come and cut her open. A fine business, what these foreigners put in our young men's heads. I swear: it is a too-bad thing. That bag should fry in Hell with the testicles of the ungodly." (*MC* 16)

Certainly Tai, like the tussock of earth, is in certain ways merely a "catalyst," another context through which the text represents Aadam's internal conflict. The confrontation with Tai markedly heightens the instability from Aadam's encounter with the prayer-mat, and further sets the scene for Saleem's own grand entrance, as it were, upon the narrative stage of his own and India's history. To a imited degree, Aadam "diagnoses" the conflict vaguely as an ideological one: "To the ferryman, the bag represents Abroad; it is the alien thing, the invader, progress . . . and yes, it sits between doctor and boatman, and has made them antagonists" (*MC* 16). Aside from this emerging pattern of conflict and resistance between 'East and West,' however, and despite the narrator's narcissistic preoccupation with his own lineage and significance within the text, the confrontation with the boatman is, paradoxically, significant for what it reveals about Tai himself. For the boatman's stand against what he correctly perceives as a threat to his way of life—and the passionate and articulate, if virulent, manner in which he delivers his verdict—is not far removed from the Macondans' resistance to technological advances they had examined and found wanting. Again, as in *Cien años de soledad,* the act of reading is forced beyond the oppositional (and Orientalist) framework of '(active) representer/ (passive) represented' to become something else, that most unsettling and uncanny *(Unheimlich)* of recognitions: no longer the unilateral impositions of a reader's mastery, but the mirror-game of simultaneously reading-and-being-read, the encountering of a subject that not only recognizes the gaze of would-be judgment but returns it, and whose agency is at least partially determined by both his demand to be recognized and his rejection of the discourses and demands of mastery—both the Western bag's and the Western reader's.

If in fact Tai is as 'defamiliarized' by the Heidelberg bag as Aadam is by his own return to Kashmir, and if we can ascribe this to some insufficiency on Tai's part—his 'ignorance' of Western advances, lack of exposure to the outside world, and so forth—we are nevertheless bound to wonder at the assumptions of Aadam's "diagnosis" (who, let us not forget, does so in his capacity as "Doctor Aziz"—the learned doctor, product of the most advanced Western scientific discourses: "Doctor Aziz begins to diagnose" [*MC* 16]). Aadam 'examines' the subject, reads him for symptoms, and would translate his findings for the 'lay audience'; his "diagnosis," and the intrusive narrator's telling aside that accompanies it, is worth repeating, this time at greater length:

> Doctor Aziz begins to diagnose. To the ferry man, the bag represents Abroad; *it is the alien thing, the invader, progress.* And yes, it has indeed taken possession of the young Doctor's mind; and yes, it contains knives, and cures for cholera and malaria and smallpox; and yes, it sits between doctor and boatman, and has made them antagonists. Doctor Aziz begins to fight, against sadness, and against Tai's anger, *which is beginning to infect him.* . . . (*MC* 16–17, emphasis added)

I have emphasized two different sections of this passage, for reasons unrelated but in fact irreducibly yoked. On the one hand it is the interpretation of the doctor's bag, or rather, the doctor's interpretation of the boatman's interpretation of it. For by a certain narrative sleight-of-hand, what is being represented here is not the bag, or even Tai's interpretation of the bag, *but Aadam's representation of the boatman's view of the bag*. This seemingly negligible point becomes more significant when we coonsider the words that Aadam's "diagnosis" puts in the boatman Tai's mouth: *"it is the alien thing, the invader, progress."* Again, as in the case of the Macondans who embark on expeditions in search of "the benefits of science" (100y 21), "progress" is always elsewhere, or more precisely and as Aadam's description suggests, it is "Abroad." It would be necessary, then, only to interrogate this signifier "progress" for its most obvious associations in this context, the notions of a culture that would be seen as 'progressive,' liberal,' 'advanced,' and so on, all part of a particular chain of signifiers that has always been indispensable to the cause of the "civilizing mission" of empire, to begin to see the structures of both the privileging of the doctor's bag as "progress" and Tai's hostility toward it.

But on the other hand and at the same time, as the civilizing "bag from Abroad" comes to invade a culture with its "foreigner's tricks" and imposes its scientific dominion upon indigenous knowledge, so there is an unanticipated and unwanted return of sorts, a supplementary exchange narrated narrated as an *infection:* "Doctor Aziz begins to fight, against sadness, and against Tai's anger, *which is beginning to infect him*. . . ." This "infection," which is apparently distressful for the compromising of the health or 'purity' of Aadam's uncritical Western-informed viewpoint, is it a moment of *resistance?* Why is the infiltration or "infection" of Western knowledge by indigenous, "magical" ones something to be avoided, even feared? In the case of Doctor Aziz, we might begin to address such questions in terms of his own 'defamiliarization,' which in this context we may read as the most profound transformation of positions in relation to the 'backward' culture he presumes to "diagnose": rather than the invader from Abroad who would occupy his former home in the name of Western civilization, Aadam becomes by virtue of this "infection" of indigenous influence literally the *inhabited* one, "infected" by the parasitical presences, echoes, specters—in short, *traces*—of his indigenous cultural memory. In this amusing twist on a Bloomian "anxiety of influence," it is paradoxically the invading neocolonial who now struggles in vain to "fight" off ("Doctor Aziz begins to fight. . . .") and to annihilate all traces of his indigenous subjectivity in order to privilege his own Western-ness.[59]

Throughout *Midnight's Children,* as in García Márquez's novel, the recourse to so-called magical discourses and knowledge may be read as a matter of strategy and of survival, of again exceeding and escaping the impositions of a Western desire or will-to-mastery. The first illustration of this strategy in *Midnight's Children,* and our first signal that Aadam is weakening in his struggle against the allegorical cultural "infection" by the boatman Tai (who is himself established within the text as one possessing indigenous, "magical" knowledge), is his falling in love with Naseem Ghani—and under the "spell" of a perforated sheet:

> In short: my grandfather had fallen in love, and had come to think of the perforated sheet *as something sacred and magical*, because through it he had seen the things which had filled up the hole inside him which had been created when he had been hit on the nose by a tussock and insulted by the boatman Tai. (*MC* 24, emphasis added)

Further complications of this chain of events, and all subsequents in Aadam's lifelong struggles with his future wife, from the "mercurochrome" episode to her eventual ascent to the familial title of Reverend Mother and Ahmed Sinai's later "utter retreat from reality" (*MC* 128), claim as their originary moment Aadam's fascination with the perforated sheet and its "magical" power over him. But Reverend Mother's (and of course Tai's, through his initial resistance to the invading "bag from Abroad") eventual victory over Aadam brings only partial closure to the cultural battle waged in "The Perforated Sheet," a discursive jihad which, through the text's compulsion to circularity and repetition of events, reaches a climax with Saleem's own magical 'flights from reality.'

But what would in a narrowly literal way be called 'circularity' or 'repetition' might also, within this context of cultural infections and transfusions, be seen as an *inheritance;* Aadam's struggles in the interstices of Western and non-Western cultural discourses also inhabit Saleem in his attempts to write a history of a family and a nation. And there is also another doctor, and another diagnosis, this one considerably less satisfactory to Saleem than his grandfather's reading of the boatman Tai:

> Believe this if you can: the fraud has pronounced me whole! "I see no cracks," he intoned mournfully, differing from Nelson at Copenhagen in that he possessed no good eye, his blindness not the choice of stubborn genius but the inevitable curse of his folly! Blindly, he impugned my state of mind, cast doubts on my reliability as a witness, and Godknowswhatelse: "I see no cracks." (*MC* 72)

Given this incident as another manifestation of the text's playing-out of the ongoing struggle between cultural discourses and a sign of Saleem's own emerging involvement with those discourses, the question still remains: Why does Saleem narrate this event so self-consciously, drawing attention to his own views outside the immediate structure of the narrative? And why make such an interruption in his narrative to include both the doctor's diagnosis and his own protest at this point in the text, especially since, as he tells us himself, such an inclusion might work to "cast doubts on [his] reliability as a witness"?

Saleem himself offers only the vaguest excuses for the digression: "I wasn't going to today, because Padma has started getting irritated whenever my narration becomes self-conscious . . . but I simply must register a protest" (*MC* 72). More to the point, however, is the fact of the self-narration itself—or rather, the fact that Saleem can represent himself and his position in this way at all, a luxury not available to either Padma or the boatman Tai, who is himself similarly maligned by the reductive "diagnosis" of the Western-educated Aziz. The fact that Saleem's "cracks" cannot be verified by the Western-informed Indian doctor—and Saleem's virulent attack upon the reliability of the doctor's accurate if too-literal diagnosis ("I see no cracks")—allow a reading of the paradox of this developing economy of knowledge: on the one hand, his self-reflexivity of the narration reveals Saleem's preoccupation with his own "reliability," a question of crucial importance if he is to be read as a credible witness to, and translator of, India for a Western audience. But on the other hand, the only way he finds to salvage his reliability is to attack that of the doctor, with the implication that the latter is incapable of properly 'seeing' the truth of Saleem's fragmented condition—or in other words, that there are things that simply lie beyond the ability of a Westerner, or even a Western-educated Indian, to see. So Saleem's gesture, then, for all its narrative virtuosity, emerges as another of the text's contradictorily coherent moments, as Saleem attacks in the Western-trained Indian doctor *precisely the same privileged discourses upon which he himself depends for his reliability as a narrator.* This is again the double bind of the Orientalist: the need to maintain credibility as an authority via the demystification of that which must remain mystical, which may be translated, mediated, and so forth, but never produced in its presence.

This series of displacements of authority, throwing into question as it does the reliability of the narrator-as-Orientalist and creating a consciousness of our own situated-ness among the text's narrator and characters, complicates the act of reading and frustrates any attempt to privilege Western knowledges over non-Western ones. Given, then, both the text's refusal to settle on an epistemological center and its tireless foregrounding of its own self-reflexivity (largely courtesy of Saleem's self-obsessed narration), it is not surprising to begin to see the characters themselves falling prey to the ambiguities of 'defamiliarization.' Toward the end of Book One the characters begin to blur, as do García Márquez's Macondans, the illusory lines between 'magical' and non-magical' knowledges in their own lives; they have, as Saleem would put it, begun to let the 'magical' and 'nonmagical' elements in their lives "bleed into" each other:

> Rumours in the city; "The statue galloped last night!" "And the stars are unfavourable!" But despite these signs of ill-omen, the city was poised, with a new myth glinting in the corners of its eyes. August in Bombay: a month of festivals, the month of Krishna's birthday and Coconut Day; and this year—fourteen hours to go, thirteen, twelve—there was an extra festival on the calendar, a new myth to celebrate, because a nation which had never previously existed was about to win its freedom, catapulting us into a world which, although it had five thousand years of history, although it had invented the game of chess and traded with Middle Kingdom Egypt, was nevertheless quite imaginary; into a mythical land, a country which would never exist except in a dream we all agreed to dream; it was a mass fantasy shared in varying degrees by Bengali and Punjabi, Madrasi and Jat, and would periodically need the sanctification and renewal which can only be provided by rituals of blood. India, the new myth—a collective fiction in which anything was possible, a fable rivalled only by the two other mighty fantasies: money and God. (*MC* 129–130)

Clearly Saleem, and by implication others as well ("Rumours in the city," etc.), are faced with the task of interpreting and reconciling a set of conflicting signs at a critical time. And Saleem throws a rather bewildering bundle of these signs at readers: on the one hand looming independence and freedom for a new nation, on the other the knowledge of the nation-as-myth-or-fiction, a colonial fantasy actually composed of a plurality of diverse cultural identities that would eventually chafe under the social and political restrictions of a single nation-state; on the one hand the drawing-up of documents and governmental decrees that would declare inception of the new state, on the other the magical signs of impending doom. Beyond even this, however, there is still the question of the position of Saleem as narrator and complicating presence, as a guide who, however, self-serving and often self-undermining, retains the dual privilege of a Third-World Orientalist and omniscient narrator. For Saleem, however unreliable or suspicious, retains the privilege of a certain omniscience; he is, for instance, able to grant the character Saleem access to the events of the narrative in such a way as would allow him to portray those events as only an all-knowing narrator (or in Saleem's words, "All-India Radio") would have access. This quality of Saleem's complicates the reading of the text, as it puts us in a 'defamiliarized' position somewhat analogous to the characters'; that is, within the interstices of conflicting knowledge: between belief and disbelief, magic and the myth of a nonmagical reality. We too are 'defamiliarized,' in that the (illusory) lines, the neat distinctions between 'magical' and 'nonmagical,' credible and incredible events, become blurred. We cannot fully and uncritically buy into accounts of magical events (even Padma, faithful listener to

Saleem's tales, cannot); yet neither can we entirely reject them and privilege a rational Western position, because both Saleem's self-reflexive narration and his status as a narrator conversant in Western knowledges and discourses preclude such a dismissive view. Indeed, despite our suspicions of him Saleem's omniscience—and his privileged position as a trafficker between cultural discourses—means that he sees and knows more about the events than we do; so that while we cannot completely trust him, we cannot overrule him either.

Given the complexity of the text to this point and the experience of 'defamiliarization,' Padma's exasperation upon finally learning the truth behind Saleem's birth is understandable: "All the time . . . you tricked me. Your mother, you called her; your father, your grandfather, your aunts. What thing are you that you don't even care to tell the truth about who your parents were?" (*MC* 136). Saleem's cryptic response to her anger ("No: I'm no monster. Nor have I been guilty of trickery") is of course double-edged; for while he resolves one set of instabilities (his birth and parentage, and the metaphoric significance of his birth and birth-date), his subsequent explanation creates new complications to be addressed in Book Two. But while Padma claims to have heard enough ("I don't want to listen"), Saleem's narrative will continue. After all, Saleem knows that we, like Padma, await eagerly the next episode of the unraveling story: "[Padma] is affecting nonchalance, jutting a careless hip in my general direction, but doesn't fool me. I know now that she is, despite all her protestations, hooked. No doubt about it: my story has her by the throat" (*MC* 38).

In the closing pages of Book One, Saleem begins to resolve some of the narrative's growing instability by revealing the circumstances surrouding his birth and parentage. Paradoxically, however, in doing so he brings the text to a more profound state of crisis by complicating our understanding of the significance of those circumstances, or more precisely, the significance of a parentage that is not his parentage, but that is nevertheless an unavoidable *inheritance*. If the inheritances of birth and class are no longer to be interpreted in a linear and inescapably deterministic fashion, as they apparently are in the case of García Márquez's Buendía family—with every Aureliano and Jose Arcadio seemingly preordained into the personality, life-style, and even fate of their respective namesakes—then Saleem can nevertheless claim himself heir to that which would override, in the manner of a dialectical overtaking or overcoming, the exigencies of class and caste:

> In fact, all over the new India, the dream we all shared, children were being born who were only partially the offspring of their parents—the children of midnight were also the children *of the time:* fathered, you understand, by history. It can happen. Especially in a country which is itself a sort of dream. (*MC* 137)

This positing of Saleem as member of, and spokesperson for, the eponymous "children of midnight" certainly reinforces the narrator's privileged position as "Third World cosmopolitan," interpreter, or translator of 'magical discourses for a Western audience, neo-Orientalist, and so on. But Saleem's position; that is, his *responsibility* for the text and the events he narrates, by the almost imperceptible turn of a single phrase, becomes explicit now, much more than at the moment of his cryptic utterance about being "handcuffed to history." The phrase does much moe than define a historical moment, a temporal specificity: "children *of the time*." And if that were not enough: "fathered, you understand, by history." By being no longer "handcuffed to" the particular contingencies of a given parentage, a given lineage, with all of the preconditions that such a lineage must inevitably entail, Saleem and the other "children of the time" are enabled, if only for the briefest of periods before their eventual ruin, to literally become children of *possibility*, by their magical powers to exceed and escape, however momentarily, the chains of that other inheritance that would otherwise be forever theirs. Or to put it yet another way: to dream an inheritance of a history, and from that history, to claim—*to dare to claim*—the inheritance of a future. A future not of the lineage (that is, of the father), a future which, otherwise, would never be. Saleem thus becomes more than a narrator of a particular national or personal history; he emerges, rather, as a narrator and protagonist of a struggle between possibilities, contingencies, and *futures*. Or more precisely: between possibilities and the end of possibilities.

IV

We are reminded from the first paragraph of Book Two that Saleem's is an "autobiographical enterprise" (*MC* 141); and certainly it is upon this 'magically' omniscient narrator, his knowledge (of Indian history, for instance, or of characters and events to which we have no other access), his views, and his 'translations' of certain 'magical' discourses, that we depend for an account of events and their possible significances. It is perhaps not surprising, then, that Saleem wastes no time in asserting his own importance or centrality within the events of the text:

> Newspapers celebrated me; politicians ratified my position. Nawaharlal Nehru wrote: "Dear Baby Saleem, My belated congratulations on the happy accident of your birth! You are the newest bearer of that ancient face of India which is also eternally young. We shall be watching over your life with the closest attention; it will be, in a sense, *the mirror of our own*." (*MC* 143, emphasis added)

To Saleem, the endorsement from an outside source apparently substantiates his claim to a position "at the centre of the universe" (*MC* 148) of his own narrative. Within the larger context of the novel, however, Nehru's letter (and indeed, the very act of invoking the name of modern India's first prime minister) takes on a much greater significance; for it reveals the text's primary structural device, and its central metaphor: Saleem as a "mirror" of his country, a characterized microcosm of the newly conceived nation and the often violent relations between the discursive entities that constitute it. It is in this context that Saleem's incessant talk of "cracks," fissures, and schisms in/on his body point most clearly to his own relation to the imagined or "dreamed" community called 'India.' For if this is the story of Saleem-as-India, then that India is itself both defamiliar-ized and -izing, is itself composed of the discourses of multiplicity and cultural entropy. Both the newly minted India and Saleem himself, then, exist precisely within and among the "cracks" or interstices that so distress the would-be chronicler. Or to put it another way: the narrative of India-as-nation exists precisely to the extent to which it is able to exceed and escape the constraints of the nation as imposed from without, imposed, that is, in large part by a colonial power that would contain its irreducibly polyglot cultural discourses within the (always illusory) borders of the nation-state. For to write about—and even more so, to seek the "mirror"—the nation is always to inscribe the "cracks" or schisms, rather than the enclosings of boundary lines (geographic or otherwise); so that Saleem's claims for his own narrative in the opening pages become the allegorical gesture by which we may read the nation as well:

> And there are so many stories to tell, too many, such an excess of intertwined lives events miracles places rumours, so dense a commingling of the improbable and the mundane! I have been a swallower of lives; and to know me, just the one of me, you'll have to swallow the lot as well. (*MC* 4)

To further complicate the reading of both the text-as-national-history and the text-as-magical-realism, Saleem narrates common everyday occurrences in a 'magical' fashion, in what constitutes a parody or critique of so-called magical realist fiction. Part of this interrogation of the narrative conventions of so-called magical realism is simply a product of the text's self-reflexive narration; the text certainly foregrounds this aspect of the narration with Saleem's comments about his own "matter of fact descriptions of the outré and bizarre, and their reverse, namely heightened, stylized versions of the everyday" as techniques by which he seeks to create "a picture of the world of startling uniformity" (*MC* 261). The text's metafictional interrogation of so-called magical realist conventions, however, isn't always this explicit; that is, it doesn't generally take the form of self-reflexive commentary. Rather, such implicit critiques of genre more often appear as part of Saleem's story-related narration, as 'magical' characteristics are imposed upon a clearly nonmagical event, only to be undermined by the narration. In Book One, Saleem initially portrays such events as Aadam Aziz's encounters with the perforated sheet and the prayer-mat (*MC* 4 and 5–6) and the prophesy of Ramram Seth (*MC* 96) as supernatural. A few paragraphs or pages later, however, Saleem contradicts himself by offering pointedly 'nonmagical' (*MC* 4), more rational explanations for the occurences: Aadam doesn't really get "punched in the nose" (*MC* 97) by the valley; Ramram Seth doesn't really levitate; and Aadam, rather than actually fall under the spell of the perforated sheet, merely "come[s] to think of [it] as something sacred and magical" (*MC* 24) because of his experience with it.

It would certainly not be difficult, given what we have already seen regarding both Saleem's tenuous between two cultures and his preoccupation with his own credibility before a Western audience, to see what is at stake here for Saleem. Thus again does Saleem's narration find itself in the double bind and double displacement of the 'Oriental Orientalist': on the one hand Saleem needs to present himself as being in a privileged position from which to critique, represent, and translate the other's culture for a Western audience, a position that demands the would-be Orientalist's proximity to or immersion, in the exoticized other; but on the other hand, the fact of his own difference in relation to that Western audience dictates that his credibility before that audience is less certain, more precarious than that of a conventional (that is, a white European) Orientalist, whose allegiance at bottom to Western cultures is more or less assumed. This is not to say, of course, that the relation of the white-European Orientalist to their object of study is itself to be accepted uncritically, as some uniform or homogeneous consistency; Said's claims to the contrary notwithstanding, the writings of T. E. Lawrence and Sir Richard Burton, to name but two of the best-known examples, are themselves fraught with the same types of ambivalences and ambiguities that surface in Saleem's narration, albeit from a different set of cultural subject-positions.[60] Nevertheless Saleem must, unlike his white-European counterparts, be constantly wary of slippages in his narration that a Western audience might read as signs of his own implication or complicity with the cultures he represents. Thus does Saleem here play the precarious role of cultural and racial 'double-agent'; that is to say that the very relation to another culture that privileges his narration is also paradoxically the measure and focus of an unspoken, unacknowledged *suspicion* for a Western audience, the narrative equivalent of a black inner-city police officer or a Chicano border patrol officer. This is not, of course, to already and in advance condemn all Western readers and 'Third World' narrators to this type of culturally bound hermeneutics of reading, or to say that Saleem functions categorically or uniformly as a sort of Indian "Uncle Tom," or that he is always suspicious to any and all white Western readers because of his cultural difference; after all, it is in *Cien años de soledad* precisely such deterministic reading practices, whereby characters' names mark them in advance as behaving in this or that manner and the texts of a gypsy are uncritically accepted as Fate, which bring about the cataclysmal destruction of Macondo. Rather, the task here is to unceasingly point out and interrogate these hierarchical structures—which are always part of the act of reading—whenever and wherever we find them.

Reading Saleem's narration in this manner, and always keeping in mind the various complications and contingencies that his interstitial position between cultures necessarily bring to bear upon the text, we can begin to see the necessary ambivalence in Saleem's narration of Amina Sinai's encounter with the soothsayer Ramram Seth. Consider that

1. Amina is only momentarily fooled by the guru's trick of "sitting on a shelf" (*MC* 97); but unlike the event of Aadam Aziz's "bewitchment" by the perforated sheet, our affective response is (albeit momentarily) not so much one of superiority and detachment as of a certain engagement and, yes, identification. We cannot laugh at Amina because we have been temporarily fooled along with her; and her embarrassment and subsequent skepticism before Seth is, to some degree, ours as well; and

2. Seth's prophesy turns out to be true after all, its accuracy vindicated by subsequent events in the text (as a rereading of p. 99 after finishing the novel, for instance, will confirm). Saleem's narration of this event, then, takes three turns: *first,* he raises expectations of a magical event by introducing the soothsayer; *second,* he undermines Seth's credibility by exposing the "shelf trick" behind the apparent levitation; and *third and finally,* fulfills the just-undermined expectations by having Seth deliver a 'real' prophesy. My point here is that Saleem's narration illustrates the profound ambivalence of his position as chronicler and translator of things Indian: the necessity of his proximity to the cultural practices of an-other's 'magical' culture, and the paradoxical necessity of not not appearing to be complicit with or having otherwise bought-into such 'magical' cultural occurrences as levitating soothsayers and their prophesies. It is the unresolvable challenge of the anthropologist 'among the natives': to know of 'magical' things, to witness and even participate in them, but in the end to remain skeptical, to reject the 'magical' as the superstitions of an inferior, less 'sophisticated' civilization in favor of the scientific rationality of the West. Such is the cultural landscape negotiated by all texts of so-called magical realism in their attempt to mediate between the demands of an interpreted culture, the text's interpretations of that culture, and the consumers of—and in turn, interpreters and further disseminators of—those interpretations.[61]

I have dwelled this much on what are essentially Book One events because Saleem's narration of them has important consequences for how we might read one of *Midnight Children*'s most crucial and ambivalent moments: the eponymous "Accident in a Washing-chest," during which young Saleem first discovers his magical powers. Saleem introduces this critical moment in the narrative by claiming that his mother "had fallen under the spell of the telephone" (*MC* 188); this narrative tease, as in the example of the prophesying soothsayer Ramram Seth, again raises expectations for a supernatural event. And again Saleem both frustrates and fulfills those expectations; for while the telephone's "spell" proves to be a narrative red herring, the real item lies concealed in the washing-chest with young Saleem. The narration soon reveals that Amina's "spell" is not magical at all; rather, it is a former lover who, when confronted by the children, pretends to be calling for a truck company:

> Silence again: the voice, which has not been able to prevent itself from speaking, considers its answer; and then, ". . . Hullo . . . This is the Shanti Prasad Truck Hire Company, please? . . ." And the Monkey [Saleem's name for his sister], quick as a flash: "Yes, what d'you want?" Another pause: the voice, sounding embarrassed, apologetic almost, says, "I want to rent a truck."
>
> but after that, the telephone rang regularly; sometimes my mother answered it, listened in silence while her mouth made fish-motions, and finally, much too late, said, "Sorry, wrong number"; at other times the Monkey and I clustered around it, two ears to earpiece, while the Monkey took orders for trucks. I wondered, "Hey Monkey, what'd you think? Doesn't the guy ever wonder why the trucks don't *arrive!*" And she, wide-eyed, flutter-voiced: Man, do you suppose . . .maybe they *do!*" (*MC* 188)

Aside from Saleem's implicit debunking of his own 'magical' introduction, the end of the passage self-consciously (and more than half-mockingly) raises the possibility of another magical event (the trucks actually arriving). One the one hand, the scene seems to parody "magical realist" conventions by illustrating how easily the children are fooled; that is, we really don't expect the trucks to arrive (although given the technique of 'defamiliarization' as previously discussed, we might accept it as plausible if they did), and by the way that the scene is narrated—the Monkey as "wide-eyed, flutter-voiced," for instance, a seemingly perfect parody of a certain kind of reader, or the fact that the words are spoken by children, further implying a certain gullibility—it is fairly obvious that we aren't meant to. More significant than the (non-) event itself, however, is how the narration leads into the 'real' magical event that occurs in the washing-chest. For as in Amina's encounter with the soothsayer, Saleem's narration in the "Accident" chapter intertwines 'fraudulent' magical events with 'real' ones (or at least ones that he doesn't undermine); and the text further complicates any ostensible clarifications by forcing us to depend upon a narrator whom we know to be unreliable to make (largely illusory) distinctions between the two.

Unlike Amina's encounter with the soothsayer, in which the narration throws a single narrative curve before fulfilling 'magical' expectations, Saleem's "accident" reveals a more complex pattern of frustration and fulfillment. After initially frustrating expectations of a magical telephone "spell," the narration again raises possibilities of 'magic' once Saleem is in the washing-chest:

> Electricity in the air. Heat, buzzing like bees. A mantle, hanging somewhere in the sky, waiting to fall gently around my shoulders . . . somewhere, a finger reaches toward a dial; a dial whirs around and around, electrical pulses dart along cable, seven, zero, five, six, one. The telephone rings. (*MC* 189)

We can read the passage's movements, in its mediation of both an audience's 'magical' expectations and its own desire for credibility with that audience, as threefold:

1. The first sentence ("Electricity in the air") is a familiar-enough structural device, an almost clichéd metaphor used to signify growing excitement or tension. As such, the passage, (again, somewhat self-mockingly) creates its own narrative tension, as we wait for something important to happen;

2. We know by this point in the text that the chapters are named for devices or events that are significant within the narrative ("The Perforated Sheet," The Fisherman's Pointing Finger," and so on). Naturally then, we expect the "Accident in a Washing-chest" to be an event of some significance within the chapter, if not the text as a whole; and most importantly

3. Saleem's referring again to the telephone in such a deliberately mystifying way ("somewhere, a finger reaches toward a dial") reopens the possibility of a magical "spell," despite previous narrative signals to the contrary. And although the narration again denies expectations of the 'magical,' in this regard, Amina's trancelike repetition of "Na. Dir. Na. . . ." seems to be a playful mockery of Saleem's own 'magical' introduction, another example of the text's apparent parodying of "magical realist" conventions—the frustration is again only temporary, a diversion that belies the telephone's other significance; for it is young Saleem's eavesdropping on his mother's conversation that leads to his magical "accident," where young Saleem first discovers his supernatural powers:

> Pajama-cord rises painfully half an inch further up the nostril. But other things are rising too: hauled by that feverish inhalation, nasal liquids are being sucked relentlessly up up up, nose goo flowing upwards, against gravity, against nature . . . there is a shock. Something electrical has been moistened.
>
> Pain.
>
> And then noise, deafening manytongued terrifying, *inside his head!* . . . Inside a white wooden washing-chest, within the darkened auditorium of my skull, my nose began to sing. (*MC* 191)

Here is a seemingly unambivalent moment, an apparent affirmation of Saleem's claim to magical powers. The possibility of dismissing the passage as merely another twist in a narration full of them is admittedly tempting; but the narration here complicates that prospect in two significant ways:

1. although we already know Saleem to be at best ambivalent, and at worst untrustworthy in his narration, he seems to be reliable enough here—he is, after all, speaking relatively "plainly," without the more ornate language that characterizes his digressions elsewhere ("It's time to talk plainly," he states [*MC* 191]); and

2. although Saleem deliberately undermines his own narration of earlier 'magical' events in the text, there is no evidence of that happening in this passage. The text is, for once, not raising expectations only to frustrate them. As a result of all this, as find ourselves once again in the position of the 'defamiliarized' reader: constantly negotiating, as are characters within the text, between the categories of belief and disbelief, 'magical' and 'nonmagical' discourses. Further complicating this act of reading is a narrator who is himself wrapped in his own double-bind, caught up between the impulse to render himself and his culture knowable to a Western audience and the impulse to constantly elude that audience, between his own implicit promise to faithfully represent the epistemological object "India" and the impossibility of delivering on that promise.

Further complicating our reader's position in relation to Saleem is the fact that he is himself unsure of his place within his own autobiographical text, within the narrative of his own familial and national histories. Much of Saleem's unreliability as a narrator is fueled by his own ambivalence, his own uncertainty; throughout the text he vacillates between contradictory impulses: the tendency to question his own agency, in the form of his and the children's purpose and role in India's future; and the equally overwhelming desire to affirm that agency, to place himself at the center of the narrative's—and

India's—most significant events. The former is a question to which Saleem brings a degree of closure by the end of the novel; the latter, however, remains pointedly unresolved, for while by text's end Saleem is resigned in his submission to the powers-that-be, his battles with "The Widow" apparently conceded, he refuses to surrender dominion over his autobiographical enterprise. We can already see glimpses of these contradictory narrative impulses in Aadam Aziz and Ahmed Sinai's respective "flights from reality" as they retreat to the apparent refuge of the 'magical'; although as we have seen in *Cien años de soledad*, what appears to be simple regression is also, read in a certain way, a move of strategic and subversive value. But nowhere is this relation of economy between 'magical' and 'nonmagical' discourses, between a nonmagical agency and the illusion of a 'magical return'—as if the 'magical' could not itself represent a kind of agency, as I have been implicitly arguing all along—than in Saleem's narration of his own life, as he chronicles the role of the supernatural in his repeated attempts, first to engage repressive and neocolonial powers, then in a manner analogous to Jose Arcadio Segundo to evade their wrath.

Significantly, Saleem's struggle between 'magical' and 'nonmagical' impulses is not neatly defined along character or plot lines; unlike *Cien años de soledad*, in which characters can generally be said to stand on one or the other side of a 'magical/nonmagical' opposition, Saleem often exhibits these contradictory impulses at the same time. Whereas García Márquez's novel presents this opposition through the characters as a totality, each with their own identifiable and more-or-less static position within the overall dichotomy, and also through the additional illusion of its distanced, 'objective' narration, *Midnight's Children* constantly deconstructs itself via a first-person narrator who is himself irremediably fractured along precisely those lines that allow us to divide or sort out the members of the Buendía clan; or in other words, Saleem in a sense *is* the struggle between 'magical' and 'nonmagical' discourses, because both his narration and his very notion of himself as a narrating subject is already defined by the fact, and the effects, of that struggle.

The washing-chest incident and its immediate aftermath show Saleem's early struggles with magic and agency—and more importantly, with the possibility of magic *as* agency. Significantly, Saleem's discovery of his magical powers occurs simultaneously with Amina's discovery of him in the washing-chest, together inspiring Saleem to act on his newfound powers, that is, to impose his burgeoning sense of what I will call his 'magical agency' upon the world, as his powers lead him to assume the role of visionary or prophet:

> Gabriel or Jibreel told Muhammed: "Recite!" And then began the Recitation, known in Arabic as Al-Quran: "Recite: in the name of the Lord thy Creator, who created Man from clots of blood. . . ." That was on Mount

> Hira outside Mecca Sharif; on a two-storey hillock opposite Breach Candy Pools, voices also instructed me to recite: "Tomorrow!" I thought excitedly, "Tomorrow!" (*MC* 193)

The attempt, of course, fails, as young Saleem is reviled by his family for his apparent blasphemy; his subsequent inability to "tell the people who mattered most about the goings-on in [his] head" (*MC* 195) leads Saleem to the next of what is to be a series of 'magical' refuges. In the clock-tower Saleem takes his first ambivalent steps toward employment of his powers in a magical agency, although not as auspiciously as his narration would have us believe: "in the solitude of rusting time, I paradoxically took my first tentative steps towards *that involvement with mighty events and lives* from which I would never again be free" (*MC* 205, emphasis added). As in Saleem's favorite childhood game, the text here becomes a narrative game of Snakes and Ladders: play between action and retreat, magic and nonmagic, *fort* and *da,* all inextricably linked in a textual web in which no single element can either take precedence or escape the play of the others.

As young Saleem struggles with the demands of magical agency, so does older narrating Saleem continue to self-consciously question his own credibility and significance within his narrative:

> Does one error invalidate the entire fabric? Am I so far gone, in my desperate need for meaning, that I'm prepared to distort everything—to rewrite the whole history of my times in order to place myself in a central role? Today, in my confusion, I can't judge. I'll have to leave it to others. (*MC* 198)

This seemingly gratuitous digression, as with others scattered throughout the novel, has significant consequences for what is to come. Consider that

1. although Saleem first discovers a factual error in his tale, leading him to openly question the validity of his whole narrative, he has already defended his narration (albeit in a qualified way) from the chapter's opening page, allowing him to "reiterate, entirely without a sense of shame" (*MC* 197) his magical claims in the following pages. Any question of reliability thus becomes moot, for in order to continue reading we must believe him to some degree—the only alternative being to throw not only Saleem's text but the act of reading itself into a state of paralysis—and so we do; additionally

2. if I am correct in my assumption about point number 1, then Saleem's digression is far from random or gratuitous. The consequences of the aside are

visceral and immediate; for if Saleem's (one?) error does invalidate the entire narrative fabric, how can we then believe the much larger burdens on his credibility: of 'magical' events and powers, and especially his claims about the Midnight's Children—a claim crucial to the rest of the novel? Clearly we are being asked to answer no to Saleem's question; the "errors" and accompanying digressions are simply part of what we are being asked to "swallow" as a precondition of the act of reading *Midnight's Children*. We must, in other words, answer no here in order to be able to say yes to Saleem's ever more elaborate claims later on; that is, in order to be able to say yes to the very *possibility* of a magical agency, we must in a sense release Saleem from the impossible demands of his own narration.

And further, as Saleem's magical claims do become larger and more elaborate, so do his attempts to justify and defend his narrative credibility grow increasingly elaborate. The explanations offered for Saleem's telepathic powers (*MC* 199–204) and the magical network of the Midnight's Children (*MC* 234–239) show none of the pattern of frustration and fulfillment, none of the self-undermining tendencies that mark his narration in previous chapters; rather, Saleem's 'magical' tales are henceforth littered with assertions of narrative credibility:

> I am coming to [the] fantastic heart of my story, and must write in plain unveiled fashion, about the midnight children. (*MC* 234)
>
> That's how it was; there can be no retreat from the truth. (*MC* 236)
>
> There, now I've said it. That is who I was—who we were. (*MC* 239)

Again and again, Saleem finds it necessary to defend both the plausibility of his recounting of 'magical' events and his own reliability as a narrator, or more specifically, his mental stability and sanity. For the former, Saleem provides reference to similar, if "admittedly lesser" (*MC* 236) stories in the media as verification of his claims. Saleem's defense of his mental state, however, comes in response to doubts expressed by Padma, who is arguably his most faithful audience:

> "O Baba!" she says at last. "Baba! You are sick; what have you said?"
>
> No, that would be too easy. I refuge to take refuge in illness. Don't make the mistake of dismissing what I've unveiled as mere delirium; or even as the insanely exaggerated fantasies of a lonely, ugly child. I have stated before that I am not speaking metaphorically; what I have written (and read

> aloud to stunned Padma) is nothing less than the literal, by-the-hairs-of-my-mother's-head truth. (*MC* 239–240)

Saleem is right, of course, to want to quell Padma's fears; for if we are to read her as a gauge, however accurate, of how an audience might read the text (or at least a characterization of what an author might anticipate in such an audience), then what Saleem faces here is much more than the loss of a single reader. Read in this context, the loss of Padma would signify nothing less than a full-scale mutiny, a crisis of credibility not just for a particular text but for an entire body of literature—or more precisely, for the very possibility of what I call a 'magical agency' and of a literature that would allow us to think of such a possibility. Or put another way: Saleem's narration, haunted as it is by its own obsession with credibility and bearing the unmistakable marks of a narrator-as-would-be-Orientalist (would-be translator of India for a Western audience), is somehow transforming, even displacing itself, into something else. To think of what this might be, we need only consider again Saleem's interstitial position between cultures—his *situatedness,* in other words, between cultural discourses, and also and most importantly his efforts (which constitute the overarching text of *Midnight's Children*) to mediate, translate, and so forth, between and among these. I have to this point implicitly critiqued Saleem's narration as one that would represent an other ("India") for Western (and Western-informed) audiences, the fantasy of a passive mimesis, an informed and privileged observer scrutinizing and representing their object of study in a detached, utterly uninvolved manner: the classic "outsider looking in." Without entering into a lengthy exposition of how this notion already deconstructs itself in the writings of the nineteenth-century Orientalists, we can nevertheless observe that it is precisely Saleem's involvement with the text's events—his drive, in other words, to place himself at the center of those events—that both undermines his claims to a neo-Orientalist authority and opens up a space from which to read the possibility of an-other agency or agency-of-the-other. What I have been calling 'magical agency,' then, emerges as that most profound, if still barely perceptible, shift in Saleem's narration, in his situatedness or subject position in relation to cultural discourses of East-West-and so forth; the move beyond a passive *representation* of otherness—at best a naive mimesis, at worst Orientalism—to a realization of a subjectivity of agency and resistance. Rather than represent and critique "India," then, Saleem's text becomes more an exegesis of its own difference, its own otherness; and it does so precisely to the extent that it articulates and defends its claims to a reality of difference in terms of, yes, *magic.*

As we have already seen, however, young Saleem is much more unsure of his significance than is his older, narrating counterpart; for while the narrator

Saleem strives to place himself at the center of events, young Saleem is embroiled in doubts about the meaning or purpose of his own life. His dealings with the Midnight's Children illustrate this concern, as young Saleem strives to find a sense of agency for the group: " 'We must think,' I said, 'what we are for' " (*MC* 273). Read in this context, Saleem's claims to being both (passive) victim and (active) protagonist of his narrative ("but Saleem Sinai, perennial victim, persists in seeing himself as protagonist" [*MC* 285]) aren't as self-contradictory as they might initially seem. To better read this apparent paradox, we must consider just what kind of protagonist is being asserted. Saleem is certainly not the kind of heroic character who is in control of their world, presented as possessing some kind of superior mental, physical, or emotional strength; he is, rather, a character who is less consistently act-*ing* than act-*ed upon*, "the sort of person to whom things have been done" (*MC* 285). The repetition of Nehru's letter, which appears again in "The Kolynos Kid" chapter (*MC* 285), is significant for its reminder of Saleem's role; that is, it reminds us that within the text, Saleem is significant not so much for what he does but for what he himself represents: an allegorical embodiment or "mirror" of nation, of an India and the precarious balances of/among its various cultural discourses (to say nothing of its relations to Western cultural imperatives). But again there must be more than a simple, passive representation going on here. For Saleem has claimed for himself the role of an active protagonist; and if his sense of agency stems not from the more conventional strengths expected of one who makes such claims, of one who would claim the role of a hero, as it were, then that leads inevitably to the single distinction that Saleem *can* claim: his magical powers. Again, the recourse to 'magic' not as a mere technical or narrative device ("exotic," Western critics have called it; "the fantastic presented in an everyday, realistic fashion," etc.[62]), but as an active alterity, the movement within the so-called magical realist text of that which escapes and exceeds what would understand, comprehend, or in any other sense master it, a movement of active difference within the text, to which we may now more accurately and appropriately return the name 'agency.' Saleem explains further:

> How, in what terms, may the career of a single individual impinge on the fate of a nation? I must answer in adverbs and hyphens: I was linked to history both literally and metaphorically, both actively and passively, in what our (admirably modern) scientists might term "modes of connection" composed of "dualistically-combined configurations" of the two pairs of opposed adverbs given above. This is why hyphens are necessary: actively-literally, passively-metaphorically, actively-metaphorically, and passively-literally, I was inextricably entwined with my world. (*MC* 185–186)

Although the scholarly tone of the passage is at least partially tongue-in-cheek,[63] Saleem's preoccupation with notions of active and passive modes of engagement is nevertheless evident; more to the point, however, is the implicit positing of the text—indeed, of the very act of writing—as an active form of involvement with and within the world, of writing itself as an act of agency. Saleem's critically conscious could, of course, be dismissed as simply consistent with a certain dimension of his character: digressive, self-aggrandizing, showing off his knowledge to an immediate audience (Padma) less versed in scholarly discourse; and Saleem does confess to having resorted to just such tactics in dissuading Padma from her disbelief ("By my show of erudition and by the purity of my accents, I have shamed them into feeling unworthy of judging me" [*MC* 254]). But this is less significant than the fact of Saleem's awareness of the act of writing as being "actively- . . . entwined" with the world, and thus of writing as a form of agency; and beyond that, the very fact of his exposition of the "modes of connection" illustrates in an inescapably self-reflexive manner his awareness of this agency, as well as his desire to share this knowledge. By doing so the text to some degree does "reveal the hands holding the strings" (*MC* 72); that is, we are now more acutely aware of the literary constructs and conventions of the text—and by extension, those of a whole body of texts known by the term 'magical realism.' By foregrounding the literariness of his narration, then, Saleem's text—and the overarching text we know as *Midnight's Children*—self-reflexively signifies its own agency; and by the slightest shift in Saleem's position between East and West, what begins as an attempt to represent India gives way to something else—to a space, as it were, for otherness *to represent itself,* to claim a stake in its own representation even as it exceeds and escapes all attempts from without to apprehend, define, and translate it into a fully knowable object.

I have attempted to this point to articulate, however sketchily, what I see as Saleem's precarious position in the text as a sort of gateway figure, one who occupies a mediating (we might say overlapping) position between cultures: cultural discourses, allegiances, knowledge, and so forth. To be known, in the words of Nehru's fictional letter, as a life that "will be, in a sense, the mirror of [India's] own" (*MC* 143), and to paradoxically turn the mirror inward and outward simultaneously; that is, to occupy at the same time the positions of translator and translated, Oriental and Orientalist—is a task that will necessarily leave its marks on the text, as it shifts and moves between/among the subject positions that it attempts to negotiate. As such, it is perhaps not surprising that as Saleem's position becomes more "fantastic," that is, as the demands of 'magic' and 'realism,' of representation and agency and credibility come to bear upon the text, so will his attempts at self-defense and justification of his claims become more emphatic. In keeping, then, with the defamiliarizing narrative pattern of 'magical' events countered by the narrator's relatively sober assertions of reliability, Saleem prepares for Book Two's final chapters by reasserting his narrative authority yet again. Saleem is again hoping that with his "show of erudition" and "purity of [his] accents" (MC 73) he can persuade us, like Padma, to believe.

Saleem's narration in the final six chapters of Book Two does in fact ask readers to "swallow" a great deal: Saleem murders a classmate by dreaming his death (*MC* 296–298) and uses his telepathic powers to take revenge on his "adulterous" mother, with disastrous results (*MC* 310–314); young Saleem also acquires a magical olfactory prowess in the wake of his telepathy-ending sinus surgery, and sleeps with a 512-year-old whore who can alter her body odors to imitate those of his family (*MC* 367–368, 381–382, respectively). There are also more playful parodies of "magical realist" (*MC* 336) conventions, as the old servant Musa is mistaken for a ghost and Saleem's childhood friend Cyrus-the-great emerges as a fraudulent holy-man (*MC* 321–324). Yet the text also approaches a certain limit or critical-mass, as events complicate and compound themselves toward their apocalyptic resolution in "How Saleem Achieved Purity." As both the narrative tension and instabilities within the events themselves (as narrated) increase, the narration grows increasingly self-conscious and unsure, of both its own claims and the as-narrated events; in the examples just cited and in later incidents, Saleem questions the facts of his own narration. We may read this most pointedly in Saleem's recounting of Jimmy Kapadia's death, his own encounter with Tai Bibi ("You may legitimately ask: Did it happen in just this. . . . And surely she couldn't have been five hundred and. . . ." [*MC* 382]), and the tremendous narration of Book Two's final chapter.

This growing ambivalence on Saleem's part is symptomatic of a corresponding and more widespread instability of the novel itself. As Book Two draws to a close, we see characters—Saleem and his family in particular, but others as well, in a manner similar to what we have already seen in *Cien años de soledad*—growing into a position analogous to that of a 'defamiliarized' reader; that is, as they become overwhelmed by the accelerating circumstances surrounding them, the characters in *Midnight's Children* find themselves increasingly unable to adopt a critical stance toward what is so rapidly happening around (and to) them. Which is to say that at this point in the novel the characters collectively lose their tenuous grip on the magical agency that Saleem had earlier labored so to construct; certainly these appear as "the sort of person[s] to whom things have been done" in the name of whom Saleem had posited himself as the magical hero. As the warring nations (India and Pakistan) and their respective citizens become engulfed in the defamiliarizing yet all-too-familiar horrors of war and Book Two hurtles toward an uncertain conclusion, all is darkness. Saleem's own observation here could hardly be more indicative of the general plight: "in a country where the truth is what it is instructed to be, reality quite literally ceases to exist" (*MC* 389).

The first major signs of instability in this part of the text emerge as rumors of magical happenings, "omens" of the coming holocaust. As in Book Two's opening chapters, Saleem passes on these reports of what he and others regard as supernatural portents of impending doom:

> According to Mary, the country was in the grip of a sort of supernatural invasion. "Yes, Baba, they say in Kurukshetra an old Sikh woman woke up in her hut and saw the old-time war of the Kurus and Pandavas happening right outside! It was in the papers and all, she pointed to the place where she saw the chariots of Arjun and Karna, and there were truly wheel-marks in the mud! Baap-re-baap, such so-bad things: at Gwallor they have seen the ghost of the Ran of Jhansi; rakshasas have been seen many-headed like Ravana, doing things to women and pulling down trees with one finger. (*MC* 293)

As in earlier examples, Saleem momentarily abandons his self-questioning ways to assume the (illusory) role of 'objective' reporter-narrator observing 'magical' events of India and translating them for his audience. But unlike previous such incidents, phrases such as "rumours relayed to me as matters of absolute fact" and "I remain, today, half-convinced" (MC 293–294) foreground Saleem's uncertainties and bring the entire text to crisis; because whereas to this point Saleem has been in apparent control of his narrative, skillfully reasserting his authority as a witness whenever necessary to maintain credibility, here his own ambivalent language forecloses in advance any such claims. Here, for the first time in the text, Saleem loses a degree of control over his narration, and undermines his own narrative authority in an apparently unwitting way, in a manner, that is, which does not seem to be part of any game of narrative give and take with readers, but rather a sign of his own exhaustion. And as we shall see, this will not be the last time for such slips in Saleem's narration.

If Saleem's history is, as he claims, inextricably linked to that of India, so are Saleem's and India's respective crises of indeterminacy, a shared crisis, we might say, of meaning, irreducibly linked to their apparent annihilation at the end of Book Two. Saleem's own growing inability to narrate his own story grows increasingly apparent, as the narration grows more self-conscious and ambivalent:

> Because I am rushing ahead at breakneck speed; errors are possible, and overstatements, and jarring alterations in tone; I'm racing the cracks, but I remain conscious that errors have already been made, and that, as my decay accelerates, *the risk of unreliability grows.* (*MC* 325, emphasis added)

As the "cracks" grow, then, Saleem finds his ability to hold together a coherent narrative greatly diminished; and appropriately for his position as a "mirror" of his country, we will see an analogous relation between 'defamiliarization' and disintegration in the chapters and events around him. As Book Two enters its final chapter, both Saleem's claims to a central role in India's history (and the implications of that claim for his own narration) and and the "modes of connection" in which he couches his argument come to at least provisional resolution; for true to his "active-metaphorical" mode of connection, both of the Sinais' struggles with their own 'defamiliarization' and their resulting descent into disintegration and chaos are reflected in the affairs of their country. More than ever, Saleem and the other Sinais' predicament "mirrors" that of the divided, confused nations, as the turmoil of the Sinai clan "bleeds into" all of India:

> gradually the confusion and ruin seeped out through the windows of the house and took over the hearts and minds of the nation, so that war, when it came, was wrapped in the same muddled haze of unreliability in which we had begun to live. (*MC* 398)

Clearly the consequences of such a wholesale descent into a defamiliarizing "unreality" by a people who in the best of times have "only the slipperiest of grasps on reality" (*MC* 369) cannot help but be catastrophic. And the text does not disappoint, for what befalls the Sinais is a catastrophe of apocalyptic proportions; in all of twentieth-century fiction, Book Two's conclusion is perhaps rivaled (*Midnight's Children*'s own powerful conclusion notwithstanding) only by the destruction of Macondo in *Cien años de soledad* for sheer narrative scope, bleakness of vision, and utter totality of annihilation. Yet along with the cataclysmal events comes a further heightening of tension within the text itself to near-crisis proportions, as Saleem's increasingly bloated narrative claims stretch his credibility to the breaking point:

> Let me state this quite unequivocally: it is my firm conviction that the hidden purpose of the Indo-Pakistani War of 1965 was nothing moe nor less than the elimination of my benighted family from the face of the earth. (*MC* 403)

This prefacing of Book Two's climactic events is Saleem's boldest narrative gambit yet, all the more so given the apparently hyperbolic nature of the assertion and what Saleem has at stake—or more precisely, what he stands to lose—at this point in the narrative.

Saleem's claim is not so much fantastic as it is simply unbelievable, even within the context of a work of so-called magical realism; and further, to examine the events "with an analytical, unprejudiced eye" (*MC* 403), as Saleem asks later in the same paragraph, is to realize that the narrative only partially substantiates his story: Yes, the bombs landed in the appropriate places, but what does that really prove? Couldn't Saleem, if his dreams really enters the minds of his rulers as he claims (*MC* 404–405), have dreamed the outcome to be otherwise? Or dreamed it out of existence altogether? Unlike previous tellings of 'magical' events through which Saleem maintains his narrative credibility, here he has, on his own terms, apparently failed, despite his erudition and "the purity of [his] accents." Saleem has, it seems, finally fallen from his oft-defended perch of narrative credibility, and to swallow this latest claim seems akin to believing that Rostand's Chantecleer's cock-a-doodle-doo really made the sun rise, or that Macondo was destroyed because someone didn't like the Buendías.

But to dismiss the narration at this point, as mere hyperbole or overstuffed metaphor, or the sort of 'fantastic' storytelling so often identified with so-called magical realism—would be equally fallacious. For we must remember that what we are reading here, and in so many other texts that belong to that limit or threshold of languages, ontologies, knowledges—known collectively as the 'post-' (-colonialism, -modernism, -feminism, etc.), is nothing more or less than a crisis of narration itself, of the ability and privilege of a given culture to narrate; that is, to represent and thus *speak for* itself from a position other than that of the known, apprehended subject. The subject that would articulate its own place in the relation with its others, which would turn to the West and say "I. . . ."—this has ever been the task of this body of texts identified from without as "magical realism." It is a task, at best, complicated from the start, and at worst rendered contradictorily coherent, by the ambivalence of the texts' positions in relation to more than one set of cultural discourses; that is, the cultural balancing-act of presenting one (non-Western) culture for the consumption or entertainment or understanding of another (Western) one. Saleem's crisis of narration, then, his own 'defamiliarization' within his own text, takes the form of a struggle for the representation of difference. It is a narrator's with the limits of his own language, and the final inadequacies of that language to convey the "unbridled reality" (García Márquez's words) of his cultural surroundings to an audience far removed from that world.

It cannot be surprising, then, for Saleem to pass his ambivalence on in the form of an uncertain narration; indeed, he is himself so defamiliarized by now that he is uncertain of the facts of his own story: "Who to believe?" (*MC* 407). Certainly no Saleem, whose disorientation grows more acute as the narrative approaches its climax:

> Aircraft, real or fictional, dropped actual or mythical bombs. It is, accordingly, either a matter of fact or a figment of a diseased imagination that of the only three bombs to hit Rawalpindi and explode, the first landed on the bungalow in which my grandmother Naseem Aziz and my aunty Pia were hiding under a table. (*MC* 407)

Faced with the growing incoherence of his narrative and the impossibility of accurately 'translating' events for his audience any longer, the failure of a naive mimesis in the face of an almost total overdetermination of meanings ("But did it or didn't it? Was that how it happened? . . . Nothing was real, nothing certain" [*MC* 406]), there is nothing left for the text but a certain closure for his "drained" characters and hopelessly lost nation. But as Saleem intimates in Book Two's closing pages, this ritual annihilation or "cleansing," unlike the final pages of *Cien años de soledad*, is anything but final; it is in fact only a provisional apocalypse or clearing *(Lichtung)* from which the narrative may continue:

> Even ends have beginnings, everything must be told in sequence. . . . By August 8th, 1965, my family history had got itself into a condition from which what-was-achieved-by-bombing-patterns provided a merciful relief. No: let me use the important word: if we were to be purified, *something on the scale of what followed was probably necessary*. (*MC* 404, emphasis added)

"Necessary." In what sense? As a strictly narrative device, to more or less conveniently dispense with the burdensome encumbrances of an increasingly complicated text and its hopelessly overdetermined events and characters, certainly (again, we may think here of García Márquez's words: "our problem has been a lack of conventional means to make our lives believable"); Saleem simply wipes the narrative slate clean and moves on, allowing himself (and his audience) a much-needed respite from the defamiliarizing excesses of Book Two's final chapter. But this ritual "purifying" or "wiping-clean" of Saleem's is also a tabula rasa in a more generalized and radical sense. I have to this point used the term 'apocalypse' advisedly, and with the biblical sense in mind (the adjective appears strategically in the conclusion of *Cien años de soledad:* "the wrath of the *biblical* hurricane" [100y 383] emphasis is added), partially in allusion to the inevitable and necessary nature of the apocalyptic moment: the apocalypse as 'final solution,' as the necessary and most extreme measure taken when resolution of another kind is no longer either possible or desirable, the most absolute of endings. And yet: Why such an event now—with fully a third of the text still to be read? To better respond to this question, and better read the cataclysm of Book Two's final pages, we need only briefly consider two more defining features of the apocalypse in general:

1. the apocalypse always comes for the purpose of purification, of "cleansing." It is always a ritual "wiping-clean" of all that is undesirable or impure—hence the tongue-in-cheek title of Book Two's final chapter: "How Saleem Achieved Purity"; and

2. this ritual purifying or "wiping-clean" is always performed in the name of something to come, a better, future world for some to come *after* the biblical destruction of the cataclysm. Thus is the apocalypse simultaneously the most thorough and absolute ending *and* the most provisional of beginnings, the paradoxical signal of both narrative closure and transition. And in the case of *Midnight's Children* the annihilation of the Sinais signifies both an end and a beginning for the remainder of the text; for unlike García Márquez's unfortunate Buendía family, Saleem is, apparently, given a second opportunity on earth.

V

Although we cannot be satisfied with calling *Midnight's Children* a historical novel, it is certainly a text based partially upon documented, to the extent that they are documentable, events: Indian independence, the Indo-Pakistani War of 1965, the Indian Emergency of 1975–1976, and so forth. In the moment of narration, however, events and incidents are transformed into something else; that is, the act of narration is also a positing of an order [telos] and a construction of meaning, the creation of an ordering discourse from occurrences conjoined in that act. To narrate, then—and especially to narrate historically—is always to bestow meaning upon events which, by the act of narration, are subsumed after the fact into one or more ordering discourses to form a history.

Saleem's narration of Book Two's closing chapter, then, based as it is on the historical event known as the 'Indo-Pakistani War of 1965,' in terms of an apocalypse—in terms, as we have already seen, of an all-purifying and necessary cataclysm performed in preparation for a future to come—cannot fail to have implications for how we read those events presented in the text as historical and apocalyptic. For the moment of apocalypse is, as narrated, always a paradox: both event and meta-event, a moment contained within an ordering history that would yet transcend that history, rupture it (again paradoxically: from both within and without), and radically alter its movement. The apocalyptic moment is, as we have noted earlier, also both end and beginning, an end point or limit that defines, encloses, all that precedes it and proceeds from it; it is both recontextualization and revision, determining the movement of all that follows rewriting all previous events as premonitory.[64]

Book Two's cataclysmal conclusion would suggest that Book Three will mark a new beginning for Saleem and his narrative. To the extent that Saleem is "stripped of past present memory time shame and love" (*MC* 409) and "wiped clean as a wooden writing chest" (*MC* 410) by the impact of the spittoon, he can begin his narration of subsequent events apparently without these things; that is, while we have not forgotten about the pasts, presents, memories, and so forth, that we have read to this point, the character Saleem apparently has.[65] Thus again emerges the Heideggerian moment of the *Lichtung*, the opening up of a space in which things may be revealed in their presence *(Anwesen)*. The apocalypse comes in the name of that which would then emerge, would be then revealed, only in its aftermath, the violent clearing of a space, making possible the subsequent moment of illumination or enlightenment (Aufklärung).

But the apocalypse never fully achieves its purpose; that is, it is always as incomplete as it is excessive. For the very fact of its narration and contextualization within a history—its being written and read—as apocalypse already signifies its failure. As both a literary and philosophical device the apocalypse retains the ambivalent trace of that which would announce both ebbdings and beginnings; it is thus both incomplete and forever deferred., ongoing. Having read Saleem's apocalyptic moment of "purification" at the end of Book Two, we may begin to read the aftermath in the first chapter of Book Three; we learn in "The Buddha" that he has suffered "a merely partial erasure, *and was only wiped clean while others were wiped out* (*MC* 413, emphasis added). But rather than reap the rewards of the postapocalyptic afterlife, in which violent purification is followed by the promise of a better world, Book Two's cataclysm has also denied Saleem the refuge of a magical afterlife:

> Grieve for Saleem! Who, barred from celestial lawns by the continued beating of his heart, awoke once again amid the clammy metallic fragrances of a hospital ward.; for whom there were no houris, untouched by man or djinn, to provide the promised consolations of eternity. (*MC* 413)

Again, young Saleem's longed-for release from the burdens of history has been frustrated. The apocalypse is not final; another end of history has come and gone, and Saleem is alive, "flung unceremoniously across the years, fated to plunge memoryless into an adulthood whose aspect grew daily more grotesque" (*MC* 414). The promised "cleansing" of the apocalypse is further flawed by the survival of Saleem's sister Jamila Singer, "whom bombs were unable to find," and (arguably, less significantly) "in India, the family of my uncle Mustapha, with whom bombs could not be bothered" (*MC* 408). Having thus been denied the comforts of a magical afterlife in camphor gardens, however, character Saleem's reconnection to a historical consciousness is not immediate; as his first adult incarnation, "The Buddha" is wary of those who would "fill

[his] head with all that history" (*MC* 419), apparently content, for the moment, to remain in his amnesiac fog.

But to remain there, disconnected from both historical and alternative discourses, is precisely what Saleem is finally unable to do. In his new role as "The Buddha," a reluctant scout for the Pakistani army, Saleem continues to find himself in situations that would demand a level of consciousness, awareness, in short, the ability to act as a witness, for which there is no magical refuge. The task of interpreting, 'translating' this postapocalyptic India for a Western audience grows ever more complicated; and through it all, questions of how character Saleem is to emerge from his "purified" state to become reconnected to a historical consciousness, as well as the continuing instabilities of the narrator Saleem's claimed historical role "at the centre of things," and where his narration will place him within the text's various oppositional dichotomies ('East/West,' 'magical/nonmagical,' etc.), remain.

As Book Three progresses, Saleem still strives to place himself in a central role within both Indian history and his own text-in-progress, but his narrative tactics change. Instead of using established events to confirm his own importance within that officially sanctioned history—with the consequence that he often more-or-less uncritically accepts that history—Saleem now begins to construct his narrative as an *alternative* history; that is, he now begins to subvert and question the accepted official versions of Indian/Pakistani/Bangladeshi history, by constantly placing himself in the position of eyewitness to events ignored or otherwise neglected by the official discourses. So that while the ambivalence and unreliability of the earlier narration is by no means forgotten—Book Two's question of whether Saleem is "prepared to distort everything—to re-write the whole history of [his] times purely to place [him]self in a central role?" (*MC* 198) remains a significant one—the focus of Saleem's self-reflexive narration is now turned *outward,* upon the sham of government manipulations of events under the guise of an "official" national history. Saleem's narrated version of what follows, then, is as he advises, "as likely to be true as anything; as anything, that is to say, except what we [are] officially told" (*MC* 400).

Remembering this relation between Saleem's penchant for fanciful narration and the apparent duplicity of government propaganda will in fact prove useful for reading Book Three, as the radical revisions of Indian history begin early on:

> The camp in the hills will be found on no maps; it is too far from the Murree road for the barking of dogs to be heard, even by the sharpest-eared of motorists. . . . Yet it does, did, exist; though its existence has been hotly denied. (*MC* 415)

> And the Tiger, "Canine Unit for Tracking and Intelligence Activities? Never heard of it. . . . No, ridiculous, damn ridiculous, if you don't mind me saying." (*MC* 453–454)

Saleem's accounts of the Pakistani army slaughtering civilians (*MC* 512) work in much the same way, placing readers between the narrator's claims and government-sanctioned versions of what happened. We are further defamiliarized by Saleem's own uncertainty, as he narrates events in utter disbelief of what he has seen:

> Shaheed saw many things which were not true, which were not possible, because our boys would not could not have behaved so badly; we saw men in spectacles with heads like eggs being shot in side-streets, we saw the intelligencia of the city being massacred by the hundred, but it was not true because it could not have been true. (*MC* 449)

Here, as in Book Two's late chapters, the narration starts to unravel; the ambivalence and self-conscious uncertainty that marks Saleem's narration in those chapters are again evident, raising expectations for yet another destructively climactic series of events. Or put another way, another apocalypse, albeit not the final one, is in sight.

As in Book Two, Saleem's narration becomes increasingly unreliable as he approaches the text's next apocalyptic event. The novel's first signal to this effect also provides a structural parallel to Book Two, as Saleem again avers that a major historical event is staged for his benefit:

> Even if Shaheed had been able to hear me, I could not then have told him what I later became convinced was the truth: that the purpose of that entire war had been to reunite me with an old life, to bring me back together with my old friends. (*MC* 446)

There is much in this part of the text that is not a departure from what we know of Book Two; aside from the obvious parallel to Saleem's introduction to the war of 1965, there is also his continued drive to place himself at the center of events, as well as the defamiliarizing description of the "dying pyramid of heads" (*MC* 445–446). Given all of this, it would not be difficult to read Saleem's claim here as the signal of another "beginning of the end"; for the hysterical grandeur of the claim, along with the returning ambivalence of the narration and our experience of having read an analogous buildup of tension before the provisional apocalypse of "How Saleem Achieved Purity," combine to raise expectations for, if not a cataclysm on the order of Book Two's conclusion, then at least another major calamity for Saleem.

The narration from this point does not disappoint this expectation: Saleem's grasp of the 'objective' facts of his story again begins to disintegrate, and again begins to self-consciously second-guess his own version of events, see, for example, his repeated "unless it was on another day" (*MC* 494), or his ambivalence about the flood that carries him out of the Sundarbans (*MC* 440)—as the "cracks" in his narrative become increasingly apparent:

> No shadow of a doubt: an acceleration is taking place. Rip crunch crack—while road surfaces split in the awesome heat, I, too, am being hurried toward disintegration. What-gnaws-on-bones will not be denied for long; and still so much remains to be told . . . so that I, too, am forced to accelerate, to make a wild dash for the finishing line; before memory cracks beyond hope of reassembly, I must breast the tape. (*MC* 459)

Also worth noting here is the return of the magical "omens" analogous to those preceding fantastic events earlier in the text:

> it seems to me, at any rate, that on the day of Parvati's return, an Indian cabinet minister was in his railway carriage, at Samastipur, when an explosion blew him into the history books; that Parvati, who had departed amid the explosions of atom bombs, returned to us when Mr. L. N. Mishra, minister for railways and bribery, departed this world for good. Omens and more omens . . . perhaps, in Bombay, dead pomfrets were floating belly-side-up to the shore. (*MC* 494)

The narrative "omens" continue throughout the chapter, culminating in the synchronous events of the Emergency and Aadam Sinai's birth (*MC* 497–500).

Thus again appears the promise of a cleansing apocalypse, another clearing of a clearing *(Lichtung),* in a series of unveilings each more bombastically 'final' than the one before; and again appears the deterioration of narrative coherence as the text approaches its next historical cataclysm. The next such 'climactic' event, then, and the narrative crisis toward which the text has been building over the last two chapters, finally occurs in "Midnight," as Saleem recounts the story of the Midnight's Children's undoing at the hands of "The Widow," the novel's fictional moniker for Indian prime minister Indira Gandhi. As in the cataclysmal conclusion of Book Two, Saleem's narration again grows increasingly ambivalent and confused. But unlike "How Saleem Achieved Purity," in which the defamiliarizing narration is a product of

Saleem's own uncertainty, here he is all to aware of the facts; and unlike the playful, teasing digressions of Book One's opening chapter, here the narrator Saleem attempts in vain to distance himself psychically from the horrible events of his story. In the chapter's opening paragraph, Saleem's reflection of horror as he reflects on events at the Widow's Hostel is evident, in a passage that vacillates but is clearly not being playful:

> No!—But I must.
>
> I don't want to tell it!—But I swore to tell it all.—No, I renounce, not that, surely some things are better left . . . ?—That won't wash; what can't be cured must be endured!—But surely not the whispering walls, and treason, and snip-snip, and the women with the bruised chests?—Especially those things.—But how can I, look at me, I'm tearing myself apart, can't even agree with myself, talking arguing like a wild fellow, cracking up, memory going, yes, memory plunging into chasms and being swallowed by the dark, only fragments remain, none of it makes sense anymore! . . . But the horror of it, I can't won't mustn't won't can't no!—Stop this; begin.—No!—Yes. (*MC* 503)

Saleem's narration here is especially significant in that it strays from one of the acknowledged conventions of so-called magical realism: the casual, matter-of-fact narration of fantastic and sometimes horrifyingly violent events. At least two well-known critics of "magical-realist" literatures claim this narrative characteristic as an important one. Angel Flores describes the literature as "an art of surprises" in terms not far removed from Formalist conventions of 'defamiliarization,' as he quotes the Surrealist painter Giorgio de Chirico:

> [Autores del realismo mágico] todos subscribirán al dicto de Chirico: "Lo que es sobre todo necesario es limpiar del arte todo de lo conocido que ha de mantener hasta ahora: cada sujeto, idea, pensamiento, y símbolo tendra que ser dejado a un lado. . . . Las cosas le aparecerán bajo un nuevo aspecto, como si fueran iluminado por una constelación que aparece por primera vez." *Es sobre todo un arte de sorpresas.*[66] (AF 189, emphasis added)

Flores goes on to list four characteristics of magical realism that have since gained general critical acceptance, one of which is the appearance of a fantastic or larger-than-life realistic, everyday occurrence, an element also noted by Juan Barroso, among others. J. E. Irby also makes mention of the frequent and excessive incidents of violence in "magical realist" fiction, which often are narrated in a matter-of-fact, almost casual manner (JEI 45–48 and 53–59).

Rather than the "terrifying, nonchalant violence" of Saleem's self-described technique in Books and Two (*MC* 261–262), here Saleem approaches a narrative critical-mass, a limit not unlike Wilson Harris's Conradian "threshold of capacity,"[67] a point at which he struggles against the limits of language and consciousness to narrate impossible truths.

Whether the product of uncertainty of self-reflexive horror, one thing is certain; that once again, as events become more and more fantastic, so does Saleem's narration become increasingly fragmented ("Scraps, shreds, fragments" [*MC* 510]). And as in Book Two's conclusion, we again read a heightening of tension via an apparently impossible narrative claim just before the climactic event, this time the battle at the magician's ghetto and the destruction of the Midnight's Children:

> and here is the secret which has lain concealed for too long beneath the mask of those stifled days: the truest, deepest motive behind the declaration of a State of Emergency was the smashing, the pulverizing, the irreversible discombobulation of the children of midnight. (*MC* 510)

The pattern initiated by Saleem's fantastic claims again completes another apocalyptic cycle, as the Children are destroyed by the tactics of the Widow's regime; their downfall appears as yet another cataclysm on the order of Saleem's birth and subsequent "purification" during the war, as the Children are rounded up, imprisoned, and ultimately "drained" of their magical powers through mass sterilization.

The demise of the Children as a "magical" force brings to apparent closure the question, raised from the moment of Saleem's first realizations of his powers and sustained to this point, of the possibility of what I have been calling 'magical agency'; that is, the opening *(Lichtung)* of a space in which to read another speaking of and for themselves, an active representing of a present-and-past in the name of a present-and-future, of what is to come—a narrating beyond that of the narrating Orientalist, for whom the other is always a mysterious exotica to be assimililated and their future an extension into eternity of the same '(writing) representer/(written) represented' opposition. Almost from the inception of Saleem's telepathic meetings with the Children's Conference, and certainly as they decline into political bickering and divisiveness, the narrator Saleem hints that the dream of organized activism might never come to fruition. Further, Saleem's intimations that "the purpose of Midnight's Children might be annihilation; that we would have no meaning until we were destroyed" (*MC* 274) continue periodically through the text, culminating in their destruction at the hands of the Widow.

But the end of the Midnight's Children is not the end of *Midnight's Children*, anymore that the conclusion of the text itself signifies the end of agency or the dream of a future. After all that happens, is yet to happen in the novel's closing chapters, for Saleem, there remains the question of the text he creates; or put another way, after the life is lived there still remains the question of the life's remains, the documents of that life and its witnessed events that lingers in the form of the written text. But the question of bearing witness, of having seen and wishing to tell, in short, of *experience* and its always slippery translation into the written text, is never a simple one-to-one correspondence of seeing to telling; and as I observe elsewhere, the text written in the name of one-who-writes is never the same as the life lived in that name.[68]

But the question here is, after all, one of agency, or rather of what happens to agency in the face of utter annihilation, demoralization, and destruction. The question thus becomes: What happens to the future after the 'end of futures' that the apocalypse would be? Is not to write, the act of writing as an act of bearing witness, a gesture always projected toward a future? And what of Saleem—what possibility of agency is there left for him after this last cataclysm, *if not the act of writing itself*—his remaining ability to document, to narrate, and to bear witness? The other—unwritten, undocumented by a certain body of Western literatures and literary criticisms—the *other* history of the literature known collectively as 'magical realism' is, to a greater or lesser degree, the history of a body of texts that do precisely that: *bear witness,* in the face of a half-millennium of disillusionment and the failure of historical action, political reforms, dissensions from within, and invasions and colonizations from without. "Magical realism" thus emerges as a literature of *agency,* perhaps even magical agency, a body of texts that would speak, in however mediated or fractional a fashion, for an other that would no longer be represented by the voice and pen and knowledges of its Orientalist translators, which would dare in the face of all that has befallen it—*is* befalling it—to say "I." We are now, perhaps, a little better equipped context to reflect once again on the words of García Márquez as he accepts the great European prize for literature:

> Poetas y mendigos, músicos y profetas, guerreros y malandrines, todas las creaturas de aquella realidad desaforada hemos tenido que pedirle muy poco a la imaginación, porque el desafío mayor para nosotros ha sido la insuficiencia de los recursos convencionales para hacer creíble nuestra vida. Este es, amigos, el nudo de nuestra soledad.[69] (*Sol* 59)

Read in this further context, Saleem's new formulation of his role as narrator, that is, as self-appointed chronicler or historian rather than prophet or activist, seems uncharacteristically self-deprecating: from now on, mine would be a role as peripheral as any redundant oldster: the traditional function, perhaps, of reminiscer, of teller-of-tales. . . ." (*MC* 534). This passage, along with Saleem's chagrin at the magicians' loss of memory (*MC* 531), constitute his final narrative position; having failed in his bid to become a magical prophet or political leader, he now claims for himself the role of historian, a spectator or interpreter rather than a mover or shaker of his world. Certainly his preoccupation with the preserving process seems a particularly apt analogy; it is in this capacity of "preserving" that Saleem would finally stake his sense of agency, for it is precisely agency that is more than ever at stake:

> One day, perhaps, the world may taste the pickles of history. They may be too strong for some palates, their smell may be overpowering, tears may rise to eyes; I hope nevertheless that it will be possible to say of them that they possess the authentic taste of truth . . . that they are, despite everything, acts of love. (*MC* 550)

And it is finally to things preserved, in texts and in pickle jars, however imperfectly or unreliably, that we must finally turn, as our guide and narrator accelerates toward his final undoing. As in *Cien años de soledad,* we reach the conclusion having read an apocalypse, the cataclysmal disintegration of a world utterly consumed. But what is perhaps most disturbing about *Midnight's Children*'s horrific conclusion, beyond its bleakness of vision and totality of destruction, is paradoxically its lack of closure:

> Yes, they will trample me underfoot, the numbers marching one two three, four hundred million five hundred six, reducing me to bits of voiceless dust, just as, in all good time, they will trample my son who is not my son, and his son who will not be his, and his who will not be his, until the thousand and first generation, until a thousand and one midnights have bestowed their terrible gifts and a thousand and one children have died, because it is the privilege and the curse of midnight's children to be both masters and victims of their times, to forsake privacy and be sucked into the annihilating whirlpool of the multitudes, and to be unable to live or die in peace. (*MC* 552)

Unlike the destruction of García Márquez's Macondo, the apocalypse here is ongoing, endlessly recurring, a vicious, spiraling cycle of cataclysm and destruction that the Saleems of the world have no power, magical or otherwise, to alter or escape. And this too is part of that other, unchronicled history of so-called magical realism: as a literature of the apocalypse—or more precisely of apocalyp-*ses,* of the recurring cataclysm and state of chronic crisis of cultures forever at the mercy of another's representations, another's cultural imperatives. Rehearsing the apocalypse thus becomes a way of life, a grotesque and exploded caricature of D. H. Lawrence's introduction to his most notorious novel:

> The cataclysm has happened, we are among the ruins, we start to build up new little habitats, to have new little hopes. It is rather hard work: there is no smooth road into the future: but we go round, or scramble over the obstacles. We've got to live no matter how many skies have fallen.[70]

Thus is the apocalypse finally, paradoxically both excessive and insufficient; its intended "purification" is ever incomplete, some of intended targets always surviving to tell the tale. The body of texts known as 'magical realism' have always been the chronicle of these excessive yet unfinished apocalypses, a mimesis of surfeit, the calling cards of others and worlds just beyond our grasp.

Conclusion

Magic, "Realism," and the "Post-"

Finally, then, there remains the requisite if naive question: "But what then *is* magical realism?" Everyone talks about "magical realism," as a literary style or mode, or even as a genre; everyone knows more or less what "magical realism" 'is,' or can point to any number of examples of it in literature or film. The same thing happens with any number of related critical terms: 'postmodernism,' 'surrealism,' even 'realism' itself, to the point at which they become near-meaningless adjectives of common parlance, all signs inflated and devalued in proportion to their distance from a distinct and rigorous critical application. But if we return to the originary texts from which the terms still circulate, say Jean-François Lyotard's *Postmodern Condition: A Report on Knowledge,*[1] or even Aristotle's discussion of mimesis in his *Poetics,*[2] what we read there is epistemically far removed from—almost unrecognizable within the context of—what has since been written, is being written, under the respective signs of 'postmodernism' and 'realism.'

With all of this in mind, then, it is curious that *The Oxford English Dictionary*[3] contains no entry for a "magic realism" or "magical realism." We do find a lengthy entry for "realism," about which more later; but more to my immediate purpose, let us turn to this very striking entry:

> **magic. 1. a.** The *pretended art* of influencing the course of events, and of producing marvellous physical phenomena, *by processes supposed to owe their efficacy to their power of compelling the intervention of spiritual beings,* or of bringing into operation some occult controlling principle of nature; sorcery, witchcraft. Also, the practice of this art. (OEDxii 185–186, emphasis added)

Also:

> **3.** *transf.* The art of producing (by legerdemain, optical illusion, or devices suggested by knowledge of physical science) surprising phenomena *resembling the pretended results of magic;* conjuring. (OEDxii 185–186, emphasis added)

Already we may note two points that will help illustrate the contradictorily coherent strategies of displacement at work in the application of the term 'magical realism':

1. On the one hand, the first passage defines the term in an obviously negative light, through the use of terms such as 'sorcery,' 'witchcraft,' and the especially damning phrase 'some occult controlling principle of nature'—the (uncharacteristically vague, for a source so renowned for its thoroughness and specificity) modifier "some" being especially telling for its implicit denial of such knowledge by either writer or reader, that is, "some strange, evil thing that we would know nothing about." This preliminary gesture of definition is already fraught with ambivalence, rendered unintelligible by its own effort to clarify its terms; for just ahead of its implicit denial of the "occult" the entry would inform us that there are apparently malevolent forces that are "supposed to owe their efficacy to their power of compelling the intervention of spiritual beings," a supposition which, removed from its context, is immediately recognizable and familiar to most of us trained in the various religious disciplines as the premise behind *prayer,* indeed behind the act of praying itself. In fact, what is prayer if not an explicit appeal for "the intervention of spiritual beings"? In this and other ways, too numerous to list here but equally astonishing, the passage deconstructs itself in the very act of casting away as "occult" that which has always been ingrained in its own complicites with the mystical, with "magic."

The passage proceeds to imbricate itself even further, entangling itself even as it would distance itself from the "magical," as it attempts to make exceptions for 'acceptable' types of magic:

> The "magic" which made use of the invocation of evil or doubtful spirits was of course always regarded as sinful; but *natural magic,* i.e., that which did not involve recourse to the agency of personal spirits, was in the Middle Ages usually recognized as a legitimate department of study and practice, so long as it was not employed for maleficent ends. Of "natural magic" as understood by mediaeval writers, typical examples are *the making of an image,* under certain astrological conditions, *in order to injure or benefit the health of the person represented;* and the application of a medicament to a weapon in order to heal the wound made by it. These things, if

> now practiced, would still be called "magic", though the qualification "natural" would seem quite inappropriate. On the other hand, the "natural magic" of the Middle Ages included much that from the standpoint of modern science is "natural", but not "magical", the processes resorted to being really, *according to the now known laws of physical causation,* adapted to produce the intended effects. (OEDxii, emphasis added)

There is certainly much in this passage that a careful reader might find astonishing, and that would reward scrutiny here if space allowed. But for now we need only mention two further points, to emphasize the very problematic nature of the assumedly 'objective' dictionary definition:

a. its primary example of what it would classify as acceptable or 'natural' magic bears a more than passing resemblance to what, within the context of "occult" practice, becomes immediately recognizable as the use of *vodun-* or *voodoo dolls,* with which the person casting the spell might control the physical well-being and overall health of the represented person; and

b. its recourse to "the now known laws of physical causation" lays bare what has been implicit in the passage all along, namely that the illusory distinctions between what is and is not considered "occult" is, in this context, predicated precisely on the practice in question being within the realm of what is *known,* that is, *familiar,* to the culture making the distinctions. At stake here is, among other things, the most intricate of complicities between the epistemological and the onto-theological; that is, between what we know and what we do not know, and thus fear, which is itself the basis for every encounter with what is alien, with what is other; and

2. at the same time as the definition would distance itself from a mysterious "occult" practice of which it would claim no knowledge, it would expose those same discourses as sham, as practices without value or meaning. The term 'magic' thus becomes a "pretended art [as opposed to a 'science']" which depends for its currency upon "processes supposed to owe their efficacy to their power of compelling the intervention of spiritual beings"; most damning of all, however, is the assertion that the discourses so ambivalently censured as "occult" are mere products of "legerdemain [the OED's definition: "tricks performed with the hands, as by a magician"; from the Old French *leger de main,* meaning 'light of hand'], optical illusion, or devices suggested by knowledge of physical science," a shallow simulacra only "resembling the pretended results of magic." Aside from the obvious contradiction of dismissing so hastily in one breath what was addressed so gravely and at such length in the previous one, this self-contradictory gesture, of lightly dismissing and apprehensively condemning, of simultaneously claiming knowledge, seeing, as it were, through

the sham of "magic," and disavowing that knowledge, the inability to see, or self-righteous averting of eyes from, what is tellingly called the 'occult' (a word that is itself ambiguous, meaning both 'dark' and 'hidden from view'), is consistent with the cultural practices of a civilization unable to recognize the others that it fears and desires, but can never fully apprehend. What is contradictorily coherent is symptomatic of the force of a desire, a manifestation of the desire to fulfill an impulse that must be suppressed.[4] Seen in this context, we can begin to read more clearly what I have been implicitly working toward all along in my theorizing of these literatures called 'magical realism': namely that the history of imperialism; that is, of the colonizing impulse, like the history of the West itself, is the history of these contradictory gestures, of the simultaneous desire to apprehend/civilize/assimilate, and suppress/vanquish/exterminate that which is experienced as alien: as other. And beyond all this, that the literature of so-called magical realism represents the first flowering, the first moment of a future fruition for the postcolonial discourses that will bring, are bringing, the remnants of a tired colonialism to its final crisis.

In *The Oxford Encyclopedia of 20th Century Art*, we learn that 'magical realism' is "a term introduced by Franz Roh in a book on post-Expressionism in 1925, and adapted by later criticism," and that it is to be associated with painters such as Wilhelm Leibl and Hans Thomas and distinguished from the German Verism of the time.[5] And so already, we are presented with an originary movement for 'magical realism' that is irreducibly European, as the term is itself wielded in the early twentieth century by a German art critic.[6] But that is not all, for then there is this:

> The term has, however, been more often used of the suggestion *of an imaginative dream reality other than the reality of daily life* which, with a strong impression of "presence", is conveyed by some naïve art, some metaphysical painting, and some surrealism. (OEA 344, emphasis added)

Bearing in mind that the entry in question seeks to define a style of German painting rather than a body of literature, one must still wonder at the appearance of the word 'naive' here, that is, one must wonder why a term that is so casually applied to texts written by Rushdie and García Márquez, by Toni Morrison and Günter Grass and Jorge Luis Borges—in short, by some of the most sophisticated writers of this or any century—would also be associated with "children's art" and "folk art," with "the art of primitive peoples and of psychotics" (OEA 413–414). In the entry for "naive art" from which I cite, we are additionally warned against confusing true "naive art" with the "false naïveté *(faux naif)*" of a Picasso or a Klee, which is apparently to be taken as a technique or affectation and distinguished accordingly from the art of the "true" other: the child, savage, madman. A reading of literary magical realism as a type of "false naive *(faux naif)*" writing, within the context of the Schklovskian model of defamiliarization with which I have been working in these pages, seems to be a very promising one, and one that would require a very careful analysis in its own right. But we can say for now that the present example again illustrates the ambivalent gesture, the Western impulse to dismiss as "magical," "naive," or otherwise exotic or unreal that which is irremediably imbricated within itself, that which is simultaneously desired and suppressed. We may begin to read the history of this gesture, to cite just two instances, in G. W. F. Hegel's denigration of the American indigenous peoples as a perpetual child: undisciplined, unfit for physical or mental labors, and utterly incapable of intellectual development,[7] or in Bartolomé De Las Casas's passionate refutation of the Spanish myth of the "civilizing mission" of colonialism—both the colonial and De Las Casas's rebuttal centered on Aristotle's attempts in the *Politics* to justify Greek rule over non-Greek or "barbarous" peoples.[8]

It is finally to this sense of the unreal or "imaginative dream reality" alluded to in this passage from the *Oxford Encyclopedia,* or rather to realities other than those most Western readers would recognize as part of their "daily life," which we must turn. For that has often been the paradoxical basis of both the limited adoption and relative marginalization of "magical realism": its sense of difference from, or more specifically its interrogation (and often willful disregard) of the mimetic norms of so-called realistic literatures, or precisely what this citation would claim as "the reality of daily life." One would have to ask: "*Whose?* Whose 'daily life'?" It should be more than clear by now that the range of incidents considered plausible or "realistic" in texts such as *Midnight's Children* or *Cien años de soledad* is unlikely to approximate that of most of its Western readers. Yet those same texts just as clearly seek to engage the political and historical discourses of the cultures they respectively represent. To the extent that they do so successfully involves, among other things, the undermining of a Western hegemony of ethnographic representation, what amounts to a canon of nineteenth- and twentieth-century ethnographic literatures; to cite one such example, we may certainly read *Midnight's Children* as just such a deconstruction of E. M. Forster' *A Passage to India*. But it is also and more importantly a dismantling of the Western dichotomy between what Amaryll Chanady calls "the nonreflexive primitive society and the Western ethnographer's discourse of knowledge."[9]

What the literatures of so-called magical realism offer, finally, is the first glimpses of a postcolonial literature that would dare to represent itself, however inadequately at first, as a space or index of difference, indeed as the very marker of that difference. Such a radical act of representation must necessarily seem to be excessive, out of all proportion with a Western literary tradition steeped in outdated notions of mimetic "realism" and tired constructs of a specious universal rationalism. We may, in this context, consider once again Gabriel García Márquez's reference to the "unbridled reality" of Latin America, or his dismissal of conventional Western notions of "realism" as inadequate to represent a "reality [which] is in itself out of all proportion."[10] "Magical realism" thus emerges as precisely a mimesis of excess, of excessive and "unbridled realit[ies]," which paradoxically turns out to be a *more* "realistic" mode of representation than conventional Western conceptions of literary "realism." Thus would certain beautiful and excessive literatures labeled 'magical realism' come to represent what is to occur, is already occurring, under the sign of the postcolonial: a recovering or reclaiming of cultural discourses dominated until now by the centralizing and suppressing impulses of an imperial culture in decline. Its arrival could hardly be more anticipated, or more welcome. And while we wait, there are always questions: those asked of us by our various cultural specters ("What will you do?"), those that we must ask of them ("What would you have me do? Why don't you leave me alone?"). The first thing any ghost would ask of us is precisely that we hear it out, that we listen to its demands; it would have us first learn to let them speak, to begin to return the speech deprived it for so long.

The rest is listening.

Notes

Introduction

1. Hegel is, of course, concerned with a phenomenological description of human existence, which is to say existence as it appears *(erscheint)* or manifests itself. The text, then, is primarily concerned with the conscious subject or "consciousness" (let us not forget that "consciousness" *[Bewusstsein]* is Hegel's standard term for "man" *[sic]* in the *Phenomenology*) as it unfolds toward a final historical culmination and a 'posthistorical' world.

But of course Hegel writes this entire history of consciousness as a completely rendered totality, having already 'seen' it all from a position of "Absolute Knowledge"; and thus he is able to set it all down in the form of the Hegelian system. Certainly I make no claims here to such a telos or metaposition; but what is significant here is less the veracity of this or that system than the fact of what we might call a *future-present;* that is, a future that is nevertheless 'present' to the philosopher, which may be glimpsed in advance of its coming-to-be.

2. Ahmad, Aijaz. "The Politics of Literary Postcoloniality" in *Race and Class* 36/3 (1995): 9.

3. Sareen, S. K. "Australian Post-coloniality" in *Interrogating Post-colonialism: Theory, Text, and Context;* Harish Trivedi & Meenakshi Mukherjee, eds. (Shimla: Indian Institute of Advanced Study, 1996) p. 111.

4. Mongia, Padmini. "Introduction" in *Contemporary Postcolonial Theory,* Padmini Mongia, ed. (London: Arnold, 1998) p.1.

5. Mukherjee, Meenakshi. 'Interrogating Post-colonialism' in *Interrogating Post-colonialism: Theory, Text, and Context,* Harish Trivedi & Meenakshi Mukherjee, eds. (Shimla: Indian Institute of Advanced Study, 1996) pp. 5–6. Hereafter cited as MM.

6. Fanon, Frantz. *The Wretched of the Earth* (1961), Constance Farrington, trans., Jean-Paul Sartre, pref. (New York: Grove, 1968) p. 209.

7. Gorra, Michael. *After Empire: Scott, Naipaul, Rushdie* (Chicago: University of Chicago Press, 1997) pp. 4–5. In the passage cited Gorra is specifically discussing Said's *Culture and Imperialism* (New York: Knopf, 1993) and JanMohamed's *Manichean Aesthetics: The Politics of Literature in Colonial Africa* (Amherst: University of Massachusetts Press, 1983), among others; I would extend Gorra's claim to encompass an entire phase of/approach to postcolonial studies beginning arguably with Said's seminal work *Orientalism* (New York: Pantheon, 1978) and breathing its last in *Culture and Imperialism*, perhaps the definitive study of English colonial literature's ideological unconscious. Hereafter cited as MG.

8 . Bhabha, Homi K. *The Location of Culture* (London: Routledge, 1994). Hereafter cited as HB.

9. Orwell, George. 'Shooting an Elephant' (1936) in *The Collected Essays, Journalism, and Letters of George Orwell, Volume 1: An Age Like This 1920–1940*, Sonia Orwell & Ian Angus, eds. (New York: Penguin, 1970) p. 269.

10. Hall, Stuart. 'New Ethnicities' in *The Post-colonial Studies Reader*, Bill Ashcroft, Gareth Griffiths, & Helen Tiffin, eds. (London: Routledge, 1994) pp. 223–227.

11. Balme, Christopher. 'Inventive Syncretism: The Concept of the Syncretic in Intercultural Discourse' in *Fusion of Cultures?* Peter O. Stummer & Christopher Balme, eds. (Amsterdam: Rodopi, 1996) p. 9, emphasis added.

12. See Stummer, Peter O., & Balme, Christopher, eds. *Fusion of Cultures?* (Amsterdam: Rodopi, 1996); and Young, Robert J. C. *Colonial Desire: Hybridity in Theory, Culture and Race* (London: Methuen, 1995).

13. Deleuze, Gilles, & Guattari, Felix. *Kafka: Toward a Minor Literature* (1975), Dana Polan, trans. (Minneapolis: University of Minnesota Press, 1986) p. 16.

14. Lee, Kyung-Won. "Is the Glass Half-Empty or Half-Full? Rethinking the Problems of Postcolonial Revisionism" in *Cultural Critique* 36/2 (Spring 1997): p 89. Hereafter cited as KWL.

15. Foucault, Michel. *Power/Knowledge: Selected Interviews and Other Writings 1972–1977*, Colin Gordon, ed. & trans. (New York: Pantheon, 1980) pp. 79–81.

16. Lest anyone think the point silly or overwrought, I offer this passage from Dirlik's best-known essay:

> My neighbors in Farmville, Virginia, are no match in power for the highly paid, highly prestigious postcolonial intellectuals at Columbia, Princeton, or Duke; some of them might even be willing to swap positions and take the anguish that comes with hybridity so long as it brings with it the power and the prestige it seems to command.

Such invective only detracts from what is in some ways a very useful analysis of the institutional dynamics at work in the presence of Third World intellectuals working in the First World academy. See Dirlik, Arif. "The Postcolonial Aura: Third World Criticism in the Age of Global Capitalism" in *Critical Inquiry* 20 (Winter 1994): 343.

17. Appiah, Kwame Anthony. "Is the Post- in Postmodernism the Post- in Postcolonial?" in *Critical Inquiry* 17/2 (Winter 1991): 353.

18. San Juan Jr., E. *Beyond Postcolonial Theory* (New York: St. Martin's, 1998). Hereafter cited as ESJ.

19. Of the three in question only Said has published a traditional memoir; but Sara Suleri has also published one; and Gayatri Spivak speaks at length of her experiences as a "Native Informant" working in the First World academy, most prominently in interview form. See Said, Edward. *Out of Place: A Memoir* (New York: Knopf, 1999); Suleri, Sara. *Meatless Days* (Chicago: University of Chicago Press, 1989); and Spivak, Gayatri Chakravorty. *The Postcolonial Critic: Interviews, Strategies, Dialogues* (London: Routledge, 1990).

20. *The Oxford English Dictionary* (2nd ed.) Vol. 10 (Oxford: Oxford University Press, 1989) pp. 1164–6116.

21. Shohat, Ella. "Notes on the 'Post-Colonial' " in *Social Text* 31/32 (1992): 101, emphasis added. Hereafter cited as ES.

22. Paul Smith provides this useful summation of these terms:

> The human *agent* will be seen here as the place from which resistance to the ideological is produced or played out, and thus as *not* equivalent to either the "subject" or the "individual" . . . The term "agent" . . . will be used to mark the idea of a form of subjectivity where, by virtue of the contradictions and disturbances in and among subject-positions, the possibility (indeed, the actuality) of resistance to ideological pressure is allowed for (even though that resistance too must be produced in an ideological context).

See Smith, Paul. *Discerning the Subject* (Minneapolis: University of Minnesota Press, 1988) p. xxxv.

23. Spivak, Gayatri Chakravorty. *The Spivak Reader,* Donna Landry & Gerald MacLean, eds. (New York: Routledge, 1996) p. 203.

24. Parry, Benita. "Problems in Current Theories of Colonial Discourse" in *Oxford Literary Review* 9 (1987): 43. Hereafter cited as BP.

25. Mahood, M. M. *The Colonial Encounter: A Reading of Six Novels* (Totowa, NJ: Rowman & Littlefield, 1977) p. 186. Hereafter cited as MMM.

26. Cherniavsky, Eva. "Subaltern Studies in a U.S. Frame" in *Boundary 2* 23/2 (1996): 85–110.

27. Chun, Allen. "Fuck Chineseness: On the Ambiguity of Ethnicity as Culture as Identity" in *Boundary 2* 23/2 (1996): 111–138 (qt. from p. 138). Hereafter cited as AC.

28. E. San Juan Jr. is even more virulent on this point, referring to cultural pluralism or what he calls the "multicultural Imaginary" as "the principal ideological strategy of the ruling bourgeoisie in the post-Cold War era" (ESJ 12) and generally echoing Chun's conviction that cultural difference without social equality is meaningless. See also San Juan Jr. E. *Beyond Postcolonial Theory* New York: St. Martin's, 1998) pp. 113–154.

29. Miyoshi, Masao. "A Borderless World? From Colonialism to Transnationalism and the Decline of the Nation-State" in *Critical Inquiry* 19 (Summer 1993): 726–751.

30. The panelist in question argues for an Indian national "core constituency" comprised of Indians of liberal sensibility and "[l]argely middle-class in attitudes and values," then proceeds to exclude Bhabha and Spivak, and by implication all diasporic Indian scholars, by way of a rhetorical question:

> Do Gayatri Chakravorty Spivak or Homi Bhabha, to name two "Indian" champions of theory, belong to the previously defined constituency? Again, the answer has to be a "no," though it would perhaps be a more qualified "no." The fact is that their stake in India and in the health of our academic culture, too, is minimal. They speak to the West, seek to modify or alter Western modes of thinking and writing.

See Paranjape, Makarand. "Coping with Post-colonialism" in *Interrogating Post-colonialism: Theory, Text, and Context,* Harish Trivedi & Meenakshi Mukherjee, eds. (Shimla: Indian Institute of Advanced Study, 1996) p. 44.

31. Belliappa, K. C. "Three Post-colonial Novelists: Ghosh, Tharoor, Advani" in *Interrogating Post-colonialism: Theory, Text, and Context,* Harish Trivedi & Meenakshi Mukherjee, eds. (Shimla: Indian Institute of Advanced Study, 1996) p. 211.

32. Griffiths, Gareth. "Representation and Production: Issues of Control in Post-colonial Cultures" in *Interrogating Post-colonialism: Theory, Text, and Context,* Harish Trivedi & Meenakshi Mukherjee, eds. (Shimla, Indian Institute of Advanced Study, 1996) pp. 22 and 32. Hereafter cited as GG.

33. Griffiths, Gareth. "The Myth of Authenticity" in *The Post-colonial Studies Reader,* Bill Ashcroft, Gareth Griffiths, & Helen Tiffin, eds. (London: Routledge, 1995) p. 237. Hereafter cited as gg.

34. Jameson, Frederic. "Third World Literature in the Era of Multinational Capitalism" in *Social Text* 15 (Fall 1986): 65 and 69.

35. In a book of interviews entitled *Positions,* Derrida explains his suspicions of a historicist narrative associated with Marxist and Hegelian readings of history ("the *metaphysical* concept of history," as he calls it), and his interest in a historiography of heterogeneity and difference. Although the interviews constitute a wide-ranging discussion of his work in general to that point, Derrida does offer substantial insights into historicism and its limits, including a hearty endorsement of Louis Althusser's critique of Hegelian concepts of history, which for Derrida "aims at showing that there is not one single history, a general history, but rather histories *different* in their type, rhythm, mode of inscription—intervallic, differentiated histories."

See Derrida, Jacques. *Positions* (1972), Alan Bass, trans. (Chicago: University of Chicago Press, 1981) pp. 46–49 and 58–60.

36. Salman Rushdie's *Midnight's Children* (New York: Knopf, 1980) and Gabriel García Márquez's *Cien años de soledad* (One Hundred Years of Solitude) (Madrid: Espasa-Calpe, 1985) emerge as prime exemplars of "historiographic metafiction" in Linda Hutcheon's discussion, as do the novels of J. M. Coetzee.

See Hutcheon, Linda. *A Poetics of Postmodernism: History, Theory, Fiction* (New York: Routledge, 1988) pp. 105–123.

37. Mohan, Rajeswari. "Dodging the Crossfire: Questions for Postcolonial Pedagogy" in *Order and Partialities: Theory, Pedagogy, and the "Postcolonial,"* Kostas Myrsiades & Jerry McGuire, eds. (Albany: State University of New York Press, 1995) p. 265. Hereafter cited as RM.

38. Ashcroft, Bill; Griffiths, Gareth; & Tiffin, Helen. *The Empire Writes Back: Theory and Practice in Post-Colonial Literatures* (London: Routledge, 1989) p. 2.

39. Jolly, Rosemary. "Rehearsals of Liberation: Contemporary Postcolonial Discourse in the New South Africa" in *PMLA: Publications of the Modern Language Association* 110/1 (January 1995): 21. Hereafter cited as RJ.

40. I address this issue at greater length in another article, "*La patria y el tirano*: José Martí and the Role of Literature in the Formation of Cuban Nationalisms, Past and Present" in *The Iowa Journal of Cultural Studies* 12(1993): 25–43.

41. Spivak herself takes the term from Antonio Gramsci's "On the Margins of History: History of the Subaltern Social Groups" *(Ai margini della storia: Storia dei gruppi sociali subalterni).*

See Gramsci, Antonio. *Selections from Prison Notebooks,* Quentin Hoare & Geoffrey Nowell Smith, trans. (London: Lawrence & Wishart, 1971) p. 26 n.

42. Spivak, Gayatri Chakravorty. "Subaltern Studies: Deconstructing Historiography" in *In Other Worlds: Essays in Cultural Politics* (New York: Routledge, 1988) p. 197. Hereafter cited as IOW.

43. MacCabe, Colin. "Foreword" in *In Other Worlds: Essays in Cultural Politics* (New York: Routledge, 1988) p. ix.

44. Young, Robert. *White Mythologies: Writing History and the West* (London: Routledge, 1990) pp. 161–162. Hereafter cited as RY.

45. Spivak, Gayatri Chakravorty. *The Postcolonial Critic: Interviews, Strategies, Dialogues* (New York: Routledge, 1990) p. 70.

46. Spivak, Gayatri Chakravorty. *A Critique of Postcolonial Reason: Toward a History of the Vanishing Present* (Cambridge: Harvard University Press, 1999) pp. 4, 9, and 51–52. Hereafter cited as CPR.

47. Certainly all of Said's examples of Orientalist scholars, from Richard Burton to T. E. Lawrence, support this formulation. This is not say that no European orientalist ever reflected or otherwise experienced any ambivalence about their work, just that in Said's estimation all finally placed their work in the service of empire: knowing the Orient, for Said, became Europe's strategy for better managing and dominating it.

See Said, Edward W. *Orientalism* (New York: Pantheon, 1978) pp.194–197, 223–225, & 240–241.

48. Shankar, S. "The Thumb of Ekalavya: Postcolonial Studies and the 'Third World' Scholar in a Neocolonial World" in *World Literature Today* 68/3 (Summer 1994): 479. Hereafter cited as SS.

49. Foucault, Michel. *The History of Sexuality, Volume 1* (1980), Robert Hurley, trans. (New York: Vintage, 1990) p. 94.

50. Specifically, San Juan Jr. refers to *Culture and Imperialism* as Said's "much more committed sequel" to *Orientalism,* its central task "the demystifying interrogation of Eurocentric discourse."

51. Spivak, Gayatri Chakravorty. "Can the Subaltern Speak?" in *The Post-colonial Studies Reader*, Bill Ashcroft, Gareth Griffiths, & Helen Tiffin, eds. (London: Routledge, 1995) p. 28.

52. Gikandi, Simon. "In the Shadow of Hegel: Cultural Theory in an Age of Displacement" in *Research in African Literatures* 27/2 (Summer 1996): 140.

53. I discuss this form of mimicry as a subversive intervention later and at greater length. See my discussion of Edward Brathwaite's poetry in chapter 2 of the present volume, "Specters of the Nation: Resistance, *Criollismo,* and the Ambivalence of the 'Neo-.' "

54. Antoni, Robert. *Divina Trace* (Woodstock, NY: Overlook, 1992). Hereafter cited as DT.

55. Rushdie, Salman. *The Ground Beneath Her Feet* (New York: Henry Holt, 1999).

56. Hutcheon, Linda. *A Theory of Parody: The Teachings of Twentieth-Century Art Forms* (New York: Methuen, 1985) pp. 5–6.

57. The date of the *Ramayana*'s composition is a major area of debate among Hindu scholars. Factions arguing for various dates have established a range of over one thousand years, claiming dates of origin between 1500 B.C. and 200 B.C. This statement by P. Lal perhaps puts it best, in his very useful introduction to his own "transcreation" of the text: "No one really knows, but one could hazard a guess anywhere between 1500 B.C. and 200 B.C." It is also worth mentioning that even if such a date of origin could be accurately determined for the text, that the *Ramayana*'s origins as an oral history far older than Valmiki's transcription would render such efforts less than conclusive.

See Lal. P., trans. & intro. *The Ramayana of Valmiki* (New Delhi: Vikas Publishing House Pvt., 1981) p. xxii.

58. Conrad, Joseph. *Heart of Darkness* (1899), Ross C. Murfin, ed. & intro. (New York: St. Martin's, 1989).

59. To read the phrase "threshold of capacity" in Harris's originary context, see Harris, Wilson. "The Frontier on Which *Heart of Darkness* Stands" in *Joseph Conrad: Third World Perspectives,* Robert Hamner, ed. (Washington, DC: Three Continents, 1990) p. 162.

60. Harris, Wilson, *The Palace of the Peacock* (London: Faber & Faber, 1960).

61. Derrida, Jacques. *Specters of Marx,* Peggy Kamuf, trans., Bernd Magnus and Stephen Cullenberg, intro. (New York: Routledge, 1994).

62. It is precisely because such suppressed knowledges lie beyond the reach of the subject's consciousness, what Sigmund Freud calls the subject's "critical faculty," that psychoanalysis has always strived in its methods to bypass the patient's conscious mental processes (first through hypnosis, later through free association) and thus preempt their ability to bring a critical (interpreting, editing, potentially censoring) activity to bear upon thoughts or ideas emerging from the unconscious. During analysis the patient is asked to suppress only that "critical faculty" that would in turn work to act upon the "involuntary ideas" of the unconscious:

> In reflection there is one more psychical activity at work than in the most attentive self-observation. . . . the man who is reflecting is also exercising his *critical* faculty; this leads him to reject some of the ideas that occur to him after perceiving them, to cut short others without following the trains of thought which they would open up to him, and to behave in such a way

> toward still others that they never become conscious at all and are accordingly suppressed before being perceived.
>
> It is thus only through such the rigorous "self-observation" of analysis, which would ensure that the emergent contents of the unconscious are not interfered with in any way, can the properly informed work of interpretation take place.

See Freud, Sigmund. *The Interpretation of Dreams* (1899) (4th English ed., 1953), James Strachey, trans. & ed. (New York: Avon, 1965) pp. 133–135. Hereafter cited as *ID*.

63. Cliff, Michelle. "Clare Savage as a Crossroads Character" in *Caribbean Women Writers: Essays from the First International Conference,* Selwyn R. Cudjoe, ed. (Wellesley, MA: Calaloux, 1990) p. 265.

64. Cliff. Michelle. "Object Into Subject: Some Thoughts on the Work of Black Women Artists" in *This Bridge Called My Back: Writings by Radical Women of Color* (2nd ed.), Cherrie Moraga & Gloria Anzaldúa, eds. (New York: Kitchen Table, Women of Color Press, 1983) p. 272.

65. Coetzee, J. M. *White Writing: On the Culture of Letters in South Africa* (New Haven: Yale University Press, 1988) p. 8.

66. Coetzee discusses these constructions of the Hottentots as "idle" as part of an Afrikaaner rhetoric of nationalist identification with the land: as harder-working, more dedicated farmers, the settler thus prove themselves more worthy heirs of the erstwhile colony than the natives. See Coetzee, J. M. *White Writing: On the Culture of Letters in South Africa* (New Haven: Yale University Press, 1988) pp. 12–35.

See also Coetzee, J. M. *Boyhood: Scenes from Provincial Life* (New York: Viking, 1997) p. 62.

67. Mowitt, John. "Breaking Up Fanon's Voice" in *Frantz Fanon: Critical Perspectives,* Anthony C. Alessandrini, ed. (London: Routledge, 1999) p. 89.

68. Sartre, Jean-Paul. "Preface" in Fanon, Frantz. *The Wretched of the Earth* (1961), Constance Farrington, trans. (New York: Grove, 1968) pp. 1–35.

69. Turner, Lou. "On the Difference between the Hegelian and Fanonian Dialectic of Lordship and Bondage" in *Fanon: A Critical Reader* (Lewis R. Gordon et al., eds. & trans. (Oxford: Blackwell, 1996) p. 138.

70. Fanon, Frantz. *Black Skin White Masks* (1952), Charles Lam Markmann, trans. (New York: Wiedenfeld, 1967) p. 134.

71. García Márquez, Gabriel. *Cien años de soledad* (1967) (Madrid: Espasa-Calpe, 1985). The best extant translation from the Spanish remains

One Hundred Years of Solitude, Gregory Rabassa, trans. (New York: Avon, 1970).

72. Rushdie, Salman. *Midnight's Children* (New York: Knopf, 1980).

73. Rushdie, Salman (conversation with Gunther Grass). "Fictions Are Lies that Tell the Truth" in *Listener* June 17, 1985: 15.

74. The quote is from the very first page of Ashcroft, Bill; Griffiths, Gareth; & Tiffin, Helen, eds. *The Post-colonial Studies Reader,* a text which, while qualifying in its general introduction the inflated claims of its title, is still populated with texts "mainly from societies which employ forms of English as a major language of communication." That a nearly five-hundred-page volume containing excerpts from eighty-six essays on "postcolonial studies," even one that would insist that its title "is not meant to claim some completeness of coverage or absolute authority," would feature but four essays by Francophone writers (two by a single writer, Frantz Fanon), and ONE by a Hispanic (José Rabassa's excellent "Allegories of *Atlas*") is symptomatic of a much larger malaise within postcolonial scholarship in general, one that would privilege the literatures of societies colonized *in English* over those from cultures dominated by others.

75. Colás, Santiago. "Of Creole Symptoms, Cuban Fantasies, and Other Latin American Postcolonial Ideologies" in *PMLA: Publications of the Modern Language Association* 110/3 (May 1995) 382–396. Hereafter cited as SC.

76. Fuson, Robert H., trans. & intro. *The Log of Christopher Columbus* (Camden, ME: International Marine, 1987).

CHAPTER ONE. "THE OTHER! THE OTHER!": CONRAD, WILSON HARRIS, AND THE POSTCOLONIAL "THRESHOLD OF CAPACITY"

Harris, Wilson. *The Four Banks of the River of Space* (London: Faber & Faber, 1990) p. 103. Hereafter cited as *4B.*

Derrida, Jacques. "'Eating Well', or the Calculation of the Subject: An Interview with Jacques Derrida," Avital Ronell, trans. in *Who Comes After the Subject?* Eduardo Cadava, Peter Connor, & Jean-Luc Nancy, eds. (New York: Routledge, 1991) p. 109.

1. Shohat, Ella, "Notes on the 'Post-Colonial'" in *Social Text* 31/32 (1992): 103.

2. The term is from Wilson Harris; I will have recourse to it again later on.

3. Clifford, Hugh, C. M. G. "The Genius of Joseph Conrad" in *Joseph Conrad: Third World Perspectives,* Robert Hamner, ed. (Washington, DC: Three Continents, 1990), pp. 11–12, emphasis added. Hereafter cited as HC.

4. Achebe, Chinua. "An Image of Africa" in *Joseph Conrad: Third World Perspectives,* Robert Hamner, ed. (Washington, DC: Three Continents, 1990) p. 124. Hereafter cited as CA.

5. Said, Edward W., "Conrad: The Presentation of Narrative" in *Joseph Conrad: Third World Perspectives,* Robert Hamner, ed. (Washington, DC: Three Continents, 1990) p. 171. Hereafter cited as ES.

6. Harris, Wilson, "The Frontier on Which *Heart of Darkness* Stands" in *Joseph Conrad: Third World Perspectives,* Robert Hamner, ed. (Washington, DC: Three Continents, 1990) p. 162. Hereafter cited as Wha.

7. Wilson Harris's own clarification of the term might be helpful here:

> *Asymmetric context* implies that the unknowable God mediates between all structures. Thus if one were to say "the sun is a rose" one would visualize—in asymmetric context—an inimitable or unstructured relation existing between *sun* and *rose.* Both *sun* and *rose,* therefore, are partial signatures of—partial witnesses to—a universal principle of mediation, a universal principle of light beyond capture or structure. That principle of mediation at the heart of all metaphor may only be perceived as an *untamable* force mediating between *sun* and *force.*
>
> *Symmetric context* on the other hand would imply a binding locality or materiality or physicality in which *sun* and *rose* are *tamable* extensions or symmetric inversions of each other. (Wha 166–167)

8. Bonney, William W. *Thorns and Arabesques: Contexts for Conrad's Fiction* (Baltimore: Johns Hopkins University Press, 1980) p. 195. Hereafter cited as WB.

9. This distinction is part of a much larger philosophical project, which is articulated much more fully in Martin Heidegger's "End of Philosophy and the Task of Thinking." *Lichtung* is, for Heidegger, an act of "clearing," the clearing or opening up of a space in which things may be revealed in their presence *(Anwesen)*: "Speculative dialectic is a mode in which the matter of philosophy comes to appear of itself and for itself, and thus becomes present *[Gegenwart]*. Such appearance necessarily occurs in luminosity. Only by virtue of some sort of brightness can what shines show itself, that is, radiate. But brightness in its turn rests upon something open, something free, which it might illuminate here and there, now and then. . . . We call this openness that grants a possible letting appear and show "clearing" *[Lichtung]*.

See Heidegger, Martin. "The End of Philosophy and the Task of Thinking" in *Basic Writings,* David Farrell Krell, ed. & trans. (San Francisco: HarperCollins, 1993) p. 441. Hereafter cited as MH.

10. Conrad, Joseph. *Heart of Darkness* (1899), Ross C. Murfin, ed. & intro. (New York: St. Martin's, 1989) p. 66. Hereafter cited as *HoD*.

11. Conrad, Joseph. *The Nigger of the "Narcissus"* (1904) (New York: Signet, 1960).

12. The law as an instrument of terror and vehicle for the construction and enforcement of homogeneous cultural imperatives is instructively addressed (albeit in a different context) in Theodor W. Adorno's *Negative Dialectics,* from which this remarkable passage:

> The total legal realm is one of definitions. Its systematic forbids the admission of anything that eludes their closed circle, of anything *quod non est in actis*. These bounds, ideological in themselves, turn into real violence as they are sanctioned by law as the socially controlling authority, in the administered world in particular. In the dictatorships they become direct violence; indirectly, violence has always lurked behind them.

It would not be difficult to demonstrate that this systematic, and its hostility toward anything existing beyond its strictures, is consistent with an entire history of Western conquest and domination. See Adorno, Theodor W. *Negative Dialectics,* E. B. Ashton, trans. (New York: Continuum, 1973) p. 309.

13. Harris, Wilson. *The Palace of the Peacock* (London: Faber & Faber, 1960) p. 10. Hereafter cited to as *PP*.

14. By way of further explanation of Wilson Harris's concept of parallel/multiple/quantum realities, I offer as a preliminary guide this passage from the preface to *The Four Banks of the River of Space* (London: Faber & Faber, 1990) (there are many such statements throughout his texts that addresses this, but typically, no single definitive passage). Here Harris quotes Anselm, the novel's fictional protagonist-narrator:

> He spoke of "two (and more) existences in parallel yet suffused with alternative rhythms". This was the pattern of his eruptive life into reformations of being and the "interior existence" was the "living dreamer". . . . in whom heart and mind may relinquish the tyranny of a closed intelligence that becomes oblivious to *subtle and fateful signals of the crisis of a civilization,* signals of reality one may have been conditioned to suppress. (*4B* xii, emphasis added)

For Harris, then, it is again not a matter of shedding or otherwise 'leaving behind' an outmoded or no longer efficacious discourses in a simply binary way, but of acknowledging and receiving that which is always already there: the multiformity/diversity of being and the illusion of the uniform sovereign subject (ego).

15. Harris, Wilson. "A Talk on the Subject Imagination" in *Explorations,* Hena Maes-Jelinek, ed. (Copenhagen: Dangaroo, 1981) p. 58. Hereafter cited as Whb.

16. Coleridge, Samuel Taylor. "Shakespeare's Judgement Equal to His Genius" (1836) in *Critical Theory Since Plato* (rev. ed.) Hazard Adams, ed. (Fort Worth, TX: Harcourt, 1992) p. 471, emphasis added.

17. Philip, Marlene Nourbese. "Managing the Unmanageable" in *Caribbean Women Writers: Essays from the First International Conference,* Selwyn R. Cudjoe, ed. (Wellesley, MA: Calaloux, 1990) p. 434.

Chapter Two. Specters of the Nation: Resistance, *Criollismo,* and the Ambivalence of the "Neo-"

For the full text of the original see Martí, José. *Poesias completas* (Complete poems) (Buenos Aires: Editorial Claridad, 1983) p. 212. Hereafter cited as PC, with translations from the Spanish provided in subsequent notes. This and subsequent translations are my own:

> What more, what greater laurel? When has martyrdom
> Not been upon the forehead the finest crown?

1. The book under discussion is *Versos Libres* (Free verse).

2. This question of the specter and its question (what we might call 'the question of the question' of the specter) is part of a much larger and developing polemic, which appears in its most comprehensive form in the recent work of Jacques Derrida. See especially *Specters of Marx,* Peggy Kamuf, trans., Bernd Magnus & Stephen Cullenberg, intro. (New York: Routledge, 1994). Hereafter cited as *SoM.*

3. For Jacques Derrida, part of the specter's time as "out of joint" (see the lengthy meditation on this phrase from *Hamlet* and its various translations into French: *SoM* 18–20) is the impossibility of attributing to it a moment of origin: "*Untimely,* it does not come to, it does not happen to, it does not befall, one day, Europe, as if the latter, at a certain moment of its history, had begun to suffer from a certain evil, to let itself be *inhabited* in its inside, that is, haunted by a foreign guest" (*SoM* 4).

4. Naipaul, V. S. "Conrad's Darkness" (1974) in *Joseph Conrad: Third World Perspectives*, Robert Hamner, ed. (Washington DC: Three Continents, 1990) p. 194, emphasis added. Hereafter cited as VSN.

5. Naipaul's acknowledgment of his 'debt' to Conrad is particularly significant, if not directly relevant for the purposes of the present argument, for the premonition (pre- or partial apparitions, if you will—a "specter of a specter"), the originary trace of entities already present in the work of the latter—specters "inherited" by the descendant Naipaul. Two moments stand out: one in which Naipaul cites Conrad as a writer who "had been everywhere before me" (VSN 194), and this statement of more-or less unabashed endorsement: "Conrad's value to me is that he is someone who sixty to seventy years ago meditated on my world, a world I recognize today" (VSN 195). Here we can clearly read the link between the writers as a mutual haunting, what one might venture to call (in more than just a tongue-in-cheek way) a *hauntology* of colonial and postcolonial fictions, to be read as a matter of not merely multiple specters but of multiple apparitions of multiple specters.

6. Fanon, Frantz. *Black Skin, White Masks* (1954), Charles Lamm Markmann, trans. (New York: Grove Weidenfield, 1967) p. 231.

7. For a fuller articulation of this type of analysis see Bhabha, Homi K. *The Location of Culture* (London: Routledge, 1994) pp. 1–18. Hereafter cited as *LoC.*

8. Derrida uses the term *différance* to simultaneously denote two different meanings: to differ and to defer. For Derrida, *différance* comes to signify the denial of presence (i.e., 'presence' as a moment always deferred) and the existence within the sign itself of that which is radically other and nonidentical. These two meanings together, difference and deferment, are both present in the French verb *différer*. The significance of this structure to questions of subjectivity, and specifically relative to the present inquiry into Naipaul, we may begin to address by saying that the position of Naipaul's neocolonial 'half-madeness' is precisely an economy of *différance*/trace; the status of the neocolonial subject in this instance is clearly in crisis, caught in the flux of its own shifting subject positions and the realization of this instability. The subject of the '-neo-' is forever caught up in this play of difference and deferral, between the nostalgia for the relative comforts of colonial status and the desire to forever defer the uncertain futures of the 'post-'.

For a more thorough discussion of the term *différance* see Derrida, Jacques. *Margins of Philosophy* (1972), Alan Bass, trans. & notes (Chicago: University of Chicago Press, 1982) pp. 1–27; and Spivak, Gayatri Chakravorty. "Translator's Preface" in Derrida, Jacques. *Of Grammatology* (1967), Gayatri

Chakravorty Spivak, trans. & pref. (Baltimore, MD: Johns Hopkins University Press, 1976) pp. ix-lxxxv.

9. Brathwaite, Edward Kamau. "History, the Caribbean Writer and *X/Self*" in *Crisis and Creativity in the New Literatures in English,* Geoffrey Davis & Hena-Maes Jelinek, eds. (Amsterdam: Rodopi, 1990) p. 23, emphasis added. Hereafter cited as HCW.

10. Brathwaite delivered his talk in Kingston, Jamaica on June 18, 1988, the transcript of which was edited by Geofrey Davis, Hena-Maes Jelinek, and Christine Pagnoulle. See Brathwaite, Edward Kamau. "History, the Caribbean Writer and *X/Self*" in *Crisis and Creativity in the New Literatures in English,* Geoffrey Davis & Hena-Maes Jelinek, eds. (Amsterdam: Rudopi, 1990).

11. Of course, the sites of such resistances and struggles in the name of a national project can be, and often are, far from limited to a single oppressing or opposing entity; nevertheless, the complexities of even the most localized nationalist struggles are often reduced, by the media, the leadership, the propaganda machines, and so forth, to binary oppositional models. It is in terms of a struggle for survival between an 'us' and a 'them' that the burgeoning nation perceives itself.

12. As the passage from Jacques Derrida alludes, this notion of the conjuring of (historical) specters and the national *Geist* owes much to the Heideggerian *being-with* and *Dasein-with (Mitsein und Mitdasein)* (this is division One, Ch. IV of *Being and Time:* "Being-in-the-world as Being-with and Being-one's-self. The 'They' "). For Martin Heidegger, not only is the relation between subjectivities a relation of being, but it is a relation on which they mutually depend for their essential being. In *Being and Time* he would divide "Being-in-the-world" into three more abstract moments ("world," "being-in," and "being"), the third of which, "being," Heidegger tells us is the "being-with" *(Mitsein).* Thus, for Heidegger, the characteristic of being of human reality is precisely its being *with* others—a relation which, as Derrida points out, stands in danger of a certain overdetermination in the current context of spectrality ("this *with* that makes *being-with* in general more enigmatic than ever for us"). For if it is in fact by making explicit what we might call a 'preontological' comprehension of self that one apprehends being-with-others as an essential characteristic of one's being—if it is in fact a *transcendental* relation to the other that constitutes being—then the other, like the specter itself, can never be a mere existence that is encountered one day, as if on a certain day we were haunted by a spectral other and never, not before then. Rather, the apparition of this other-as-specter—that which, let us clarify, must be distinguished from the spirit (*Gespenst* from *Geist*) as that which appears to inhabit, to threaten the

latter from without, constitutes a *limit* and a reckoning. I offer from Jean-Paul Sartre's fruitful meditation on the Heideggerian *Mitsein,* in *Being and Nothingness,* this brief excerpt, one that in its way finds its echoes in Derrida: "The Other is the *ex-centric limit* which contributes to the constitution of my being. He is the test of my being inasmuch as he throws me outside of myself toward structures which at once both escape me and define me; it is this test which originally reveals the Other to me." See Heidegger, Martin. *Being and Time* (1933), John Macquarrie & Edward Robinson, trans. (San Francisco: HarperCollins, 1962) pp. 149–168; and Sartre, Jean-Paul. *Being and Nothingness* (1947), Hazel E. Barnes, trans. & intro. (New York: Philosophical Library, 1956) pp. 244–245 & 413–430.

13. Freud, Sigmund. *Civilization and Its Discontents* (1930), James Strachey, ed. & trans. (New York: Norton, 1950) pp. 83–84.

14. Fuson, Robert H., trans. & intro. *The Log of Christopher Columbus* (Camden, ME: International Marine, 1987).

15. "Abandoned by its original discoverers Barbadoes continued unfrequented till the year one thousand six hundred and five. . . . Here they erected a cross, and took possession of the island in the name of their sovereign; inscribing these words on a tree in the vicinity of the place where they landed, 'James, King of England and of this island.' " See Poyer, John. *The History of Barbadoes* (1808) (London: Frank Cass & Co., 1971) p. 4. Hereafter cited as JP. See also Ligon, Richard. *A True and Exact History of the Island of Barbadoes* (1873) (London: Frank Cass & Col., 1971).

16. Again from the colonial historian Poyer:

> Placed at the south-eastern extremity of the great American archipelago, [Barbados] remained unknown, or unnoticed, for upwards of a century after the bold and enterprising genius of Columbus had extended the bounds of the habitable globe, and added a new world to the dominions of Spain. (JP 1–2)

17. Marlow's narration in Conrad's *Heart of Darkness,* for example, is besieged with this sort of trace-structure; the narration is paralyzed at every turn by the encounter with the fact of the jungle's radical and untamable otherness.

18. Thanks to A. R. Abdallah.

19. Rushdie, Salman. "The Empire Writes Back with a Vengeance" in *The Times* July 3, 1982: 10.

20. Hutcheon, Linda. *A Poetics of Postmodernism: History, Theory, Fiction* (New York: Routledge, 1988) pp. 3–6. (qt. from p. 3):

> we hear of discontinuity, disruption, dislocation, decentering, indeterminacy, and antitotalization. What all of these words literally do (precisely by their disavowing prefixes *-dis, de, in, anti*) is incorporate that which they aim to contest. . . . I would like to begin by arguing that, for me, postmodernism is a contradictory phenomenon, one that uses and abuses, installs then subverts, the very concepts it challenges. . . .

21. Brathwaite, Edward Kamau. *Contradictory Omens: Cultural Diversity and Integration in the Caribbean,* Monograph No. 1 (Mona, Great Britain: Savacou, 1974) p. 21. Hereafter cited as *CO.*

22. There is also a dimension of parody in all of this, this mimicry of the exterior forms and concepts of a colonizing order that nonetheless serves to emphasize and foreground only difference, otherness. In *A Theory of Parody* Linda Hutcheon submits these instructive definitions of what for her holds to the limits of an artistic, aesthetic genre, but that nevertheless allows us to glimpse some of the implications in her notion of parody as an imitation that retains within it the surplus or supplement of *difference,* the coherent contradiction of an ironic mimesis, for postcolonial constructions of creole mimicry: "Parody, therefore, is a form of imitation, *but imitation characterized by ironic inversion* not always at the expense of the parodied text. . . . [it] is, in another formulation, repetition with critical distance, *which marks difference rather than similarity.*"

See Hutcheon, Linda. *A Theory of Parody: The Teachings of Twentieth-Century Art Forms* (New York: Methuen, 1985) p. 6 emphasis added.

23. Brathwaite, Edward Kamau. *The Arrivants: A New World Trilogy* (Oxford: Oxford University Press, 1989) p. 222. Hereafter cited as *TA.*

24. López, Alfred. "*La patria y el tirano*: José Martí and the Role of Literature in the Formation of the Cuban Nations, Past and Present" in *Iowa Journal of Cultural Studies* 12 (1993): 25–43.

25. The book under discussion is *Versos Sensillos* (Simple poetry).

26. To the grave on the farm / Where the father is buried, / Comes the son, a soldier / of the invader; comes the son. / The father, a hero in the war, / wrapped in his patriot's flag / rises, and with a blow / cuts him, dead, to the ground. / The sun shines; wind / blows over the land / the father picks up his son / and carries him to the grave (*PC* 143).

Chapter Three. Whiteness and the Colonial Unconscious

Thanks to the members of the postcolonial-studies course, "Whiteness After Empire," which I taught at Florida International University during the summer of 1998. These are excerpts from their anonymous written responses, on the first day of the course, to my in-class essay prompt: "Whiteness is. . . ." Hereafter cited as R1 & R2, respectively.

Thanks also to Donald Watson, Chair of the Department of English at Florida International, for his help in making my course proposal a reality.

1. It is important to note here that I am not applying the concept of "ideology" as it commonly appears in much Marxist literary theory. Rather, the reader should understand "ideology" in this context as standing closer to a Saidian application; that is, reading the concept of colonialism itself in terms of an "invention of tradition" in the sense that it represents a group of irregular, unorganized discourses from a wide range of disciplines and methodologies (from, say, philology to historiography, popular culture to opera) that together articulate a national project formulated in terms of some *ideal*—of national culture, national interests (wealth, defense, prestige, etc). Said argues that such a decentralized alignment of discourses has the effect of collectively constituting a rhetoric of justification for empire; or as he puts it, "an imperial personality becomes distinct" as a composite of the discourses of colonial interests.

This is especially important to bear in mind as my own term bears some similarity to Fredric Jameson's "political unconscious"; even a cursory look at Jameson's remarkable book, however, will reveal just how different conceptually the present essay is from his more narrowly Marxist approach.

See Said, Edward W. *Culture and Imperialism* (New York: Pantheon, 1993) pp. 97–110; and Jameson, Fredric. *The Political Unconscious: Narrative as a Socially Symbolic Act* (Ithaca, NY: Cornell University Press, 1981) pp. 9–14.

2. It is precisely because such suppressed knowledges lie beyond the reach of the subject's consciousness, what Sigmund Freud calls the subject's "critical faculty," that psychoanalysis has always strived in its methods to bypass the patient's conscious mental processes (first through hypnosis, later through free association) and thus pre-empt their ability to bring a critical (interpreting, editing, potentially censoring) activity to bear upon thoughts or ideas emerging from the unconscious. During analysis the patient is asked to suppress only that "critical faculty" that would in turn work to act upon the "involuntary ideas" of the unconscious:

> In reflection there is one more psychical activity at work than in the most attentive self-observation . . . the man who is reflecting is also exercising his *critical* faculty; this leads him to reject some of the ideas that occur to him after perceiving them, to cut short others without following the trains of thought which they would open up to him, and to behave in such a way toward still others that they never become conscious at all and are accordingly suppressed before being perceived.

> It is thus only through such the rigorous "self-observation" of analysis, which would ensure that the emergent contents of the unconscious are not interfered with in any way, can the properly informed work of interpretation take place.

See Freud, Sigmund. *The Interpretation of Dreams* (4th English ed., 1953), James Strachey, ed. & trans. (New York: Avon, 1965) pp. 133–135 emphasis added. Hereafter cited as *ID*.

3. Freud is unswerving, especially in his later "metapsychological" works, in his view that the desire for aggression is an irreducible part of humanity's collective instinctual endowment:

> The result is that their neighbor is to them not only a possible helper or sexual object, but also a temptation to them to gratify their aggressiveness on him, to exploit his capacity to work without recompense, to use him sexually without his consent, to seize his possessions, to humiliate him, to cause him pain, to torture and kill him. *Homo homini lupus* [Man is to man a wolf]; who has the courage to dispute it in the face of all the evidence in his own life and in history? This aggressive cruelty usually lies in wait for some provocation, or else it steps into the service of some other purpose, the aim of which might as well have been achieved by milder measures. In circumstances that favour it, when those forces in the mind which ordinarily inhibit it cease to operate, it also manifests itself spontaneously and reveals men as savage beasts to whom the thought of sparing their own kind is alien. Anyone who calls to mind the atrocities of the early migrations, of the invasion by the Huns, or by the so-called Mongols under Jenghiz Khan and Tamurlane, of the sack of Jerusalem by the pious Crusaders, even indeed the horrors of the [First] World War, will have to bow his head humbly before the truth of this view of man.

Freud asserts that, because of this "primary hostility of men *[sic]* toward one another," civilization can only maintain its constantly imperiled cohesion by turning the society's internal aggressions beyond its own borders and onto its others; he considers this "narcissism of minor differences" a convenient and effective way of both channeling a society's aggressive tendencies and reinforcing the individual subjects' loyalty to each other.

See Freud, Sigmund. *Civilization and its Discontents* (1930), James Strachey, ed. & trans. (New York: Norton, 1950) pp. 40–43.

4. Bhabha, Homi K. *The Location of Culture* (London: Routledge, 1994) p. 149. Hereafter cited as *LoC*.

5. In chapter One of the present volume, "'The Other! The Other!': Conrad, Wilson Harris, and the Postcolonial 'Threshold of Capacity,'" I more

or less cast Conrad's Marlow as the repressed/ repressing colonial agent *par excellence.*

6. Cliff, Michelle. *The Land of Look Behind* (Ithaca, NY: Firebrand, 1985) p. 14. Hereafter cited as *LB.*

7. Derrida, Jacques. *Margins of Philosophy* (1972), Alan Bass, trans. & notes (Chicago: University of Chicago Press, 1982) p. 213.

8. Of course this is not always the case, and even when it is such a process of national socioeconomic transformation does not magically occur on the eve of independence. Although it is true that the new nation will benefit to some extent from such material wealth as the colonial regime has to leave behind (infrastructure comes to mind: roads, buildings, and so on), we must not forget that the whole point of the colonial enterprise is to produce wealth *for the colonizing country;* it is thus often the case that the new nation formed in the wake of empire is quite impoverished as a result of its having been systematically sacked of much of its resources for decades or centuries. Colonies served to expand economic trade—and therefore production—by opening up new and secure (because colonized) markets for European products while also providing new sources of raw materials; additionally, new colonies constituted fields for profitable investment of capital often not available at home.

Certainly much of the "new imperialism" of the late-19th century owes much of its vigor to a combination of economic and political factors, or what D. K. Fieldhouse considers a 'politicization' of economic imperatives:

> Economic factors were present and in varying degrees influential in almost every situation outside Europe which led ultimately to formal empire; and the specific value of many of these territories to Europeans lay in trade, investment opportunities or other forms of economic activity. . . . At one extreme such problems directly affected what European officialdom regarded as "first-class" national interests. At the other they raised minor political difficulties such as the instability of an indigenous political régime or obstruction by other Europeans to satisfactory trade or investment. But in virtually every case the ultimate explanation to formal annexation was that the original economic issue had to some degree become "politicized" and therefore required a political solution.

See Brewer, John, & Porter, Roy, eds. *Consumption and the World of Goods* (London: Routledge, 1993); Fieldhouse, D. K. *Economics and Empire 1830–1914* (Ithaca, NY: Cornell University Press, 1973 pp. 475–476) Semmel, Bernard. *The Liberal Ideal and the Demons of Empire: Theories of Imperialism from Adam Smith to Lenin* (Baltimore, MD: Johns Hopkins University

Press, 1993); and Wolff, Richard D. *The Economics of Colonialism: Britain and Kenya, 1870–1930* (New Haven, CT: Yale University Press, 1974).

9. The Promotion of National Unity and Reconciliation Act of 1994 enabled President Mandela to convene the Truth and Reconciliation Commission (TRC), whose purpose is threefold: (1) to induce a full acknowledgment of guilt by those who had been guilty of human rights violations during the apartheid regime; (2) to offer amnesty to those who make a full confession; and (3) to grant relief, reparation, and/or remuneration to those who had suffered what the act deemed "a gross violation of human rights," or failing that, to their survivors—including victims of those who receive amnesty from the commission. An amended bill, further emphasizing the rights and needs of the victims of violence, passed into law in July 1995

The TRC, chaired by Archbishop Desmond Tutu, has received heightened media coverage in recent months during the appearance before it of the former Mrs. Mandela under suspicion of human rights abuses, and for the continued refusal of former president P. W. Botha to appear.

See Davenport, T. R. H. *The Birth of a New South Africa: The 1995 Joanne Goodman Lectures* (Toronto: University of Toronto Press, 1998) pp. 96–105; and Truth and Reconciliation Commission. *Truth and Reconciliation Commission of South Africa Report.* 5 vols. (Cape Town, S.A.: Truth and Reconciliation Commission, 1998).

10. The reference is to Marlow's aunt in *Heart of Darkness,* whom he visits before his departure for the Congo. The full quotation is narrated by Marlow, and it reveals something of his ambivalence toward the mission upon which he is to embark: "She talked about 'weaning those ignorant millions from their horrid ways,' till, upon my word, she made me quite uncomfortable." This matter of Marlow's colonial angst—and *Heart of Darkness*'s own ambivalent relation with postcolonial discourses—is one I take up more thoroughly in chapter 1 of this volume, "'The Other! The Other!": Conrad, Wilson Harris, and the Postcolonial "Threshold of Capacity.'"

See Conrad, Joseph. *Heart of Darkness* (1899), Ross C. Murfin, ed. & intro. (New York: St. Martin's, 1989) pp. 26–27.

11. Again I will have recourse to Derrida's seminal essay "White Mythology," in which he develops his theory of whiteness as Eurocentrism. For Derrida, Eurocentrism is the name or index of an irreducible relation between the myth of white superiority and colonial domination.

See Derrida, Jacques. *Margins of Philosophy* (1972), Alan Bass, trans. & notes (Chicago: University of Chicago Press 1982) pp. 187–236.

12. For Frantz Fanon, this is precisely the existential dilemma of the colonial subject of color:

> the educated Negro suddenly discovers that he is rejected by a civilization which he has none the less assimilated . . . if, however, he forgets his place, if he takes it into his head to be the equal of the European, then the said European is indignant and casts out the upstart—who, in such circumstance, in this "exceptional case," pays for his own rejection of dependence with an inferiority complex.

See Fanon, Frantz. *Black Skins, White Masks* (1954), Charles Lam Markmann, trans. (New York: Grove Weidenfeld, 1967) p. 93. Hereafter cited as *BSWM.*

13. The model is of course Freudian, based specifically upon Freud's reading in *Totem and Taboo* of Darwin's "primal horde" and the murder of the primal father. Freud is interested in tracing the lines of development from Darwin's posited scene, in which a single violent and jealous father keeps all the females for himself and drives away the sons as they mature, to what he observes in tribal organizations, in which groups of males share equal rights and observe the two restrictions of the totemic system: murder and incest.

Freud's hypothesis that such a tribal culture could only come after the band of banished sons return to murder and devour their father, and that such a primal scene is the hidden foundation of all social, moral, and religious organization, draws heavily from that arrived at by J. J. Atkinson in his anthropological study *Primal Law.* Atkinson asserts that Darwin's primal father's most dreaded fear is the return of the banished brothers, who in time would gain sufficient strength and organization to topple the paternal tyrant; this scene would be followed by a period of fratricidal struggle for power among the surviving brothers. This period would be brought to an end, and the nucleus of a tribal society thus facilitated, by the intervention of the maternal love on behalf of the sons; first the youngest—but sooner or later the others too—would be allowed through the intervention of the mother to remain with the horde, in exchange for the sons' acknowledgment of their father's sexual privilege and renouncement of all claims upon their mothers and sisters. Freud thus sees the tribal "totem meal," described by William Robertson Smith as a ritual in which clansmen mourn, then rejoice over the killing and devouring of the totem animal, normally a forbidden act, as a repetition and commemoration of the primal patricide: "The ambivalent emotional attitude, which to this day characterizes the father-complex in our children and which often persists into adult life, seems to extend to the totem animal in its capacity as substitute for the father."

Freud's hypothesis becomes particularly relevant to the postindependence reckoning with the absence of the colonial father in two of its features: the clansmen's identification with the totem; and the compulsory nature of both participation in the ritual and the subsequent mourning. Freud emphasizes both of these points in a single passage:

> The clansmen are there, dressed in the likeness of the totem and imitating it in sound and movement, as though they are seeking to stress their identity with it. Each man is conscious that he is performing an act forbidden to the individual and justifiable only through the participation of the whole clan; nor may anyone absent himself from the killing and the meal. When the deed is done, the slaughtered animal is lamented and bewailed. The mourning is obligatory, imposed by dread of a threatened retribution. As Robertson Smith remarks of an analogous occasion, its chief purpose is to disclaim responsibility for the killing.

We need not read this scene in the literal sense, of a literal murder and cannibalistic consumption of a biological father, to see its analogic value in helping us read the postindependence scene of desire, denial, and mourning for the departed colonial father.

See Atkinson, J. J. *Primal Law* (London: Longmans, Green & Co, 1903) pp. 220–231; Freud, Sigmund. *Totem and Taboo* (1913), James Strachey, trans. & ed. (New York: Norton, 1989) pp. 172–183; and Smith, William Robertson. *Lectures on the Religion of the Semites* (1894) (New York: Ktav Publishers, 1969) pp. 412–419 (qt. from p. 175).

14. Within a postcolonial context, South Africa is no doubt the best-known among recent examples of white angst in the face of the electoral empowerment of a majority of color; there is no shortage of studies focusing on the long and arduous negotiation process leading to the ANC's victory in the 1994 national elections. But South Africa is far from unique in this manifestation of white ambivalence toward nonwhite suffrage, as the history of such struggles in Great Britain and the United States will attest.

See Davenport, T. R. H. *South Africa: A Modern History* (4th ed.) (Toronto: University of Toronto Press, 1991); Elliott, Ward E.Y. *The Rise of Guardian Democracy: The Supreme Court's Role in Voting Rights Disputes, 1845–1969* (Cambridge: MA: Harvard University Press, 1974); Pugh, Martin. *Electoral Reform in War and Peace 1906–18* (London: Routledge, 1993); Rich, Paul B., ed. *Reaction and Renewal in South Africa* (Houndsmills, Great Britain: Macmillan, 1996); and Worden, Nigel. *The Making of a Modern Africa* (2nd ed.) (Oxford: Blackwell, 1995).

15. Luo, Ting-yao. *Crossing the White Country: J. M. Coetzee and Postcolonial Agency*, Diss. State University of New York-Buffalo, 1993 (Ann Arbor, MI: University Microfilms International, 1994) p. 1.

16. I say "relative" here as a concession to socioeconomic class. In a context in which whites retain most of the national capital, as is the case in Jamaica and postapartheid South Africa, the nominal equality of white and non-white citizens does not necessarily coincide with parity in political or economic power. Racial ghettos remain, and middle-class whites retain the option of "retreating" to the comfort of enclaves and communities where their less-affluent new fellow citizens cannot afford to live. Grant Farred elaborates on this phenomenon as it exists in postapartheid South Africa:

> South Africa is a society in which the black working class and its unemployed and unemployable cohorts continue to bear the brunt of apartheid's historic inequities, and this scenario promises to be the experience for generations to come. Whites, on the other hand, now enjoy the benefits of those disparities in its post-apartheid formation, albeit in the increasingly gated, if relatively safe, suburban neighborhoods they have always occupied.

See Farred, Grant. "Bulletproof Settlers: The Politics of Offense in the New South Africa" in *Whiteness: A Critical Reader,* Mike Hill, ed. (New York: New York University Press, 1997) pp. 63–78 (qt. from p. 66).

17. At the time of the writing of this chapter, two unfortunately fine examples of the latter rage in Rwanda and the Kosovo region of the former Yugoslavia, where warring factions are divided not by race, but by cultural, religious, or tribal identifications.

18. One might think here of Charles Dickens's Pip and Oliver Twist, each of whom rises up out of poverty and social marginalization to occupy, by their respective novels' conclusions, a position of considerable wealth and privilege. Surprisingly, few critics have attempted to mine this potentially fruitful intersection of the novel as bildungsroman and a critique of socioeconomic class, and particularly as part of a larger interrogation of colonial and postcolonial narratives that depict an indivudual subject's struggle to achieve class mobility within a race- and culture-based social hierarchy.

Happily, a few such studies do exist in this fertile but so-far overlooked area of postcolonial studies. See McCully, Michael. "Beyond 'The Covenant and the Cottage': A Reconsideration of Disraeli's Sybil" in *College Language Association Journal* 29/3 (March 1986): 318–335 (not postcolonial in its orientation, but still useful as a reading of the bildungsroman in terms of a critique of class); Porter, Abioseh Michael. "Second Class Citizen: The Point of Departure for Understanding Buchi Emecheta's Major Fiction" in *International Fiction Review* 15/2 (Summer 1988): 123–129; and especially Lima, Maria

Helena. "Revolutionary Developments: Michele Cliff's *No Telephone to Heaven* and Merle Collins's *Angel*" in *ARIEL: A Review of International English Literature* 24/1 (January 1993): 35–56.

19. This autobiographical element generally present in Michele Cliff's work has surfaced as a topic in a number of interviews with the author; but there has only appeared in print one careful critical exposition to date of *Abeng* in its problematical status as an autobiographical novel. As regards the former, see Adisa, Opal Palmer. "Journey Into Speech—A Writer Between Two Worlds: An Interview with Michelle Cliff" in *African American Review* 28/2 (Summer 1992): 273–281; Raiskin, Judith. "The Art of History: An Interview with Michelle Cliff" in *The Kenyon Review* 15/1 (Winter 1993): 57–71; and Schwartz, Meryl F. "An Interview with Michelle Cliff" in *Contemporary Literature* 34/4 (Winter 1993): 595–619.

For a useful critical analysis of *Abeng* specifically as an autobiographical text, see Lionnet, Francoise. "Of Mangoes and Maroons: Language, History, and the Multicultural Subject of Michelle Cliff's *Abeng*" in *De/colonizing the Subject: The Politics of Gender in Women's Autobiography,* Sidonie Smith & Julia Watson, eds. (Minneapolis: University of Minnesota Press, 1992) pp. 321–345.

20. Coetzee, J. M. *Boyhood: Scenes from Provincial Life* (New York: Viking, 1997).

21. Paul Smith has observed that the term 'subject' is susceptible to a certain overdetermination in its usage. Briefly, the assumed synonymity of "subject" with the unitary "individual" as a controlling consciousness is often conflated with the notion of the "subject" as that which is under scrutiny, which is studied or observed. And as Smith points out, the word takes on a further meaning as one who is "subjected" to a particular ruler or ruling discourse:

> Equally, in political discourse, the "subject" maintains one of its older sense and signifies a person who is subjected, exactly, to a particular form of rule or domination. And the use of that word—in a phrase such as "a British subject," for example—has been extended to include one who is subject to ideology, to particular hegemonic formations, or to power in general.

Although it is certainly plausible to think of Clare Savage and the young protagonist of Boyhood as "subjects" in all of these ways, I will endeavor whenever possible (and relevant) to distinguish between these usages.

See Smith, Paul. *Discerning the Subject* (Minneapolis: University of Minnesota Press, 1988) p. xxxiii.

22. In G. W. F. Hegel's *Phenomenology of Spirit*, the highest stage of "Absolute Knowing" can only occur when the subject (Self) "surmounts the object of consciousness,"or learns to see Spirit *[Geist]* not as a form of self-consciousness for itself but as a perfect identification with self-consciousness *itself*. That is, the individual learns to understand the other as the "externalized" form of self-consciousness, and thus achieves a union with Spirit in which the Self realizes itself as both an extension and externalization of Spirit; or as Hegel puts it: "this externalization [of the Self in Spirit] is in its own self externalized, and just as it is in its extension, so it is equally in its depth, in the Self." Thus for Hegel "Absolute Knowing" represents the highest possible stage and resolution of the dialectic: perfect union, and in fact, indistinguishablity, of individual and collective, Self and Spirit.

In his post-Auschwitz critique of Hegel, however, Theodor W. Adorno finds such a utopian merging of subject and state dangerously flawed:

> What is realized by means of individuality and plurality is the cause of the many, and again it is not their cause: they have less and less control over it. *Their totality is their otherness at the same time;* this is the dialectic carefully ignored by the Hegelian one. Insofar as the individuals are at all aware of their taking a back seat to unity, its priority reflects to them the being-in-itself of the universal which they encounter in fact: *it is inflicted upon them,* all the way into their inmost core, even when they inflict it on themselves. The line ἦθος ἀνθρώπῳ δαίμων—that the character of men, as such always moulded by the universal, is their fate—has more truth to it than the truth of a characterological determinism. The universal by which every individual is determined at all, as one of his particular kind, that universal is borrowed from what is extraneous and therefore as heteronomous to the individual as anything once said to have been ordained for him by demons.

For Adorno, then, the universal is always an *a priori* category by which the individual's "character" is measured; the Self's union with Spirit, then, always comes at the expense of his own individuality, and is thus represents a submission, conscious or not—"even when they inflict it on themselves"—to the cultural imperatives of the state. Further, for Adorno, perfect union is not possible even in the hypothetical case of the Self's complete identification with Spirit, for as but an individual contained within a larger entity, "the knowing subject must reflect on itself as a moment of the universal that is to be known, without being quite like that universal."

See Hegel, G. W. F. *The Phenomenology of Spirit* (1807), J. V. Miller, trans. (Oxford: Oxford University Press, 1977) pp. 479–480 and 492–493; and Adorno, Theodor W. *Negative Dialectics* (1966), E. B. Ashton, trans. (New York: Continuum, 1973) pp. 314–315, emphasis added.

23. Cliff, Michelle. *Abeng* (1984) (New York: Penguin, 1991) p. 3. Hereafter cited as *Ab*.

24. Of course, this image does not reflect all of the individual acts of resistance that always take place in the colonial encounter. But such is one of the more unfortunate effects of metaphor, or what in Freudian terms is called 'condensation'—the process by which complex dream-thoughts are reduced by the dream-work into the pictographic script of the dream-symbol; the metaphoric image, then, is but a fragmentary remnant of the text's sum of significations and referents, but a powerful and efficacious one nevertheless.

Much of *Abeng*, in fact, is concerned with reinscribing into Jamaican history just such resistances to British rule, particularly in chapters 2 and 3 narration of the organized resistance of the Windward Maroons and their legendary leader Nanny (*Ab* 14 and 18–22).

25. See in chapter 2 of the present volume, "Specters of the Nation: Resistance, *Criollismo*, and the Ambivalence of the 'Neo-,' " in which I explain the larger psychic significance of Columbus's arrival in the so-called New World for nations he did not physically encounter himself, but that were later colonized by other imperial powers. In the present example, Edward Kamau Brathwaite refers to his home island of Barbados, which was colonized by Britain and actually came to be known among the Caribbean colonial territories as 'Little England'; Columbus makes no mention of Barbados in his travel logs, and it is unlikely that he ever saw the island.

26. The names in the passage belong to key figures in South African colonial history. The first three, Riebeeck, Stel, and Somerset, were early (pre-Great Trek) governors of the Cape Town colony during Dutch and English rule respectively; the Dutch Riebeeck, who founded Cape Town as a Dutch colony in 1652, is revered by Afrikaaners as a founding father of Afrikaans nationalism, while the Lord Somerset is reviled by the same as being especially representative of repression under British colonial rule. Pretorius and Martz are honored by Afrikaaners as leaders of the Great Trek, the massive migration of Afrikaaners from Cape Town into what is now the northern part of South Africa in repudiation of increasingly liberal British colonial rule (freeing of Afrikaaners' slaves, returning recently annexed lands to African tribes, etc.); Pretorius is especially honored by Afrikaaners as a nationalist leader and general for his military battles against the Zulus and British in the 1830s–1840s. Pretorius's son, Marthinus Pretorius, established the city of Pretoria and named it for his father.

There is a wide range of useful historical accounts from this period of South African history. See for example Keegan, Timothy J. *Colonial South Africa and the Origins of the Racist Order* (Charlottesville: University Press of Virginia, 1996); Elphick, Richard. *Kraal and Castle: Khoikhoi and the Founding of White South Africa* (New Haven, CT: Yale University Press, 1977; Elphick, Richard, & Giliomee, Hermann, eds. *The Shaping of South African Society, 1652–1840* (2nd ed.) (Middlestown, CT: Wesleyan University Press, 1989); and Walker, Eric A. *The Great Trek* (5th ed.) (London: A. & C. Black, 1965).

27. The Boer War, also known as the 'Anglo-Boer War' and the 'South African War' (October 11, 1899-May 31, 1902), transpired between the British colonial army and two Boer republics (Transvaal and the Orange Free State). Britain's troops greatly outnumbered Boers (almost five hundred thousand to about ninety thousand), but struggled for much of the war against the additional obstacles of hostile terrain and Boer "guerrilla" tactics (hiding behind rocks, ambushes, sabotage, etc).

The war ostensibly started over South African Republic (Transvaal) president Paul Kruger's refusal to grant political rights to the "Uitlander" (non-Dutch foreign, mostly British) population of the mining areas of the Witwatersrand, and the uncompromising attitude on this point of British colonial administrators. Also at stake, however, was the control of a large gold-mining operation in Transvaal at a time when British colonialism was becoming ever more dependent on gold to finance its endeavors. After a protracted and bloody war, which saw large losses on both sides as well as the death of over twenty thousand Boer civilians in concentration camps, the Boers signed the Peace of Vereeniging (May 1902), effectively conceding their independence to the British.

28. Another important South African writer, Breyten Breytenbach, also strives to articulate a whiteness in opposition to Afrikaaner nationalism and apartheid. Breytenbach's memoir of his years in prison for anti-apartheid activities explains his own motivations for fighting against apartheid, and addresses the problems faced by whites in South Africa who wish to dissasociate themselves from the dominant regime and its racist politics:

> How could I, as a White man, express my opposition to the system, which means to the exploitation and the degradation, effectively whilst identifying myself with the cause of the Black majority? How could I relate to them? I could do so on the plain of ideas, concerning the absolutes of justice and dignity and freedom, even of socialism.
>
> I repeat: my revulsion to Apartheid could not only be because of what it is doing to all the 'un-whites', could not be really resilient if motivated by a 'do-good' approach, but because of how it was affecting *me*.

Breytenbach distances himself from Afrikaaner racism by positioning himself as a subject in a relation of ideological solidarity with black South Africans, and siding with them against their oppressors.

See Breytenbach, Breyten. *The True Confessions of an Albino Terrorist* (New York: Farrar, 1985) pp. 73–74.

29. Chambers, Ross. "The Unexamined" in *Whiteness: A Critical Reader*, Mike Hill, ed. (New York: New York University Press, 1997) p. 193.

30. This concept borrowed from metaphysics, namely that the center of a structure serves to facilitate and delimit the play of that structure, thus establishing its "margins" or limits, is among the basic insights of deconstruction. Perhaps its most well-known exposition is from one of Derrida's important essay "Structure, Sign, and Play in the Discourse of the Human Sciences":

> structure—or rather the structurality of structure—although it has always been at work, has always been neutralized or reduced, and this by a process of giving it a center or of referring it to a point of presence, a fixed origin. The function of this center was not only to orient, balance, and organize the structure—one cannot in fact conceive of an unorganized structure—but above all to make sure that the organizing principle of the structure would limit what we might call the *play* of the structure. By orienting and organizing the coherence of the system, the center of a structure permits the play of its elements inside the total form. And even today the notion of a structure lacking any center represents the unthinkable itself.

See Derrida, Jacques. "Structure, Sign, and Play in the Discourse of the Human Sciences" in *Writing and Difference* (1967), Alan Bass, trans, intro, & notes (Chicago: University of Chicago Press, 1978) pp. 278–279.

31. In Jamaican Creole, *buckra* signifies a white person, specifically one representing the dominant (British) class; the word *smaddy* broadly means 'somebody'(as the cited passage and others in the text illustrate, the word is used in a variety of connotations); *wunna* simply means 'you'; *fe* is a fairly generic preposition whose meaning varies depending on its context, most commonly functioing in a sentence as 'for,' 'of,' or 'to'; and a *pickney* is a child or children; the word is the same for both singular and plural usage.

32. This is not at all to say that a productive reading of the more narrowly sexual elements of the narrative—particularly as it applies to the homoerotic dimension of Clare and Zoe's relationship—would not yield a useful interpretation of the text. But since sexuality is not in-itself a central focus of my work in this chapter, I would just as soon address only those sexual elements that apply more-or-less directly to my thesis here. The possibility of a "queer postcolonial" reading of Michelle Cliff's work, and the implications of such a reading for postcolonial theory in general, is, I believe, a worthy topic for another article.

33. Significantly, the memoir is subtitled "Scenes from Provincial Life"; the narrative develops as a series of such "scenes" narrated in the third-person and present tense.

34. My claims here are informed by what Jacques Lacan has taught us about the nature of the desiring subject. For Lacan, desire is an ongoing effect of symbolic articulation; rather than a definable and satisfiable appetite, it is fundamentally insatiable. One of the irreducible conditions of the Lacanian subject, in fact, is that it *wants;* that is, it experiences itself in terms of a lack; all speech, then, is the exterior of a demand, which presupposes the other to whom it is addressed. And in fact Lacan explicitly addresses this Hegelian characterization of desire as a drive that is intimately bound up with the subject's will to knowledge as an *overtaking* or mastering of the object of the to-be-known:

> And the enigmas that desire seems to pose for a "natural philosophy"—its frenzy mocking the abyss of the infinite, the secret collusion with which it envelops the pleasure of knowing and of dominating with *jouissance,* these amount to no other derangement of instinct than being caught in the rails—eternally stretching forth towards the *desire for something else*—of metonymy. Hence its "perverse" fixation at the very suspension-point of the signifying chain where the memory-screen is immobilized and the fascinating image of the fetish is petrified.

The term *jouissance* is best translated into English by the phrase "guilty pleasure," or that symptom to which the subject has attached and from which it derives pleasure, but that nevertheless produces guilt in the subject.

See Lacan, Jacques. *Ecrits: A Selection*, Alan Sheridan, trans. (New York: Norton, 1977) pp. 166–167; also *The Seminar of Jacques Lacan—Book 7: The Ethics of Psychoanalysis, 1959–1960,* Jacques-Alain Miller, ed., Sylvana Tomaselli, trans. (New York: Norton, 1992).

35. I am referring here primarily to Theroux's short fiction, particularly but not exclusively the series of stories featuring the narration of U.S. Consulate employee Spencer Savage and collected under the titles "The Consul's File" and "The London Embassy"; and Hilary Mantel's novels *Eight Months on Ghazzah Street* and *A Change of Climate,* which focus on the experiences of English expatriates in Saudi Arabia and South Africa, respectively.

See Theroux, Paul. *The Collected Stories* (New York: Viking, 1997); and Mantel, Hilary. *Eight Months on Ghazzah Street* (New York: Marian Wood/Owl, 1988); and *A Change of Climate* (New York: Marian Wood/Owl, 1986).

36. Garvey, John, & Ignatiev, Noel. "Toward a New Abolitionism: A *Race Traitor* Manifesto" in *Whiteness: A Critical Reader,* Mike Hill, ed. (New York: New York University Press, 1997) p. 346.

CHAPTER FOUR. "TOWARD A NEW HUMANISM. . . .": FANON, HEGEL, AND THE CRISIS OF MASTERY

Lacan, Jacques. *The Seminar of Jacques Lacan—Book 2: The Ego in Freud's Theory and in the Technique of Psychoanalysis 1954–1955,* Jacques-Alain Miller, ed., Sylvana Tomaselli; trans. (New York: Norton, 1988) p. 71. Hereafter cited as *SJL.*

1. Ashcroft, Bill; Griffiths, Gareth; & Tiffin, Helen, eds. "General Introduction" in *The Post-colonial Studies Reader* (London: Routledge, 1995) p. 1.

2. Mongia, Padmini, ed. "Introduction" in *Contemporary Postcolonial Theory: A Reader* (London: Arnold, 1998) p. 3.

3. Gates, Henry Louis Jr. "Introduction: Writing 'Race' and the Difference It Makes" in *"Race, Writing, and Difference*, Henry Louis Gates Jr., ed. (Chicago: University of Chicago Press, 1988) p. 6. Hereafter cited as HLG.

4. Young, Robert J. C. *White Mythologies: Writing History and the West* (London: Routledge, 1990) pp. 1–6.

5. Gikandi, Simon. "In the Shadow of Hegel: Cultural Theory in an Age of Displacement" in *Research in African Literatures* 27/2 (Summer 1996): 140.

6. See Bhabha, Homi K. *The Location of Culture* (London: Routledge, 1994) pp. 40–65, hereafter cited as *LoC;* and Gordon, Lewis R. *Fanon and the Crisis of European Man: An Essay on Philosophy and the Human Sciences* (London: Routledge, 1995), hereafter cited as LG.

7. Fanon, Frantz. *Black Skin White Masks* (1952), Charles Lam Markmann, trans. (New York: Wiedenfeld, 1967) p. 217. Hereafter cited as *BSWM.*

8. Sartre, Jean-Paul. *Being and Nothingness* (1947), Hazel E. Barnes, trans. & intro. (New York: Philosophical Library, 1962) pp. 233–252. Hereafter cited as *BN.*

9. A comprehensive listing of literary and philosophical texts informed by "Lordship and Bondage" would obviously be beyond the scope of my work here. It is worth noting, however, that Robert J. C. Young's *White Mythologies: Writing History and the West* is the most thorough analysis to date of G. W. F. Hegel and his continuing impact upon contemporary theories and theorists. Also useful as an introduction to Hegel's thought and system are Alexandre Kojève's *Introduction to the Reading of Hegel,* which contains a fine and careful

exposition of "Lordship and Bondage," and Jean Hyppolite's *Introduction to Hegel's Philosophy of History*.

It is sufficient for present purposes to observe that the Hegelian dialectic remains as both explicit subject and unacknowledged context for critical theories ranging from the existential phenomenology of Sartre, Merleau-Ponty et al. to Lacanian and neo-Lacanian psychoanalysis, from Foucault's New Historicist rethinkings of the relations between knowledge and power to Derridean deconstruction and Levinasian poststructuralist philosophy, to its current incarnations in the work of postcolonial critics as diverse as Edward Said and Homi Bhabha, Gayatri Spivak and Paul Gilroy.

Aside from Robert J. C. Young, *White Mythologies: Writing History and The West* (London: Routledge, 1990), see Kojève, Alexandre. *Introduction to the Reading of Hegel* (1947), Allan Bloom, trans., James H. Nichols Jr., ed. (Ithaca, NY: Cornell University Press, 1969), hereafter cited as AK; and Hyppolite, Jean. *Introduction to Hegel's Philosophy of History* (1948), Bond Harris & Jacqueline Bouchard Sperlock, trans., Arkady Plotnitsky, foreword (Gainesville: University Press of Florida, 1996).

10. All references to the *Phenomenology* will be from A.V. Miller's 1977 English translation, which is itself based on the 5th edition (1831) as edited by J. Hoffmeister. See Miller, A.V., ed. *Hegel's Phenomenology of Spirit*, J. N. Findlay, analysis & foreword (Oxford: Oxford University Press) p. 111. Hereafter cited as PHN.

11. Karl Marx's most forceful and succinct articulation of the worker's alienation comes from *the Economic and Philosophic Manuscripts of 1844*, in which he avers that "[o]n the basis of political economy itself, in its own words, we have shown *that the worker sinks to the level of a commodity* and becomes indeed the most wretched of commodities" (emphasis added). For Marx this alienation is paradoxically only exacerbated by the workers' increased production and by the heightening of competition for capital, to the point at which the worker is finally and utterly separated from the fruits of their labor on a collective level:

> finally the distinction between capitalist and land renter, like that between the tiller of the soil and the factory worker, disappears and . . . the whole of society must fall apart into the two classes—the property *owners* and the propertyless *workers*. (emphasis added)

See Marx, Karl. *The Economic and Philosophic Manuscripts of 1844*, Dirk J. Struik, ed. & intro., Martin Milligan, trans. (New York: International Press, 1964) p. 106.

12. It would be productive to read this section of *Being and Nothingness* (1947), Hazel E. Barnes, trans. & intro. (New York: Philosophical Library, 1962) as a transitional philosophy leading to the more explicitly Marxist-informed *Critique of Dialectical Reason*, Sartre's more systematic attempt to reconcile the radical alienation of his existential phenomenology with the homogenization of the proletariat—and thus conflation of otherness—characteristic of traditional (in the Lukacsian sense) Marxism.

See Sartre, Jean-Paul. *Critique of Dialectical Reason, Volume 1: Theory of Practical Ensembles* (1960), Alan Sheridan-Smith, trans., Jonathan Ree, ed. (London: Verso, 1991); and Lukacs, Georg. *History in Class Consciousness Studies in Marxist Dialectics* (1922), Rodney Livingstone, trans. (Cambridge: Massachusettes Institute of Technology Press, 1971).

13. Sartre, Jean-Paul. "Preface" in Fanon, Frantz. *The Wretched of the Earth* (1961), Constance Farrington, trans. (New York: Grove, 1963) p. 10. Hereafter cited as *WE*.

14. I will discuss the Hegelian Unhappy Consciousness, specifically within the context of Fanon's work, in greater detail in this chapter. To read this section of the dialectic see Miller, A. V. ed. *Hegel's Phenomenology of Spirit*, J. N. Findlay, analysis & forward (Oxford: Oxford University Press) pp. 199–238.

15. For a useful exposition of this apparently contradictory phrase and for its significance for Frantz Fanon's writings, see Onwuanibe, Richard C. *A Critique of Revolutionary Humanism: Frantz Fanon* (St. Louis: Warren H. Green, 1983).

See also Geismar, Peter, & Worsley, Peter. "Frantz Fanon: Evolution of a Revolutionary" in *Monthly Review* 21/1 (May 1969): 22–49; and Grohs, G. K. "Frantz Fanon and the African Revolution" in *The Journal of Modern African Studies* 6/4 (Summer 1979): 42–72.

16. Lewis R. Gordon points out that Frantz Fanon's work is heavily informed by the existential phenomenology of Jean-Paul Sartre, which is to say that Fanon generally eschews traditional ontological categories in favor of an existential analysis of the colonized subject's being-in-the-world: "Fanon's investigations amount to a rejection of ontology, the study of being, *from* which, *of* which, and *in* which, it seems, the very notions of the objective and the subjective can make sense" (LG 9–10).

17. By "recognition" in this context I do not mean the official government act of recognizing the former colony as a sovereign state, as for example when Great Britain recognized India's sovereignty immediately upon dissolving its own colonial rule of India in 1947. Rather, I mean "recognition in the strictly Hegelian, phenomenological sense; that is, the mutual recognition of

an intersubjective relation, in short, of equals or peers. It would take very little to demonstrate that such a relation seldom exists between former colonizers and their erstwhile colonies; one notable exception, which only illustrates how rare such a relation is, would be the postcolonial relations between Great Britain and the United States—an example which, admittedly, hardly applies here.

18. For a more thorough discussion of the Sartrean existentialist term 'bad faith' as it applies to Fanon's writings, see Gordon, Lewis *R. Fanon and the Crisis of European Man: An Essay on Philosophy and the Human Sciences* (London: Routledge, 1995), pp. 6–24.

Chapter Five. Reason, "the Native," and Desire: A Theory of "Magical Realism"

"But what is all the history of America if not a chronicle of *lo real maravilloso* (marvelous reality)?"

See Carpentier, Alejo. *El reino de este mundo* (Barcelona: Seix Barral, 1967) p. 18. Hereafter cited as AC. Translations from the Spanish are my own, except where noted.

1. Indeed González Echevarria, in his groundbreaking study of Alejo Carpentier's work, repudiates the term utterly, asserting that "The theoretical import of the concept does not deserve to be recounted here, because, as shall be seen, magical realism lies in a theoretical vacuum. . . ." He does, however, find an analysis of the history of 'magical realism' as a critical term to be quite useful in his readings of Carpentier's 1940s work; and González Echevarria is among the first to recognize the relations between the literatures of so-called "magical realism," the dissemination of the term in being attached to these literatures, and the complicity of certain critical discourses with the cultural imperatives of empire:

> The widespread use of the concept stems from its being part of a question that goes beyond literature: the question about the place of the New World in the scheme of universal history, stemming from the dissemination of the works of Hegel and Spengler in Spanish. As applied to literature, however, the concept refers specifically to narrative fiction. It is an effort to account for a narrative that could simply be considered fantastic; that is to say, one that does not depend on natural or physical laws or on the usual conception of the real in Western culture—a narrative, in other words, in which the relation between incidents, characters, and setting could not be based upon or justified by their status within the physical world or their normal acceptance by bourgeois mentality.

See González Echevarria, Roberto. *Alejo Carpentier: The Pilgrim at Home* (Ithaca, NY: Cornell University Press, 1977) pp. 107–129. Hereafter cited as RGE. For an essay which, although not specifically concerned with Latin American or Caribbean texts, is nevertheless a fine discussion of magical realism's intersections with postcoloniality in an English/Canadian literary context, see Slemon, Stephen. "Magical Realism as Postcolonial Discourse" in *Magical Realism: Theory, History, Community,* Lois Parkinson Zamora & Wendy B. Faris, eds. (Durham, NC: Duke University Press, 1995) pp. 407–426. Hereafter cited as *MR*.

2. When Uslar Pietri first invoked the term *realismo mágico*, it had already been in circulation for over 20 years; the German art critic Frank Roh was the first to give *Magischer Realismus* critical currency within the context of post-Expressionist painting of the 1920s. Irene Guenther, in her very useful article "Magical Realism, New Objectivity, and the Arts During the Weimar Republic," points out that Roh's term reached Latin American literary circles through the Spanish translation and publication of his work by the influential *Revista de occidente* in 1927; and that it was perhaps further disseminated through "the unprecedented cultural migration from Europe to the Americas in the 1930s and 1940s, as the muses fled the horrors of the Third Reich" (*MR* 61).

See Uslar Pietri, Arturo. "*Realismo mágico*" in *Godos, insurgentes, y visionarios* (Barcelona: Seix Barral, 1986); and Roh, Franz. *Nach-Expressionismus, Magischer Realismus, Probleme der neusten Europäischen Malerei* (Leipzig, Germany: Klinkhardt und Biermann, 1925).

3. This is a point most succinctly put by Gayatri Chakvavorty Spivak in (amusingly enough) her translator's preface to Jacques Derrida's *Of Grammatology:* "It is clear that, as it is commonly understood, the text harbors a lie." The context for Spivak's observation is at once G. W. F. Hegel's preface to *The Phenomenology of Mind;* Derrida's extrapolation of a theory of signifier and signified that is articulated, in part, within a critique of the Hegelian *Aufhebung;* and a self-reflexive exploration of her preface's own problematic position within this polemic. This problematic of the preface as abstract generality to the text's self-moving activity of knowing (i.e., of knowledges) is one that I will return to later on. For now let us just say that the Derridean critique of the preface, the deconstruction of the relation 'preface/text,' will prove instructive for our own understanding of the relations between Carpentier's preface and the body of work he wishes to call "marvelous reality."

See Spivak, Gayatri Chakravorty. "Translator's Preface" in Derrida, Jacques. *Of Grammatology* (1967) (Baltimore, MD: Johns Hopkins University Press, 1974) pp. x-xiii; Derrida, Jacques. *Dissemination,* Alan Bass, trans. & notes (Chicago: University of Chicago Press, 1976) pp. 15–21; and Hegel, G. W. F. *The Phenomenology of Mind* (1800) (2nd ed.), J. B. Baillie, trans. &

intro. (London: George Allen & Unwin, 1931) pp. 67–130. *Of Grammatology* hereafter cited as *OG*.

4. The book under discussion is *El reino de este mundo* (The kingdom of this world).

5. In late 1943 I was fortunate to visit the kingdom of Henri Christophe—the ruins, so poetic, of Sans-Souci; the vastness, impressively intact despite storms and earthquakes, of the Citadel of La Ferriere—and to know the still-Norman Cape Town—the Cap Français of the ancient colony—, where a street of impossibly long balconies leads to the stone palace once inhabited by Pauline Bonaparte. *After experiencing the very real sorcery of the lands of Haiti, having witnessed magical symbols along the red paths of the Central Meseta, having heard the drums along the Petro and the Rada,* I have come to associate this recently-experienced marvelous reality with the exhaustive position of influencing the marvelous element that has characterized certain European literatures of the past thirty years. The marvelous, sought by means of the old clichés of the forests of Britain, of the Knights of the Round Table, of the sorcerer merlin and the cycle of Arthur. The marvelous, poorly suggested by the tricks and deformities of characters at a fair—will the young French poets never tire of the freaks and clowns of the *fête foraine,* to whom Rimbaud had already bid farewell in his *"Alchemie du verbe"*? The marvelous, obtained through tricks of sleight-of-hand, combining objects which would normally never meet: the old tall-tale of the chance encounter of umbrella and sewing-machine on a dissection table, seashells and falling rain inside a taxi, the lion's head in the pelvis of a widow, of surrealist expositions. Or still, the literary-marvelous: the king in Sade's *Juliet,* Jarry's supermacho, Lewis' monk, the spine-chilling devices of the English Gothic novel: ghosts, ministers entombed alive behind stone walls, werewolves, mysterious hands knocking on a castle door. (emphasis added)

6. We might think also, if only in passing, of the marked contrast between Alejo's Carpentier's wonder-filled acknowledgment of the Haitian drums and Marlow's reaction of fear and foreboding when faced with an analogous experience in Joseph Conrad's text. For a more thorough discussion of *Heart of Darkness* in its relation to postcolonial literatures, see chapter 1 in this volume: "'The Other! The Other!': Conrad, Wilson Harris, and the Postcolonial 'Threshold of Capacity.'"

7. Fanon, Frantz. *The Wretched of the Earth* (1961), Constance Farrington, trans. Jean-Paul Sartre, pref., (New York: Grove, 1963) p. 237.

8. I am thinking particularly of Brennan's *Salman Rushdie and the Third World* (New York: St. Martin's, 1989), part of which appears in Homi K. Bhabha's collection *Nation and Narration* (London: Routledge, 1990). See also Brennan, Timothy J. "The National Longing for Form" in *Nation and Narration.*

9. Fuson, Robert H., trans. & intro. *The Log of Christopher Columbus* (Camden, ME: International Marine, 1987).

10. Edward W. Said gives this concise definition of the Orientalist's job:

> For decades the Orientalists had spoken about the Orient, they had translated texts, they had explained civilizations, religions, dynasties, cultures, mentalities—as academic objects, screened off from Europe by virtue of their inimitable foreignness. The Orientalist was an expert, like Renan or Lane, whose job in society was to interpret the Orient for his compatriots. The relation between Orientalist and Orient was essentially hermeneutical: standing before a distant, barely intelligible civilization or cultural monument, the Orientalist scholar reduced the obscurity by translating, sympathetically portraying, inwardly grasping the hard-to-reach object. Yet the Orientalist remained outside the Orient, which, however much it was made to appear intelligible, remained beyond the Occident.

See Said, Edward W. *Orientalism* (New York: Pantheon, 1978) p. 222; see also pp. 196–197, 222–225, 228–231, and 237–246. Hereafter cited as ES.

11. Without having planned it in a systematic way, the following text has responded to this order of preoccupations. In it there is a succession of extraordinary events, occurring on the island of Santo Domingo, during a span not quite the length of a human life, allowing for the marvelous to flow freely from a reality strictly portrayed in all its details. Because it is important to state that the story you are about to read has been established upon extremely rigorous documentation that not only respects the historical truth of events, the names of characters—even secondary ones—, of places and even streets, but also conceals, behind its apparent intemporality, a meticulously detailed comparison of dates and chronologies. And yet, for the dramatic singularity of its events, for the fantastic nature of the characters who find themselves, at a certain moment, at the magical crossroads of the Ciudad del Cabo, *it is a magical history that would be impossible to situate in Europe, and yet is as real as any successive chronicle consigned, for pedagogical edification, to the scholarly journals.* But what is all the history of America if not a chronicle of marvelous reality?

12. "Poets and beggars, musicians and prophets, soldiers and scoundrels, all creatures of that unbridled reality, we have had to ask little of imagination, for our problem has been a lack of conventional means to make our lives believable. This is, friends, the crux of our solitude." See García Márquez, Gabriel. *La soledad de America Latina/Brindis por la poesia* (Cali, Colombia: Carvajal S. A., 1983) p. 8. Hereafter cited as *Sol.*

13. 'Nudo' in the original.

14. On the lighter side, a potentially catchy T-shirt slogan: It's a Solitude Thing—You Wouldn't Understand.

15. Heidegger, Martin. "The End of Philosophy and the Task of Thinking" in *Basic Writings,* David Farrell Krell, ed. & trans. (San Francisco: HarperCollins, 1993) p. 441.

16. García Márquez, Gabriel. *Cien años de soledad* (1967) (Madrid: Espasa-Calpe, 1985) p. 59. Hereafter cited as *100Y.* Translations from the Spanish are from *One Hundred Years of Solitude,* hereafter cited as 100y: "Many years later, as he faced the firing squad, Colonel Aureliano Buendia was to remember that distant afternoon when his father took him to discover ice" (100y 11).

17. The specific reference is to Angel Flores's influential essay "Magical Realism in Spanish American Fiction," which claims European origins for magical-realist texts (particularly Kafka) and presents a fairly thorough (and persuasive) list of formal characteristics for them. Flores's fledgling attempts at a poetics are further amplified and developed by, among others, Juan Barroso, whose book on magical realism is also instructive in its treatment of Carpentier's term "marvelous reality"; and J. E. Irby, who cites William Faulkner as a primary influence upon Latin American magical-realists.

See Flores, Angel. "Magical Realism in Spanish American Fiction" in *Hispania* 38 (May 1955): 187–192, hereafter cited as AF; Barroso, Juan. *Realismo mágico y lo real maravilloso* (Miami: Ediciones Universal, 1977); and Irby, J. E. *La influencia de William Faulkner en cuatro narradores hispanoamericanos* (Mexico City: Editorial Mimeográfica de Juan Ruiz Velasco, 1957). Hereafter cited as JEI.

18. Williamson, Edwin. "Magical Realism and the Theme of Incest in *One Hundred Years of Solitude*" in *Gabriel García Márquez: New Readings,* Bernard McGuirk & Richard Cardwell, eds. (Cambridge: Cambridge University Press, 1987) p. 46. Hereafter cited as McG.

In the same volume, Gerald Martin's "On Magical and Social Realism in García Márquez" is also of interest as an exploration of Latin American themes in the novel, as well as a useful critique of North American imperialism in Gabriel García Márquez's work in general.

19. This is an argument methodically dismantled by Jorge Luis Borges, for whom "magic" is a narrative effect, a product of causal relations in narrative—thus constituting itself as a telos, no less than the "realistic" discourses to which so-called magical realist (or at the time of Borges's essay, simply "magical" or "fantastic") texts are so often mistakenly opposed. Borges sees so-called magical discourses as observing many of the same structural and rhetorical rules as the novel, rendering them both *un juego preciso de vigilancias, ecos y afinidades* (a precise game of vigilances, echoes and affinities) and thus neatly

deconstructing both the misguided notion of a naïve or merely nostalgic "magic" and the supposedly rationalist "reality" upon which more traditionally mimetic fictions are based.

See Borges, Jorge Luis. "*El arte narrativo y la magia*" in *Discusión* (Madrid: Alianza Editorial, 1964) pp. 71–79.

20. Indeed, there is little in Gabriel García Márquez's novel to support the blatantly Europocentric view of Gerald Martin, for whom it exemplifies "the dialectic between prescientific and scientific visions of reality" (McG 103).

21. González Echevarria, Roberto. *Myth and Archive* (Cambridge: Cambridge University Press, 1990) p. 13, emphasis added. Hereafter cited as *M&A.*

22. Then, for more than ten days, they did not see the sun again. The ground became soft and damp, like volcanic ash, and the vegetation was thicker and thicker, and the cries of the birds and the uproar of the monkeys became more and more remote, and the world became eternally sad. The men on the expedition became overwhelmed by their most ancient memories in that paradise of dampness and silence, going back to before original sin, as their boots sank into pools of steaming oil and their machetes destroyed bloody lilies and golden salamanders. For a week, almost without speaking, they went ahead like sleepwalkers through a universe of grief, lighted only by the tenuous reflection of luminous insects, and their lungs were overwhelmed by a suffocating smell of blood. They could not return because the strip that they were opening as they went along would soon close up with a new vegetation that almost seemed to grow before their eyes. "It's all right", Jose Arcadio Buendía would say. The main thing is not to lose our bearings." (100Y 20)

23. "Frente a ellos, rodeado a helechos y palmeras, blanco y polvoriento en la silenciosa luz de la mañana, estaba un enorme galeón español" (*100Y* 69).

24. I am aware of the insuficiency of terms such as 'the reader,' 'implied reader,' and 'ideal reader,' and use the term 'Western reader' advisedly. It is, of course, not without its perils to create a fantasy subject in this manner, one who would read this text in such-and-such a way because of environmental or cultural or experiential factors; such is, however, the tyranny of the example, of the so-called illustration that always also illustrates its own limits, indicates above all else what it is unable to reveal. Thus emerges once again the subtle, almost imperceptible distinction between Aufklärung and *Lichtung,* from an illusory enlightenment to a more efficacious clearing of that space which is not, after all, to be illuminated.

25. Shklovsky, Victor. "Art as Technique" (1917) and Eichenbaum, Boris. "The Theory of the 'Formal Method' " (1926) in *Russian Formalist Criticism: Four Essays,* Lee T. Lemon & Marion J. Reis, eds. & trans. (Lincoln:

University of Nebraska Press, 1965) pp. 151–159 & 201–216. Hereafter cited respectively as VS and BE.

26. Freud, Sigmund. *Civilization and Its Discontents* (1930), James Strachey, ed. & trans. (New York: Norton, 1950) p. 5.

27. "When it was opened by the giant, the chest gave off a glacial exhalation. Inside there was only an enormous, transparent block with infinite internal needles in which the light of the sunset was broken up into colored stars" (100Y 25–26).

28. "El mundo era tan reciente, que muchas cosas carecían de nombre, y para mencionarlas había que señalarlas con el dedo" (*100Y* 59).

29. "[Jose Arcadio Buendía] pagó otros cinco reales, y con la mano puesta en el témpano, como expresando un testimonio sobre el texto sagrado, exclamó:

> Este es el gran invento de nuestro tiempo." (*100Y* 75)

30. "Los forasteros, por supuesto, pensaron que Remedios, la bella, había sucumbido por fin a su irrevocable destino de abeja reina, y que su familia trataba de salvar la honra con la patraña de la levitación" (*100Y* 280).

31. Thanks to Luis Palacios, Universidad de Guanajuato, Mexico.

32. "It was as if God had decided to put to the test every capacity for surprise and was keeping the inhabitants of Macondo in a permanent alternation between excitement and disappointment, doubt and revelation, to such an extreme that no one knew for certain where the limits of reality lay" (100y 212).

33. The belief that Macondo is an island, and thus from outside 'civilization,' leads Buendía to this bewildered lament: <Nunca llegaremos a ninguna parte—se lamentaba ante Ursula—. Aquí nos hemos de pudrir en vida sin recibir los beneficios de la ciencia> (*100Y* 70).

34. They became indignant over the living images that the prosperous merchant Bruno Crespi projected in the theater with the lion-head ticket windows, for the character who had died and was buried in one film and for whose misfortune tears of affliction had been shed would reappear alive and transformed into an Arab in the next one. The audience, who paid two cents apiece to share the difficulties of the actors, would not tolerate that outlandish fraud and they broke up the seats. The mayor, at the urging of Bruno Crespi, explained in a proclamation that the cinema was a machine of illusions that did not merit the emotional outbursts of the audience. *With that discouraging explanation many felt that they had been the victims of some new and showy gypsy business and they decided not to return to the movies,* considering that they already

had too many troubles of their own to weep over the acted-out misfortunes of imaginary beings. Something similar happened with the cylinder phonographs that the merry matrons from France brought with them as a substitute for the antiquated hand organs and that for a time had serious effects on the livelihood of the band of musicians. At first curiosity increased the clientele on the forbidden street and there was even word of respectable ladies who disguised themselves as workers in order to observe the novelty of the phonograph from first hand, *but from so much and such close observation they soon reached the conclusion that it was not an enchanted mill as everyone had thought and as the matrons had said, but a mechanical trick that could not be compared with something, so human, and so full of everyday truth as a band of musicians.* It was such a serious disappointment that when phonographs became so popular that there was one in every house they were not considered objects for amusement for adults but as something good for children to take apart." (100y 211–212, emphasis added)

35."Pero cuando Aureliano Segundo abrió las ventanas entró una luz familiar que parecía acostrumbrada a iluminar el cuarto todos los dias, y *no había el menor rastro de polvo o telaraña, sino que todo estaba barrido y limpio, mejor barrido y más limpio que el día del entierro. . . .*" (*100Y* 230, emphasis added).

36. Todo era tan reciente, que varias semanas después, cuando Ursula entró al cuarto con un cubo de agua y una escoba para lavar los pisos,no tuvo nada que hacer" (*100Y* 230).

37. Una vez [el Coronel Aureliano Buendía] abrió el cuarto de Melquíades, buscando los rastros de un pasado anterior a la guerra, y sóol encontró los escombros, la basura, los montones de porquería acumulados por tantos años de abandono. En las pastas de los libros que nadie había vuelto a leér, en los viejos pergaminos macerados por la humedad había prosperado una flora lívida, y en el había sido el más puro y luminoso de la casa flotaba un insoportable olor de recuerdos podridos. (*100Y* 284)

38. "For Colonel Aureliano Buendía it was the most appropriate name, because while the rest of the family was still amazed by the fact that Melquíades's room was immune to dust and destruction, he saw it turned into a dunghill" (100y 244).

39. [Narrator:] There was the same pureness in the air, the same clarity, the same respite from dust and destruction that Aureliano Segundo had known in childhood. . . . (100y 289)

[Officer:] It's obvious that no one has been in that room for at least a hundred years. . . . There must even be snakes in there. (100y 289)

40. "Pero la noche en que los militares lo miraron sin verlo . . . Jose Arcadio Segundo llego a la conclusión de que el Coronel Aureliano Buendía no fue más que un farsante o un imbecil" (*100Y* 349).

41. "In Melquíades's room, on the other hand, protected by the supernatural light, by the sound of the rain, by the feeling of being invisible, he found that he had not had for one single instant during his previous life" (100y 289–290).

42. Freud, Sigmund. *Totem and Taboo* (1913) James Strachey, trans. & ed. (New York: Norton, 1989) pp. 92–93.

43. See Foucault, Michel. *Madness and Civilization,* Richard Howard, trans. (New York: Random, 1965); Lifton, Robert Jay. *The Nazi Doctors: Medical Killing and the Psychology of Genocide;* (San Francisco: Basic Books, 1986); and Mackenzie, Angus. *Secrets: The CIA's War at Home,* David Weir, foreword (Berkeley: University California Press, 1997).

44. This comment by Edwin Williamson is representative of such a view:

> [After Jose Arcadio Segundo's withdrawal] the Buendías lose all vestige of objectivity, and, with it, the capacity to discriminate between elementary differential categories such as truth and falsehood. As a result, the town as a whole suffers the fate that had previously befallen the characters individually. (McG 42–63)

This reading, and others like it, finally prove inadequate to the novel's true complexity on at least two counts: (1) it fails to account for the fact that such categories as "truth and falsehood" are, as illustrated in my close reading, constantly being put into question by the text; and (2) that Macondo's downfall finally has at least as much to do with the havoc wreaked by the colonizing forces as with the loss of a specious "objectivity" suffered by the town's inhabitants.

45. "Llovió cuatro años, once meses y dos dias" (*100Y* 351).

46. "Su fervor por la palabra era una urdimbre de respeto solemne e irreverencia comadrera. Ni sus propios manuscritos estaban a salvo de esa dualidad" (*100Y* 432).

47. The parchments are clearly Aureliano's basis for his claims that "Everything is known [Todo se sabe]" (100y 344, 352, & *100Y* 407 and 415 respectively).

48. "Aturdido por dos nostalgias enfrentadas como dos espejos, perdió su maravilloso sentido de la irrealidad, hasta que terminó por recomendarles a todos que se fueran de Macondo. . . ." (*100Y* 434).

49. Again we may read Williamson's position as representative of Eurocentric critical attitudes toward this novel in particular and so-called "magical realist" texts in general:

> Systematically, [the Catalonian] condemns the effects of magical realism: the fascination with the past, the escape from history into memory, the longing to recover a pristine innocence, and the surrender to mindless erotic desire. (McG 60)

50. "[Aureliano Babilonia] leía con avidez hasta muy altas horas de la noche, aunque por la forma en que se refería a sus lecturas, Gastón pensaba que no compraba los libros para informarse sino para verificar la exactitud de sus conocimientos, y que ninguno le interesaba más que los pergaminos, a los cuales dedicaba las mejores horas de la mañana" (*100Y* 415).

51. "[El último Aureliano e]ra un pellejo hinchado y reseco, que todas las hormigas del mundo iban arrastrando trabajosamente hacia sus madrigueras por el sendero de piedras del jardin. Aureliano no pudo moverse. No porque lo hubiera paralizado el estupor, sino porque en aquel instante prodigioso se le revelaron las claves definitivas de Melquíades, y vio el epígrafe de los pergaminos perfectamente ordenado en el tiempo y el espacio de los hombres: *El primero de la estirpe está amarrado en un árbol y al último se lo están comiendo las hormigas*. (*100Y* 446)

52. Two very useful discussions of the conclusion of *Cien años de soledad* may be found in Roberto González Echevarria's *Myth and Archive* (*M&A* 24–30) and in Emir Rodriguez Monegal's "*One Hundred Years of Solitude:* The Last Three Pages" in *Books Abroad* 47 (1973): 485–489. Each comments extensively on Aureliano Babilonia in the act of reading Melquíades's parchments, González Echevarria's chapter focusing especially on Melquíades's room as what he calls the 'Archive' *(arché)*, or epistemological center of knowledge for the novel.

53. "Macondo ya era un pavoroso remolino de polvo y escombros centrifugado por la cólera del huracán bíblico. . . ." (*100Y* 447).

54. "Only then did he discover that Amaranta Ursula was not his sister but his aunt, and that Sir Francis Drake had attacked Riohacha only so that they could seek each other through the most intricate labyrinths of blood until they would engender the mythological animal that was to bring the line to an end" (100y 382–383).

55. Linda Hutcheon has used the term "historiographic metafiction" to describe *Midnight's Children,* citing at greater length what I have just sketched out.

See Hutcheon, Linda. *A Poetics of Postmodernism: History, Theory, Fiction* (New York: Routledge, 1988) pp. xii and 161–164.

56. For Sigmund Freud, paranoia is the state or disorder in which the subject regresses to an earlier stage of their psychosexual development that predates their ability to distinguish the "inner world" of their own psyche from the outside "real world." The paranoiac thus projects their own mental fantasy world onto reality, and lives as if there were no difference between the "real world" and their own mental productions. Thus Don Quixote, to cite the most famous example, lives the life of a knight-errant, slaying windmills and so on, never affected in the slightest by the fact that none of it is at all true in the external world; the paranoiac's ego in a sense *is* the world.

For Freud's definitive case history of paranoia as well as his most systematic exposition of it, see Freud, Sigmund. "Psycho-analytic Notes on an Autobiographical Account of a Case of Paranoia (Dementia Paranoides)" (1911) in *Three Case Histories,* James Strachey, trans., Philip Rieff, intro. & ed. (New York: Touchstone, 1996) pp. 83–160.

57. Rushdie, Salman. *Midnight's Children* (New York: Knope, 1980) p. 3 Hereafter cited as *MC.*

58. Heidegger, Martin. "The End of Philosophy and the Task of Thinking" in *Basic Writings,* David Farrell Krell, ed. & trans. (San Francisco: HarperCollins, 1993) p. 441. Hereafter cited as MH.

59. For Harold Bloom, literary history may be read as a series of psychic battles between literary "fathers" and their descendants. His term "anxiety of influence" refers to the writer's fear that their works are dependent upon the texts of predecessors that always already exist before and beyond their own, and thus assume essential and irrevocable priority over their own writings. This model of literary "paternity" is of course overwhelmingly Oedipal, as it posits the need for the poet to enter into mythical "battle" with his literary "father" and destroy him, thus asserting his own phallocentric authority as artist.

See Bloom, Harold. *The Anxiety of Influence* (London: Oxford University Press, 1973).

60. See Lawrence, T. E. *The Seven Pillars of Wisdom: A Triumph* (1926, reprint ed.) Garden City, NY: Doubleday, 1935); and Burton, Richard Francis. *Personal Narrative of a Pilgrimage to al-Madinah and Meccah, in Two Volumes* (1855), Isabel Burton, ed. (New York: Dover, 1964).

61. Although the distinctions I make here are, admittedly, too neat, I nevertheless find them provisionally useful. Rather than read them as a master schema or blueprint from which to analyze "magical realist" narrators, I would suggest that they be taken as one especially felicitous possible framework for reading. I would additionally advise against constructing as part of any such reading the spurious separation of a text, its interpreters, and the cultures in which they are irreducibly enmeshed.

62. Although these passages are not directly cited from any specific source, I offer them as a loose composite, a general paraphrase of all the misreadings, misstatements, and so forth, I have encountered across a range of critical texts addressing so-called magical realism.

63. It's true: actively metaphorically so.

64. For a more thorough discussion of this relation between history and apocalypse see Berger, James. "Ghosts of Liberalism: Morrison's *Beloved* and the Moynihan Report" in *PMLA: Publications of the Modern Language Association* 111/3 (1996): 408–420.

65. I say the "character Saleem" here to further emphasize the distinction between character, or *experiencing* subject, and the narrator Saleem, or *narrating* subject. The narrative distance between these two entities varies throughout the text, as it would in any such autobiographical narrative structure; but an awareness of it seems especially useful to maintain at this point in the text.

66. "[Magical-realist writers] will all subscribe to Chirico's dictum: 'What is most of all necessary is to rid art of everything of the known which it has held until now: every subject, idea, thought, and symbol must be put aside. . . . Things may appear to it under a new aspect, as though they are illuminated by a constellation now appearing for the first time'. *It is predominantly an art of surprises*" (emphasis added).

67. See chapter One of the present volume: "'The Other! The Other!': Conrad, Wilson Harris, and the Postcolonial "Threshold of Capacity,'" for further discussion of this term.

68. López, Alfred. "*La Patria y el tirano*: José Martí and the Role of Literature in the Formation of the Cuban Nations, Past and Present" in *Iowa Journal of Cultural Studies* 12 (1993): 25–43.

69. "Poets and beggars, musicians and prophets, soldiers and scoundrels, all creatures of that unbridled reality, we have had to ask little of imagination, for our problem has been a lack of conventional means to make our lives believable. This is, friends, the crux of our solitude."

70. Lawrence, D. H. *Lady Chatterley's Lover* (New York: Doubleday, 1938) p. 1.

CONCLUSION. MAGIC, "REALISM," AND THE "POST-"

1. Lyotard, Jean-François. *The Postmodern Condition: A Report on Knowledge,* Geoff Bennington & Brian Massumi, trans. (Minneapolis: University Minnesota Press, 1984).

2. Aristotle. *Aristotle's Poetics,* James Hutton, trans. & intro. (New York: Norton, 1992) pp. 45–47.

3. *The Oxford English Dictionary* (2nd ed.) Vol. 9 (Oxford: Oxford University Press, 1989). Hereafter cited as OEDxii.

4. I refer here to Freud's theories of neurotic symptoms and dream-interpretation, in which the dream-symbol is interpreted in terms of an economy: it represents both the desire to fulfill an impulse and the desire to suppress it. Frued's theories, of course, are themselves taken up into a much larger polemic that finds its fullest expression in the writings of Jacques Derrida. A good place to begin to read Derrida's overarching thesis that logic and coherence are each within themselves contradictory entities—the basis for the Derridean concept of *différance,* the economy of what Derrida calls "writing," would be the essays "Structure, Sign, and Play in the Discourse of the Human Sciences" in *Writing and Difference* (1967), Alan Bass, trans., intro., & notes (Chicago: University of Chicago Press, 1978) pp. 278–293; and "Plato's Pharmacy" in *Dissemination* (1972), Barbara Johnson, trans. & notes (Chicago: University of Chicago Press, 1981) pp. 61–172. This latter is an especially fine example of how Derrida applies the Freudian model of dream-interpretation in his critiques of philosophical "coherence."

5. The entry makes no mention of 'magical realism' as a literary term, but it is at some pains to distinguish the term *(Magischer Realismus)* from another critical movement of the time, known as the *Neue Sachlichkeit* (New Objectivity), which effectively eclipsed Franz Roh's term in the art world of the Weimar Republic.

See *The Oxford Encyclopedia of 20th-Century Art* (Oxford: Oxford University Press, 1994) pp. 343–344. Hereafter cited as OEA.

6. Roh, Franz. *Realismo mágico, postexpresionismo: problemas de la pintura europea mas reciente,* Fernando Vela, trans. (Madrid: Revista de Occidente, 1927). The original text by Roh is entitled *Nach-Expressionismus, Magischer Realismus: Probleme der neuesten Europaischen Malerei* (Leipzig, Germany: Klinkhardt & Biermann, 1925).

7. Hegel, G. W. F. *The Philosophy of History* (1831), J. Sibree, trans. (New York: Dover Press, 1956) pp. 257–258.

8. De Las Casas, Bartolomé. *A Selection of His Writings,* George Sanderlin, ed. & trans. (New York: Knopf, 1971) pp. 142–146.

9. Chanady, Amaryll. *Magical Realism and the Fantastic: Resolved Versus Unresolved Antinomy* (New York: Garland, 1985) p. 16.

10. Mendoza, Plinio Apuleyo & García Márquez, Gabriel. *The Fragrance of Guava,* Ann Wright, trans. (London: Verso, 1983) p. 60.

Bibliography

Adisa, Opal Palmer. "Journey Into Speech—A Writer Between Two Worlds: An Interview with Michelle Cliff" in *African American Review* 28/2 (Summer 1992): 273–281.

Adorno, Theodor W. *Negative Dialectics* (1966), E. B. Ashton, trans. (New York: Continuum, 1973).

Ahmad, Aijaz. "The Politics of Literary Postcoloniality" in *Race and Class* 36/3 (1995): 1–20.

Antoni, Robert. *Divina Trace* (Woodstock, NY: Overlook, 1992).

Appiah, Kwame Anthony. "Is the Post—in Postmodernism the Post—in Postcolonial?" in *Critical Inquiry* 17/2 (Winter 1991): 336–357.

Aristotle. *Aristotle's Poetics,* James Hutton, trans. & intro. (New York: Norton, 1992).

Ashcroft, Bill; Griffiths, Gareth; & Tiffin, Helen. *The Empire Writes Back: Theory and Practice in Post-Colonial Literatures* (London: Routledge, 1989)

———(eds.). *The Post-colonial Studies Reader* (London: Routledge, 1995).

Atkinson, J. J. *Primal Law* (London: Longmans, Green & Co, 1903) pp. 220–231.

Barroso, Juan. *Realismo mágico y lo real maravilloso* (Miami: Ediciones Universal, 1977).

Berger, James. "Ghosts of Liberalism: Morrison's *Beloved* and the Moynihan Report" in *PMLA: Publications of the Modern Language Association* 111/3 (1996): 408–420.

Bhabha, Homi K. *The Location of Culture* (London: Routledge, 1994).

———(ed.). *Nation and Narration* (London: Routledge, 1990).

Bloom, Harold. *The Anxiety of Influence* (London: Oxford University Press, 1973).

Bonney, William W. *Thorns and Arabesques: Contexts for Conrad's Fiction* (Baltimore: Johns Hopkins University Press, 1980).

Borges, Jorge Luis. "*El arte narrativo y la magia*" in *Discusión* (Madrid: Alianza Editorial, 1964) pp. 71–79.

Brathwaite, Edward Kamau. *Contradictory Omens: Cultural Diversity and Integration in the Caribbean,* Monograph No. 1 (Mona, Great Britain: Savacou, 1974).

———. *The Arrivants: A New World Trilogy* (Oxford: Oxford University Press, 1989).

———. "History, the Caribbean Writer and *X/Self*" in *Crisis and Creativity in the New Literatures in English,* Geoffrey Davis & Hena-Maes Jelinek, eds. (Amsterdam: Rodopi, 1990) pp. 22–30.

Brennan, Timothy. *Salman Rushdie and the Third World* (New York: St. Martin's Press, 1989).

Brewer, John, & Porter, Roy, eds. *Consumption and the World of Goods* (London: Routledge, 1993).

Breytenbach, Breyten. *The True Confessions of an Albino Terrorist* (New York: Farrar, 1985).

Burton, Richard Francis. *Personal Narrative of a Pilgrimage to al-Madinah and Meccah, in Two Volumes* (1855), Isabel Burton, ed. (New York: Dover, 1964).

Carpentier, Alejo. *El reino de este mundo* (Barcelona: Seix Barral, 1967).

Chanady, Amaryll. *Magical Realism and the Fantastic: Resolved Versus Unresolved Antinomy* (New York: Garland, 1985).

Cherniavsky, Eva. "Subaltern Studies in a U.S. Frame" in *Boundary 2* 23/2 (1996): 85–110.

Chun, Allen. "Fuck Chineseness: On the Ambiguity of Ethnicity as Cuulture as Identity" in *Boundary 2* 23/2 (1996): 111–138.

Cliff, Michelle. "Object Into Subject: Some Thoughts On the Work of Black Women Artists" in *This Bridge Called My Back: Writings by Radical Women of Color* (2nd ed.), Cherrie Moraga & Gloria Anzaldúa, eds. (New York: Kitchen Table, Women of Color Press, 1983) pp. 271–288.

———. *The Land of Look Behind* (Ithaca, NY: Firebrand, 1985).

———. "Clare Savage as a Crossroads Character" in *Caribbean Women Writers: Essays from the First International Conference,* Selwyn R. Cudjoe, ed. (Wellesley, MA: Calaloux, 1990) pp. 71–75.

———. *Abeng* (1984) (New York: Penguin, 1991).

Coetzee, J. M. *White Writing: On the Culture of Letters in South Africa* (New Haven: Yale University Press, 1988).

———. *Boyhood: Scenes from Provincial Life* (New York: Viking, 1997).

Colás, Santiago. "Of Creole Symptoms, Cuban Fantasies, and Other Latin American Postcolonial Ideologies" in *PMLA: Publications of the Modern Language Association* 110/3 (May 1995): 382–396.

Coleridge, Samuel Taylor. Shakespeare's Judgement Equal to his Genius" (1836) in *Critical Theory Since Plato* (rev. ed.), Hazard Adams, ed. (Fort Worth, TX: Harcourt, 1992) pp. 469–471.

Conrad, Joseph. *Heart of Darkness* (1899), Ross C. Murfin, ed. & intro. (New York: St. Martin's, 1989).

———. *The Nigger of the "Narcissus"* (1904) (New York: Signet, 1960).

Davenport, T. R. H. *South Africa: A Modern History (4th ed.)* (Toronto: University of Toronto Press, 1991).

———. *The Birth of a New South Africa: The 1995 Joanne Goodman Lectures* (Toronto: University of Toronto Press, 1998).

De Las Casas, Bartolomé. *A Selection of His Writings,* George Sanderlin, ed. & trans. (New York: Knopf, 1971).

Deleuze, Gilles, & Guattari, Felix. *Kafka: Toward a Minor Literature* (1975), Dana Polan, trans. (Minneapolis: University of Minnesota Press, 1986).

Derrida, Jacques. *Of Grammatology* (1967), Gayatri Chakravorty Spivak, trans. & pref. (Baltimore, MD: Johns Hopkins University Press, 1976).

———. *Writing and Difference* (1967), Alan Bass, trans, intro, & notes (Chicago: University of Chicago Press, 1978).

———. *Margins of Philosophy* (1972), Alan Bass, trans. & notes (Chicago: University of Chicago Press, 1982).

———. *Positions* (1972), Alan Bass, trans. (Chicago: University of Chicago Press, 1981).

———. "'Eating Well,' or the Calculation of the Subject: An Interview with Jacques Derrida" in *Who Comes After the Subject?* Peter Connor & Avital Ronell, trans., Connor Eduardo Cadava & Jean-Luc Nancy, eds. (New York: Routledge, 1991).

———. *Specters of Marx,* Peggy Kamuf, trans., Bernd Magnus & Stephen Cullenberg, intro. (New York: Routledge, 1994).

Dirlik, Arif. "The Postcolonial Aura: Third World Criticism in the Age of Global Capitalism" in *Critical Inquiry* 20 (Winter 1994): 328–356.

Elliott, Ward E. Y. *The Rise of Guardian Democracy: The Supreme Court's Role in Voting Rights Disputes, 1845–1969* (Cambridge: Harvard University Press, 1974).

Elphick, Richard. *Kraal and Castle: Khoikhoi and the Founding of White South Africa* (New Haven: Yale University Press, 1977.

Elphick, Richard, & Giliomee, Hermann, eds. *The Shaping of South African Society, 1652–1840 (2nd ed.)* (Middlestown, CT: Wesleyan University Press, 1989).

Fanon, Frantz. *Black Skin White Masks* (1954), Charles Lam Markmann, trans. (New York: Wiedenfeld, 1967).

———. *The Wretched of the Earth* (1961), Constance Farrington, trans., Jean-Paul Sartre, pref. (New York: Grove, 1968).

Fieldhouse, D. K. *Economics and Empire 1830–1914* (Ithaca, NY: Cornell University Press, 1973).

Flores, Angel. "Magical Realism in Spanish American Fiction" in *Hispania* 38 (May 1955): 187–192.

Foucault, Michel. *Madness and Civilization,* Richard Howard, trans. (New York: Random, 1965).

———. *Power/Knowledge: Selected Interviews and Other Writings 1972–1977,* Colin Gordon, ed. & trans. (New York: Pantheon, 1980).

———. *The History of Sexuality, Volume 1* (1980), Robert Hurley, trans. (New York: Vintage, 1990).

Freud, Sigmund. *The Interpretation of Dreams* (1899) (4th English ed. 1953), James Strachey, ed. & trans. (New York: Avon, 1965).

———. "Psycho-analytic Notes on an Autobiographical Account of a Case of Paranoia (Dementia Paranoides)" (1911) in *Three Case Histories,* James Strachey, trans., Philip Rieff, intro. & ed. (New York: Touchstone, 1996) pp. 83–160.

———. *Totem and Taboo* (1913), James Strachey, trans. & ed. (New York: Norton, 1989).

———. *Civilization and Its Discontents* (1930), James Strachey, ed. & trans. (New York: Norton, 1950).

Fuson, Robert H., trans. & intro. *The Log of Christopher Columbus* (Camden, ME: International Marine, 1987).

García Márquez, Gabriel. *Cien años de soledad* (1967) (Madrid: Espasa-Calpe, 1985).

———. *One Hundred Years of Solitude,* Gregory Rabassa, trans. (New York: Avon, 1970).

———. *La soledad de America Latina/Brindis por la poesia* (Cali, Colombia: Carvajal S. A., 1983)

Gates Jr., Henry Louis, ed. *Race, Writing, and Difference* (Chicago: University of Chicago Press, 1988)

Gikandi, Simon. "In the Shadow of Hegel: Cultural Theory in an Age of Displacement" in *Research in African Literatures* 27/2 (Summer 1996): 139–150.

Gordon, Lewis R. *Fanon and the Crisis of European Man: An Essay on Philosophy and the Human Sciences* (London: Routledge, 1995).

Gorra, Michael. *After Empire: Scott, Naipaul, Rushdie* (Chicago: University of Chicago Press, 1997).

Gramsci, Antonio. *Selections from Prison Notebooks,* Quentin Hoare & Geoffrey Nowell Smith, trans. (London: Lawrence & Wishart, 1971).

Geismar, Peter, & Worsley, Peter. "Frantz Fanon: Evolution of a Revolutionary" in *Monthly Review* 21/1 (May 1969): 22–49.

González Echevarria, Roberto. *Alejo Carpentier: The Pilgrim at Home* (Ithaca, NY: Cornell University Press, 1977).

———. *Myth and Archive* (Cambridge: Cambridge University Press, 1990).

Grohs, G. K. "Frantz Fanon and the African Revolution" in *The Journal of Modern African Studies* 6/4 (Summer 1979): 42–72.

Hamner, Robert, ed. *Joseph Conrad: Third World Perspectives* (Washington, DC: Three Continents, 1990).

Harris, Wilson. *The Palace of the Peacock* (London: Faber & Faber, 1960).

———. *The Four Banks of the River of Space* (London: Faber & Faber, 1990).

———. *Jonestown* (London: Faber & Faber, 1995).

Hegel, G. W. F. *The Phenomenology of Mind* (1800) (2nd ed.), J. B. Baillie, trans. & intro. (London: George Allen & Unwin, 1931).

———. *The Phenomenology of Spirit* (1807), J. V. Miller, trans. (Oxford: Oxford University Press, 1977).

———. *The Philosophy of History* (1831), J. Sibree, trans. (New York: Dover Press, 1956).

Heidegger, Martin. *Being and Time* (1933), John Macquarrie & Edward Robinson, trans. (San Francisco: HarperCollins, 1962).

———. *Basic Writings,* David Farrell Krell, ed. & trans. (San Francisco: Harper Collins, 1993).

Hill, Mike, ed. *Whiteness: A Critical Reader* (New York: New York University Press, 1997).

Hutcheon, Linda. *A Theory of Parody: The Teachings of Twentieth-Century Art Forms* (New York: Methuen, 1985).

———. *A Poetics of Postmodernism: History, Theory, Fiction* (New York: Routledge, 1988).

Hyppolite, Jean. *Introduction to Hegel's Philosophy of History* (1948), Bond Harris & Jacqueline Bouchard Sperlock, trans., Arkady Plotnitsky, foreword (Gainesville: University Press of Florida, 1996).

Irby, J. E. *La influencia de William Faulkner en cuatro narradores hispanoamericanos* (Mexico City: Editorial Mimeográfica de Juan Ruiz Velasco, 1957).

Jameson, Frederic. *The Political Unconscious: Narrative as a Socially Symbolic Act* (Ithaca, NY: Cornell University Press, 1981).

———. "Third World Literature in the Era of Multinational Capitalism" in *Social Text 15* (Fall 1986): 65–88.

JanMohamed, Abdul. *Manichean Aesthetics: The Politics of Literature in Colonial Africa* (Amherst: University of Mass Press, 1983).

Jolly, Rosemary. "Rehearsals of Liberation: Contemporary Postcolonial Discourse in the New South Africa" in *PMLA: Publications of the Modern Language Association* 110/1 (January 1995): 17–29.

Keegan, Timothy J. *Colonial South Africa and the Origins of the Racist Order* (Charlottesville: University Press of Virginia, 1996).

Kojève, Alexandre. *Introduction to the Reading of Hegel* (1947), Allan Bloom, trans., James H. Nichols Jr., ed. (Ithaca, NY: Cornell University Press, 1969).

Lacan, Jacques. *Ecrits: A Selection,* Alan Sheridan, trans. (New York: Norton, 1977).

———. *The Seminar of Jacques Lacan: Book II: The Ego in Freud's Theory and in the Technique of Psychoanalysis 1954–1955,* Jacques-Alain Miller, ed., Sylvana Tomaselli, trans. (New York: Norton, 1988).

———. *The Seminar of Jacques Lacan: Book VII: The Ethics of Psychoanalysis 1959–1960,* Jacques-Alain Miller, ed., Sylvana Tomaselli, trans. (New York: Norton, 1992)

Lal, P., trans. & intro. *The Ramayana of Valmiki* (New Delhi: Vikas Publishing House Pvt., 1981).

Lawrence, D. H. *Lady Chatterley's Lover* (New York: Doubleday, 1938).

Lawrence, T. E. *The Seven Pillars of Wisdom: A Triumph* (1926) (reprint ed.) Garden City, NY: Doubleday, 1935).

Lee, Kyung-Won. "Is the Glass Half-Empty or Half-Full? Rethinking the Problems of Postcolonial Revisionism" in *Cultural Critique* 36/2 (Spring 1997): 89–117.

Lemon, Lee T., & Reis, Marion J., eds. & trans. *Russian Formalist Criticism: Four Essays* (Lincoln: University of Nebraska Press, 1965).

Lifton, Robert Jay. *The Nazi Doctors: Medical Killing and the Psychology of Genocide.* (San Francisco: Basic Books, 1986).

Ligon, Richard. *A True and Exact History of the Island of Barbadoes* (1873) (London: Frank Cass & Col., 1971).

Lima, Maria Helena. "Revolutionary Developments: Michele Cliff's *No Telephone to Heaven* and Merle Collins's *Angel*" in *ARIEL: A Review of International English Literature* 24/1 (January 1993): 35–56.

Lionnet, Francoise. "Of Mangoes and Maroons: Language, History, and the Multicultural Subject of Michelle Cliff's *Abeng*" in *De/colonizing the Subject: The Politics of Gender in Women's Autobiography*, Sidonie Smith & Julia Watson, eds. (Minneapolis: University of Minnesota Press, 1992) pp. 321–345.

López, Alfred. "*La patria y el tirano*: José Martí and the Role of Literature in the Formation of Cuban Nationalisms, Past and Present" in *Iowa Journal of Cultural Studies* 12 (1993): 25–43.

———. "Meaningful Paradox: The 'Strange Genius' of Wilson Harris" in *Conradiana* 28/3 (1996): 190–205.

Lukacs, Georg. *History in Class Consciousness Studies in Marxist Dialectics* (1922), Rodney Livingstone, trans. (Cambridge: Massachusetts Institute of Technology Press 1971).

Luo, Ting-yao. *Crossing the White Country: J. M. Coetzee and Postcolonial Agency.* Diss. State University of New York-Buffalo, 1993 (Ann Arbor, MI:University Microfilms International, 1994).

Lyotard, Jean-François. *The Postmodern Condition: A Report on Knowledge*, Geoff Bennington & Brian Massumi, trans. (Minneapolis: University of Minnesota Press, 1984).

Mackenzie, Angus. *Secrets: The CIA's War at Home*, David Weir, foreword (Berkeley: University of California Press, 1997).

Mahood, M. M. *The Colonial Encounter: A Reading of Six Novels* (Totowa, NJ: Rowman & Littlefield, 1977).

Mantel, Hilary. *A Change of Climate* (New York: Marian Wood/Owl, 1986).

———. *Eight Months on Ghazzah Street* (New York: Marian Wood/Owl, 1988).

Martí, José. *Poesias completas (Complete poems)* (Buenos Aires: Editorial Claridad, 1983).

Marx, Karl. *The Economic and Philosophic Manuscripts of 1844*, Dirk J. Struik, ed. & intro., Martin Milligan, trans. (New York: International P, 1964).

McCully, Michael. "Beyond 'The Covenant and the Cottage': A Reconsideration of Disraeli's Sybil" in *College Language Association Journal* 29/3 (March 1986): 318–335.

McGuirk, Bernard, & Cardwell, Richard, eds. *Gabriel García Márquez: New Readings* (Cambridge: Cambridge University Press, 1987).

Mendoza, Plinio Apuleyo (interview with Gabriel García Márquez). *The Fragrance of Guava*, Ann Wright, trans. (London: Verso, 1983).

Miyoshi, Masao. "A Borderless World? From Colonialism to Transnationalism and the Decline of the Nation-State" in *Critical Inquiry* 19 (Summer 1993): 726–751.

Monegal, Emir Rodriguez. "*One Hundred Years of Solitude:* The Last Three Pages" in *Books Abroad* 47 (1973): 485–489.

Mongia, Padmini, ed. & intro. *Contemporary Postcolonial Theory: A Reader* (London: Arnold, 1998).

Mowitt, John. "Breaking Up Fanon's Voice" in *Frantz Fanon: Critical Perspectives,* Anthony C. Alessandrini, ed. (London: Routledge, 1999) pp. 89–98.

Myrsiades, Kostas, & McGuire, Jerry, eds. *Order and Partialities: Theory, Pedagogy, and the "Postcolonial"* (Albany: State University of New York Press, 1995).

Onwuanibe, Richard C. *A Critique of Revolutionary Humanism: Frantz Fanon* (St. Louis: Warren H. Green, 1983).

Orwell, George. 'Shooting an Elephant' (1936) in *The Collected Essays, Journalism, and Letters of George Orwell, Volume 1: An Age Like This 1920–1940,* Sonia Orwell & Ian Angus, eds. (New York: Penguin, 1970) pp.265–272.

Oxford Encyclopedia of 20th Century Art (Oxford: Oxford University Press, 1994).

Oxford English Dictionary (2nd ed.). (Oxford: Oxford University Press, 1989).

Parry, Benita. "Problems in Current Theories of Colonial Discourse" in *Oxford Literary Review* 9 (1987): 27–58.

Philip, Marlene Nourbese. "Managing the Unmanageable" in *Caribbean Women Writers: Essays from the First International Conference,* Selwyn R. Cudjoe, ed. (Wellesley, MA: Calaloux, 1990) pp. 297–301.

Porter, Abioseh Michael. "Second Class Citizen: The Point of Departure for Understanding Buchi Emecheta's Major Fiction" in *International Fiction Review* 15/2 (Summer 1988): 123–129.

Poyer, John. *The History of Barbadoes* (1808) (London: Frank Cass & Co., 1971).

Pugh, Martin. *Electoral Reform in War and Peace 1906–18* (London: Routledge, 1993).

Raiskin, Judith. "The Art of History: An Interview with Michelle Cliff" in *The Kenyon Review* 15/1 (Winter 1993): 57–71.

Rich, Paul B., ed. *Reaction and Renewal in South Africa* (Houndsmills, Great Britain: Macmillan, 1996).

Roh, Franz. *Nach-Expressionismus, Magischer Realismus, Probleme der neusten Europäischen Malerei* (Leipzig, Germany: Klinkhardt und Biermann, 1925).

———. *Realismo mágico, postexpresionismo: problemas de la pintura europea mas reciente,* Fernando Vela, trans. (Madrid: Revista de Occidente, 1927).

Rushdie, Salman. *Midnight's Children* (New York: Knopf, 1980).

———. "The Empire Writes Back with a Vengeance" in *The Times* July 3, 1982: 8–10.

———(conversation with Gunther Grass). "Fictions Are Lies that Tell the Truth" in *Listener* June 17, 1985: 15–17.

———. *The Ground Beneath Her Feet* (New York: Henry Holt, 1999).

Said, Edward W. *Orientalism* (New York: Pantheon, 1978).

———. *Culture and Imperialism* (New York: Pantheon, 1993).

———. *Out of Place: A Memoir* (New York: Knopf, 1999).

San Juan Jr. E. *Beyond Postcolonial Theory* (New York: St. Martin's, 1998).

Sartre, Jean-Paul. *Being and Nothingness* (1947), Hazel E. Barnes, trans. & intro. (New York: Philosophical Library, 1956).

———. *Critique of Dialectical Reason, Volume 1: Theory of Practical Ensembles* (1960), Alan Sheridan-Smith, trans., Jonathan Ree, ed. (London: Verso, 1991).

Schwartz, Meryl F. "An Interview with Michelle Cliff" in *Contemporary Literature* 34/4 (Winter 1993): 595–619.

Semmel, Bernard. *The Liberal Ideal and the Demons of Empire: Theories of Imperialism from Adam Smith to Lenin* (Baltimore, MD: Johns Hopkins University Press, 1993).

Shohat, Ella. "Notes on the 'Post-Colonial' " in *Social Text* 31/32 (1992): 103–127.

Shankar, S. "The Thumb of Ekalavya: Postcolonial Studies and the 'Third World' Scholar in a Neocolonial World" in *World Literature Today* 68/3 (Summer 1994): 479–487.

Smith, Paul. *Discerning the Subject* (Minneapolis: University of Minnesota Press, 1988).

Smith, William Robertson. *Lectures on the Religion of the Semites* (1894) (New York: Ktav Publishers, 1969).

Spivak, Gayatri Chakravorty. *In Other Worlds: Essays in Cultural Politics,* Colin McCabe, foreword (New York: Routledge, 1988).

———. *The Postcolonial Critic: Interviews, Strategies, Dialogues* (London: Routledge, 1990).

———. *The Spivak Reader,* Donna Landry & Gerald MacLean, eds. (New York: Routledge, 1996).

———. *A Critique of Postcolonial Reason: Toward a History of the Vanishing Present* (Cambridge: Harvard University Press, 1999).

Stummer, Peter O., & Balme, Christopher, eds. *Fusion of Cultures?* (Amsterdam: Rodopi, 1996).

Suleri, Sara. *Meatless Days* (Chicago: University of Chicago Press, 1989).

Theroux, Paul. *The Collected Stories* (New York: Viking, 1997).

Trivedi, Harish, & Mukherjee, Meenakshi, eds. *Interrogating Post-colonialism: Theory, Text, and Context* (Shimla: Indian Institute of Advanced Study, 1996).

Truth and Reconciliation Commission. *Truth and Reconciliation Commission Report.* 5 vols. (Capetown, S.A.: Truth and Reconciliation Commission, 1998).

Turner, Lou. "On the Difference between the Hegelian and Fanonian Dialectic of Lordship and Bondage" in *Fanon: A Critical Reader,* Lewis R. Gordon et al., eds. & trans. (Oxford: Blackwell, 1996) pp.134–151.

Uslar Pietri, Arturo. "*Realismo mágico*" in *Godos, insurgentes, y visionarios* (Barcelona: Seix Barral, 1986).

Walker, Eric A. *The Great Trek (5th ed.)* (London: A. & C. Black, 1965).

Wolff, Richard D. *The Economics of Colonialism: Britain and Kenya, 1870–1930* (New Haven: Yale University Press, 1974).

Worden, Nigel. *The Making of a Modern Africa (2nd ed.)* (Oxford: Blackwell, 1995).

Young, Robert J. C. *White Mythologies: Writing History and the West* (London: Routledge, 1990).

———. *Colonial Desire: Hybridity in Theory, Culture and Race* (London: Methuen, 1995).

Zamora, Lois Parkinson, & Faris, Wendy B., eds. *Magical Realism: Theory, History, Community* (Durham, NC: Duke University Press, 1995).

Index

A

Achebe, Chinua, 3, 45, 46
Adorno, Theodor W.
  Negative Dialectics, 221 n.12
    critique of Hegel in, 235 n.22
Africa, 43, 50, 62, 64, 101, 137
Afrikaans language, 103–104, 117
Afrikaners, 104–105
agency, 11, 22, 28, 36, 97, 159, 161–162, 183, 188
  magical, 184–187, 201
  writing as, 189, 202
Ahmad, Aijaz, 2
alienation, 125, 131–2, 135–137, 241 n.9, 242 n.12
alterity, 143–145, 150, 156–157
Althusser, Louis, 215 n.35
America (as "New World"), 146–147, 236 n.25
Anglophilia, 104
Anerkennen (recognition), 127
Anwesen (presence), 152, 166–7, 196
anthropology, 153
Antoni, Robert, 30, 31
  Divina Trace, 30–35
Appiah, Kwame Anthony, 9
apocalypse, 194–196, 199, 202–204
Aristotle
  catharsis, 164
  mimesis, 39, 162, 187, 194, 204, 210
    as discussed in *Poetics*, 205
  Politics, 209
Arthur, King, 146
Ashcroft, Bill, 19–20
Atkinson, J. J.
  Primal Law, 231–232 n.13; see also "Freud, Sigmund: *Totem and Taboo*"
Aufklärung (Enlightenment), 49, 52, 56, 156, 166, 168–169, 196, 248 n.24
Austen, Jane, 61
Australia, 20
authenticity, 16

B

bad faith, 10, 131, 137, 141, 243 n.18
Bahamas, the, 74
Balme, Christopher, 5
Bandung Conference (1955), 19
Barbados, 36, 72, 74–75, 77, 81
  as "Little England", 74, 236 n.25
Barroso, Juan, 200, 247 n.17
Barrow, Errol, 74
Bhabha, Homi K., 4, 5, 9, 11–12, 15, 25–27, 30, 87–88, 130-131, 241 n.9, 214 n.30
  hybridity, 4, 5, 12, 13–14, 17, 27–28, 30–32, 34
  Location of Culture, The, 122
  mimicry, 4, 28–30, 78–79, 216 n.53, 226 n.22
  "Signs Taken for Wonders", 29–30
Biko, Steven, 39
Bildungsroman (narrative of progress), 37, 97–101, 107, 118, 233 n.18
blackness, 96, 105

Bloom, Harold
anxiety of influence, 172, 253 n.59
Bonney, William W., 48–49, 53
Borges, Jorge Luis, 208, 247 n.19
Brathwaite, Edward Kamau, 36, 70–71, 73–4, 77–81, 83, 100, 216 n.53, 236 n.25
Contradictory Omens, 81
"Negus", 79–80
Brennan, Timothy, 147
Breytenbach, Breyten, 8
True Confessions of an Albino Terrorist, 237–238 n.28
British Empire, 48, 56–57, 73–74, 76, 104
Buendía family, See "García Márquez, Gabriel: *Cien años de soledad*"
Burton, Richard (Sir), 179, 216 n.47

C

Canada, 20
capitalism, 9, 13, 241 n.9
global, 14–15, 17
Caribbean, the, 27, 30, 36–37, 64, 70–78, 80, 83
novel, 30, 33
woman, 88–89
writer, 70–1, 78
Carpentier, Alejo, 143, 168
real maravilloso, lo (marvelous reality), 144–149, 247 n.17
Preface to *reino de este mundo, El*, 144, 244 n.3, 244 n.6
Cas, Fidel, 21
Catholic Church, 30
Chambers, Ross, 105
Chanady, Amaryll, 209
Cherniavsky, Eva, 13–14
Chirico, Giorgio de, 200, 254 n.66
Chun, Allen, 13–14, 214 n.28
class, 10, 17, 22–23, 69, 88–89, 96, 176
as barrier to social equality, 233 n.16
Cliff, Michelle, 8, 37, 88–89, 96, 97–100
Abeng, 97, 99–103, 105–111, 116–119, 234 n.19, 236 n.24
homoerotic dimension of, 238 n.32
Clifford, Hugh C. M. G. (Sir), 45, 47
Coetzee, J. M., 8, 37
as child/adolescent, see "*Boyhood*"
as writer of "historiographic metafiction", 215 n.36
Boyhood, 38, 97, 99, 103–106, 111–119, 239 n.33
White Writing, 218 n.66
Colás, Santiago, 40
Coleridge, Samuel Taylor, 62–63
colonial unconscious, 37–38, 85–86, 88, 90, 99, 108, 119, 125
colonialism, *passim*
and its legacy, 11–12, 36–37, 86, 92, 97, 108, 115, 119, 123, 229–230 n.8
as "civilizing mission", 11, 29, 48, 50–51, 53, 62, 86–87, 94, 121, 136, 172, 209
as myth-of-origins, 89–90
and desire of/for the Other, 39, 97, 110–116, 143–144, 147–150, 208
and identification with the land, 113–118
Columbus, Christopher, 11, 74–75, 81, 83, 91, 100
as *Cristobal Colón*, 40
Log of Cristopher Columbus, The, 41, 147–148, 236 n.25
Commonwealth literature, 3, 6, 19
comparative literature, 144
Congo, the, 49, 53, 230 n.10
Conrad, Joseph, 6, 43–52, 55–56, 58–59, 60–62, 68, 151, 201, 223 n.5
Heart of Darkness, 35–36, 41, 46–61, 116, 145, 225 n.17, 230 n.10, 244 n.6
Nigger of the "Narcissus", 51
corporations, transnational, 14–15
Creole, 78–83
language (Jamaican), 238 n.31
society, 78, 83

creolization, 27, 79–80
criollismo (creoleness), 36, 81, 216 n.53, 236 n.25
Cuba, 11, 18, 36, 72, 74, 83
1895 War of Independence, 21, 82
Battle of Dos Rios (1895), 65
Castro regime, 21
criollos (creoles), 81–82
voluntários (Spanish sympathizers), 82
culture, 4–7, 12, 14, 28, 39, 146, 153, 189, 203–4
national, 83, 125, 139–140, 180, 227 n.1
tribal, 231 n.13; see also "Freud, Sigmund: *Totem and Taboo*"
Western, 123, 158
as determinant of "reality", 162

D

De Las Casas, Bartolomé , 209
Deleuze, Gilles, 6
Derrida, Jacques, 6, 18, 27, 36, 66–67, 76, 80, 89, 241 n.9
critique of the Preface, 144
differance, 27, 70, 79, 223 n.8
"Eating Well", 43
Of Grammatology, 153, 244 n.3; see also "Spivak, Gayatri Chakravorty: Translator's Preface to"
"Plato's Pharmacy", 255 n.4
Positions, 215 n.35
relève (*Aufhebung*, resolution), 70, 144
Specters of Marx, 36, 222 n.2, 222 n.3, 224–225 n.12
specter, 65, 70, 71, 76, 83, 216 n.53, 222 n.2, 223 n.5, 236 n.25
"Structure, Sign, and Play in the Discourse of the Human Sciences", 238 n.30, 255 n.4
"White Mythology", 230 n.11
diaspora, 7, 13–14
Chinese, 14
Cuban, 21–22
Dickens, Charles
Pip, 233 n.18
Oliver Twist, 233 n.18
difference, 11–12, 13, 16, 30–32, 35, 46, 73, 110, 116, 143, 145, 151, 187–188, 209–210, 226 n.22
cultural, 27, 125, 130
exhuming, 61
racial, 125
representation of, 193
Dirlik, Arif, 9, 12–13, 14
"Postcolonial Aura, The", 212–213 n.16
diversity, cultural, 27, 40, 78

E

Egypt, 175
Eleguá, see "*Legba*"
Elizabeth II, Queen, 105–106
Enargeia (self-evident truth), 52
England, 3, 19, 31, 75, 104–105, 110
English department, 3
English language, 78, 117, 219 n.74
"Englishness", 104–105
Enlightenment, 49, 51, 123
post-, 121
epistemology, 137
ethnicity, 10, 14, 17, 22–23, 28
Europe, 50, 92, 107, 125, 136, 138–142, 146, 149, 216 n.47, 222 n.3
Eurocentrism, 89, 230 n.10
Europocentrism, 4, 90, 126, 158
European Union, 15
exile, 159
internal, 169–170

F

Fanon, Frantz, 4, 8, 121–142, 146, 219 n.74, 242 n.16
Black Skins White Masks, 69, 125, 136–137, 139, 230–231 n.12
"The Negro and Hegel", 124–125, 127, 138–139
Wretched of the Earth, The, 38–39, 132, 136–142

Faulkner, William as influence on "magical-realist" literature, 247 n.17
Fieldhouse, D. K., 229 n.8
First World, 9, 11, 13, 17, 19, 23–24
narrative perspective, 153
theory, 15
Flores, Angel, 200
"Magical Realism in Spanish American Fiction", 247 n.17
Forster, E. M.
Passage to India, A, 209
Foucault, Michel, 8, 24, 162, 241 n.9
Frank, Anne, 107–109
Diary of Anne Frank, The, 107
freedom, 44–45, 56–57, 69, 129, 135, 137, 175
Freud, Sigmund, 72, 87–88, 155; see also "subject, Freudian"
Civilization and its Discontents, 72
narcissism of minor differences, 228 n.3
Interpretation of Dreams, The, 217–218 n.62, 227–228 n.2
condensation (of dream-thoughts), 236 n.24
narcissism, 165
neurotic symptoms, definition of, 161–162, 255 n.4
"Psycho-analytic Notes on an Autobiographical
Account of a Case of Paranoia", 253 n.56
paranoia, 165
Totem and Taboo
primal horde, Darwin's, 231–232 n.13
Unheimlich (Uncanny), 157, 171
frontier, 43–44, 48, 54, 59–60
as substitute for "margin", 44, 64

G

Gandhi, Indira, 199
García Marquez, Gabriel, 39, 150–151, 153, 172, 176, 195, 208
Cien años de soledad (*One Hundred Years of Solitude*), 39, 151–165, 171, 180, 184, 190, 192 194, 209
as"historiographic metafiction", 215 n.36; see also "Hutcheon, Linda"
Nobel acceptance speech, 150–151, 194, 202, 210
Gates Jr., Henry Louis, 122
gaze, 92, 158–159, 171
gender, 10, 17, 22–23
General Agreement on Tariffs and Trade (GATT), 15
geography, 17
Gegenwart (arrival, becoming present), 151, 167
Gikandi, Simon, 26, 122–123
Gilroy, Paul, 241 n.9
Black Atlantic, The, 122
González Echevarria, Roberto, 143, 147, 153
Alejo Carpentier: The Pilgrim at Home, 243–244 n.1
Myth and Archive, 252 n.52
Gordon, Lewis, 137, 142
Fanon and the Crisis of European Man, 122, 242 n.16, 243 n.18
Gorra, Michael, 4, 7, 12, 15, 19
After Empire, 212 n.7
Gramsci, Antonio
"On the Margins of History", 215 n.41; see also "Spivak, Gayatri Chakravorty"
Grass, Günter, 208
Great Britain, 19, 21, 103, 146, 236 n.25, 242 n.17
non-white suffrage in, 232 n.14
Greece, ancient, 72, 73
Griffiths, Gareth, 16, 19–20
Guattari, Felix, 6
Guenther, Irene
"Magical Realism, New Objectivity, and
the Arts During the Weimar Republic", 244 n.2
Guyana, 59–60

H

Haiti, 144–147, 149
Hall, Stuart, 5
Harris, Wilson, 3, 8, 15, 35, 41, 43, 46, 55–64, 201
  Four Banks of the River of Space, 43, 221–222 n.14
  "The Frontier on Which *Heart of Darkness* Stands", 46–47, 220 n.7
  "threshold of capacity", 35, 46, 55, 217 n.59, 244 n.6
  Jonestown, epigraph
  Palace of the Peacock, 35, 55, 57–59, 63
Hegel, G. W. F., 1, 38, 121–142, 209; see also "subject, Hegelian"; see also "Hyppolite, Jean," "Kojève, Alexandre," and "Young, Robert J. C.: *White Mythologies*"
  Anerkennen (recognition), 127–132, 137–139, 242–243 n.17
  Aufhebung (resolution, *relève*), 70, 115, 130, 144–145, 244 n.3
  dialectic, 122, 124, 235 n.22, 241 n.9
  Geist (Spirit), 37, 71, 81, 224 n.12, 235 n.22
  Gespenst (Specter), 81
  historicism, 123
  Phenomenology of Mind, The, 244 n.3
  Phenomenology of Spirit, The, 126, 130, 133–4
    "Absolute Knowledge", 115, 133, 211 n.1
    as highest stage of the dialectic, 235 n.22
    "Lordship and Bondage", 38, 122, 124–135, 240–241 n.9
    "Unhappy Consciousness", 128, 135–136, 140, 142
  Self-consciousness, 127–129, 131–132, 135, 235 n.22
hegemony, 12, 13, 15, 23, 30, 56, 77
Heidegger, Martin, 125
  Being and Time
    Dasein (Being-in-the-world), 224 n.12, 242 n.16
    Mitdasein (*Dasein*-with), 224 n.12
    Mitsein (being-with), 37, 224–225 n.12
  "End of Philosophy and the Task of Thinking, The", 220 n.9
    aletheia (clearing, *clarière*), 52, 55–6, *220 n.9*
    Lichtung (Unconcealment), 49, 55, 156, 166–168, 194, 196, 199, 201, 220 n.9, 248 n.24
Hispaniola, 74
historiography, 16, 18–19, 22–3
  Western, 122
  postmodern, 165
  of heterogeneity, difference, 215 n.35
history, 7, 10, 19, 30, 39, 47, 70–78, 88–89, 152–153, 161–162, 164, 166, 173, 177, 195–197, 203
  European, 222 n.3
  Freud's view of, 228 n.3
  Indian, 168, 170, 177, 197–198
  Jamaican, 236 n.24
  metaphysical concept of, 215 n.35
  of empire/colonialism, 64, 68–69, 89, 100–101, 119, 136, 165, 208
  of meanings (*sens*), 72
  of the West, 208
  medical, 162
  pre-colonial, 75–6, 86–87, 89
  South African, 236 n.26
History, 122
Hong Kong, 11, 19
Hottentots, 38, 97, 99, 218 n.66
humanism, 121
  "revolutionary," new, 136, 138, 140–142
Husserl, Edmund, 125
Hutcheon, Linda
  Poetics of Postmodernism, A, 225–226 n.20

Hutcheon, Linda *(cont.)*
historiographic metafiction, 18, 215 n.36, 252 n.55
postmodern paradox, 78
Theory of Parody, A, 32–33, 226 n.22
Hyppolite, Jean
Introduction to Hegel's Philosophy of History, 241 n.9

I

identity, 5–6, 7, 14, 30, 69
national, 125
ideology, 227 n.1
imperialism, 10, 13, 21, 50, 56, 77–78
North American, 247 n.18
India, 12, 20, 21, 31, 43, 165–168, 174–175, 178, 183–184, 187- 189, 191–192, 197, 214 n.30, 242 n.17
Independence Day, 166, 242 n.17
Indo-Pakistani War of 1965, 195
Emergency, the, 195, 199, 201
Iran, 38
Irby, J. E., 200, 247 n.17
Ivanhoe, 107

J

Jamaica, 20, 74, 97, 99–101, 107
class barriers in, 233 n.16
Jameson, Fredric, national allegory, 17–18
Political Unconscious, The, 94, 227 n.1
JanMohammed, Abdul, 4
Manichean Aesthetics, 212 n.7
Jews, extermination of, 107
Jolly, Rosemary, 21

K

Kafka, Franz, 6, 247 n.17
Kojève, Alexandre, 127
Introduction to the Reading of Hegel, 240–241 n.9
Kosovo, 233 n.17
Kruger, Paul, 237 n.27; see also "South Africa: Transvaal"

L

Lacan, Jacques, 125, 127–128, 241 n.9; see also "subject, Lacanian"
jouissance, 239 n.34
Seminar of Jacques Lacan: Book II, 121
"Freud, Hegel, and the Machine", 133–135
Lal, P.
Ramayana of Valmiki, The, 217 n.57; see also "*Ramayana*, origins of"
Latin America, 34, 40, 210
Lawrence, D. H., 204
Lawrence, T. E. , 179, 216 n.47
Legba, 80
Leibl, Wilhelm, 208
Lévi-Strauss, Claude, 153
Light Brigade, the, 105
logos (reason, knowledge), 69, 150, 159
López, Alfred, "*La patria y el tirano*," 215 n.40
Lyotard, Jean-François
Postmodern Condition: The, 205

M

MacCabe, Colin, 22
Macondo, See "García Márquez, Gabriel: *Cien años de soledad*"
magic, 152–153, 156, 163, 187–189, 205–208
as *telos*, 247 n.19; see also "Borges, Jorge Luis"
"magical realism", 39–40, 143–205, 208–210, 254 n.62, 255 n.5
as literature of agency, 202
as "theoretical vacuum", 243–244 n.1
Mahood, M. M., 12, 35–36, 37
Mandela, Nelson, 94, 230 n.9
Manicheanism, 4, 77
Mantel, Hilary, 116
Eight Months on Ghazzah Street, 239 n.35
Change of Climate, A, 239 n.35

Maritz, Geerit, 103, 236 n.26
Marlow, see "Conrad, Joseph: *Heart of Darkness*"
as unreliable narrator, 52
Martí, José, 21, 36, 65, 67, 71, 74, 81–83, 215 n.40
Versos libres (*Free Verses*), 65
Versos sensillos (*Simple Verses*), 81
Martin, Gerald
"On Magical and Social Realism in García Márquez", 247 n.18
Marx, Karl, 131–132, 134
Economic and Philosophic Manuscripts of 1844, 241 n.11
Marxism, 12, 242 n.12
mastery, 38–39, 121, 126, 128, 134
colonialism and, 115–119, 136
and desire for the Other, 143-144, 148–150
reading as (will-to-), 148–150, 152, 164, 168, 171
memory, 74, 76–77, 91, 163, 200, 203
-trace, (Freud), 155
Merlin, 146
mestizaje (mixture of races), 28
Mexico, 146
Miyoshi, Masao, 15
Mohan, Rajeswari, 19
Mongia, Padmini, 2, 121
Mowitt, John, 38
Morrison, Toni, 12, 208
Mukherjee, Meenakshi, 3, 19
multiculturalism, 5, 13, 27
myth, 30, 153, 168
of forgetting, 155

N

Nachträglichkeit (deferred action), 28
Naipaul, V. S., 67–69, 71, 74
Conrad's influence on, 223 n.5
naive art, 208–209
narration, 153–154, 165–168, 170, 173–174, 180–184, 186, 193, 195, 225 n.17
self-reflexive, 176, 178–179, 190–192, 198, 201
nation, 17, 65, 92–3, 126, 137–140, 178, 188, 216 n.53, 229–230 n.8, 236 n.25
as fatherland (*patria*), 81–83
as geographical location, 82
as myth-of-origins, 28, 71–72, 93, 175
as *natio*, 64, 72, 73
-formation, 71
nationalism, 14, 16, 17, 28, 73, 82–83, 87
Afrikaans, 21, 103–104, 218 n.66, 236 n.26, 237 n.28
Chinese, 14
Cuban, 21–22, 81–83
Cuban-American, 21–22
natives
as "innocent", 148
Native Informant, 24–25
Third World scholar as, 25
nativism, 144
Nehru, Jawaharlal, 177–178, 188–189
neo-, 36, 68–70, 216 n.53, 236 n.25
as nostalgia, 68
Ngugi wa Thiongo, 3
Nigeria, 20
North American Free Trade Association(NAFTA), 15

O

ontology, 70, 136–137, 144, 242 n.16
Orinoco rain forest, 30, 31–32
Orwell, George, 4
Other, the, 12, 28, 29, 43, 56, 60, 87–88, 129–131, 141, 144, 147, 225 n.12, 244 n.6
Overseas Contract Workers (OCWs), 15
Oxford Encylopedia of Twentieth-Century Art, 208–209
Oxford English Dictionary, The, 10, 205–207, 209

P

palimpsest, 89–90
Panama Canal, 19

Papa Labá, See *"Legba"*
Parry, Benita, 11, 25–26
parody, 32–33
phallogocentrism, 44
phenomenology, 123, 125, 242 n.12
philosophy, Western, 122–123
Philip, Marlene Nourbese, 64
Platt Amendment, 21
post-, 1, 70, 78, 193, 205
Post-colonial Studies Reader, The, 121, 219 n.74; see also "Ashcroft, Bill," Griffiths, Gareth," and "Tiffin, Helen"
postcolonialism, *passim*
  objections to, 10–17
  response to objections, 17–19
postmodernism, 1, 10, 12, 205
power, 11, 12–13, 15, 90, 96, 121, 123, 125–126
Poyer, John
  History of Barbadoes, The, 225 n.15, 225 n.16
praxis, 11
Pretorius, Andres, 103, 236 n.26
Pretorius, Marthinus, 236 n.26
psychoanalysis, 123, 126, 155, 217–218 n. 62, 227–228 n.2, 241 n.9

R

Rabassa, Jose
  "Allegories of *Atlas*", 219 n.74
race, 10, 17, 28, 69, 83, 122, 125, 136
Ramayana, 33–34
  origins of, 217 n.57
Rastafarians, 106
reader, Western, 248 n.24
realism, 39, 205, 210
Reason *(Logos)*, 39–40, 69, 143, 152–153, 156, 159
regression, 155
repression, 86, 90, 126
resistance, 11–12, 13, 16, 30, 36, 41, 71–73, 77–78, 82, 119, 121, 172, 216 n.53, 236 n.24, 236 n.25
  as national project, 224 n.11
Rhys, Jean, 25
  Wide Sargasso Sea, 25–27
Riebeeck, Jan van, 97, 103, 236 n.26
Robin Hood, 104–105
Rodriguez Monegal, Emir
  "*One Hundred Years of Solitude*: The Last Three Pages", 252 n.52
Roh, Franz, 208
  Magischer Realismus, 244 n.2, 255 n.5
  as opposed to *Neue Sachlichkeit* (New Objectivity), 255 n.5
Round Table, Knights of the, 146
Royal African Company of London, 101
Rushdie, Salman, 6, 17, 31, 78, 208
  Ground Beneath Her Feet, The, 31
  Midnight's Children, 39, 165–203, 209
    as"historiographic metafiction", 215 n.36, 252 n.55
  Satanic Verses, The, 12
Rwanda, 233 n.17

S

Said, Edward W., 4, 9, 26, 46, 148, 241 n.9
  Culture and Imperialism, 26, 212 n.7, 216 n.50, 227 n.1
  Orientalism, 212 n.7, 216 n.47, 216 n.50
    Orientalist, the, 23–24, 201–202, 246 n.10
      as postcolonial narrator, 148, 154, 167–168, 174–177, 179, 187, 189
  Out of Place, 213 n.9
San Juan Jr., E., 11, 13–14, 15, 26, 216 n.50
  Beyond Postcolonial Theory, 9, 214 n.28
santería, 34, 80

Sartre, Jean-Paul, 38, 125, 132, 134, 142, 241 n.9, 242 n.16
Being and Nothingness, 125, 129–135, 242 n.12
Being-for-itself, 129
Being-for-others, 130
indifference-toward-others, 131, 134, 137
Mitsein, critique of, 225 n.12; see also "Heidegger, Martin: *Being and Time: Mitsein*"
Us-object, 133–134
We-subject, 133–134
Critique of Dialectical Reason, 242 n.12
Saudi Arabia, 239 n.35
Saussure, Ferdinand de, 69
Savage, Clare, See "Cliff, Michelle: *Abeng*"
Scheherazade, 167
Second World, 19
Shakespeare, William, 61–62
Hamlet, 222 n.3
Shankar, S., 24
Shariati, Ali, 38
Shklovsky, Victor
"Art as Technique", 155
defamiliarization *(ostranenie)*, 155–156, 165, 172, 174–176, 181, 193, 209
Shohat, Ella, 10–11, 13, 19, 41, 43
Siboney Indians, 81
Sinai, Saleem, See "Rushdie, Salman: *Midnight's Children*"
as omniscient narrator, 175–177
as unreliable narrator, 167–168, 183–184
Smith, Paul
Discerning the Subject, 213 n.22, 234 n.21
Smith, William Robertson, 231–232 n.13; see also "Freud, Sigmund: *Totem and Taboo*"
Somerset, Lord Charles, 103, 236 n.26
South Africa, 18, 20, 21, 39, 88, 97, 239 n.35
1948 elections, 103
1994 elections, 96, 232 n.14
apartheid, 99, 237 n.28
Boer War, 103–104, 237 n.27
Cape Town colony, 236 n.26
class barriers (post-apartheid), 233 n.16
Coloureds, 97–99, 111–114
Great Trek, the, 103, 117, 236 n.26
Orange Free State, 237 n.27
Transvaal, 237 n.27
Truth and Reconciliation Committee (TRC), 92, 94, 230 n.9; see also "Mandela, Nelson"
Spivak, Gayatri Chakravorty, 4, 9, 11–13, 15, 18, 22, 26, 214 n.30, 241 n.9
as "Native Informant", 24, 213 n.19
Critique of Postcolonial Reason, 25
Postcolonial Critic, The, 213 n.19
subaltern, 5, 11, 22, 25, 56
term's origins in Gramsci, 215 n.41
Subaltern Studies Group, 22–23
"Translator's Preface" to *Of Grammatology*, 244 n.3
Stel, Simon van der, 103, 236 n.26
subject, 4, 5, 11, 22, 28, 38, 47, 98, 126, 193, 230–231 n.12; see also "Smith, Paul"
Freudian, 86, 162, 217–218 n. 62
Hegelian, 115, 140, 144
Lacanian, 239 n.34
narrating, 184
split-, 36, 110–111, 115–118, 128–129, 138
"Westernized", see "split-"
subject-effect, 28–30
subject-positions, 24, 30, 37, 60, 125, 179

subjectivity, 4, 36, 137
  collective (a people's), 44
Suleri, Sara
  Meatless Days, 213 n.19
Surrealism, 205
syncretism, 5, 27

T

Taino Indians, 81
techne (tool), theory as, 45
telos (order), 3, 69, 70, 80, 195
Theroux, Paul, 116
  short fiction of, 239 n.35
Third World, 2, 9–10, 11, 15, 17, 19, 56, 142, 146–147, 149–150
  cosmopolitan, 143, 145, 147–148, 153, 177
  narrator, 179
  scholar/writer, 23–25, 38, 144
Thomas, Hans, 208
Tiffin, Helen, 19–20
Ting-Lao Yuo, 96
Trinh Minh-ha, 4, 18
Trinidad and Tobago, 30, 34
Turner, Lou, 38
Tutu, Desmond (Archbishop), 230 n.9; see also "South Africa: Truth and Reconciliation Committee (TRC)"

U

United States, 19, 20, 21–22, 31, 243 n.17
  as internal colonial power, 13–14
  non-white suffrage in, 232 n.14
Uslar Pietri, Arturo, 144
  realismo mágico, 244 n.2

V

Valdes, Zoe, 17
Verism, 208
Verwoerd, Handrik, 21
Victoria Cross, the, 105, 106
veld (farm), 116
volk (people), 117
volksmond (people's mouth), 117
voyeurism, 113

W

West, the, 4, 11, 15–16, 17, 19, 68, 158, 180, 193, 214 n.30
  as universal authority, 122
  Western canon (literary), 144
whiteness, 37–38, 85–86, 88, 90–100, 113–116, 125, 136, 237 n.28
  as colonial imperative, 88–92, 94–95, 98
  as cultural history, 94, 97, 99
  as cultural aesthetic/ideal, 94–95, 103–107, 110
  as ontological relation, 95–96
  without mastery, 118–119
Williamson, Edwin, 251 n.44, 252 n.49
wish-fulfillment, 115
world literature, 144

Y

Young, Robert J. C. , 6, 23, 29, 122
  White Mythologies, 240 n.9